Healthcare Entrepreneurship

Entrepreneurship in the healthcare sector has received increased attention over the last two decades, both in terms of scholarly research and number of innovative enterprises. Entrepreneurial activities and innovations have emerged from and will continue to be driven by several actors along the healthcare value chain, but especially from non-traditional healthcare players. In this new volume, we present the reader with several critical issues in healthcare entrepreneurship and innovation, covering a comprehensive set of research topics. We bring together the latest academic research and management practice, with contributions by authors from entrepreneurship, medical sciences, and management, who provide in-depth and practical insights into designing and managing entrepreneurship in healthcare. Upon providing a systematic review of the research field, we discuss several important macro-, meso-, and micro-level issues in healthcare entrepreneurship, such as opportunity identification, the entrepreneurial ecosystem including accelerators, the benefits of open innovation for the sector, and social entrepreneurship in healthcare.

These topics open up avenues for nurturing entrepreneurship in healthcare through both education and policy. Building on this trend, the book is organized around levels of analysis and specifies which cross-disciplinary efforts are needed to advance understanding of how entrepreneurs discover opportunities and start viable and innovative businesses.

Healthcare Entrepreneurship will be of interest to scholars of healthcare and entrepreneurs alike, but also managers of innovative healthcare enterprises as well as policymakers in the health sector.

Dr. Ralf Wilden is an Associate Professor at Macquarie University in Sydney, Australia and former Director of the Newcastle Business School, Sydney.

Dr. Massimo Garbuio is a Senior Lecturer at the University of Sydney Business School.

Dr. Federica Angeli is Associate Professor at the School of Social and Behavioral Sciences at Tilburg University.

Dr. Daniele Mascia is Associate Professor of Management and Organizations at the University of Bologna.

Routledge Studies in Health Management
Edited by Ewan Ferlie

The healthcare sector is now of major significance, economically, scientifically and societally. In many countries, healthcare organizations are experiencing major pressures to change and restructure, while cost containment efforts have been accentuated by global economic crisis. Users are demanding higher service quality, and healthcare professions are experiencing significant reorganization while operating under increased demands from an aging population.

Critically analytic, politically informed, discursive and theoretically grounded, rather than narrowly technical or positivistic, the series seeks to analyze current healthcare organizations. Reflecting the intense focus of policy and academic interest, it moves beyond the day to day debate to consider the broader implications of international organizational and management research and different theoretical framings.

Analysing Health Care Organizations
A Personal Anthology
Ewan Ferlie

Managing Modern Healthcare
Knowledge, Networks and Practice
Mike Bresnen, Damian Hodgson, Simon Bailey, Paula Hyde and John Hassard

Challenging Perspectives on Organizational Change in Health Care
Louise Fitzgerald and Aoife McDermott

Healthcare Entrepreneurship
Ralf Wilden, Massimo Garbuio, Federica Angeli, and Daniele Mascia

Healthcare Entrepreneurship

Ralf Wilden, Massimo Garbuio,
Federica Angeli, and Daniele Mascia

Routledge
Taylor & Francis Group
NEW YORK AND LONDON

First published 2018
by Routledge
711 Third Avenue, New York, NY 10017

and by Routledge
2 Park Square, Milton Park, Abingdon, Oxon, OX14 4RN

Routledge is an imprint of the Taylor & Francis Group, an informa business

Library of Congress Cataloging-in-Publication Data
A catalog record for this book has been requested

ISBN: 978-1-138-06840-7 (hbk)
ISBN: 978-1-315-15799-3 (ebk)

Typeset in Sabon
by Apex CoVantage, LLC

Contents

Authors' Biographies

Authors

Dr. Federica Angeli is Associate Professor at the School of Social and Behavioral Sciences at Tilburg University, the Netherlands. Federica strives to understand how organizations—in their profit, non-for-profit or hybrid declination—can play an active role in tacking complex societal issues, or "grand challenges," such as inclusive healthcare delivery and poverty alleviation

By using a multidisciplinary, multi-level interpretive lens at the intersection between organizational sociology and public policy, her research has investigated the complex interactions of policy reforms with organizational strategies in the healthcare and biopharmaceutical sector; the effectiveness of multi-strategy policy interventions in improving maternal and child care indicators in emerging contexts; the influence of organizational culture in shaping patient-perceived quality of health service; and the role of inter-organizational collaborative networks in defining patient outcomes. Federica's research spans across multiple geographies and institutional environments, including Italy, the Netherlands, India, and Sub-Saharan Africa.

Federica's research is synergic with her educational activity at Tilburg University, where she is Academic Director of the Master's Program in Global Management of Social Issue.

Federica also serves as Associate Editor of BMC Health Services Research and has convened since 2015 a conference track at the European Group of Organizations Studies (EGOS) yearly Colloquium, to reflect on contemporary challenges for healthcare organizations.

Federica's work has won several research prizes, awarded among others by the Academy of Management (Healthcare Management Division and International Management Division), Strategic Management Society, and Academy of International Business. Her research has been published in outlets such as *Social Science and Medicine*, *PLOS One*, *Health Policy*, *Health Policy and Planning*, *Regional Studies*, *Organization & Environment*, *Long Range Planning*, and *Pharmacoeconomics*.

Dr. Massimo Garbuio is a Senior Lecturer at the University of Sydney Business School.

Working at the intersection of entrepreneurship, design thinking and strategy, Massimo's work explores how executives think about strategy and innovation and allocate resources. He works with companies as well as startups operating in financial services, healthcare and more broadly the Internet of Things.

Massimo's research has shown the critical importance of strategic conversations over financial analysis in the success of strategic decisions such as market entries, capital investments and M&As. As result of his research, Massimo has developed an Index, the Australian Corporate Innovation Index, which measures to what extent Australian companies are organized to thrive in dynamic and disruptive environments. The Index appeared in the report entitled "The Venture Capital Effect," published by the Australian Private Equity & Venture Capital Association in 2017.

Massimo is regularly invited to speak at international conferences and is published in *Academy of Management Learning & Education, California Management Review*, *Design Studies*, *Journal of Management*, *Long Range Planning*, *McKinsey Quarterly*, and *McKinsey on Finance.*

Massimo holds a Ph.D. from the University of Western Australia and has Masters from the University College London and the University of Pennsylvania. He is a member of the Strategic Management Society and the Academy of Management, and is on the Editorial Board for the *Journal of Management.*

Dr. Daniele Mascia is Associate Professor of Management and Organizations at the University of Bologna. Prior to Bologna, he was on the faculty at the Università Cattolica del Sacro Cuore. In the past, he has held a number of visiting fellowships at various academic institutions, among them The University of Sydney Business School, the KTH Royal Institute of Technology (Stockholm), the Chalmers University of Technology (Gothenburg), and the University of Lugano USI. In 2017, he was appointed Honorary Adjunct Professor at the University of Technology Sydney. For his research, Daniele received a number of awards and distinctions from, among others, the Academy of Management.

Daniele's current research interests include the administration and management of healthcare organizations, the study of inter-personal and inter-organizational networks, and the analysis of learning dynamics in the context of medical innovation. His work has been published in journals such as *American Journal of Sociology*, *Social Science and Medicine*, *Regional Studies*, *Social Networks*, *Medical Care* and *Health Care Management Review.* Daniele is evaluator of research projects and individual profiles on behalf of the Italian Ministry of

Research and Education, the Swiss National Foundation for Scientific Research and the Netherlands Organisation for Health Research and Development. He has been advisor of public and private organizations in the health sector (hospitals, pharmaceutical companies and medical device manufacturers).

Daniele is on the editorial board for the Health Care Management Review journal and has convened several conference subthemes at the European Group of Organizations Studies (EGOS) yearly Colloquium. He currently serves as the international representative for the Academy of Management's Health Care Management (HCM) Division.

Dr. Ralf Wilden is an Associate Professor at Macquarie University in Sydney, Australia and former Director of the Newcastle Business School, Sydney. He is passionate about helping organizations deal with change. Ralf leads projects on service-oriented business models and organizational change to help organizations sense, shape and seize market opportunities and improve their strategic performance. Ralf worked for multinational organizations in the automotive (BMW Group), telecommunications (O2 Telefónica) and consulting industries.

His research interests focus predominantly on the question of how organizations can improve performance. In order to derive and solve interesting and relevant research questions, he uses core strategy theories, and the resource-based and dynamic capability views of firm strategy in particular, as well as (open) innovation and service strategy literature. He has used these lenses to investigate managerially relevant problems, such as service-dominant business models, and the impact of market sensing and reconfiguring activities on operational capabilities.

Ralf's work has been recognized by several international and national associations, and he has authored journal publications in outlets such as *Academy of Management Annals*, *Journal of the Academy of Marketing Science*, *Journal of Product Innovation Management*, *Strategic Organization*, and *Journal of Service Research*. Ralf's work has won several research prizes, such being included in the Academy of Management's best paper proceedings. He also serves as the global representative for the Academy of Management's Strategic Management Division and is on the Technology and Innovation Management division's panel for the Best Paper Award.

Chapter Contributors

Jeroen Gruiskens is a Ph.D. student at the Care and Public Health Research Institute (CAPHRI) School of Public Health and Preventive Medicine of Maastricht University, currently investigating the relationship between micro-, meso-, and macro-determinants of social entrepreneurship and the development of social impact measurement in the health sector. He has a Bachelor's degree in Medicine and a Master's degree in Global Health, and he has co-founded NGOs and social enterprises.

Jan Hohberger is a Senior Lecturer at the University of Technology Sydney (UTS). He earned his Ph.D. in Management at ESADE Business School. His research focuses on innovation strategies, alliances, and collaborations, and has appeared in journals such as *Research Policy*, *Industrial and Corporate Change*, *Journal of Product Innovation Management*, and *Journal of International Business Studies*.

Valentina Iacopino, Ph.D., is Postdoctoral Researcher in Organization Studies and Human Resource Management at the Catholic University of Rome, Department of Management. Her research interests and publications focus on the adoption processes of innovations in healthcare. Valentina applies social network analysis techniques to understand inter-organizational and professional networks' role in the adoption and diffusion of medical technologies. She deals with policy issues and governance of innovations both at organizational and institutional level.

Emre Karali is a Ph.D. Candidate in Strategic Management at the Rotterdam School of Management. He is affiliated with the Erasmus Centre for Business Innovation and with the Erasmus School of Accounting and Assurance. Emre seeks to unravel why some organizations are successful while others are not and focuses for this purpose on organizational change and innovation in relation to organizational design, (in)tangible resources and products/services.

Nidthida Lin is a Senior Lecturer at Newcastle Business School, University of Newcastle, Australia. Nidthida's scholarly interests are in the areas of innovation management, strategic outsourcing and global sourcing, and managerial decision-making. Nidthida has a Ph.D. in Strategic Management from Australian Graduate School of Management (AGSM), University of New South Wales and University of Sydney.

Francesca Pallotti is a Senior Lecturer in Economic Sociology at the Centre for Business Network Analysis, University of Greenwich (UK). She holds a Ph.D. from the Catholic University of Rome (Italy) and a MSc from the University of Birmingham (UK). She has been postdoctoral researcher and Swiss National Science Foundation fellow at the University of Italian Switzerland, Lugano, where she is currently an international fellow of the Social Network Analysis Research Center. Her research draws upon a network perspective to examine how the structure of social relations develops and affects individual opportunity and outcomes.

Dr. Jarrod Ormiston is an Assistant Professor in Social Entrepreneurship in the Maastricht Centre for Entrepreneurship (MC4E), Maastricht

University. His research interests include social entrepreneurship, social innovation and social impact investment, refugee entrepreneurship, Indigenous entrepreneurship, and innovative pedagogies in entrepreneurship education. Jarrod has worked as a consultant to the Australian Government, OECD, and the UN on entrepreneurship and education.

William Page recently completed an MBA at MGSM (Macquarie Graduate School of Management) and is currently undertaking a Ph.D. at the University of Sydney where he is focusing on the impact of open innovation on the development, growth and potential success of accelerators. Outside of academia, William is an entrepreneur who has co-founded FilmDoo, a diversified media company utilizing disruptive technology to enable people to discover the best in entertainment, cultural, and language learning content.

Dr. Krithika Randhawa is an Assistant Professor of Innovation at the University of Technology Sydney (UTS). Her research focuses on open innovation, with a special interest in collaborative networks, crowdsourcing and community-based innovation. Her work has been published in journals such as *Journal of Product Innovation Management* and *Journal of Knowledge Management*. Her research on innovative healthcare and manufacturing management practices has been published in the *International Journal of Production Economics*, *International Journal of Production Research*, and *Journal of Health Organization and Management*.

Dr. Jatinder S. Sidhu is an Associate Professor of Strategic Management at the Rotterdam School of Management, Erasmus University. He obtained his Ph.D. degree at the Tinbergen Institute, Erasmus School of Economics, Rotterdam, Netherlands. His current research focuses on issues related to identity, gender, and diversity in organizations, the upper echelons of management, organizational learning, and innovation. He is the National Representative of the Netherlands at the European Academy of Management and serves as Associate Editor for the *European Management Review*. His work has appeared in various journals including *International Business Review*, *Journal of Business Research*, *Journal of Management*, *Journal of Management Studies*, *Journal of Product Innovation Management*, and *Organization Science*.

Prof. Dr. Onno van Schayck is Professor of Preventive Medicine at Care and Public Health Research Institute (CAPHRI) at Maastricht University, the Netherlands. Professor van Schayck's core area of expertise relates to prevention and treatment of asthma, COPD, and pulmonary conditions in general. Prof. van Schayck has been acknowledged to be the most cited researcher in the world in his area of expertise in

2010 and 2011. He co-authored more than 450 international and 100 national peer-reviewed articles. Total funding obtained until 2016 adds up to €46 million in governmental and charity grants, obtained from prestigious funding organizations, such as the Netherlands Organisation for Scientific Research (NWO), the Netherlands Organisation for Health Research and Development (ZonMW), the Lung foundation, Prevention fund, and others.

Prof. Dr. Henk W. Volberda is Professor of strategic management and business policy and Academic Director of the Erasmus Centre for Business Innovation at the Rotterdam School of Management, Erasmus University. He obtained his Ph.D., cum laude, in business administration at the University of Groningen, the Netherlands. His research focuses on strategic renewal and innovation, strategic flexibility, hyper-competition, new organizational forms, and the co-evolution of firms and industries. His research has been published in numerous leading journals such as *Academy of Management Journal*, *Journal of Management*, *Journal of Management Studies*, *Management Science*, *Organization Science*, and *Organization Studies*, *Strategic Management Journal*.

Dr. Daan Westra obtained his Ph.D. in 2017 after defending his dissertation on the competitive and cooperative dynamics in inter-organizational networks between healthcare organizations. He is currently Assistant Professor at Maastricht University's department of Health Services Research at CAPHRI (Care and Public Health Research Institute). His research focuses on matters relating to the industrial organization of healthcare markets, healthcare management, and networks in healthcare. Since 2015, Daan has been a member of the Young Advisory Committee of the European Healthcare Management Association.

Preface

Entrepreneurship underlies the discovery of opportunities for new ideas and ventures, as well as their realization. Entrepreneurship is a major driver of innovation across industries and is important for both developing and developed economies. Despite its importance, as a research area entrepreneurship is still a relatively young scholarly field, and entrepreneurship in healthcare specifically is only emerging in these days.

Healthcare has undergone significant changes in the last decade, providing greater power to individuals; for example, through wearable devices, as well as clinicians and nurses with a wealth of digital devices that improve their daily operations. Entrepreneurial activities and innovations have emerged from and will continue to be driven by several actors along the healthcare value chain but especially from non-traditional healthcare players. Besides significant innovations around new drugs and technologies affecting healthcare, other more service-related health innovations have significantly affected the industry. For example, the significance of products and services that are related to healthcare—but are not in the form of more traditional offerings such as drugs, hospitals, and medical appliances—can be seen in the many collaborations emerging between established companies and startups, as well as companies from other industries entering the healthcare space.

This book reaches the audience at a crucial time. It presents the reader with several critical issues in the area of healthcare entrepreneurship and innovation, covering a comprehensive set of research topics. We bring together the latest academic research and management practice on entrepreneurship and innovation in healthcare, with contributions by co-authors from entrepreneurship, medical sciences and management, who provide in-depth and practical insights into designing and managing entrepreneurship in healthcare. This is achieved through cutting-edge research contributions, practical examples and implementations, and illustrative cases.

This book is organized into three parts, which in combination discuss important aspects of healthcare entrepreneurship and innovation. These parts cover a range of topics, both emergent and traditional. We aim to highlight central topics in healthcare entrepreneurship as well as introduce novel approaches and provide an understanding of related research streams. In doing so, this book provides an overview of healthcare entrepreneurship and innovation on three levels of analysis: micro, meso, and macro. The authors of this book have sought help from a select group of co-authors for the various chapters.

In Chapter 1, "Entrepreneurship in Healthcare: Past Contributions and Future Opportunities," we review existing work on healthcare entrepreneurship and set the stage for future research in this domain. It starts by providing an overview of healthcare entrepreneurship, including key characteristics that distinguish healthcare from other sectors. This systematic review applies a novel text mining approach using Leximancer to identify key themes and concepts underlying previous research in the field. Special attention is given to investigate differences between relevant research published in medical versus management journals. The chapter concludes with suggestions for future research relevant to macro-, meso-, and micro-levels of analysis. Several of these suggestions are then addressed throughout the remainder of the book.

The subsequent four chapters are dedicated to **macro-level** topics relevant to healthcare entrepreneurship. In Chapter 2 entitled "Defining and Delivering Value in the Healthcare Sector," Angeli and Westra discuss the concept of value, which serves as the fundamental principle in healthcare. After exploring the concept of value and value-based healthcare, we shift our focus to value delivery by healthcare organizations and adopt the lens of hybrid organizations to understand how healthcare providers deliver value and what organizational challenges they face in doing so.

Chapter 3, "Competition and Institutional Forces in Healthcare" by Westra and Angeli, investigates the opportunities and constraints that the healthcare institutional context may pose on entrepreneurs considering entering the healthcare market. First, we describe the relevant institutional frameworks, which differ in terms of governmental regulation, competitive environment, barriers to entry and private-public co-existence. The Dutch and Italian healthcare systems serve as ideal examples, due to their polar opposite characteristics on many relevant dimensions. The idea of managed competition and the scholarly as well as policy debate around the benefits of pro-competitive policy reforms are addressed. The chapter then considers how competition and rivalry may trigger new venture creations. Empirical measurement of competition plays an important role in guiding scholars in this context, as well as the subjective perception of competition by professionals and practitioners. Finally, the chapter will discuss the opportunities and entry barriers for entrepreneurs related to varying levels of competition in the market. The Dutch context, and the rise of Independent Treatment Centers in the Netherlands after the introduction of pro-competitive policy, will provide empirical illustration.

Chapter 4 by Mascia, Pallotti and Iacopino investigates factors "Beyond Competition: Exploring Collaboration for Entrepreneurship in Healthcare Organizations." Previous research suggests that entrepreneurial opportunities in a given industry are strongly affected by the environmental conditions that both individuals and organizations face. This chapter presents the various forms of planned and unplanned collaborative arrangements that organizations can adopt in healthcare. We discuss the main trajectories of change in hospitals and how planned and unplanned collaborations may sustain initiatives for the development and commercial exploitation of new knowledge.

Chapters 5–8 turn their attention to **meso-level** aspects relevant to healthcare entrepreneurship. Chapter 5 by Page, Garbuio and Wilden deals with "The Role of Incubators and Accelerators in Healthcare Innovation." This chapter focuses on how accelerators and incubators as part of the wider entrepreneurial ecosystem support healthcare entrepreneurs in their new venture creation. These institutions provide startups with access to a wide pool of complementary technological and important organizational resources. We provide an overview of the different types of incubators and accelerators that work with healthcare organizations and startups. We highlight the variety of ways in which they seek to revolutionize the healthcare industry. We will use a number of practical and relevant examples to illustrate the different approaches that can be used.

In Chapter 6, "Understanding Healthcare Innovation through a Dynamic Capabilities Lens," Angeli together with Karali, Sidhu, and Volberda focus on innovation in healthcare entrepreneurship. They start with introducing one of the most eminent frameworks in strategy research, the dynamic capability view of the firm. Subsequently, they identify critical factors within the healthcare sector that obstruct innovation. Finally, the dynamic capability literature is applied to specific examples to show how it can aid in explaining innovation within healthcare.

In Chapter 7 entitled "Open Service Innovation for Healthcare Organizations," Wilden and Randhawa focus on how healthcare entrepreneurs can source innovation outside their own organizational boundaries. Specifically, much previous research on innovation in the healthcare industry has focused on product manufacturers such as pharmaceutical companies and medical instrument manufacturers. Significantly less research has investigated service innovation, such as the innovative activities of healthcare service providers. We turn our attention to what is labeled open service innovation, which represents a departure from the traditional innovation paradigm by highlighting the importance of both internal and external paths to developing and commercializing inventions. Using an illustrative case study, this chapter provides an overview of possible advantages of using crowdsourcing, a popular open innovation mechanism, to drive innovation in healthcare, with a particular focus on healthcare service providers such as hospitals.

Following up on the idea of using collaborations to drive entrepreneurship and innovation, Chapter 8 entitled "How Corporate Entrepreneurs Use Interfirm Collaboration in the Search for Emerging Knowledge in Biotech Innovation," Hohberger and Wilden discuss the idea of collaborative entrepreneurship; that is, the creation of value based on new, cooperatively generated ideas resulting from sharing information and knowledge between firms. More specifically, this chapter investigates how firms access and search for emerging knowledge, which is crucial especially for firms in the biotechnology industry.

The last part of the book deals with topics related to **micro-level** phenomena in healthcare entrepreneurship. In Chapter 9, Garbuio and Lin apply a cognitive lens to discuss how entrepreneurs may best identify opportunities in healthcare. In the chapter "Entrepreneurial Opportunities in Healthcare: A Cognitive Perspective," through cognitive acts we exemplify how healthcare entrepreneurs develop and explore ideas related to new business opportunities. Focusing on framing, analogical reasoning, abductive reasoning, counterfactual reasoning and mental simulation, we explicate how these cognitive acts enable healthcare entrepreneurs to identify entrepreneurial opportunities. The chapter concludes by suggesting promising avenues for future theoretical and empirical research in healthcare entrepreneurship.

Finally, in Chapter 10 entitled "Understanding the Emergence of Social Entrepreneurial Action in Healthcare," Angeli together with Gruiskens, Ormiston and van Schayck explore the emergence of individual's social entrepreneurial action in healthcare through an exploratory study of the antecedents of social entrepreneurial action by Ashoka Fellows active in the healthcare sector. To do so, this chapter uses a qualitative biographical approach. Findings uncover four interlinked aggregate dimensions of social entrepreneurial antecedents, which altogether are driven by 14 antecedents. The study suggests that the dimensions of multidisciplinarity, exposure, connectedness, and pro-social orientation are the core antecedents for social entrepreneurial pathways in healthcare. While the study focuses on the profiles of highly successful social entrepreneurs in general, this research provides novel insights on the emergence of social entrepreneurial action in healthcare.

The aim of this book is too appeal to a broad set of target audiences, due to its broad coverage of the topic area. Scholars and young researchers in entrepreneurship as well as healthcare are the primary audience. Especially, research students will find this book useful to get a comprehensive understanding of the healthcare entrepreneurship field, of its complexities and opportunities in both private industry and public sectors. Our hope is that it will spark conversations across disciplines and guide them in their search for research avenues. More senior academic researchers will benefit from the various literature streams presented on the topic of healthcare entrepreneurship, as well as the various pointers for areas of future research that we discuss.

Managers, healthcare professionals, public sector officials, and future healthcare entrepreneurs may benefit from the practical examples and case studies provided in this book. Rather than prescribing to only one theoretical lens, we make use of a several frameworks emerging from both medical, entrepreneurship, and innovation research.

Ralf Wilden—Massimo Garbuio—Federica Angeli—Daniele Mascia

1 Entrepreneurship in Healthcare

Past Contributions and Future Opportunities

Massimo Garbuio and Ralf Wilden

Introduction

The number of startups listed on the New York Stock Exchange that are active in healthcare-related industries has grown significantly, such that they now comprise the largest number of company listings in the New York Stock Exchange in 2014. In September 2015, the *New York Times* counted over 165,000 smartphone applications available in the US to help people stay healthy or monitor medical conditions.[1] Innovation in healthcare is expected to be significantly fueled by new entrants and entrepreneurs using digital technologies, "Internet of Things" applications, and/or low-cost business models to solve problems more cheaply and effectively (Teece, 2010; Christensen, 1997). It has been highlighted that starting a business may be the most valuable lesson for medical students (Ryu, 2017). Similarly, it has been claimed that anesthesiologists could become the next leaders in innovative medical entrepreneurism (Kwon et al., 2017).

Despite its promise, entrepreneurship in the healthcare context faces several unique barriers (Phillips and Garman, 2006). First, because the majority of healthcare revenue (which is primarily generated from third parties, such as governments and insurance providers) is directly linked to specific provided services, healthcare organizations have little room to use their revenues for other activities (Robinson, 2001), such as building up risk capital to allocate to entrepreneurial activities (Phillips and Garman, 2006). Second, the hierarchical structure of healthcare organizations and competition for scarce resources often discourages collaboration between organizations with similar capabilities. Finally, the high degree of professional autonomy of healthcare professionals and their discomfort with risk taking given the traditional scope of their work hinders entrepreneurship.

A better understanding of the unique context and challenges that the healthcare sector provides will help to advance entrepreneurship research in general. For example, digitalization and the large availability of mobile devices in both advanced and developing economies allow for new business models, often driven by entrepreneurs previously not active in healthcare. Further, the Internet of Things, and wearable devices more specifically, permit us to monitor health conditions and address them in new ways, even remotely. Finally, pay per product is being replaced with pay-per-usage and subscription models, and even free models, as when income is generated by advertising or cross-selling to other market segments. As these examples suggest, it is becoming easier for healthcare entrepreneurs to reach large numbers of people.

Most of the entrepreneurship research using a healthcare context has been published in healthcare and medical journals, with little reference to management theories and journals. That is of some concern, given the wealth of knowledge that entrepreneurship and management literature have developed over the years. We aim to contribute to the current debate with two key contributions. First, we explore the research progress that has been made in the area of healthcare entrepreneurship. To do so, using text mining, we conduct systematic content analysis of the abstracts 909 articles published in relevant health and management journals. More precisely, we explore the dominant *content themes* of existing research, as well as changes in these content themes over time. Second, to improve our understanding of research in healthcare entrepreneurship, we suggest themes that can be leveraged to shape future research endeavors and foster collaborations across fields (Ireland and Webb, 2007). Indeed, to increase the chances of discovering valuable opportunities and starting viable businesses in healthcare, much of the work from entrepreneurship and management more broadly can be leveraged further. We do so by presenting our research directions in a multi-level framework, distinguishing among macro-, meso-, and micro-level research, as established in entrepreneurship research. We provide key themes for each and suggest entrepreneurship, management, innovation, and marketing theories that may help guide further research.

Methodology

To examine the impact of entrepreneurship in healthcare research and develop a framework for future theory building and testing, we conduct a systematic review of published articles in the area of entrepreneurship in healthcare (Tranfield et al., 2003). We validate the extrapolation of relevant themes and concepts through textual analysis using the Leximancer software. To conduct a systematic literature review, we primarily drew on Tranfield et al. (2003) and Macpherson and Jones (2010), in addition to Lee (2009), Rashman et al. (2009), and Wang and Chugh (2014). We followed a systematic approach to increase the validity of our findings by providing a clear set of steps that can be replicated. Given that our sample spans multiple disciplines, from entrepreneurship to management to medical care, we followed Lee (2009), Rashman et al. (2009), and Wang and Chugh (2014) in considering systematic reviews as a "guiding tool" that allows us to shape the review according to our research focus and objectives rather than as a methodology with rigid rules.

Data Collection

Using *Scopus*, one of the most comprehensive research platforms available (Zupic and Čater, 2015), we looked for articles that explicitly included the terms "entrep*" AND "healthcare" OR "health care" in their titles, keywords, and/or abstracts.[2] We focused our search on only journal articles published in English. Thus, we did not include other published outputs, such as in book chapters and conference proceedings. Books (similar to working papers and book chapters) do not undergo as rigorous editorial review process as journals, and including these sources may impact the quality of the data and results.

The comprehensive search resulted in 1,289 articles (909 available abstracts), out of which 145 articles were published in journals classified in as belonging to business, management, accounting, economics, finance, or econometrics, and 912 articles were published in journals related to medicine, nursing, or health professions. We focus our analysis on these two broad categories of academic research, and include all articles for which abstracts were available (135 abstracts in the former and 671 articles in the latter category).

Analysis Method

To provide a detailed analysis of core publications in entrepreneurship in healthcare, we analyze the manuscripts using unstructured ontological discovery. We therefore shift the level of analysis to the *words* used by the authors instead of investigating authors and their citation patterns. The result is a systematic, unbiased, and content-driven review of the literature (Biesenthal and Wilden, 2014). We apply the textual data-mining software Leximancer 4.0, a valuable tool for narrative inquiry of a research field (Sowa, 2000; Stubbs, 1996). This text mining tool has been used in previous literature reviews in areas such as open innovation (Randhawa et al., 2016), dynamic capabilities (Wilden et al., 2016), and service-dominant logic (Wilden et al., 2017). The assumption underlying this type of analysis is that co-occuring words reflect categories (i.e., concepts) that carry specific meanings and that words are defined by the context within which they occur. Leximancer differs from manual coding of words, as it bootstraps an expanded list of related terms that signify a concept from the text data. This machine-based identification of concepts exhibits close agreement with expert judgment (Campbell et al., 2011; Rooney, 2005; Wilden et al., 2017). It is therefore appropriate for sophisticated exploratory research due to its high reliability and reproducibility of concept extractions and thematic grouping.

A Bayesian learning algorithm underlies Leximancer to identify: (i) the most frequently used concepts within the text data, and (ii) the relationships between these identified concepts. Thus, Leximancer first systematically uncovers key concepts within the healthcare entrepreneurship paradigm by using a small number of seed words from the text (thematic analysis). To do so, the software generates a thesaurus of words that are closely related to a concept to define its content. Identified concepts are more than just keywords; they represent collections of words that carry related meaning (Campbell et al., 2011). Second, Leximancer reveals how concepts are linked based on the frequency and co-occurrence of words within their contexts (semantic analysis). The result is an investigation of concepts (i.e., common text elements) and themes (i.e., groupings of uncovered concepts) (Mathies and Burford, 2011).

The results of this thematic and semantic analysis are represented in "maps of meaning." The black dots represent identified concepts; the relationships between concepts are then identified and aggregated into themes.[3] The color of the circles (brighter circles are more important) and their size (which indicates how many concepts have been clustered to form a given theme) indicate the importance of the themes. The distance between concepts on these "maps of meaning" indicate how closely the concepts are related. Hence, concepts that are weakly related semantically will be mapped far apart from each other and vice versa (Campbell et al., 2011; Rooney, 2005). Summing up, Leximancer aids researchers in interpreting and visualizing the structure of complex text data.

State of Entrepreneurship in Healthcare Research

Publication Statistics

In a first analysis step, we analyzed the publication trends. To do so, we analyzed all 909 available abstracts included in our sample, not restricting the list of journals to any specific research area. Figure 1.1 shows that the number of publications has steadily increased.

As summarized in Figure 1.1, research on entrepreneurship in the healthcare sector has attracted growing interest over the past 40 years. Furthermore, our analysis reveals that entrepreneurship in healthcare research is beginning to reach a broad audience, indicating interest within multiple domains. More specifically, the majority of our sample articles were published in medical and nursing journals rather than in entrepreneurship or management journals. In fact, only six articles were published in leading management or strategy journals, such as: *Research Policy* (two articles), *R&D Management* (one), *Journal of Business Venturing* (two), *Journal of Business Ethics* (three), and *Harvard Business Review* (four). In fact, medicine, nursing, or health professions journals

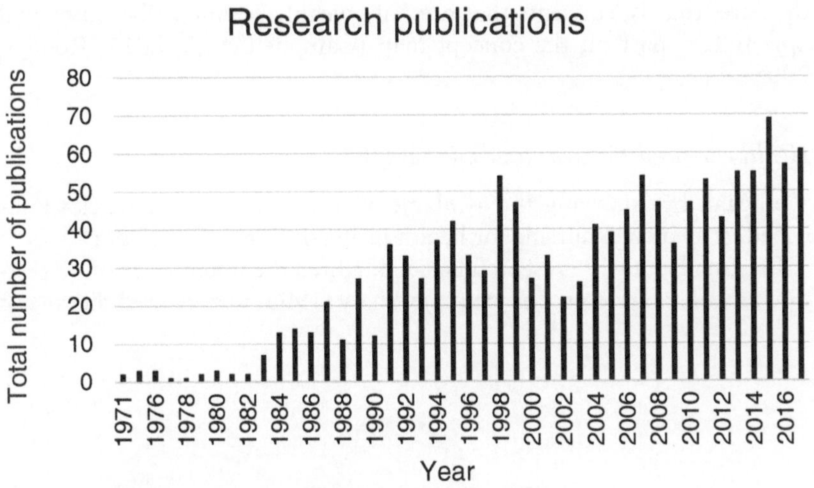

Figure 1.1 Publications Per Year

correspond to 71% of our total entrepreneurship in healthcare research sample, and business, management, accounting, economics, finance, or econometrics articles for 11%, revealing that the impact of former three fields has been more significant than that of other disciplines. Overall, our review suggests that entrepreneurship in healthcare research has yet to reach a broad audience in management as well as marketing. However, we notice a promising trend toward increased research in this area.

Textual Analysis Findings

In the following sections, we conduct a text-mining-based content analysis of the identified article abstracts to systematically decipher key concepts and themes. To conduct the analysis, all text data was used as input into the analysis, and concept seeds were created through the software—the equivalent of assuming a "diffuse prior" of theoretical concepts. Patterns that arose between concepts were identified and aggregated into themes. We illustrated the relationship between concepts and themes through concept maps. We structured our textual analysis in two steps. First, we analyzed all article abstracts published in medical journals and in management-related journals separately. Second, we compared the findings of these two sets of articles.

In the "maps of meaning" discussed and presented hereafter, circles represent themes derived from the articles, and relevant concepts are located within each theme. The importance of themes is shown by the color and size of the circles, with darker and bigger circles being more important.

The distance between concepts on the map indicates how closely related they are; that is, concepts that are only weakly semantically linked will appear far apart on the concept map (Campbell et al., 2011; Rooney, 2005).

Healthcare and Medical Journals Sample

We began by analyzing the available abstracts of the 671 articles published in medicine, nursing, or health professions journals (Figure 1.2).

Existing healthcare research has highlighted the importance of innovation as well as systems. For example, Shaw (1993) investigated the role of

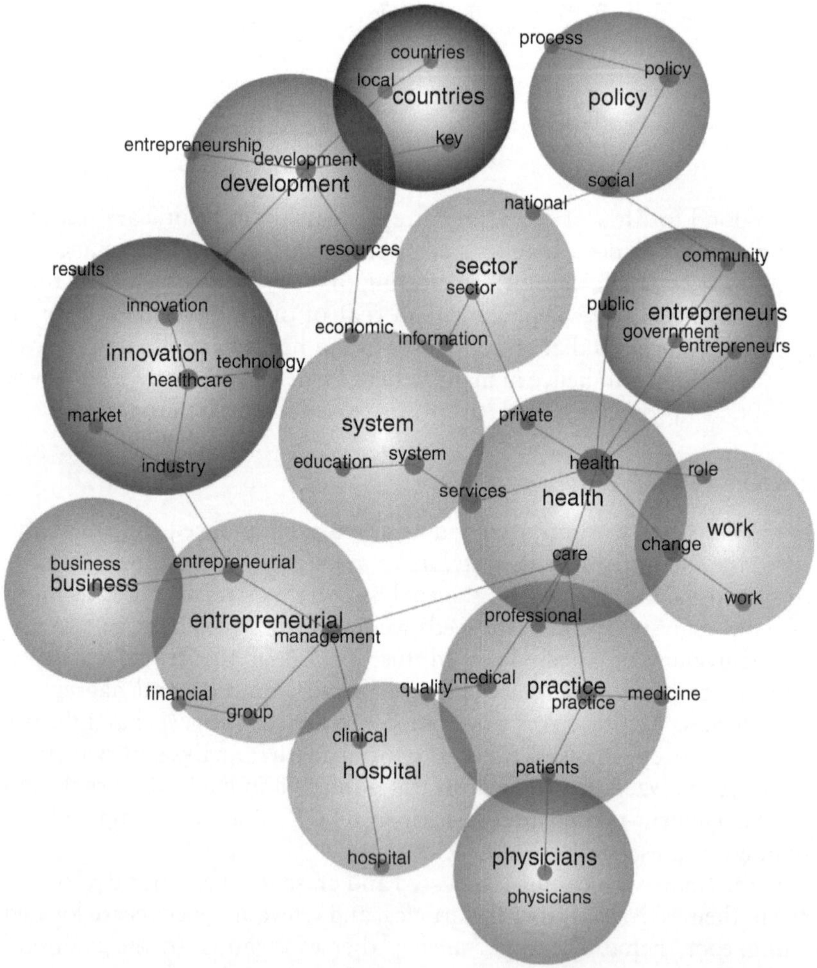

Figure 1.2 Themes and Concepts Based on Medical Journals Abstracts

entrepreneurs' networks to foster innovation and found that consultant clinicians and physicians play an important role in new product development processes and marketing of innovative products. For example, research has investigated the use of six sigma, a set of techniques and tools for process improvement, in healthcare services and research and development (R&D) processes (Rehn and Abetti, 2013). Furthermore, Janssen and Moors (2013) have investigated the role of entrepreneurial strategies in developing sustainable innovations for the structural change of healthcare systems.

The themes policy and entrepreneurs (comprising concepts such as community, public, and government) appear in close proximity on the map. In particular, previous macro-level research has investigated the role of public policies and governments on the healthcare industry, innovation, and entrepreneurship. For example, Tuohy (2012) compares reforms in Canada, the UK, and the Netherlands, and the implications of these reforms for institutional entrepreneurs. Field (2011) investigates the role of government in the healthcare market. Furthermore, the role of the community and community involvement in healthcare has been the focus of existing research. Dalvit et al. (2013) have investigated the importance of innovation and technology in providing healthcare service to remote communities.

In the theme of systems, a main concept is education. For example, Souba (1996) investigates the strategies that academic medical centers used to address these challenges and finds that a change from medical individualism to entrepreneurial teamwork is crucial. Colyvas et al. (2012) investigated whether gender differences exist in the innovative behavior of scientists. They find differences in the number of inventions reported and demonstrate that gender effects are contingent on the employment context and available resources. Their research also shows the growing interest in women in healthcare entrepreneurship. Furthermore, Marques et al. (2013) empirically investigate the motivations and entrepreneurial orientations among diagnostic and therapy technicians. Entrepreneurs' psychological and cognitive characteristics are identified, and implications for healthcare managers to establish conditions for business ventures more readily are provided.

More recently, Cohen (2017) has identified how the vast majority of surgeons and medical students have no formal educational training on innovation process from idea to commercial implementation. To address this challenge, Cohen presents a study on the University of Michigan recently creating the first pathway of excellence for medical students to develop skills and interests in medical innovation and entrepreneurship. In his words, "This program has been transformative for building a new culture of young, motivated medical innovators, many of whom have dedicated their talents already to addressing several key problems in surgical patient care" (pp. 989).

An area that we expected to feature more prominently on the map would be a theme around value. In particular, the idea of value creation, delivery, and capture through business model design appears to be of central interest to researchers in management and entrepreneurship, but not here in healthcare entrepreneurship. Some exceptions are previous research on the role of incubators in healthcare innovation (Chakma et al., 2010), new web-based business models for pharmacists (Alston and Waitzman, 2013), and the role of venture capitalists (Anthony, 2012; Davila et al., 2003). These are all relatively recent contributions. The value theme should also be closely related to the concept of technology, indicating the importance of technology in entrepreneurship in healthcare research (e.g., Gottlieb and Makower, 2013; Camarillo et al., 2004). Again, these contributions are rather recent relative to the time span of the articles examined in our research.

Interestingly, we do not see the concept *nurses* despite their importance in healthcare delivery. For example, Roggenkamp and White (1998) identified factors that influence nurses' decisions to become entrepreneurs (e.g., love of nursing, the belief they could make a difference, the influence of their family, and outside business setup assistance) and how healthcare managers may capitalize on this trend as an effective method of strategic adaptation. More recent research has highlighted that nurses are often recognized as creative, knowledgeable professionals with many versatile skills (Hong, 2017).

These examples are consistent with what can be observed in the marketplace. New enterprises in healthcare have been shifting from low-technology, low-innovation enterprises to those that are more heavily based on technology, innovation, and new business models, and particularly on digital technologies. This shift raises the question of the extent to which research in healthcare and the medical field is ready to understand the challenges of these new forms of enterprise in healthcare, both from the point of view of how opportunities are discovered and of what it takes to make these enterprises successful.

Management Journals Sample

We then analyzed all abstracts published in management-related journals. Figure 1.3 indicates that the focus of research in management on this topic has been on entrepreneurial activities on a higher level; that is, with little focus on the micro-foundations of healthcare entrepreneurship. This is highlighted by the absence of concepts such as nurse, manager, individual, physician, etc., but the occurrence of concepts such as organizational, management, industry, companies, and institutional. Related, the data indicate that the role of nurses has received limited empirical attention in business research. The only micro-level term that appears is entrepreneur, which is closely related to the concept market. This indicates some discussion on market orientation, or a set of individual entrepreneurs' behaviors and processes aimed at continuously monitoring

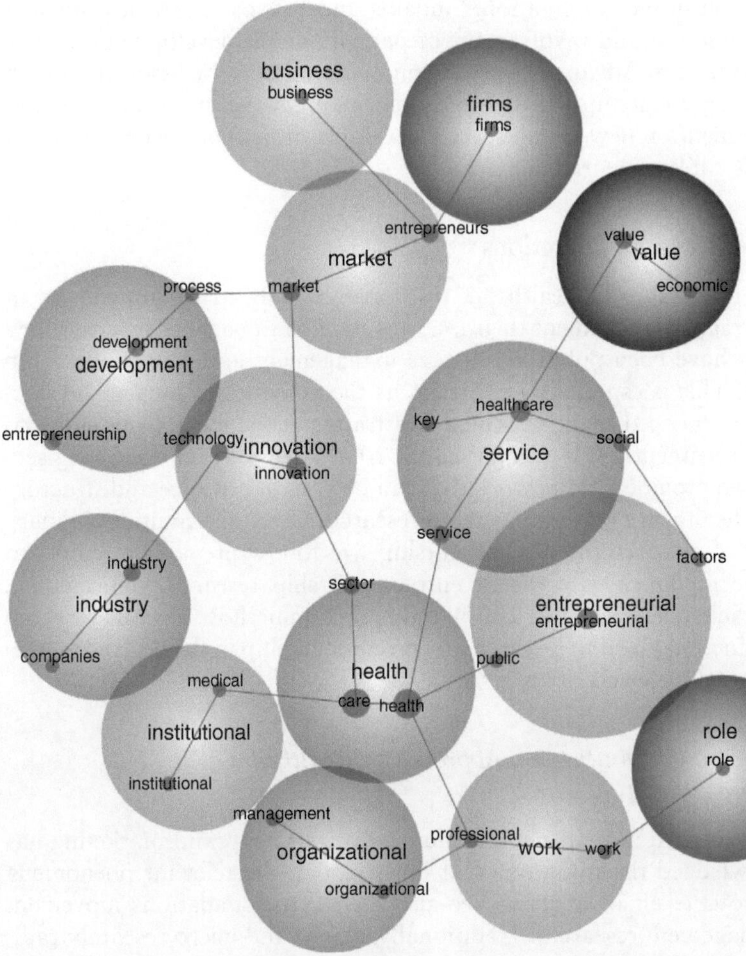

Figure 1.3 Themes and Concepts Based on Management Journals Abstracts

and surveying the external environment (Matsuno et al., 2002). A higher market orientation is typically associated with greater proactivity among entrepreneurs, as well as with their ability to recognize and create superior customer value (Zhou et al., 2005).

We further find that research has investigated the economic value of healthcare and healthcare services. One example of value is the study in the context of organizational values and how they affect doctors' receptiveness to strategy implementation (Spyridonidis and Calnan, 2011).

Finally, the results indicate that research has investigated healthcare services. An interesting study that goes across service delivery, entrepreneurship, and healthcare has investigated continuous service innovation for the first time in the healthcare context, with particular emphasis on a firm's customer orientation. Sindakis and Kitsios (2016) investigated the interaction and involvement of patients in the development of new health services. Advancing service innovation theory by associating with the entrepreneurship theory, the study highlight the importance of user involvement on new health service development and in the enhancement a firm's entrepreneurial activity.

Future Research Directions

Entrepreneurship in healthcare research has only made limited use of mainstream management theories. This may be in part because very few articles have been published in core management and entrepreneurship outlets. This is especially important, as the activities of nurses and doctors is influenced by institutional constraints at the local, firm, industry, and government levels (Knight et al., 2016). Thus, in the following sections, we provide a framework that can be used to advance and structure future healthcare entrepreneurship research. Given the multidisciplinary nature of research in entrepreneurship, we follow previous attempts to provide guidance to areas of entrepreneurship research (Short et al., 2009; Schendel and Hitt, 2007) and we examine how various research disciplines may add to research on entrepreneurship in the healthcare sector on various levels of analysis.

Encouraging a Multi-Level Approach to Healthcare Entrepreneurship Research

Much research in management, innovation, strategy, and marketing has acknowledged the importance of investigating the relevant phenomena at various levels of analysis (see also the micro-foundations movement in management research). Traditionally, macro and micro research traditions in social science research in general, and in management-related research in particular, have experienced tension (Felin et al., 2015). Partially rooted in discussions in economics, scholars following a macro-level research tradition stress the importance of history, culture, and structure, among others. Micro-level researchers, on the other hand, focus on individuals and their interactions. In the context of entrepreneurship research, the differences and interactions of micro-, meso-, and macro-level concepts are of particular interest (Syed et al., 2012; De Bruin et al., 2007; Jamali, 2009).

Our conceptual model is founded in general entrepreneurship research and adapted from Syed and Özbilgin (2009), as illustrated in Figure 1.4. The historical context affects macro-level analysis, which in turn comprises meso-organizational factors as well as micro-level individual factors and their relationships.

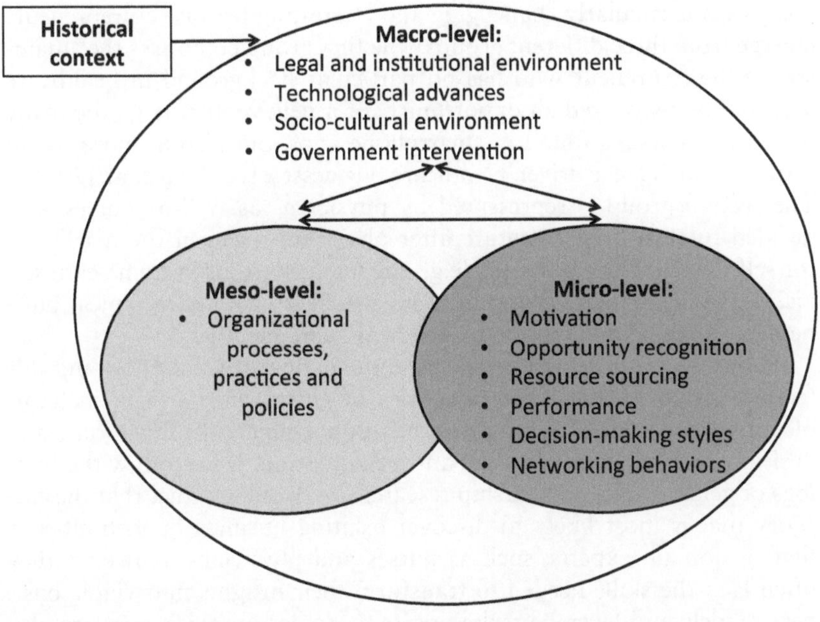

Figure 1.4 Levels of Analysis in Healthcare Entrepreneurship

Micro-Level

General research at the micro-level of entrepreneurship has advanced our knowledge by focusing on factors such as opportunity recognition, motivation, resource sourcing, decision-making, and networking behaviors. Opportunity recognition is considered to be a fundamental issue in entrepreneurship and a key source of competitive advantage (Ardichvili et al., 2003; Wilden and Gudergan, 2015; Vogel, 2017; Dong et al., 2016). Cardon et al. (2012) discuss the concept of "hot cognition" in which emotions, moods, and feelings affect entrepreneurial cognition and reasoning. Grégoire et al. (2011) articulates the importance of the mind and the environment on entrepreneurial actions. The motives for pursuing an entrepreneurial venture have also received widespread attention in general entrepreneurship, as well as in healthcare entrepreneurship research. Performance has been subject to analysis not only in terms of the financial performance of entrepreneurial ventures, but also in terms of self-growth and achievement of personal goals, particularly in the case of nurses as entrepreneurs (De Bruin et al., 2007; Lehoux et al., 2017). Decision-making styles and the management of trade-offs and paradoxes are another area of investigation that is likely to provide insights on the success of the myriad of healthcare startups (Jahanmir, 2016).

For entrepreneurship in healthcare, the micro- (individual) level of analysis is particularly challenging and interesting because entrepreneurs emerge from three different groups. The first group comprises the "mainstream" entrepreneur who has no particular background in healthcare and simply discovered an opportunity for a new venture (e.g., the many healthcare startups found in smartphone apps, but also in more recent artificial intelligence driven healthcare businesses; see Zang et al. [2015]). The second group is represented by physicians as well as nurses who decided to start a new venture after observing a gap in the market or for self-development purposes (e.g., the many startups in home-care services). Finally, the last group includes managers who have typical business background and have managed healthcare facilities.

From a future research perspective, the extent of similarities and differences among these three categories of entrepreneurs (e.g., in terms of entrepreneurial traits, motivations, opportunity identifications, and decision-making styles) remains an open question. If we follow the findings of general entrepreneurship research, we would predict that the category that is most likely to discover exciting business opportunities is that of domain experts, such as nurses and physicians. However, they often lack the skills needed to transform their insights into viable business models and leverage technologies to do so. Entrepreneurs are also resource orchestrators, an increasingly relevant skill when competitive advantage is likely to be based on the use of advanced technologies or novel business models; these technical and business resources are often not part of a physician's toolkit, having been sourced elsewhere.

Extant research informs us about the relevant cognitive mechanism, attitudes, and orientation of entrepreneurs and innovators that typically leads to the identification of market opportunities (Ireland and Webb, 2007; Busenitz et al., 2003; Garbuio et al., 2015). Although the analysis of competition and the assessment of potential profits of new ventures created are at the heart of market orientation, our analysis reveals that these characteristics in healthcare are complemented by relevant constructs such as "quality of care" and "value for the patient." The identification of market opportunities and the establishment of new entrepreneurial activities are substantially driven by the recognized opportunity to improve outcomes that matter to patients, relative to the cost sustained to treat them. The patient is not the only stakeholder considered in this perspective; the concept of value highlights the necessity of considering the affordability of treatments. Healthcare organizations, insurance companies, and public agencies are all stakeholders that individual entrepreneurs are increasingly taking into account when assessing market potential in this industry.

Abundant general entrepreneurship research has investigated differences between entrepreneurs and managers along personality and cognitive traits, in addition to social network differences. Although few personality differences have been found between entrepreneurs and non-entrepreneurs (Brockhaus and Horwitz, 1986; Low and MacMillan, 1988), there has been clearer empirical support for the existence of cognitive and social network differences (Dyer et al, 2008). Innovative entrepreneurs are not only able to act on opportunities by combining resources, but they also look at problems differently and leverage their networks to come up with original ways to address market needs in the first place (Berns, 2008). Extant general entrepreneurship research has also broadly investigated the managerial skills of managers and physicians alike (see Lega et al. [2013] for a recent literature review). However, the debate about the importance of such skills and traits in the healthcare context overlooks broader changes in society and the economy, as reflected by a call from Brown and McCool (1987) for managers in healthcare organizations to adopt entrepreneurial rather than managerial skills. The question of medical schools as a pathway to innovative entrepreneurship has also been raised (Cohen, 2017; Ryu, 2017). Similarly, Cutler (2010a, 2010b) argues more recently that healthcare entrepreneurs can address the market imperfections affecting healthcare, particularly the mismatch between the medical care that people *should* receive and the care they *actually* receive. Doing so could help to address the fact that about one-third of medical expenditures are not associated with improved outcomes, thus reducing the efficiency of the medical system overall.

Finally, the entrepreneurial orientation of the entrepreneur (rather than the firm itself) is a critical topic of research in entrepreneurship broadly (Lumpkin and Dess, 1996), and an important one in healthcare entrepreneurship. Researchers have agreed that entrepreneurial orientation is basically a combination of three aspects: the tendency to support new ideas, the proactiveness, and risk-taking propensity (Cooper and Gimeno-Gascon, 1992; McClelland, 1987; Rauch and Frese, 2000; Wiklund, 1999). Helm et al. (2010) argue that innovativeness mediates the motivation and the success of entrepreneurs. That is, the entrepreneurial orientation of the founders influences new venture performance through its generation of innovativeness. In their study of 165 spinoffs in Germany, Helm et al. (2010) show that in high-technology sectors and in fast-growing markets—such as biotechnology, healthcare, information technology, and optics—where innovation is necessary, enduring a pronounced entrepreneurial orientation is important.

The study of intrapreneurship in healthcare is also of primary importance. For example, Heinze and Weber (2015) used qualitative data from two integrative medicine (IM) programs inside large healthcare organizations to understand how institutional intrapreneurs work to integrate the IM logic in highly institutionalized institutions. Their results highlight the importance of understanding of the organizational context to explain the fate of early-stage efforts toward institutional change. In another interesting study, Hinz and Ingerfurth (2013) show how organizational entrepreneurship, in terms of proactiveness, innovativeness, and risk taking, affects hospital performance.

Meso-Level

The meso-level of analysis includes organizational processes, practices, and policies that affect entrepreneurial and innovative behavior. These include routines, decision-making processes, politics, and organizational cultures that affect employees' ability to explore and exploit opportunities within organizational boundaries. For example, organizational culture and structure usually create shared values, commitments, and beliefs that are essential to organizational functioning and success (Wilden et al., 2013). Culture, in turn, will affect employees' comfort with tackling ambiguous problems, proposing out-of-the-box solutions, and taking the risks needed to establish entrepreneurial opportunities. Both Syed and Özbilgin (2009) and Bourdieu (1990) talk about "habitus" as deeply structured dispositions that have a direct influence upon action within organizational contexts.

At the meso-level, future healthcare entrepreneurship research will benefit from investigating the interactions between individual entrepreneurs within organizational boundaries and entrepreneurial processes, behaviors, and outcomes to create innovation (Ireland and Webb, 2007). Innovation is necessary for the continued success of an organization (Tushman and Anderson, 2004). Given that multiple stakeholders, such as hospitals, patients, and nurses, are involved in healthcare-related innovation, the growing research stream on *open innovation* may inform research on healthcare business models and how best to create and capture value (Randhawa et al., 2016). Open innovation research provides alternative perspectives of innovation that focus on externally driven and non-firm-centric models. Open innovation assumes that, as attempting to advance their technology, firms use both "external and internal ideas, as well as internal and external paths to market, as the firms look to advance their technology" (Chesbrough, 2003: 24). Given these challenges, healthcare providers should step over existing firm boundaries to cooperate and exchange knowledge with external actors to enable innovation (e.g., Chesbrough, 2003; West and Gallagher, 2006). This line of investigation has the potential to identify insights into the dynamics that enable value co-creation, particularly for collaborative innovation.

Furthermore, to investigate the idea of innovation across organizational boundaries, the *service-dominant logic of marketing* (Lusch and Vargo, 2006; Vargo and Lusch, 2004) may be a useful lens (Wilden et al., 2017). This logic is based on the idea of value co-creation of market actors (Prahalad and Ramaswamy, 2004; Sawhney et al., 2005). By its very nature, healthcare is based on service provision, thus opening healthcare research up to the idea of services marketing and "open service innovation" (Chesbrough, 2011). Service (eco)system research (e.g., Vargo and Akaka, 2012) may help to develop an improved conceptualization of open service innovation in healthcare (e.g., Ordanini and Parasuraman, 2011; Gustafsson et al., 2012). Relatedly, research on "user innovation" (e.g., Von Hippel, 1986) should inform future healthcare entrepreneurship research, given the role of patient centrality in healthcare and in today's networked and service-led environments (Randhawa and Scerri, 2014).

Relatedly, *social ties* have been viewed traditionally as "pipes" through which relevant resources are channeled and acquired by individual entrepreneurs (Podolny, 2001). At the firm level, these links, which can be either formal or informal and may be encompassed by different degrees of heterogeneity (Davis and Greve, 1997), often take the form of strategic alliances and franchising initiatives. These typical entrepreneurship strategies allow access to external resources and their integration with the stock of internally available resources, thus overcoming resource constraints and internal barriers to new opportunities. For example, research on biotechnology scientists has found that the extent to which a firm's scientists collaborate externally on scientific articles positively influences the firm's innovation output (Almeida et al., 2011).

By contrast, the healthcare entrepreneurship literature seems to have been much less focused on this "egocentric" perspective, recalling instead the importance of professional communities for nurses, physicians, and other healthcare profiles. In this context, identity and professional legitimation are relevant socially constructed resources. Community represents the milieu in which healthcare entrepreneurs gain access to vital resources to develop entrepreneurial activities. Healthcare entrepreneurs' affiliation with professional communities grants them access to and interaction with peers. The analysis of 'boundaries', often discussed in entrepreneurship research, enlarges from single firms to broader communities in healthcare. The legitimacy received by peers is important for entrepreneurial processes and outcomes in this field. We emphasize the strong collective nature of healthcare entrepreneurship, despite the more traditional organizational lenses adopted in entrepreneurship research.

Disruptive innovation has become increasingly important, as digital technologies allow a cheaper source of resources for the startup and management of enterprises (McQuivey, 2013); at the same time, innovation from emerging economies has spread to advanced economies (Govindarajan and Trimble, 2012). *Disruptive innovation theory* explains how expensive, complicated products and services are often supplanted by inexpensive, simple ones when capabilities of cutting-edge innovations overshoot the demands of existing customers (Christensen, 1997). Consider, NxStage Medical created a portable dialysis machine that can fit behind a bed in an intensive-care unit. The output of the machine is not as good as that of state-of-the-art dialysis machines, but it has several other advantages, such as the fact that it is portable and thus allows patients to clean their blood more often, potentially helping them to stay healthier. In fact, large competitors such as Fresenius have started introducing their own portable dialysis units. Although senior managers of large organizations have difficulty releasing their focus on current clients and technologies, incumbents are promoting the adoption of inexpensive, potentially promising and disruptive solutions. This pattern has repeated itself across industries, countries, and time periods, threatening entire industries (Christensen and Raynor, 2003). As such, disruptive innovation is also likely to become an organizing framework for the discovery and development of entrepreneurial ideas in the healthcare sector, which is currently being disrupted by students and small companies, as noted earlier.

As in other industries, healthcare organizations do not work in isolation, and competition between providers is increasing. Inefficiencies in the healthcare sector may open doors for new organizations to enter. Indeed, inefficiencies in the healthcare sector *are* being addressed by innovative entrepreneurs as well as by entrepreneurial entities in the healthcare value chain. An entrepreneurial mindset is not only essential to coping with newly competitive conditions but also is effective beyond any concerns regarding the transparency of physician-industry financial relationships (including calls for restricting collaboration). In a recent study, Smith and Sfekas (2013) concluded that physicians are an important source of medical device innovation. On average, physician-founded companies account for 11% of the information in pre-market approval applications as compared to 4% from non-physician-founded companies. Moreover, incumbents are significantly more likely to cite physician-founded companies' patents and incorporate them into new devices. Trends in new technologies, especially digitalization, *applification*, and gamification, appear to have taken the healthcare sector by surprise. Whereas in the past, healthcare management was the prerogative of specific healthcare organizations, many services now can be offered by smartphone applications, and therefore by startups and entrepreneurs rather than hospitals. Consequently, entrepreneurs can push hospitals toward being more innovative and adaptive to the changing landscape, while also making better use of fewer resources.

Macro-Level

The macro-level of analysis comprises structural conditions such as the legal and institutional environment, the state of the technology, the sociocultural environment, and the degree and type of governmental intervention that influence healthcare entrepreneurship and innovation within the broader context (Syed and Özbilgin, 2009). Macro-level research usually investigates organizations, treating individuals and groups as "black boxes" on the assumption that durable and coherent structures take prevalence over the discrete elements of which they consist (Kyriakidou and Özbilgin, 2006). However, it also has been established that individuals and groups substantially influence macro-national phenomena through their behaviors of new venture creation.

At the macro-level, research on entrepreneurship in healthcare should consider the characteristics of this highly regulated industry as well as implications linked to the presence of major stakeholders with well-defined regulatory roles in the market (Maguire et al., 2004). For example, agencies such as the US Food and Drug Administration and the European Medicines Agency in the European Union are responsible for the scientific evaluation of drugs developed by pharmaceutical companies. New products must be approved before being commercialized and used by clients. The cost-effectiveness analysis of new technologies in hospitals is also becoming important, asking for careful assessments of new technologies and comparison of their performance with the costs of their acquisition and maintenance. Entrepreneurship in healthcare should take into account the actual effectiveness of new products and emphasize the evidence-based nature of adoption decisions rather than simply the impact of ideas and innovation in the market. Another relevant characteristic of entrepreneurship in healthcare is its R&D nature, in contrast to the much more discussed finance perspective fund in the more general entrepreneurship research (Ireland and Webb, 2007). For example, some of the papers analyzed discuss the role of scientist-entrepreneurs engaged in the formation of new biotech or healthcare ventures. Relevant areas of future research may concern the adoption of new models to close the gap between academia and industry; the integration of scientific, managerial, and entrepreneurial competencies; and the possibility of using both patenting and publishing behaviors to spread entrepreneurial achievements.

Threats to established healthcare providers may also come from organizations on different levels of the traditional value chain, which are now empowered to substitute the services of more traditional healthcare providers. In fact, a favorable regulatory environment and technological advances, such as the diffusion of electronic medical records, are substantially changing adjacent industries and will affect the role of healthcare providers in the near future (Greene et al., 2011; Blumenthal and Tavenner, 2010). Developments in communication and computing technologies have indeed changed the traditional balance between customers—patients, in healthcare—and suppliers (Teece, 2010). Customers now have more choices, and their particular needs and desires can be satisfied more easily as the supply of alternative solutions becomes more transparent. In addition, customers now expect basic services to be provided for free, often via the Internet and smartphone applications. These expectations put pressure on businesses to become more customer-centric and to find new business models. In fairness, the development of such technologies also lowers the costs of collecting information (so-called "big data"), which in turn can be exploited to provide more customized solutions at cheaper prices. The associated regulatory framework of how to deal with big data will also influence the sector. Due to the impact of population wellbeing and quality control on the effectiveness of new product and services (no harm, first of all), efforts to nurture entrepreneurship in healthcare raise important questions for policymakers.

Conclusion

The current landscape in healthcare organizations is threatened by the entrance of innovative entrepreneurs and other innovative actors in the value chain, which are leveraging the power of digital technologies, Internet of Things, and innovative business models to reach an increasing number of users from around the world. Users are also becoming more educated about what constitutes exceptional customer experience, and they expect more services to be provided for free with their privacy being protected. The healthcare sector has not been spared by these trends; if anything, it so far has seen a great number of such enterprises emerging and successfully moving toward becoming large, public organizations.

Our review and analysis shows that healthcare is a promising context for future entrepreneurship research and that more research is required to shape this research area into a more impactful one, as called for by Brown and McCool (1987) and Cutler (2010a, 2010b). The lack of collaboration between medical and entrepreneurship and management scholarship implies a serious missed opportunity to develop theories and empirical studies that could shed light on the true impact of entrepreneurship and innovation in healthcare and move the field forward in light of current challenges brought by the digital landscape and cost-cutting pressures. As the need for entrepreneurship and innovation in healthcare becomes increasingly urgent, our contribution will indeed inform the debate regarding the role of managers and clinicians at the head of healthcare structure. We identified critical themes worthy of investigation and then addressed related fields of research that could inform and enrich the healthcare entrepreneurship debate.

As in any study, some limitations underlie our study. First, our dataset may lack contributions to entrepreneurship in healthcare found in books, papers published in non-ranked journals, and conference proceedings. Finally, by focusing on the terms "entrepreneur*" and "healthcare" OR "health care," we may leave out research on related constructs, in particular innovation. Bringing in innovation would have led us to include papers in areas such as the pharmaceutical industry and biotechnology, which are not relevant to the current investigation. Given that the motivation of this study was to investigate the core concepts and themes of entrepreneurship in healthcare research specifically, articles that did not explicitly include this search term may not need to be linked to this research area.

For research in healthcare entrepreneurship research in healthcare to progress in a timely manner, it needs to build stronger bridges between healthcare scholars and entrepreneurship scholars, on the one hand, but also encourage the many possible contributions from related fields, such as management, innovation, sociology, etc. In doing so, we will be able to generate an improved understanding of the determinants and success factors of entrepreneurship in this crucial sector. This new understanding of entrepreneurship in healthcare will provide scholars with a nuanced and practical view on how to nurture entrepreneurial traits and skills in nurses and physicians as well as potential entrepreneurs from related domain, including but not limited to high tech, and ultimately increase the likelihood of effectiveness and success for new startups in the healthcare sector.

Notes

1. www.nytimes.com/aponline/2015/09/17/business/ap-us-health-app-growth-study.html?ref=international
2. The data collection was completed in February 2018.
3. We deleted words such as "study," "case," "data," etc. from the text so as to not bias the creation of concepts and themes.

References

Alston, G. L., and Waitzman, J. A. 2013. The I-Tribe Community Pharmacy Practice Model: Professional pharmacy unshackled. *Journal of the American Pharmacists Association*, 53(2): 163–171.

Almeida, P., Hohberger, J., and Parada, P. 2011. Individual scientific collaborations and firm-level innovation. Industrial and Corporate Change, 20(6): 1571–1599.

Anthony, S. D. 2012. The new corporate garage. *Harvard Business Review*, 90(9): 44–53.

Ardichvili, A., Cardozo, R., and Ray, S. 2003. A theory of entrepreneurial opportunity identification and development. *Journal of Business Venturing*, 18: 105–123.

Berns, G. 2008. *Iconoclast: A Neuroscientist Reveals How to Think Differently*. Cambridge, MA: Harvard Business School Press.

Biesenthal, C., and Wilden, R. 2014. Multi-level project governance: Trends and opportunities. *International Journal of Project Management*, 32(8): 1291–1308.

Blumenthal, D., and Tavenner, M. 2010. The 'meaningful use' regulation for electronic health records. *New England Journal of Medicine*, 363(6): 501–504.

Bourdieu, P. 1990. *The Logic of Practice*. Stanford, CA: Stanford University Press.

Brockhaus, R. H., and Horwitz, P. 1986. The psychology of the entrepreneur. In D. L. Sexton, and R. W. Smilor (Eds.), *The Art and Science of Entrepreneurship*. Cambridge, MA: Ballinger Publishing.

Brown, M., and McCool, B. P. 1987. High-performing managers: Leadership attributes for the 1990s. *Health Care Management Review*, 12(2): 69–75.

Busenitz, L. W., West III, P. G., Sheperd, D., Nelson, T., Chandler, G. N., and Zacharakis, A. 2003. Entrepreneurship research in emergence: Past trends and future directions. *Journal of Management*, 29(3): 285–308.

Camarillo, D. B., Krummel, T. M., and Salisbury, J. K. 2004. Robotic technology in surgery: Past, present, and future. *American Journal of Surgery*, 188(4A): 2S–15S.

Campbell, C., Pitt, L., Parent, M., and Berthon, P. 2011. Understanding consumer conversations around Ads in a Web 2.0 world. *Journal of Advertising*, 40(1): 87–102.

Cardon, M. S., Foo, M., Shepered, D., and Wiklund, J. 2012. Exploring the heart: entrepreneurial emotion is a hot topic. *Entrepreneurship Theory and Practice*, 36(1): 1–10.

Chakma, J., Masum, H., and Singer, P. A. 2010. Can incubators work in Africa? Acorn Technologies and the entrepreneur-centric model. *BMC International Health and Human Rights*, 10.

Chesbrough, H. 2003. *Open Innovation: The New Imperative for Creating and Profiting From Technology*. Boston, MA: Harvard Business School Press.

Chesbrough, H. 2011. Bringing open innovation to services. *MIT Sloan Management Review*, 52(2): 85–90.

Christensen, C. M. 1997. *The Innovator's Dilemma: When New Technologies Cause Great Firms to Fail*. Boston, MA: Harvard Business School Press.

Christensen, C. M., and Raynor, M. E. 2003. *The Innovator's Solution: Creating and Sustaining Successful Growth*. Cambridge, MA: Harvard Business School Press.

Cohen, M. S. 2017. Enhancing surgical innovation through a specialized medical school pathway of excellence in innovation and entrepreneurship: Lessons learned and opportunities for the future. *Surgery*, 162(5): 989–993.

Colyvas, J. A., Snellman, K., Bercovitz, J., and Feldman, M. 2012. Disentangling effort and performance: A renewed look at gender differences in commercializing medical school research. *Journal of Technology Transfer*, 37(4): 478–489.

Cooper, A., and Gimeno-Gascon, F. 1992. Entrepreneurs, process of founding and new venture performance. In *The State of the Art in Entrepreneurship*. Boston, MA: PWS Kent Publishing Co.

Cutler, D. M. 2010a. Where are the health care entrepreneurs? *Issues in Science and Technology*, 27(1): 49–56.

Cutler, D. M. 2010b. Where are the health care entrepreneurs? The failure of organizational innovation in health care. *Innovation Policy and the Economy*, 11(1): 1–28.

Dalvit, L., Gumbo, S., Ntshinga, L., and Terzoli, A. 2013. *TeleWeaver: An Innovative Telecommunication Platform for Marginalized Communities in Africa*. Proceedings of the 13th European Conference on Egovernment: 152–159.

Davila, A., Foster, G., and Gupta, M. 2003. Venture capital financing and the growth of startup firms. *Journal of Business Venturing*, 18(6): 689–708.

Davis, G. F., and Greve, H. R. 1997. Corporate elite networks and governance changes in the 1980s. *American Journal of Sociology*, 103(1): 1–37.

De Bruin, A., Brush, C. G., and Welter, F. 2007. Advancing a framework for coherent research on women's entrepreneurship. *Entrepreneurship Theory and Practice*, 31(3): 323–339.

Dong, A., Garbuio, M., and Lovallo, D. 2016. Generative sensing: A design perspective on the microfoundations of sensing capabilities. *California Management Review*, 58(4): 97–117.

Dyer, J. H., Gregersen, H., and Christensen C. 2008. Entrepreneur behaviors, opportunity recognition, and the origins of innovative ventures. *Strategic Entrepreneurship Journal*, 2(1): 317–338.Felin, T., Foss, N. J., and Ployhart, R. E. 2015. The microfoundations movement in strategy and organization theory. *Academy of Management Annals*, 9(1): 575–632.

Field, R. I. 2011. Government as the crucible for free market health care: Regulation, reimbursement, and reform. *University of Pennsylvania Law Review*, 1669–1726.

Garbuio, M., Lovallo, D., Porac, J. F., and Dong, A. 2015. A design cognition perspective on strategic option generation. In G. Gavetti, and W. Ocasio (Eds.), *Advances in Strategic Management*, Vol. 32. Bingley, UK: Emerald, 437–465.

Gottlieb, S., and Makower, J. 2013. A role for entrepreneurs an observation on lowering healthcare costs via technology innovation. *American Journal of Preventive Medicine*, 44(1): S43–S47.

Govindarajan, V., and Trimble, C. 2012. *Reverse Innovation: Create Far From Home, Win Everywhere*. Cambridge, MA: Harvard Business Press.

Greene, J. A., Choudhry, N. K., Kilabuk, E., and Shrank, W. H. 2011. Online social networking by patients with diabetes: A qualitative evaluation of communication with Facebook. *Journal of General Internal Medicine*, 26(3): 287–292.

Grégoire, D. A., Corbett, A. C., and McMullen, J. S. (2011). The cognitive perspective in entrepreneurship: An agenda for future research. *Journal of Management Studies*, 48(1): 1443–1477.

Gustafsson, A., Kristensson, P., and Witell, L. 2012. Customer co-creation in service innovation: A matter of communication? *Journal of Service Management*, 23(3): 311–327.

Heinze, K. L., and Weber, K. 2015. Toward organizational pluralism: Institutional intrapreneurship in integrative medicine. *Organization Science*, 27(1): 157–172.

Helm, R., Mauroner, O., and Dowling, M. 2010. Innovation as mediator between entrepreneurial orientation and spin-off venture performance. *International Journal of Entrepreneurship and Small Business*, 11(4): 472–491.

Hinz, V., and Ingerfurth, S. 2013. Does ownership matter under challenging conditions?: On the relationship between organizational entrepreneurship and performance in the healthcare sector. *Public Management Review*, 15(7): 969–991.

Hong, S. 2017. New nurse entrepreneur: Reflection and guidance. *Nurse Leader*, 15(5): 352–356.

Ireland, R. D., and Webb, J. D. 2007. A cross-disciplinary exploration of entrepreneurship research. *Journal of Management*, 33(6): 891–927.

Jahanmir, S. F. 2016. Paradoxes or trade-offs of entrepreneurship: Exploratory insights from the Cambridge eco-system. *Journal of Business Research*, 11(69): 5101–5105.

Jamali, D. 2009. Constraints and opportunities facing women entrepreneurs in developing countries: A relational perspective. *Gender in Management: An International Journal*, 24(4): 232–251.

Janssen, M., and Moors, E. H. M. 2013. Caring for healthcare entrepreneurs: Towards successful entrepreneurial strategies for sustainable innovations in Dutch healthcare. *Technological Forecasting and Social Change*, 80(7): 1360–1374.

Knight, K., Kenny, A., and Endacott, R. 2016. From expert generalists to ambiguity masters: Using ambiguity tolerance theory to redefine the practice of rural nurses. *Journal of Clinical Nursing*, 25(11–12): 1757–1765.

Kwon, A. H., Marshall, Z. J., and Nabzdyk, C. S. 2017. Why anesthesiologists could and should become the next leaders in innovative medical entrepreneurism. *Anesthesia & Analgesia*, 124(3): 998–1004.

Kyriakidou, O., and Özbilgin, M. 2006. *Relational Perspectives in Organizational Studies: A Research Companion*. Cheltenham, UK: Edward Elgar Publishing.

Lee, R. 2009. Social capital and business and management: Setting a research agenda. *International Journal of Management Reviews*, 11(3): 247–273.

Lega, F., Prenestini, A., and Spurgeon, P. 2013. Is management essential to improving the performance and sustainability of health care systems and organizations? A systematic review and a roadmap for future studies. *Value in Health*, 16(1): S46–S51.

Lehoux, P., Miller, F. A., Daudelin, G., and Denis, J.-L. 2017. Providing value to new health technology: The early contribution of entrepreneurs, investors, and regulatory agencies. *International Journal of Health Policy and Management*, 6(9): 509.

Low, M. B., and MacMillan, I. C. 1988. Entrepreneurship: Past research and future challenges. *Journal of Management*, 14(2): 139–161.

Lumpkin, G. T., and Dess, G. G. 1996. Clarifying the entrepreneurial orientation construct and linking it to performance. *Academy of Management Review*, 21(1): 135–172.

Lusch, R. F., and Vargo, S. L. 2006. Service-dominant logic: Reactions, reflections and refinements. *Marketing Theory*, 6(3): 281–288.

Macpherson, A., and Jones, O. 2010. Editorial: Strategies for the development of international journal of management reviews. *International Journal of Management Reviews*, 12(2): 107–113.

Maguire, S., Hardy, C., and Lawrence, T. B. 2004. Institutional entrepreneurship in emerging fields: HIV/AIDS treatment advocacy in Canada. *Academy of Management Journal*, 47(5): 657–679.

Marques, C. S. E., Ferreira, J. J. M., Ferreira, F. A. F., and Lages, M. F. S. 2013. Entrepreneurial orientation and motivation to start up a business: Evidence from the health service industry. *International Entrepreneurship and Management Journal*, 9(1): 77–94.

Mathies, C., and Burford, M. 2011. Customer service understanding: Gender differences of frontline employees. *Managing Service Quality*, 21(6): 636–648.

Matsuno, K., Mentzer, J. T., and Özsomer, A. 2002. The effects of entrepreneurial proclivity and market orientation on business performance. *Journal of Marketing*, 66(3): 18–32.

McClelland, D. C. 1987. *Human Motivation*. New York: Cambridge University Press.

McQuivey, J. 2013. *Digital Disruption: Unleashing the Next Wave of Innovation*. Las Vegas, NV: Amazon Publishing.

Ordanini, A., and Parasuraman, A. 2011. Service innovation viewed through a service-dominant logic lens: A conceptual framework and empirical analysis. *Journal of Service Research*, 14(1): 3–23.

Phillips, F. S., and Garman, A. N. 2006. Barriers to entrepreneurship in healthcare organizations. *Journal of Health and Human Services Administration*, 28(4): 472–484.

Podolny, J. M. 2001. Networks as the pipes and prisms of the market. *American Journal of Sociology*, 107(1): 33–60.

Prahalad, C. K., and Ramaswamy, V. 2004. Co-creation experiences: The next practice in value creation. *Journal of Interactive Marketing*, 18(3): 5–14.

Randhawa, K., Wilden, R., and Hohberger, J. 2016. A bibliometric review of open innovation: Setting a research agenda. *Journal of Product Innovation Management*, 33(6): 750–772.

Rashman, L., Withers, E., and Hartley, J. 2009. Organizational learning and knowledge in public service organizations: A systematic review of the literature. *International Journal of Management Reviews*, 11(4): 463–494.

Rauch, A., and Frese, M. 2000. Psychological approaches to entrepreneurial success: A general model and an overview of findings. *International Review of Industrial and Organizational Psychology*, 15: 101–142.

Rehn, U., and Abetti, P. A. 2013. Transition of R&D and product development procedures after mergers and acquisitions: A case study of Intermagnetics General and Philips Healthcare. *International Journal of Technology Management*, 61(2): 109–131.

Robinson, J. C. 2001. Academic medical centers and the economics of innovation in health care. In H. J. Aaron (Ed.), *The Future of Academic Medical Centers*. Washington, DC: Brookings Institution Press, 49–60.

Roggenkamp, S. D., and White, K. R. 1998. Four nurse entrepreneurs: What motivated them to start their own businesses. *Health Care Management Review*, 23(3): 67–75.

Rooney, D. 2005. Knowledge, economy, technology and society: The politics of discourse. *Telematics and Informatics*, 22(4): 405–422.

Ryu, A. J. 2017. My most valuable learning experience: Starting a business. *Surgery*, 161(4): 885–886.

Sawhney, M., Verona, G., and Prandelli, E. 2005. Collaborating to create: The Internet as a platform for customer engagement in product innovation. *Journal of Interactive Marketing*, 19(4): 4–17.

Schendel, D., and Hitt, M. A. 2007. Comments from the editors introduction to volume 1. *Strategic Entrepreneurship Journal*, 1(1): 1. Wiley-Blackwell Commerce Place, 350 Main St, Malden 02148, MA USA.

Shaw, B. 1993. Formal and informal networks in the UK medical equipment industry. *Technovation*, 13(6): 349–365.

Short, J. C., Moss, T. W., and Lumpkin, G. T. 2009. Research in social entrepreneurship: Past contributions and future opportunities. *Strategic Entrepreneurship Journal*, 3(2): 161–194.

Sindakis, S., and Kitsios, F. 2016. Entrepreneurial dynamics and patient involvement in service innovation: Developing a model to promote growth and sustainability in mental health care. *Journal of the Knowledge Economy*, 7(2): 545–564.

Smith, S. W., and Sfekas, A. 2013. How much do physician-entrepreneurs contribute to new medical devices? *Medical Care*, 51(5): 461–467.

Souba, W. W. 1996. Professionalism, responsibility, and service in academic medicine. *Surgery*, 119(1): 1–8.

Sowa, J. 2000. *Knowledge Representation: Logical, Philosophical, and Computational Foundations*. Pacific Grove, CA: Brooks Cole.

Spyridonidis, D., and Calnan, M. 2011. Are new forms of professionalism emerging in medicine? The case of the implementation of NICE guidelines. *Health Sociology Review*, 20(4): 394–409.

Stubbs, M. 1996. *Text and Corpus Analysis: Computer-Assisted Studies of Language and Culture*. Oxford: Blackwell.

Syed, J., and Özbilgin, M. 2009. A relational framework for international transfer of diversity management practices. *International Journal of Human Resource Management*, 20(12): 2435–2453.

Syed, S. B., Dadwal, V., Rutter, P., Storr, J., Hightower, J. D., Gooden, R., Carlet, J., Nejad, S. B., Kelley, E. T., Donaldson, L., and Pittet, D. 2012. Developed-developing country partnerships: Benefits to developed countries? *Globalization and Health*, 8.

Teece, D. J. 2010. Business models, business strategy and innovation. *Long Range Planning*, 43: 172–194.

Tranfield, D., Denyer, D., and Smart, P. 2003. Towards a methodology for developing evidence-informed management knowledge by means of systematic review. *British Journal of Management*, 14(3): 207–222.

Tuohy, C. H. 2012. Reform and the politics of hybridization in mature health care states. *Journal of Health Politics Policy and Law*, 37(4): 611–632.

Tushman, M. L., and Anderson, P. 2004. *Managing Strategic Innovation and Change*. Oxford: Oxford University Press.

Vargo, S. L., and Akaka, M. A. 2012. Value cocreation and service systems (re) formation: A service ecosystems view. *Service Science*, 4(3): 207–217.

Vargo, S. L., and Lusch, R. F. 2004. Evolving to a new dominant logic for marketing. *Journal of Marketing*: 1–17.

Vogel, P. 2017. From venture idea to venture opportunity. *Entrepreneurship Theory and Practice*, 41(6): 943–971.

Von Hippel, E. 1986. Lead users: A source of novel product concepts. *Management Science*, 32(7): 791–805.

Wang, C. L., and Chugh, H. 2014. Entrepreneurial learning: Past research and future challenges. *International Journal of Management Reviews*, 16(1): 24–61.

West, J., and Gallagher, S. 2006. Challenges of open innovation: The paradox of firm investment in open-source software. *R&D Management*, 36(3): 319–331.

Wiklund, J. 1999. The sustainability of the entrepreneurial orientation—Performance relationship. *Entrepreneurship Theory and Practice*, 24(1): 37–48.

Wilden, R., Akaka, M. A., Karpen, I. O., and Hohberger, J. 2017. The evolution and prospects of service-dominant logic. *Journal of Service Research*, 20(4): 345–361.

Wilden, R., Devinney, T. M., and Dowling, G. R. 2016. The Architecture of dynamic capability research. *The Academy of Management Annals*, 10(1): 997–1076.

Wilden, R., and Gudergan, S. 2015. The impact of dynamic capabilities on operational marketing and technological capabilities: Investigating the role of environmental turbulence. *Journal of the Academy of Marketing Science*, 43(2): 181–199.

Wilden, R., Gudergan, S., Nielsen, B. B., and Lings, I. 2013. Dynamic capabilities and performance: Strategy, structure and environment. *Long Range Planning*, 46(1–2): 72–96.

Zang, Y., Zhang, F., Di, C.-A., and Zhu, D. 2015. Advances of flexible pressure sensors toward artificial intelligence and health care applications. *Materials Horizons*, 2(2): 140–156.

Zhou, K. Z., Yim, C. K., and Tse, D. K. 2005. The effects of strategic orientations on technology-and market-based breakthrough innovations. *Journal of Marketing*, 69(2): 42–60.

Zupic, I., and Čater, T. 2015. Bibliometric methods in management and organization. *Organizational Research Methods*, 18(3): 429–472.

Part 1

Macro-Level Topics in Healthcare Entrepreneurship

2 Delivering Value in the Healthcare Sector Through the Lens of Hybrid Organizing

Federica Angeli and Daan Westra

Introduction

Value creation is a critical area of research in entrepreneurship research and in particular in the context of business model design (Teece, 2010). Here we want to take a step back and start by looking at the definition of value before delving into the typical issues of value in healthcare entrepreneurship.

The English Oxford Living Dictionary defines value as "the regard that something is held to deserve; the importance, worth, or usefulness of something." If we were to ask anybody in the world about what he/she values in life the most, "being healthy" is bound to be among the most frequently heard answers. If we would ask any politician about his/her agenda for the upcoming election, healthcare is bound to be an issue raised by many. In fact, most will agree that it is the sign of a developed nation to be able to provide citizens with universal access to healthcare. In other words, the importance of good health, and consequently high-quality healthcare, is recognized by most people. Health and healthcare are thus of great value in modern day societies. Being a fundamental principle in healthcare, this chapter revolves around the concept of value. It is divided into two sections. In the first section, we explore the concept of value and value-based healthcare, providing the reader with a basic understanding of what it is and why it is of importance. In the second section, we shift our attention to value delivery by healthcare organizations and we will adopt the lens of hybrid organizations to understand how healthcare providers deliver value and what organizational challenges they face in doing so.

An Introduction to Value

While there might be consensus regarding the need and importance of good health and high-quality healthcare, there is less agreement regarding the matter of how to operationalize both of these concepts. Or, in other words, there is less agreement on what actually constitutes health and high-quality healthcare. Larson (1999) has, for example, identified four different models of health: the medical model, the World Health Organization (WHO) model, the wellness model, and the environmental model. In the medical model, health is considered the absence of disease. In the WHO model, health is a state of complete physical, mental, and social wellbeing. In the wellness model, health equals optimal personal fitness for full, fruitful, creative living. In the environmental model, health is defined as the ability of an organism to maintain a balance with its environment, with relative freedom from pain, disabilities, or limitations, including social abilities. The debate surrounding the definition of health has not stopped at these four models. More recently, scholars have once again critiqued the existing models of defining health, arguing that they are insufficiently aligned with the increasing prevalence of chronic diseases, and with the ability of chronic patients to cope with the disease and conduct a socially, physically, and mentally fulfilling life. Huber et al. (2011) have consequently defined health as "the ability of patients to adapt and self-manage," therefore emphasizing to the quality of "resilience or capacity to cope, maintain and restore one's integrity, equilibrium, and sense of wellbeing" (Huber et al., 2011: 344). We therefore identify Huber's definition as the "resilience model." It is clear that each of these models operationalizes health in different ways, ranging from a rather narrow and physical definition in the medical model, to a broad and more all-encompassing definition in the environmental model and the model presented by Huber and colleagues. While health might be considered of the utmost importance to many people, they can have vastly different perceptions as to what it is that they actually find important. Table 2.1 reports the main perspectives on the concept of health, and related definitions.

Similar to the various ways of defining health, there is a plethora of indicators that have the ambition to measure quality of healthcare. The academic literature on this topic is vast and different measures have

Table 2.1 Definitions of Health. Adapted from Larson (1999)

Model	*Definition*
1. Medical model	The absence of disease or disability
2. World Health Organization (WHO) model	State of complete physical, mental, and social wellbeing, and not merely the absence of disease or infirmity
3. Wellness model	Health promotion and progress toward higher functioning, energy, comfort, and integration of mind, body, and spirit
4. Environmental model	Adaptation to physical and social surroundings—a balance free from undue pain, discomfort, or disability
5. Resilience model	Ability of patients to adapt and self-manage

surfaced for different segments of the healthcare sector, and at different levels. Examples range from clinical measures related to specific diseases to generic measures such as safety, satisfaction, and quality of life at the patient level; to measures such as readmission rates to examine quality of care at the level of healthcare organizations, and ultimately to international, aggregated rankings measuring the effectiveness and efficiency of whole healthcare systems (such as the Euro Health Consumers Index, or the Bloomberg ranking for healthcare systems). For some of these indicators, a range of measurement instruments have been developed. The Dutch Healthcare Inspectorate publishes annually more than 1,000 indicators to rank hospitals according to the quality of care delivered, at condition, specialty, and hospital level. In this *mare magnum* of metrics, the most common distinction regarding quality of care indicators relates to structure, process, and outcome indicators introduced by Donabedian (1988). The notions of measuring structure and process indicators are that they ultimately constitute a prerequisite to generating positive health outcomes for patients.

Operationalizing health and high-quality healthcare is only one side of the value equation, however. That is, most economists will define value not only as how the quality or usefulness of a given product or service, but rather as the amount of money a consumer is willing to pay for that good or a service. In other words, value ultimately depends on the wants and needs of consumers. Having established that most people want, and in many cases need, high-quality healthcare services, value in the healthcare sector should thus consider the monetary worth of these services. Despite the widespread academic debate surrounding the definition of health and the way in which quality of healthcare is best operationalized, the concept of value in healthcare has remained relatively under-debated for quite some time. The concept had received attention from scholars in the field of economic evaluations, in which interventions are typically compared based on their relative cost-effectiveness, in journals such as *Value in Health*, the official journal of the International Society for Pharmacoeconomics and Outcomes Research (ISPOR). However, it was not until the economist Michael Porter argued that value in healthcare remained largely misunderstood and formally defined the concept as "health outcomes achieved per dollar spent" (Porter, 2010: 2477) that value-based healthcare became arguably one of the most talked-about concepts in the realm of health policy and management.

The concept of value in healthcare formalized by Porter (2010) illustrates the inherent interrelation between outcomes and costs. So much so, that he equates value to efficiency and states that competition is considered the most appropriate way to maximize value (Porter and Teisberg, 2004) (see Chapter 3 for more on competition in the healthcare sector). He states that improving value should constitute the goal of stakeholders in the healthcare sector. In his paper, Porter furthermore takes several clear stances surrounding value and the interrelation between costs and outcomes (i.e., quality) in the healthcare sector. First, he posits that value can and should only be defined around the patient, making all activities, products and processes, which do not have value for the patient superfluous. Second, he argues that value cannot be measured at the level of one organization, as the creation and delivery of healthcare inherently transcends organizational boundaries (see also Chapter 6 on open innovation in healthcare). Consequently, both costs and outcomes should be measured across the full range of care pathway. Third, Porter argues that the focus should be on outcome indicators, rather than on structure or process indicators.

Although Porter was not the first to note that outcomes are what ultimately matter to patients, notable health economists have long indicated that it is difficult for patients to assess the quality of the outcome of medical treatments (Arrow, 1963; Dranove and White, 1994). In his description of value in healthcare, Porter concedes that outcomes are indeed seldom collected rigorously and systematically. Nonetheless, he describes so-called comprehensive outcome measures as useful in determining value in the healthcare sector. According to this line of reasoning, a single outcome measure is by definition inappropriate, as it is unable to capture all of the dimensions which patients consider relevant. In fact, some of the outcomes could even contradict one another. He considers it important to include both short-term and long-term outcome measures, and introduces a tiered hierarchy of outcome measures to define value. The first tier includes health outcomes such as survival and degree of recovery. The second tier focuses on the speed of recovery and the burden of the recovery process. The third and last tier assesses the long-term effects of the treatment and whether or not the attained health status is sustained over a prolonged period of time. Porter argues that, in order to define value in an appropriate way in the healthcare domain, there should be a set of tiered outcome measures for each medical condition.

The increased attention for the concept of value in healthcare, or value-based healthcare, over the past decade has not been confined to the realm of academics. Instead, it has made its way into practice in various forms. Perhaps the most notable of these are financial incentives introduced to improve the quality of care delivered by providers. Such schemes are known as pay-for-performance or value-based purchasing, and the US and UK are considered to be frontrunners in the adoption of these methods (Bonfrer et al., 2018). Under these schemes, those providers that offer services with the highest value to patients are contracted or receive additional payments. However, a recent study by Bonfrer et al. (2018) suggests that these incentives have only a very limited effect in terms of patient outcomes. The authors offer several explanations for this lack of value improvement. First, they note that the financial incentives are typically small. Second, they argue that value-based purchasing programs can be complex for providers. Third, the authors suggest that the fact that the financial gains were distributed once a year could have stifled quality improvements, as well. What this study shows is that even though providers and purchasers attempt to improve value of healthcare services, achieving this goal is not a straightforward process. It should be recognized that although patient outcomes remain the ultimate goal for all stakeholders in the healthcare domain, each organization faces peculiar challenges, based on its position in the market and specific business model. In particular, most healthcare providers faced inherent duality by negotiating with insurers/governments on service, while delivering these services to an entirely different target group: the patients. In the remainder of this chapter, we focus on healthcare providers, and shift our attention to the tensions arising from the co-existence within healthcare organizations of pressures towards both high service quality and financial efficiency. Specifically, we will refer to the literature and theories addressing hybrid organizations, which hold both a social and financial mission. We will then use this lens to understand the challenges faced by healthcare providers.

Understanding Healthcare Providers Through the Lens of Hybrid Organizations

A crucial decision of healthcare entrepreneurs and managers more generally is to decide on the business model and how to best structure their organization to maximize patients' value. The concept of value-based healthcare has placed the patients more central than ever before in the delivery of healthcare services and in the assessment of healthcare organizations' performance. This paradigm shift ensures that healthcare services and providers remain patient-centered and emphasizes the social responsibility of healthcare organizations. At the same time, the skyrocketing healthcare expenditures facing Western countries, and the consequent pro-competitive policy reforms introduced by several governments (e.g., Westra et al., 2015) produced increasing pressures towards efficiency and financial sustainability for healthcare providers. A tension between counteracting forces hence emerges. On the one side, value-based healthcare requires a strong focus on the patient, in the form of customized diagnostic and therapeutic services, highly responsive systems with enough capacity to deal (also) with emergency situations, but also *ad hoc* multidisciplinary teams for complex conditions, and innovative (technological) solutions to ensure better quality of life, for example, to elderly and chronic patients. On the other side, the transition towards more value- and patient-oriented models needs to happen with fewer resources, and hence more efficient organizational processes, technologies, and organizational models, to contain otherwise unsustainable healthcare costs. The deriving tensions and challenges can be fierce, and the need for entrepreneurs and intrapreneurs to drive technological as well organizational innovation in the healthcare sector is unparalleled and higher than ever before.

Hybrid Organizations

The lens of hybrid organizations is very suitable to develop an understanding of how healthcare entrepreneurs face counteracting institutional forces, which result in conflicting institutional logics. Hybrid organizations pursue a social mission while using a commercial business model; therefore, they present entrenched duality, in the form of coexisting socially oriented values as well as profit-oriented processes and competencies (Santos et al., 2015). Hybrid organizational forms are often found to complement governments and third sector organizations in tackling complex social challenges, because of their unique capabilities to scale up and develop long-term action through self-sustained models. These organizations hence transcend the profit/non-profit differentiation, blurring the boundary between business and charity (Battilana and Lee, 2014; Haigh et al., 2015), while attempting to reconcile private interests and public good.

Santos et al. (2015) note how hybrid organizations flourish particularly in market segments where value spillover is contingent on organizational actions and where transactions are hindered by demand-side obstacles, for example, inability to pay or access the product, or unwillingness to pay because of lack of awareness about the benefits. Value spillover is a crucial notion to understand hybrid organizing. In some cases, the value spillover—namely, the social benefit for the organizations' beneficiaries—occurs naturally and automatically when one of the services or products is delivered. Providing electricity generators or health check-ups in urban slum settings constitute examples of products and services which have an immediate and visible use, the value of which is immediately recognized by the communities. In other cases, the value spillover is instead contingent on organizational actions. Santos et al. (2015) provide the example of microfinance, which delivers social values only if the lenders employ the money to start up commercial activities and to generate for themselves and for the communities. Hence, mentoring activities are often necessary to ensure that the microloans achieve their social potential. Another example is provided by the French work integration social enterprises (WISEs) explored by various authors (Battilana et al., 2015; Pache and Santos, 2013). A WISE's social goal is to reduce long-term unemployment by helping individuals with a disadvantaged background to re-enter the job market. WISEs therefore hire unemployed people for two years, and produce goods or services such as gardening or recycling that are then sold in the free market (Battilana et al., 2015). The ultimate social benefit is to requalify the skills and experience of the long-term unemployed to create new (stable) job opportunities for them. In order for this long-term social mission to be achieved, in addition to the work experience offered by WISE, these disadvantaged groups also need to be supported by coaching, training, and mentoring services, to be able to fully re-entered the market with their newly acquired competencies.

Another core feature of hybrid organizations relates to the degree of overlap between customers—individuals or entities that pay for the organizations' commercial services—and beneficiaries, who identify the target group of the organization's social activities (Santos et al., 2015). The previously cited case of WISEs illustrates a situation in which customers do not overlap with beneficiaries. The target group of WISEs' social activities (the unemployed) is in fact disconnected from WISEs' customers (the individuals who buy products/services). Another example is the widespread model of non-government organizations (NGOs), who provide services to disadvantaged communities (the beneficiaries) through the funding provided by donor agencies worldwide, which can then be seen as the NGOs' customers, as income generators. Finally, a third noteworthy illustration is provided by the many business models relying on customers' cross-subsidization, a well-known mechanism to achieve sustainable business models for inclusive healthcare delivery (Angeli and Jaiswal, 2016). Examples are known in healthcare models, for example, in the case of Aravind Eye Care, a world-renowned eye hospital that operates in India and charges the full fee for eye surgery to wealthy patients (customers) and partially uses the consequent profit margin to cover healthcare costs of low-income individuals (beneficiaries). Such examples can also be appreciated in sectors that are becoming more socially aware, with models that attach a donation with each product purchase. It is the case of Tom—a famous brand of espadrilles shoes—which has established a just as famous philanthropic model of buy one/give one, in which each purchase subsidizes a pair of shoes for a child living in poverty around the world.

Based on these two dimensions, *value spillover* and *overlap between customers and beneficiaries*, Santos et al. (2015) developed a typology of organizational hybrids. The four types—namely Market hybrids, Bridging hybrids, Blending hybrids, and Coupling hybrids—present important differences that are likely to profoundly affect their structure, missions, leadership style, degree of professionalization, inter-organizational partnerships, relationship with governmental agencies, etc. (Battilana and Lee, 2014). While investigating challenges faced by hybrid organizations, several studies have particularly focused on coupling hybrids, which represent the most complex and fragile category of business models. Social and financial logics are often difficult to balance, requiring opposing organizational actions, clashing allocation of resources, and different human resources strategies. Evidence proves that social imprinting does depress economic productivity (Battilana et al., 2015). The difficult act of balancing conflicting institutional logics can lead such organizations to paralyze or even perish over time (Pache and Santos, 2013; Tracey and Jarvis, 2006), and poses a substantial risk of mission drift and loss of organizational identity (Battilana and Dorado, 2010). Constant alignment and attention posed to design structures, governance mechanisms, and human resource management systems are crucial to overcome such challenges (Santos et al., 2015). Fosfuri et al. (2016) have added to this supply-side perspective a demand-side perspective, highlighting how the necessity to scale up through intra-industry growth may compromise customers' identification by diluting the product symbolic value, thereby undermining legitimacy.

We argue here that these four organizational types can fruitfully inform the understanding of healthcare organizations. Because this typology has proven extremely valuable to the understanding of social enterprises, it can shed new light on the understanding of the market positioning of entrepreneurial ventures in the healthcare sector. Figure 2.1 represents the typology developed by Santos et al. (2015) and applied to the healthcare sector.

Healthcare Market Hybrids: The Case of Cardiovascular Care in India

Market hybrids in healthcare are organizations that are able to transact with their patients as customers. The business model in this case is

	Payers = patients	*Payers <> patients*
Automatic value spillover	**Healthcare Market hybrids** *Case: Indian cardiovascular care – Narayana Health*	**Healthcare Bridging hybrids** *Case: Dutch specialized care – AzM*
Contingent value spillover	**Healthcare Blending hybrids** *Case: Health-enhancing technologies among BoP – Sulabh International*	**Healthcare Coupling hybrids** *Case: Dutch mental healthcare – Mondriaan*

Figure 2.1 Hybrid Organizations Typology Applied to Healthcare Organizations

relatively simple, as the social impact is achieved through a straightforward commercial formula, in which the patients pay directly for the care they receive. Santos et al. (2015) illustrate three main obstacles that hinder customers from being able to pay for services: inability to pay because of affordability issues; unwillingness to pay because of inability to recognize added value in the service/product, despite the actual benefit this would bring; and difficulty to access the product and services. These dimensions partially overlap with the aspects of affordability, awareness, availability, and acceptability to be considered when offering services and products to base-of-the-pyramid customers (Angeli and Jaiswal, 2015). Healthcare market hybrids are care providers that managed to create a type of service able to overcome patients' inability or unwillingness to pay for the service. It should also be noted, however, that most healthcare systems in industrialized countries strongly restrict direct (so-called out-of-pocket) patient payments for a large part of healthcare services, instead using third-party payers (governments or insurance companies) to mediate between patients and providers. The underpinning logic is to curb system-level healthcare costs, avoid catastrophic individual expenditures and reduce the cost of services by increasing bargaining power on the demand side. Within this systemic configuration, which allows in most countries for large and almost universal healthcare coverage, the space for healthcare market hybrids is limited. This type of model can be seen, for example, in Western countries in the area of elective or cosmetic care, which is typically not included in insurance packages. In emerging contexts however, where medical insurance systems are less developed, or in contexts where insurance coverage can be limited, such as the US, market hybrids can be present also for life-threatening conditions such cardiovascular diseases. It is the case of Narayana Hrudayalaya (NH), a world-renowned heart hospital headquartered in Bangalore, India (Angeli and Jaiswal, 2016). NH has been able to develop a business formula that delivers heart surgery for 1% of the price of what it would cost in the US and EU, with comparable after-surgery infection and recovery rates. The average cost of a bypass surgery at NH is US$1,500 (INR 99,000) in comparison with US$144,000 in the US. NH's mortality and infection rates are 1.27% and 1%, respectively, for coronary artery bypass graft operations, which are comparable to US hospitals. Part of the success is due to economies of scale, where volume drives down costs and speeds up learning curves, thereby improving quality. NH is a 1,000-bed hospital in Bangalore that conducts on average 35 major heart surgeries per day and a maximum of 60 per day in its 24 operation theaters, making it one of the largest cardiac hospitals in the world. By contrast, the largest heart hospital in the UK has 270 beds and five operating theaters, and conducts 58 operations a week.

This is enabled by an "assembly line model,"[1] in which junior doctors do early stage tasks, which enables surgeons to do three surgeries a day instead of one. Human resource management is also important: in order to maintain the knowledge, attrition rate must be low. NH has an attrition rate close to zero, where personnel is strongly intrinsically motivated by "passion and compassion"[2] (Narayana Hrudayalaya Limited, 2016). The third important point is the savvy use of technology such as telemedicine, and strategic partnerships to suppliers. Founded in 2001 by Dr. Devi Prasad Shetty, by 2014, NH had 26 hospitals in 16 cities with 6,900 beds, 13,000 employees and 1,500 doctors (Angeli & Jaiswal, 2016). Because of its striking performance indicators, NH has been object of wide media attention (e.g., Indian hospital series on the broadcaster Al Jazeera), as well as business cases and scholarly publications.

Bridging Hybrids: The Case of Secondary Care in the Netherlands

Bridging hybrid healthcare providers are those organizations delivering care treatments that have immediate and recognizable value for the patients (automatic value spillovers), who however do not overlap with the customers. These organizations, therefore, present a split between beneficiaries and payers. Most healthcare organizations in Western countries—where third payers are employed by healthcare systems to mediate between patients and providers—are bridging hybrids. Dutch hospitals, for example, deliver specialized care to patients (their beneficiaries) while receiving reimbursements from insurance companies. Since government-fixed prices (tariffs) for treatments have mostly been abolished in the Netherlands with the Health Insurance Act in 2006, a large share (the so-called "B segment," which currently comprises more than 70% of treatments) of prices for care delivered within the diagnostic-related group systems are subject to negotiation between care providers and (private) insurance companies (Schut & Varkevisser, 2017). It is important to note that such negotiation process can present several complexities, especially in those cases where information asymmetry is high (e.g., rare diseases), when several co-morbidities are present (e.g., diabetes) and when long-term treatment is required (e.g., heart diseases).

The complexity created by the co-existence of multiple institutional logics is very tangible, and particularly evident in the Dutch healthcare system. It is perhaps most pronounced in the case of academic hospitals. Academic hospitals typically treat the most complex patients of a given population (e.g., patients with a specific disease or condition). While treating these complex patients is inherent to their role as teaching hospitals and research centers, the costs of treating these patients are typically higher than the costs of treating less complex patients in the same population. Consequently, the value spillover is largest for these beneficiaries, as they are treated by an organization equipped to do so when no other organization is. Yet, given the diagnosis-related groups (DRG)-like system used to pay healthcare providers in the Netherlands, academic hospitals are typically only reimbursed the standard rate per

DRG, which constitutes the price paid for an "average" patient of a given population. The mismatch between the value delivered to patients and the monetary reimbursement received from third-party payers presents these organizations with a difficult balancing task of the competing logics of social value versus financial efficiency. The increasing number of independent treatment centers which have entered the market since the pro-competitive reforms in the Netherlands (see Chapter 3 for more on that matter), are typically perceived as organizations following the inverse of this logic. That is, they are often accused of cherry-picking the easiest patients from a population and treating these against lower costs but while receiving the average per-DRG price from payers.

The introduction and expansion of the B-segment has exposed hospitals and care providers to substantial financial pressures, especially in relation to the high bargaining that the four major insurance groups enjoy in the Netherlands. This is often perceived as a constraint by specialists and hospitals at large, which find limited financial slack to invest in innovative medical technologies, and new business model innovations. Also, organizational resources and attention need to be shifted towards improving process efficiency and standardization, which is at times perceived as conflicting with the *ad hoc* nature of several segments of patient care, often requiring treatment customization and patient-centered, rather than disease-centered, approach. Finding the balance between financial performance and quality of care/patient satisfaction is perceived by clinicians and hospital managers to be difficult, especially when budget cuts are severe and require financial reassessment in a short span of time.

Blending Hybrids: The Case of Health-Enhancing Technologies in Urban Slums

Healthcare blending hybrids are those organizations who deliver services and products that have an immediate health benefit, which however fails to be recognized by the users, unless organizational efforts are devoted to increase awareness, discover value together with the users, and essentially co-create patient needs (Angeli and Jaiswal, 2016). Slum-dwellers present very idiosyncratic health-seeking behavior and perception on curative value of treatment and technologies, arising from a complex nexus of religion, gender, marital status, employment, ethnicity, and literacy level (Das et al., 2018). Interesting examples can be drawn from the case of health-enhancing product innovations, which private companies, governmental agencies, and NGOs alike have tried to introduce in disadvantaged, low-income settings. The fact that these technologies are not utilized, despite the wide improvement that they could produce in the health conditions of disadvantaged communities, is a well-known wicked problem in global health (Banerjee and Duflo, 2012). Idiosyncratic norms, values, and beliefs of target clients who live in poor conditions have to be carefully understood, to be able to successfully introduce new products and induce behavioral change.

Sulabh International is an enterprise that succeed where others failed: improving toilet use among slum-dwellers and rural poor (Angeli and Jaiswal, 2016). The problem of open-air defecation is widespread in India. In 2014, half of the Indian population did not have regular access to sanitation facilities, including toilets. This has important public health consequences, with more than 600,000 deaths yearly directly related to infectious diseases and diarrheic conditions spurred by unhealthy and bacteria-prone environments, as estimated by the World Health Organization report in 2014. However, individuals living in resource-constrained settings are often not fully aware of the health hazards related to open defecation. Instead, when toilets are installed in-house, their use is very limited because people are reluctant to dispose of human waste in the same restricted space where they also eat and sleep, a behavior that seems to be associated with lower castes, and with religious and socio-cultural beliefs (Mehrotra, 2014). In addition to that, free public toilets are often considered unhygienic and hence are seldom used (O'Reilly and Louiss, 2014). The interplay of the two trends results into a difficult-to-eradicate habit of slum-dwellers and rural villagers of defecating in the open, which compromises the health status of the communities and poses challenges to women's safety. Leveraging in-depth knowledge of these dynamics and of the socio-cultural context of the disadvantaged communities, Sulabh International successfully introduced pay-per-use public toilets, which charge a small amount for the use of common toilets outside homes. The affordable rate ensures cleanliness and for a small markup clients can enjoy a "service experience," which includes bath, laundry, and accommodation services. Because the public health importance of proper human waste disposal is not immediately evident for consumers, Sulabh International has engaged in a number of activities to raise awareness among the target communities. Sulabh International Institute of Health and Hygiene and the Sulabh International Museum of Toilets were specifically created to promote sanitation and hygiene and while training teachers, school children, volunteers, and associates involved in promoting hygienic practices. Sulabh International Institute of Health and Hygiene educated over 8,000 female workers towards creating awareness about the relationship between sanitation and health (Kumar Rastogi, 2013).

While Sulabh International represents a successful case of blending hybrids in the healthcare value chain, the history and evolution of blending hybrids is punctuated by challenges, especially that of creating a model that can incorporate the necessary financial lack to sustain health awareness campaigns. Improved cooking stoves that reduce toxic indoor pollution by using modern technologies and less polluting fuels still struggle to reach scale among urban slums and rural villages in emerging countries (Lewis and Pattanayak, 2012).

Coupling Hybrids: The Case of Dutch Mental Healthcare

Coupling hybrid organizations are by far the most widely studied in the literature, as they present the highest level of complexity, risks of mission drifts, and difficulty of achieving financial sustainability and maintaining their legitimacy among the relevant stakeholders (Fosfuri et al., 2016). Along the two-dimensional typology developed by Santos et al. (2015), coupling hybrids are those organizations that witness a split between customers and beneficiaries and that deliver value that is contingent on organizational actions. In the healthcare domain, this translates into health providers that operate in a system that uses third-party payers and whose services do not have immediately observable value or whose value manifests in the longer term, and/or is complex to measure through immediate metrics. This is the case with mental healthcare organizations. Mental healthcare providers have the difficult task of delivering treatment that is often complex and long term for conditions that are often ambiguous, subjective, and highly idiosyncratic, both with inpatient and outpatient approaches, often struggling with patients' reluctance to treatment and tendency to deviate from the prescribed care pathway of therapy, in addition to patients' delayed care-seeking because of the stigma that is still associated with mental health issues (Westra et al., 2016). Furthermore, in the case of youth mental healthcare, the Netherlands has recently reformed its system to favor a more community-based perspective including multiple stakeholders, in inpatient as well as everyday settings, so that teachers, family members, and formal caregivers need to coordinate and collaborate for the treatment to be effective and long-lasting. However, disparate viewpoints and values held by multiple stakeholders often collide when defining the mental health policy problem and potential solutions, which brings mental healthcare to be increasingly seen as a "wicked problem" for policymakers (Hannigan and Coffey, 2011). For example, while community-based approaches have found support from many policymakers, some scholars argue that these might also be responsible for too much or too little monitoring of service users, by enforcing top-down solutions that factually offset the expected benefits of community-centered care (Hannigan and Coffey, 2011; Molodynski et al., 2010). Another point of fierce discussion relates to the dominant view in relation to what constitutes a preferred treatment trajectory, with the biomedical route being often favored over alternative, more therapy-based care trajectories.

On the financing side, the mental healthcare sector has been undergoing major changes in most industrialized countries, with the UK and the Netherlands being prominent examples (Hannigan and Coffey, 2011; Westra et al., 2016). Worldwide, the incidence and relevance of mental healthcare conditions are rising steeply, along with increasing awareness of the previous large underestimation of the problem (Vigo et al.,

2016; World Health Organization, 2013). It is now estimated that the economic losses due to untreated mental disorders, in terms of lower productivity, lower employment rates, foregone taxes, and increased welfare costs amount to more than 10 billion days of lost work annually—the equivalent of US$1 trillion per year (Chisholm et al., 2016). Between 76% and 85% of people in low-income and middle-income countries with severe mental disorders do not receive treatment, a percentage which ranges between 35% and 50% in high-income countries (World Health Organization, 2013). The reasons for this lie in the complex interplay of diagnosis-related stigma, lack of specialized workforce, lack and/or little understanding of the diseases, complexity of specialized treatment, and poor socio-economic conditions such as poverty, unemployment, poor housing, poor education, and substance abuse. Sadly, many young individuals also suffer from mental health disorders, with mental conditions accounting for a large share of illness affecting youth, and suicide being the second most common cause of death for young people worldwide (World Health Organization, 2013). Mirroring the trend, the incidence of mental healthcare issues is sharply on the rise also in the Netherlands, especially among the youth. More than 1 out of 5 Dutch youth has experienced a severe mental health episode by the age of 19, and 75% of mental health conditions manifest before the age of 25,[3] complicated by the fact that young people on average wait longer before seeking help.[4] And these numbers are rising. In 2016, 4% of young individuals declared to have suffered from depression for more than six months, more than double than in 2014.[5] This poses the issue on how to best tackle the rising demand in a financially sustainable way. In this light, the Dutch mental healthcare sector has undergone various policy changes in several waves, with the idea being to promote (cheaper) outpatient-based, community-centered business models, away from the institutionalization perspective that ruled in past centuries. The complex institutional environment, the difficult target segment, the challenges deriving from a shifting regulatory framework and from increasing financial pressure, and the difficulty of balancing multiple institutional logics arising from (clashing) interests of buyers and patients have resulted in the current critical situation of the Dutch mental healthcare sector. This is reflected in the severe financial situation of large incumbent mental healthcare providers in the Dutch landscape, with many providers producing losses or even going bankrupt in the past few years.

Mondriaan Mental Health Foundation constitutes an example of such a large incumbent provider. Mondriaan is a mental healthcare provider, which diagnoses and treats a wide range of mental health problems for children, youth, adults, and elderly in more than 40 locations. With 1,662 full-time equivalent (FTE) personnel, Mondriaan is one of the largest employers in Southern Limburg, and the organization treated approximately 11,000 patients in 2015. Although Mondriaan's presence in the mental health sector is wide and long-lasting, the organization had €136 million turnover in 2015, which amounts to a loss of €2.6 million, and failed to meet the bank's financial criteria. Recent and rapid market developments have contributed to Mondriaan's hardship. In particular, pro-competitive regulation introduced in 2006 and then in 2014 specifically for mental healthcare services has opened up price negotiations between providers and insurance companies over specialized mental health care. This mechanism has increased external pressure on Mondriaan's operations, which currently face a difficult tension between cost-effectiveness and quality of care. Such tension reflects within the internal environment of the organizations, in balancing short-term vs. long-term solutions, and weighing the multifaceted perspectives offered by managers, specialists, board members, patients, and families. The specific structure of the market, with few medical insurance companies, and the increasing regulatory pressures towards the shift from (expensive) inpatient to (cheaper) outpatient care have created the need for a short-term rethinking of Mondriaan's business model. However, the size and the tenure of the organization in the market constitute important inertial factors. To add complexity, the Child and Youth section of Mondriaan, which targets patients in the 0–23 years old age range, has undergone specific regulatory changes and faces peculiar challenges. The child and youth care segment of mental healthcare has been moved to the youth act, shifting the responsibility for purchasing youth mental healthcare from insurance companies to municipalities. While negotiations with insurers had posed challenges and caused market power imbalances, the shift to municipalities worsened the issue, increasing monopoly on the buyer side as well as transaction costs related to wider information asymmetries between municipal authorities and providers of specialized mental healthcare (Westra et al., 2016) Mondriaan's Child and Youth department, which had roughly €15 million in turnover during 2015, has been trying to rethink its value proposition for psychiatric services to adolescents, given the severe budget cuts over the past year. In October 2017, it was announced that Mondriaan will have to significantly downsize its child and youth department because of the unbearable workload on psychiatrist and nurses. In an interview with Dutch newspaper NRC,[6] the organization declared "it is not possible to continue" and that families and caregivers of the share of the 500 children currently admitted for treatment at Mondriaan will be referred to other providers. This is the second provider that has decided to turn to interrupt the provision of child mental healthcare in a very short span of time. A few days before Mondriaan's announcement, the organization for child protection William Schrikker Groep in Dordrecht and surroundings declared that they were not in the financial condition to be able to continue offering their services, because the reimbursements are too low to maintain the necessary quality levels (Westra et al., 2016). For children of 300 families, it is not clear now what the future will hold in 2018. As the third example of the extreme challenges faced by Dutch mental healthcare organizations in comes from of Mondriaan's most prominent competitor, Virenze, which has very recently declared bankruptcy.[7] Virenze's business model seemed initially better placed to respond to the newly introduced policy framework, because of its patient mix comprising of both complex and milder cases, which allowed a financially more sustainable balance between high margin/low complexity outpatient cases and lower margin/higher complexity inpatient treatments. However, the low reimbursements paid by municipalities for the youth segment and by insurance companies for the adult segments have been insufficient to ensure quality and to maintain productivity. Virenze served 10,000 patients and employed 465 professionals, which underlines the implosion the mental healthcare sector is facing. Also, a bankruptcy of this is considered an "exceptional case," as mostly financially fragile organizations with such a central societal responsibility are savaged through mergers with competitors.

Conclusions

At the core of any business and organization lies the concept of value, and any organization is unique in the type of configuration that allows it to deliver value to its customers and capture part of it for its own growth. This chapter delineated an understanding of the multifaceted concept of value in the case of healthcare delivery, characterized by multiple constituencies and by the rapidly evolving concept of health, from a purely medical view to a more encompassing state of wellbeing. Value-based healthcare is now a paradigm that guides and defines most policy reforms and organizational strategic choices in the healthcare sector, and provides an important framework of reference for any entrepreneurial venture in this domain. Against this backdrop, the lens of hybrid organizations enables focus on important challenges and complexities that healthcare ventures are bound to face: the ones related to the co-existence of multiple constituencies, often holding clashing claims—such as patients and insurance companies in the case of Dutch hospitals; or municipalities and youth patients, in the case of child and youth mental healthcare providers; and the ones pertinent to value that does not automatically spill over to the beneficiaries: the patients, as in the case of health-enhancing technologies among disadvantaged communities.

Being cognizant of these challenges provides an important starting point to devise appropriate strategies, commercial formulas to deliver value—perceived and internalized as such by the beneficiaries—and appropriate value to ensure sustainability, so that the needs of the various constituent groups are met. The healthcare entrepreneur is faced with a difficult, yet challenging, orchestration work, which can, however, unleash enormous impact for society and patients alike.

Notes

1. PBS Newshour (2015). How this Indian medical chain makes heart surgery affordable. [video] Available at: https://www.youtube.com/watch?v=qaI5WBHVGmo [Accessed 22 Apr. 2018].
2. PBS Newshour (2015). How this Indian medical chain makes heart surgery affordable. [video] Available at: https://www.youtube.com/watch?v=qaI5WBHVGmo [Accessed 22 Apr. 2018].
3. GGZnieuwz (2015). At least 3000 young people with serious mental problems per year. Available at: https://www.ggznieuws.nl/home/minimaal-3000-jongeren met-ernstige-psychische-problemen-per-jaar/ [Accessed 22 Apr. 2018].
4. GGZnieuwz (2017). Young people wait a long time to find help with psychiatric disorders. Available at: https://www.ggznieuws.nl/home/jongeren-wachten-lang-zoeken-hulp-psychiatrische-stoornissen/.
5. Nji.nl. (2018). Depression. Available at: https://www.nji.nl/nl/Databank/Cijfers-over-Jeugd-en-Opvoeding/Cijfers-per-onderwerp/Cijfers-per-onderwerp-Depressie.
6. Vriesema, I. (2017). Limburgse instelling staakt deel jeugd-ggz binnenkort. NRC.nl. Available at: https://www.nrc.nl/nieuws/2017/10/01/limburgse-instelling-staakt-deel-jeugd-ggz-binnenkort-13287294-a1575600.
7. Vriesema, I. (2017). Ggz-instelling Virenze failliet: gevolg voor patiënten ongewis. NRC.nl. Available at: https://www.nrc.nl/nieuws/2017/12/19/ggz-instelling-virenze-failliet-gevolg-voor-patienten-ongewis-a1585603.

References

Angeli, F., and Jaiswal, A. K. 2015. Competitive dynamics between MNCs and domestic companies at the base of the pyramid: An institutional perspective. *Long Range Planning*, 48: 182–199.

Angeli, F., and Jaiswal, A. K. 2016. Business model innovation for inclusive health care delivery at the bottom of the pyramid. *Organization and Environment*, 29.

Arrow, K. J. 1963. Uncertainty and the welfare economics of medical care. *The American Economic Review*, 53: 141–149.

Banerjee, A. V., and Duflo, E. 2012. *Poor Economics*. London: Penguin Books.

Battilana, J., and Dorado, S. 2010. Building sustainable hybrid organizations: The case of commercial microfinance organizations. *Academy of Management Journal*, 53: 1419–1440.

Battilana, J., and Lee, M. 2014. Advancing research on hybrid organizing—Insights from the study of social enterprises. *The Academy of Management Annals*, 8: 397–441.

Battilana, J., Sengul, M., Pache, A. C., and Model, J. 2015. Harnessing productive tensions in hybrid organizations: The case of work integration social enterprises. *Academy of Management Journal*, 58: 1658–1685.

Bonfrer, I., Figueroa, J. F., Zheng, J., Orav, E. J., and Jha, A. K. 2018. Impact of financial incentives on early and late adopters among US hospitals: Observational study. *BMJ*, 360: j5622.

Chisholm, D., Sweeny, K., Sheehan, P., Rasmussen, B., Smit, F., Cuijpers, P., and Saxena, S. 2016. Scaling-up treatment of depression and anxiety: A global return on investment analysis. *The Lancet Psychiatry*, 3: 415–424.

Das, M., Angeli, F., Krumeich, A. J. S. M., and van Schayck, O. C. P. 2018. Patterns of illness disclosure among Indian slum dwellers: A qualitative study. *BMC International Health and Human Rights*, 18.

Donabedian, A. 1988. The quality of care: How can it be assessed? *JAMA*, 260: 1743–1748.

Dranove, D., and White, W. D. 1994. Recent theory and evidence on competition in hospital markets. *Journal of Economics & Management Strategy*, 3: 169–209.

Fosfuri, A., Giarratana, M. S., and Roca, E. 2016. Social business hybrids: Demand externalities, competitive advantage, and growth through diversification. *Organization Science*, 27: 1275–1289.

Haigh, N., Walker, J., Bacq, S., and Kickul, J. 2015. Hybrid organizations: Origins, strategies, impacts, and implications. *California Management Review*, 57: 5–12.

Hannigan, B., and Coffey, M. 2011. Where the wicked problems are: The case of mental health. *Health Policy*, 101: 220–227.

Huber, M., Knottnerus, J. A., Green, L., van der Horst, H., Jadad, A. R., Kromhout, D., Leonard, B., Lorig, K., Loureiro, M. I., and van der Meer, J. W. M. 2011. How should we define health? *BMJ: British Medical Journal*, 343.

Kumar Rastogi, S. 2013. *A Case Study of Sulabh International* Social *Service Organization*. Retrieved from http://www.sulabhinternational.org/wp-content/uploads/2015/07/SISSO-Case-Study-IIM-Ahmedabad.pdf

Larson, J. S. 1999. The conceptualization of health. *Medical Care Research and Review*, 56: 123–136.

Lewis, J. J., and Pattanayak, S. K. 2012. Who adopts improved fuels and cookstoves? A systematic review. *Environmental Health Perspectives*, 120: 637–645.

Mehrotra, K. 2014. *India's Toilet Race Failing as Villages Don't Use Them*. Retrieved from https://www.bloomberg.com/news/articles/2014-08-03/india-s-toilet-race-failing-as-villages-don-t-use-them

Molodynski, A., Rugkåsa, J., and Burns, T. 2010. Coercion and compulsion in community mental health care. *British Medical Bulletin*, 95: 105–119.

Narayana Hrudayalaya Limited (2016). Annual Report Narayana Health. [online] Retrieved from https://www.narayanahealth.org/annual-report-2016.pdf [Accessed 22 Apr. 2018].

O'Reilly, K., and Louiss, E. 2014. The toilet tripod: Understanding successful sanitation in rural India. *Health and Place*, 29: 43–51.

Pache, A. C., and Santos, F. 2013. Inside the hybrid organization: Selective coupling as a response to competing institutional logics. *Academy of Management Journal*, 56.

Porter, M. E. 2010. What is value in health care? *New England Journal of Medicine*, 363: 2477–2481.

Porter, M. E., and Teisberg, E. O. 2004. Redefining competition in health care. *Harvard Business Review*: 64–77.

Santos, F., Pache, A.-C., and Birkholz, C. 2015. Making hybrids work. *California Management Review*, 57: 36–59.

Schut, F. T., and Varkevisser, M. 2017. Competition policy for health care provision in the Netherlands. *Health Policy*, 121(2): 126–133.

Teece, D. 2010. Business models, business strategy and innovation. *Long Range Planning*, 43: 172–194.

Tracey, P., and Jarvis, O. 2006. An enterprising failure: Why a promising social franchise collapsed. *Stanford Social Innovation Review*, 4: 66–70.

Vigo, D., Thornicroft, G., and Atun, R. 2016. Estimating the true global burden of mental illness. *The Lancet Psychiatry*, 3: 171–178.

Westra, D., Angeli, F., Carree, M., and Ruwaard, D. 2015. Understanding competition between healthcare providers: Introducing an intermediary inter-organizational perspective. *Health Policy*, 121: 149–157.

Westra, D., Wilbers, G., and Angeli, F. 2016. Stuck in the middle? A perspective on ongoing pro-competitive reforms in Dutch mental health care. *Health Policy*, 120: 345–349.

World Health Organization. 2013. *Mental Health Action Plan 2013–2020*. WHO Library Cataloguing-in-Publication DataLibrary Cataloguing-in-Publication Data: 1–44.

World Health Organization. 2014. *Progress on Drinking Water and Sanitation—2014 Update; Joint Monitoring Programme for Water Supply and Sanitation*. WHO Library Cataloguing-in-Publication DataLibrary Cataloguing-in-Publication Data: 1–78.

3 Competition and Institutional Forces in Healthcare

The Case of the Netherlands

Daan Westra and Federica Angeli

Introduction

In many developed countries around the globe, healthcare constitutes a major source of expenditure. The most recent statistics of the Organisation for Economic Co-operation and Development (OECD) indicate that OECD countries spend on average 9% of their Gross Domestic Product, approximately US$186 billion per year on health. This includes all health-related activities such as preventive services, curative and rehabilitative care, and long-term care. On average, three-fourths of the expenditure (i.e., 6.5% of GDP) is financed from compulsory, or government-funded, schemes and the remaining 25% consists of voluntary and out-of-pocket payments (OECD, 2017). The share of GDP countries spend on health has furthermore increased steadily over the past two decades. In 2000, for example, the average OECD country spent approximately 7.2% of its GDP on health, which has risen to 9% in 2016. Gaynor et al. (2015) even calculate that if the US healthcare system would be an economy on its own, it would constitute the sixth largest economy in the world. It would only be surpassed by the economies of the US as a whole, China, Japan, Germany, and France, but it would exceed that of countries such as the UK, Italy, and Russia.

The high and increasing amounts of expenditure on healthcare compel nations to design their healthcare systems in the most efficient way possible. The stakes are simply too high, both economically as well as ethically, to tolerate otherwise. In other words, maximizing value (see Chapter 2 for more on the concept of value in healthcare) can be considered the overarching goal of any health system. However, a uniform and widely accepted way to structure a health system, which optimizes value, does not exist. The ways in which countries have designed their healthcare systems consequently vary greatly. Some countries have a healthcare system which is based on private insurers and providers, while others are entirely tax-funded and the government constitutes the main payer. Within countries, the structure, costs, and access of healthcare systems constantly ignite wide and fierce political debates. Looming healthcare reforms are bound to generate reaction from citizens and politicians alike and are rarely, if ever, passed without being heavily debated and contested. The upheaval surrounding the repeal of the Affordable Care Act in the US is perhaps the most recent and explicit example of such a debate. Similarly, in countries like Germany and the Netherlands, the structure of the health system has been a considerable point of debate during their most recent national elections. In the Netherlands, the debate revolved around abandoning the private insurance system and instead introducing one national health insurance. In Germany, the main point of contention was removing the divide between public and privately insured patients, which according to some parties led to great inequalities in the country's healthcare sector. In sum, healthcare provision, and the optimal systemic structure, can be considered a wicked problem which occurs in an ever-changing environment, punctuated by important socio-economic changes, such as an aging population, rise of chronic conditions, increasing socio-economic inequalities, and similar developments.

Against this backdrop, this chapter will unpack competition as a driving institutional force in the healthcare industry. We will assess the assumptions underpinning competition in the healthcare sector as the reasons to pass pro-competitive healthcare reforms. Next, we assess what competition actually means in the context of healthcare, where it originates from, and which types of competition exist in the healthcare industry. Last, we will focus on the effects of competition and discuss how competition can either hinder or facilitate entrepreneurship within the domain of healthcare.

Understanding Pressure for Competitive Reforms in Healthcare Systems

The distinction between the Bismarck and Beveridge systems has long been the most widely accepted and used way to distinguish between counties' healthcare systems. The Beveridge model, named after William Beveridge, the designer of the National Health Service in the UK, revolves around tax-funded and government-directed healthcare. In these systems, healthcare is typically financed by the state with collective taxes generating the funds necessary to do so. In these systems, the state generally owns most of the healthcare providers such as hospitals as well. The Bismarck model, named after German chancellor Otto von Bismarck, refers to a healthcare system based on a (social) insurance model. In these models, individuals contribute to the insurance schemes of (private) insurers to finance the healthcare sector and healthcare providers are typically private (i.e., non-state-owned) organizations. The healthcare systems to date are no longer exact replications of these two archetypical systems. That is, in many countries elements of both models can be identified. However, the Bismarck and Beveridge models still represent the two most prominent regulatory frameworks on which healthcare sectors in various countries are based.

Scott (1995) describes regulatory frameworks, or regulatory elements, together with normative and cognitive elements, as the three pillars of institutions. The regulatory elements consist of the rules and regulations under which organizations operate. These determine which actions are considered legitimate and which are illegitimate and subject to legal punishment. In other words, the type of health system a country utilizes will determine what actions organizations in the system can undertake. Normative elements are those elements which are considered appropriate throughout the industry. Cognitive elements refer to the framing which gives rise to meaning within an industry. Together, the normative, cognitive, and regulatory elements form the institutions which govern an industry. According to institutional theorists, these institutions shape organizational behavior in multiple ways. Most prominently, they have a strong influence on the actions undertaken by organizations in a similar field (i.e., adhering to similar institutions). In other words, organizations will behave in ways which are strongly influenced by the rules, regulations, and norms within a specific field. Different sets of rules and regulations will hence generate different levels of organizational performance. Adequately designing the structure of the healthcare system within a country is thus a prerequisite to reaching favorable health outcomes.

In an attempt to maximize the value of their healthcare systems, countries frequently opt to reform or restructure their healthcare system. As the Institute of Medicine (IOM) has indicated, in order to maximize value, these reforms should focus on the system level. Westra et al. (2017) argue that the decisions to pass health system reforms are typically driven by unsatisfactory outcomes of the healthcare system in place. These can include outcomes in terms of costs, quality, and accessibility. In a study of people's satisfaction with their country's healthcare system, Donelan et al. (1999) show, for example, that a large majority of people are far from content with their country's healthcare system. More recent evidence, for example from the Netherlands, reveals that healthcare is still top of mind to many people when inquired about challenges for the future. This is despite the fact that in many international comparisons, the Dutch healthcare system is ranked among the very best in the world. It is these levels of discontent, either with how the system works, or with the outcomes of the system, that will drive politicians to introduce healthcare reforms in their country.

In his review of reforms in the healthcare sectors of various countries, Cutler (2002) identified three waves of reforms which have shaped the way healthcare systems around the globe were structured. Universal access and coverage constitutes the first. While most industrialized countries made significant strides in this area in the post-World War 2 era, the WHO still considers universal coverage as a high priority in many low- and middle-income countries today. Controlling expenditures and rationing constitute the second wave of reform, according to Cutler. As health expenditures began to exceed affordable levels, countries began to realize that a more stringent control of these expenditures was necessary. This was either done through limiting the access to services or introducing cost-sharing schemes. Incentive-based reforms followed as the third wave of medical care reforms around the turn of the century. These can be categorized into three categories: cost sharing at the patient level, competition at the level of insurers, and incentives within the provider community. Of these three, introducing competition arguably constitutes the largest and most significant restructuring of the healthcare system. It thus has the greatest influence on the institutions (i.e., particularly the regulatory elements which make up those institutions) of a country's healthcare system.

Competition as a Value-Creating Institutional Force

The concept of competition in healthcare is often interpreted in a plethora of ways. In a study in which they inquired various actors in the Dutch healthcare industry (including government representatives, insurers, providers, and patients) about their views towards competition, Paulus et al. (2003) found that competition in healthcare is interpreted by some as perfect competition, while it refers to increased cooperation to others. The authors note that many different definitions in between those two extremes are referenced by respondents. The confusion about what competition (in healthcare) actually is and how it works does not help in facilitating an understanding of the concept and assessing whether it is indeed an appropriate tool to maximize value in the healthcare industry. Let us, towards that purpose, therefore commence with identifying what competition is, how it works in the healthcare industry, and what its underlying assumptions are.

The Oxford dictionary defines competition as: "the activity or condition of striving to gain or win something by defeating or establishing superiority over others." It is synonymous to terms such as rivalry, opposition, conflict, and battling. To many, these terms are the very reason why competition does not apply well to the healthcare sector. They consider it unjust or unethical to compete "for" and "over" patients. From an economic perspective, however, competition refers to a situation in which two organizations vie for the same resources and for the same goals. In more technical terminology, they occupy the same resources space (Ingram and Yue, 2008). In these situations, competitors can only reach their own goals when their competitors fail to reach theirs.

The major point of contention regarding the practicalities of competition in healthcare among scholars is the level at which competition should occur to produce optimal results. In other words, scholars are not in agreement as to who should compete with whom in order to reach the goal of optimizing (the outcomes of) the healthcare sector. Enthoven and Tollen (2005) identify two schools of thought regarding this point. The first argues that competition should occur between integrated delivery systems of payers, primary and secondary care providers. The second posits that competition should instead occur between independent healthcare providers. To understand the differences between these two, it is worthwhile to first assess the basic elements of competition in the healthcare sector.

The Structure of Competition in Healthcare

The concept of competition in the healthcare sector has been championed by the American economist Alain Enthoven. In his paper "The History and Principles of Managed Competition," he defines competition in the healthcare sector as:

> a purchasing strategy to obtain maximum value for money for employers and consumers. It uses rules for competition, derived from rational microeconomic principles, to reward with more subscribers and revenue those health plans that do the best job of improving quality, cutting costs, and satisfying patients.
>
> (Enthoven, 1993: 29)

Although some argue otherwise, the most common view is that for competition in healthcare to occur, a rather fundamental criterion has to be met, namely the existence of private purchasing organizations (also known as third-party payers). While perhaps so blatantly obvious to most economists that it remains largely unarticulated, the existence of private purchasing organizations is not self-evident within the realm of healthcare. In countries that use a Beveridge-like healthcare system, healthcare delivery has traditionally been a hierarchical, state-controlled service (Smith et al., 2012). This is the case in countries like the UK, Denmark, Italy, and Norway, and hospitals are (to a large extent) public, state-owned organizations in those countries (Mossialos et al., 2015). In countries utilizing Bismarck-type healthcare systems, hospitals and other healthcare providers are typically not state-owned but are instead private organizations. This is the case in countries such as the Netherlands and the US. It is the private nature of healthcare organizations, also known as the purchaser-provider split within the context of healthcare (Toth, 2010), which constitutes the fundamental prerequisite for price-competition to occur in the healthcare sector.

Several reasons can be found for the existence of third-party payers. The most common explanation is that the information asymmetry between patients and healthcare providers is so grave that a default model of transactions between those two groups does not function properly. Instead, third-party payers take up this role and negotiate favorable contracts with healthcare providers on behalf of patients. This logically beckons the question of which organizations are considered purchasers of healthcare services. In his recent article, Zweifel (2017) argues that the effect of competition in healthcare will ultimately depend on which type of organization is charged with the responsibility to act as prudent purchasers of healthcare services. He identifies six organizations which can take up the role of purchaser: employers, private health insurers, local governments, medical associations, uniform social health insurance (i.e., a single insurer), and national governments. While all of these organizations can fulfill the same role, Zweifel argues that their incentives and ability to make competition work effectively differ greatly.

Regardless of which type of organization takes up the responsibility of purchaser, the purchaser/provider split creates so-called option-demand markets. The term option-demand refers to the fact that citizens seek out health insurance to ensure that they will be reimbursed for their costs in case they need healthcare services, at which point they utilize the services from providers contracted by the health insurer from which they purchased their insurance policy. Consequently, competition ensues in different stages and between different types of organizations. Gaynor et al. (2015) describe a five-stage model of competition in the healthcare industry. In the first stage, healthcare providers (e.g., hospitals) "determine" their quality levels by making specific quality-related investments. In the second stage, these providers, given their quality levels, negotiate with insurers (or other third-party payers) over the price of their services and whether or not the organization is included in the insurer's network, a process often referred to as selective contracting. In the third stage, insurers set the premium for their health plans based on the agreements they have made with providers in the second stage. In the fourth stage, consumers decided which insurer they prefer and enroll in one of their plans. In the fifth and final stage, patients who fall ill decide from which provider they wish to seek out care. The five stages described by Gaynor and his colleagues are often simplified to three stages by combining stage 1 and 2 in a first stage of selective contracting, combining stage 3 and 4 in a second stage of enrollment, and referring to the last stage as the service delivery stage (see Figure 3.1).

Healthcare markets thus consist of three main groups of actors: citizens (i.e., potential patients), third-party payers (e.g., health insurers), and healthcare providers (e.g., hospitals), all of which operate on mutually dependent markets as illustrated in Figure 3.1. In these types of health systems, the role of the national government is typically limited to overseeing the effectiveness of the system as a whole and ensuring that favorable outcomes are reached. Third-party payers are positioned in arguably the most crucial position within the system, namely the one which seeks to match supply and demand for healthcare services. That is,

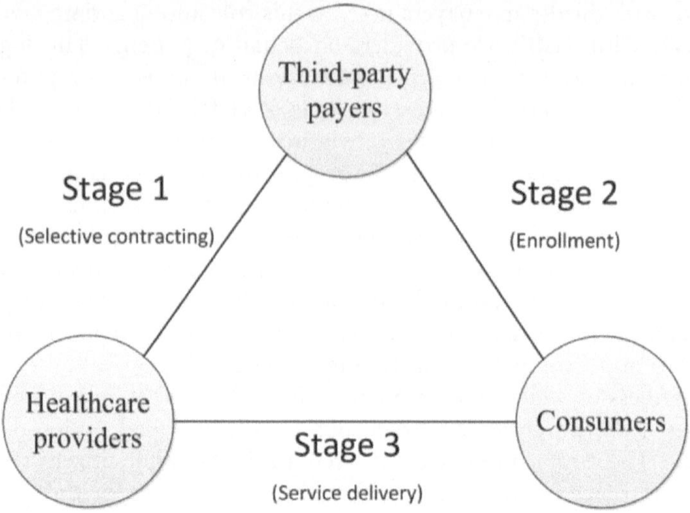

Figure 3.1 Schematic Representation of Competitive Healthcare Industries Based on Gaynor and Town (2012)

they are to contract services from providers which offer to citizens insurance policies with high value for money (i.e., price/quality ratios), which will enable them to offer high value for money (i.e., covering services of high-quality providers against affordable monthly rates).

Even within each of the competitive stages, the specific nature of competition can differ across health systems. This is most notably the case in the first stage of selective contracting and, to a considerable extent, depends on which party fulfills the purchasing role within the system. Within this stage, we can distinguish price-competition and non-price-competition. In the former case, purchasers contract providers based on the price and quality of the services they offer. Prices are thus determined by and in the selective contracting market. As Enthoven points out, competition based on price does not dismiss features such as quality of delivered services from the competitive arena. Rather, it implies that price, just like quality, is one of the features based on which competition occurs. In the latter case, purchasers are not free to negotiate the price of services offered by healthcare providers. In these cases, prices are typically set by a central authority (i.e., they are considered (pre-determined). It should be noted that in cases where there is only a single purchaser (e.g., a national health insurer) which holds full monopsony power, price can also be considered pre-determined. That is, the purchasing organization can singlehandedly raise or lower the price paid for specific services.

Although in his detailed explanation of the theory and principle of managed competition, Enthoven argues that competition in healthcare should revolve around price-competition, many healthcare systems (partially) revolve around non-price competition. In the Netherlands, for example, roughly 8% of all specialized care services were subject to price-competition upon introduction of competition in the sector in 2006. The percentage has been gradually increased to 70% of all specialized care services being subject to price-competition since 2012 (Schut & Varkevisser, 2017). However, a considerable amount of the specialized care services still revolves around prices which are pre-determined by the country's health authority. Similarly, the NHS in the UK mandated that all patients be given a choice of five different hospitals from which they could receive treatment. Hospitals were in turn paid fixed prices for treating these patients. Consequently, a situation of non-price competition was created in which quality, in its multifaceted sense, was the only factor on which hospitals could differentiate themselves in an attempt to draw patients to their organization.

Theoretical Assumptions Underpinning Competition in Healthcare

According to some, using the terms competition and healthcare in the same sentence should be avoided at all costs. According to others, uniting these two concepts is the only way to avoid apocalyptic health expenditures. The public and political debate regarding this matter is highly polarized in some countries. The Netherlands is a prime example of a country in which views on this matter are greatly polarized. In its core, the debate surrounding the desirability of competition in healthcare is a debate whether competition indeed drives value creation in this sector. The argumentation towards competition as a value-creating system in the healthcare sector ultimately hinges on two lines of reasoning.

The first explanation as to why competition between organizations benefits consumers is a classic microeconomic one. That is, according to microeconomic theory, markets are the best way to allocate resources efficiently. Competitive markets will reach an equilibrium state in which the unit price per output is such that the quantity of units produced by producers is equal to the quantity of units demanded by consumers. In other words, microeconomic theory assumes that competition forces all organizations to produce in the most efficient way possible and to sell their products at the market-determined price. Organizations that set their price higher will not sell any outputs, and organizations cannot sell for a lower price. If they could, all organizations would sell at the lower price. These theoretical predictions are based on the assumptions of perfectly competitive markets. In perfectly competitive markets, a large numbers of sellers are free to enter and exit a market (i.e., there are no entry barriers), act independently of each other, and sell as many identical products as they want to a large number of buyers who possess perfect information (Lipczynski et al., 2005). The opposite extreme is a monopoly situation, in which only one organization sells outputs to consumers. It is thus free to dictate the price of the outputs which, in case the organization seeks to earn abnormal profits, could negatively affect consumer

In practice, markets rarely conform to the extreme cases of perfectly competitive markets or monopolies, giving rise to theories of "imperfect competition" such as monopolistic competition and oligopoly (Robinson, 1969). Monopolistic competition refers to a situation in which a large number of organizations compete based on the price of their products as well as on non-price dimensions. An oligopoly, on the other hand, violates the condition of a large number of organizations. Instead, it is characterized by a low number of interdependent organizations (Lipczynski et al., 2005). The interdependence of the organizations in oligopolistic markets again leads economists to theorize two extreme scenarios in these markets, namely pure independent action of all organizations, of which price wars are an example, and pure collusion, of which price fixing is a prominent example. Again, practice is more nuanced and several types of behavior within oligopolistic markets exist, as initially described by Machlup (1952).

The assumption towards introducing competition in healthcare is thus that it will force healthcare providers to provide their services in the most efficient way possible, ultimately maximizing value for money. It should, however, be noted that the deviations from the perfectly competitive model have been well established within the healthcare industry on multiple occasions. In seminal work by Kenneth Arrow (1963) as early as the 1960's, information asymmetry and uncertainty towards an individual's health were readily identified as a deviation from the competitive model. Furthermore, healthcare markets have been described as highly localized markets (Sohn, 2002), which ultimately violates the assumption of many sellers and healthcare providers do not produce homogenous outputs. Last, although the introduction of diagnosis-related groups (DRGs) is best interpreted as an attempt to create uniform and homogenous products across hospitals, healthcare providers do not produce homogenous outputs. Assuming that these imperfections can effectively be overcome, however, competition should lead healthcare providers to produce their services in the most efficient way possible. Those who fail to do so will not be selectively contracted by purchasers, as there will be cheaper alternatives available.

The second argument as to why competition between organizations benefits consumers is related to innovation. In his book, Baumol (2002: 1) describes this process as the "free-market innovation machine." The assumption is that in competitive markets, innovation is the only way for organizations to acquire a competitive advantage over their rivals and consequently enjoy higher profits, at least for a while. The promise of abnormal profits places firms in a rat race in which they continuously seek to one-up their competitors. Firms will therefore keep seeking opportunities to improve their current products or services. As long as customers are willing to pay for these improved products and services, they will thus be better off. Baumol argues that it is precisely this race to the top which explains why capitalism has been able to produce the rapid growth rates that it has over the past centuries. In competitive markets, innovation thus becomes a competitive tool driven by entrepreneurial activity. Competition thus occurs primarily on the basis of the introduction, adoption, and diffusion of innovation rather than merely on price and quality (i.e., efficiency) dimensions.

The innovation argument of competition rests primarily on Joseph Schumpeter's view that technological change and economic growth are two crucial components to creative destruction (Antonelli, 2009). In his view, entrepreneurs are considered destroyers of existing market equilibria. That is, through innovation, entrepreneurs are able to introduce new products or services which are an improvement over existing products or services. Given the hybrid nature of healthcare organizations (i.e., they do not necessarily only seek to maximize their profits; see Chapter 2 for more on hybrid organizations), quality-improving innovations can be considered especially relevant in the healthcare industry. This is particularly true in markets in which prices are pre-determined. A crucial aspect of the effectiveness of the innovation mechanism and innovation as a competitive tool is the existence of entry barriers (or the lack thereof). For entrepreneurs to successfully take up the role of destroyers of existing equilibria, entry barriers should be as low as possible (or non-existent, according to the description of perfectly competitive markets). Although entrepreneurs could have great products or services to offer to consumers, their inability to enter the market will render these useless, locking markets into a state of inertia. To this extent, Porter (1980) considers entry barriers (along with buyer power, seller power, and threat of substitutes) as one of the crucial forces determining the level of competition in an industry. In industries with high entry barriers, incumbent organizations will hence not experience a great deal of competition, and consumer welfare may be sub-optimal as a result.

Effects of Pro-Competitive Regulation for Efficiency, Innovation, and Entrepreneurial Behavior

This chapter illustrates how different countries make use of different types of healthcare systems. Over time, many countries have introduced elements of competitive reform in their healthcare systems with the aim to improve the efficiency of—and ultimately, the outcomes delivered by—the systems. We have furthermore discussed what competition means in the context of healthcare, how it is typically structured, and which assumptions underpin the belief that competition will indeed foster better outcomes. However, the proof of the pudding is ultimately in the eating. Although it has been well established that the healthcare sector violates some important assumptions of competitive markets, several countries have nonetheless structured their healthcare systems on the premise that competition between healthcare providers will benefit patients. The US and the Netherlands are arguably the two most prominent examples of such systems. Others, like the UK and Italy, utilize National Health Services, which do not revolve around private organizations and price-competition. It should therefore be possible to assess to what extent this is indeed the case.

So it would at least seem. Although it is true that competition plays a more important role in the healthcare system of some countries than it does in that of others, many countries have hybrid health systems in which elements of price-competition and non-price-competition are interwoven. It is therefore often difficult to disentangle the effect of both of these elements in a rigorous scientific way. In those instances where it is possible to do so, it should be noted that each health system is unique in terms of its structure and financing methods. Elements which are investigated in one setting are therefore not by definition transferable to elements studied in other settings. While the Netherlands and the US are both considered competitive, insurance-based healthcare systems, they are far from being identical systems. In the Netherlands, citizens are obliged to take out a basic insurance package and insurers are not allowed to refuse applications for this package. Both features are markedly different in the US, where no mandatory insurance package exists and medical underwriting is common practice. The type of providers that are active in the industry is another prime example of differences between both sectors. Although private hospitals are common in both countries, all hospitals in the Netherlands are not-for-profit organizations whereas hospitals in the US can either be for-profit or not-for-profit. Also, vertical integration between purchasers and providers is uncommon in the Netherlands—a bill was even proposed to make vertical integration between insurers and providers illegal—but it is considerably more common in the US.

Besides being aware of the structural differences of health systems between different countries, it is wise to also take into account which section of the healthcare market one is studying when assessing the effects of competition in health systems, or the functioning of health systems in general for that matter. That is, 'the' healthcare market is essentially non-existent. Rather, the term healthcare market should be considered an overarching term for several distinct sub-markets. Based on the assumption that competitors within a market sell homogenous products or services to consumers, further specification of the provider market is required in order to undertake rigorous comparisons within or across countries. General practitioners, for example, largely offer different services (and thus do not compete with) specialized care organizations such as hospitals, which are different again from pharmacies, which differ in turn from mental healthcare providers, and so forth. To illustrate: within the mandatory basic insurance package in the Netherlands, roughly 11 cost categories are typically distinguished: specialized care, general practitioners, pharmaceuticals, mental healthcare, dental care, physical therapy, maternity care, ambulance services, supportive care, other paramedical care, and cross-border care. Because different providers offer different services within these domains, these roughly translate into 11 separate and distinguishable markets. The realm of healthcare organizations depicted in Figure 3.1 is therefore best subdivided, as is represented in Figure 3.2 (in which the markets have been arbitrarily placed and sized).

For the purpose of our argument, another distinction between the markets represented in Figure 3.2, apart from the types of services offered within each of these, is the degree to which services are indeed selectively

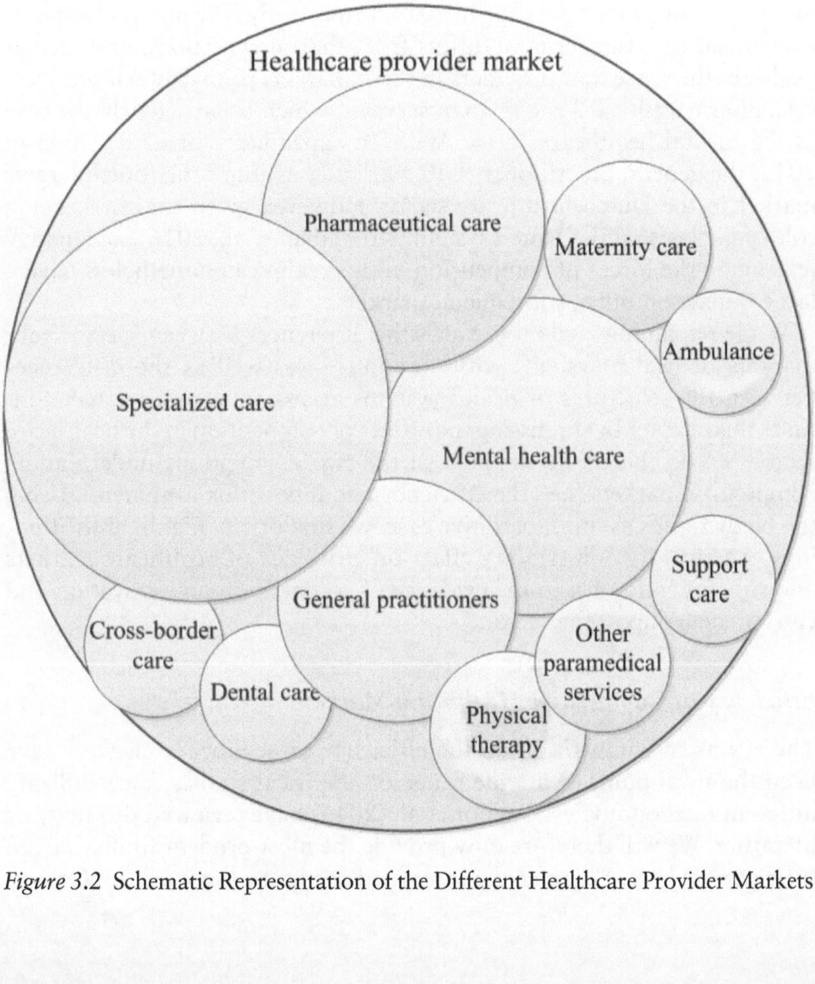

Figure 3.2 Schematic Representation of the Different Healthcare Provider Markets

contracted. In other words, the degree to which (price-)competition actually occurs in the sector and the forces of competition consequently apply can vary across these markets. Dutch insurers rarely, if ever, (selectively) contract healthcare providers in other countries. The level of (price-) competition in cross-border care is thus markedly different from those in specialized care in which providers are selectively contracted on (among other factors) based price-dimensions. Along similar lines, the size of each of the sub-markets, and hence the potential magnitude of the effects of competition, also varies. In terms of expenditure, specialized care is the largest of these markets in the Netherlands. It constituted more than half of the spending within the basic insurance package (i.e., €20 billion) in 2013 (Vektis, 2015). Furthermore, it is also the market in which competition has been most prominently implemented (Van de Ven and Schut, 2009). The market for pharmaceutical care (i.e., through ambulatory pharmacies) and the market for mental healthcare constitute the second and third largest markets in the Dutch healthcare system with an expenditure of approximately €4.5 billion and €3.5 billion under the mandatory insurance package in 2013, respectively. The market for pharmaceutical care furthermore differs from that of specialized and mental health in the sense that providers in these markets primarily sell products (i.e., pharmaceuticals) rather than services, which is particularly the case in the mental healthcare sector. With an expenditure of €2.3 billion in 2013, the general practitioner (GP) market constitutes the fourth largest market in the Dutch healthcare sector. However, given the gatekeeping role of GPs within the Dutch system (Kroneman et al., 2016), adequately leveraging the forces of competition in this realm can nonetheless have a large impact on other, subsequent, markets.

While remaining vigilant towards the differences between specific submarkets of health systems within countries, as well as the differences between the structures of health systems across countries, we will continue this chapter by discussing the effects of competition in the healthcare sector. We do this along the lines of the two assumptions underpinning competitive markets (i.e., the efficiency and innovation argument). Using the Netherlands as our illustrative case, we first briefly highlight the findings in terms of competition's effect on efficiency of healthcare markets and subsequently turn to the evidence of competition on innovation and entrepreneurship in the sector.

Efficiency of Competitive Healthcare Markets

The effects of competition on the efficiency of healthcare markets have been the focal point of a wide range of empirical studies, each utilizing different methodologies. Gaynor et al. (2015) have reviewed this body of literature. We will therefore only provide the most prudent findings from their review here. We refer the interested reader to the work by Gaynor and colleagues for a more detailed description of each of the studies undertaken in this field. In their review of the scientific literature, Gaynor and colleagues make a clear distinction between the effect of competition in markets with pre-determined prices (i.e., non-price-competition) and those in which price is determined by the market (i.e., price-competition). They furthermore distinguish between effects expressed in terms of quality of care and those expressed in terms of price and between empirical and theoretical studies. As far as empirical research is concerned, the authors additionally make a distinction between different methodologies employed in the studies which they reviewed.

The review by Gaynor et al. (2015) indicates that theoretically competition has a positive effect on the quality of services in markets in which prices are pre-determined (i.e., non-price-competitive markets), in case the pre-determined price exceeds the marginal costs of providers. In these cases, providers are expected to increase the quality of their services. The authors furthermore find that this prediction is generally supported in empirical studies. They point out that while there indeed seems to be a relation between the level of competition in a market and the quality of care delivered by providers in these markets, it is unlikely that hospitals in less competitive markets deliberately choose to deliver lower quality of care. Instead, Gaynor and colleagues suggest that hospitals in less competitive markets lack the pressure from competitors, which leads to lower efforts than in hospitals in more competitive markets. Under conditions of price-competition, the theoretical prediction is that price and quality will either increase or decrease depending on price- and quality-elasticity of demand. That is, whether competition will increase or decrease price and quality will depend on how price- and quality-sensitive consumers are. In other words, it will depend on whether consumers are willing to pay for higher levels of quality of care. The empirical evidence indicates that the effect of competition on quality of care does indeed seem to vary. Some studies find a positive effect, others find a negative effect, and some find no effect of competition on quality of care. In terms of price, most empirical studies indicate that price-competition decreases prices.

The review by Gaynor and colleagues helps in understanding whether competition is indeed able to improve the efficiency of healthcare markets. As such, it is a valuable resource to test the assumption of the allocative efficiency properties of competitive markets. However, the review also indicates that much of the empirical literature regarding hospital quality has adopted a rather one-sided operationalization of quality. That is, for a long time, scholars in the industrial organization field have modeled quality of care as Acute Myocardial Infarctions (AMI) mortality rates. The argument can be made that hospital-wide quality improvements will ultimately improve the quality of care in the hospital as a whole, including the quality of care for AMI patients. On the other hand, approximately one-third of the AMI patients are believed to arrive at the hospital by ambulance, indicating that hospitals do not actively compete for these patients. Furthermore, mortality rates constitute only a single dimension of quality of care. Other dimensions such as structure or process indicators or dimensions of a hospital's hospitality are hence disregarded in these studies. These might nevertheless constitute an important aspect of quality of care to many people.

Innovation and Entry Barriers

Unlike the effects of competition on efficiency parameters such as price and quality of care, the effect of competition as an institutional force in the healthcare industry on entrepreneurial behavior and innovation within the industry has not been thoroughly reviewed. Some aspects have, however, been subject to empirical analysis and scientific testing and theorizing. These include, but are not limited to, the spread and adoption of innovation, the role of entry barriers, and signs of market entry. In this section, we will discuss and familiarize the reader with some of these aspects.

Despite the fact that healthcare is often credited with major scientific advancement and innovations (from new drugs to innovative ways of treating patients and curing diseases), healthcare organizations are generally perceived to be rather inert and slow to adopt changes. The gap between the readily available, scientifically proven medical knowledge and the actual application of said knowledge has, for example, given rise to the evidence-based medicine, or evidence-based decision-making movement. This movement strongly promotes the use of scientific evidence in medical decision-making in order to avoid the use of ineffective, inefficient, and ultimately wasteful health services. Various explanations have been put forth explaining the failure to disseminate innovations across the healthcare sector. Perhaps the most prominent is the decision-making autonomy of medical professionals. Based on an extensive case study in the UK's NHS, Ferlie et al. (2005) furthermore suggest that the social and cognitive boundaries between different professional groups in healthcare frustrate the spread of innovations. They argue that professionals typically focus on their own community of practice and have difficulties adopting innovations which stem from different professional groups.

The difficulties in innovation adoption thus make the healthcare sector a difficult setting to scale up innovative products or services. From an entrepreneurial perspective, the conditions thus do not seem optimal in the healthcare industry. These are further worsened by the fact that the healthcare industry is known for having considerable barriers to entry. This holds true for individuals wishing to practice medicine as well as for organizations seeking to enter the provider market. At the individual level, in most countries, practicing medicine is limited to those individuals who possess the required medical license to do so. While definitely a desirable safeguard of patient's safety and security, becoming a certified medical professional takes years of training. Consequently, the barriers to entering this market are considerable. Introducing competition in the sector will furthermore have little to no effect in terms of lowering this barrier to entry. In the Netherlands, for example, the number of students admitted to medical school has long been determined by the central government. Similarly, the number of residencies towards becoming a medical specialist is also restricted.

At the organizational level, entering the healthcare provider market with new or improved products or services can also be impeded by several barriers to entry. This is true in the provider market, as well as in the insurer market. Investments constitute an obvious example. Opening a new hospital requires capital investments (i.e., buildings and equipment such as scanners and operating rooms), which make it difficult to enter the hospital market. It is thus no surprise that hospital markets in the US, the UK, and the Netherlands have become increasingly consolidated (i.e., hospitals have primarily left the market) rather than having seen a wave of new entrants (Gaynor et al., 2015). Similarly, in a recent study, the Dutch antitrust authority concluded that high entry barriers in the insurer market impede effective competition in that sector. The antitrust authority identified three major barriers to entering the insurers market; the solvency requirements at the European Union (EU) level, the license requirements from the Dutch bank, and various sources of regulatory uncertainty. Although the antitrust authority indicates that lowering entry barriers in the insurer market is an important policy point, they also acknowledge that the barriers are in place to safeguard consumers from negative consequences.

Competition-Induced Entrepreneurship in Healthcare: The Case of Dutch Independent Treatment Centers

Although the insurer market and he hospital market might be difficult to enter, different sub-markets of healthcare provision can be more attractive, especially when the competition (partially) revolves around treatment prices. By introducing price-competition and opportunities for negotiation over prices, the policy reform in the Netherlands has remarkably spurred the increase of a specific form of healthcare providers: the independent treatment centers (ITCs). Independent treatment centers are relatively small ambulatory centers which employ at least two medical specialists and which typically offer only a selected number of treatments to patients in specific specialties, such as dermatology, ophthalmology, and orthopedics (NZa, 2011). Contrary to private clinics, ITCs in the Netherlands offer services which are covered by the mandatory basic insurance package. As such, these clinics are direct competitors to incumbent hospitals, whereas private clinics commonly offer services which are paid for out of pocket because they are not covered by the insurance package.

The Dutch health authority provides an extensive report of entrepreneurial activity related to ITCs (NZa, 2012). After the reforms in 2006, the number of independent treatment centers has rapidly increased from a few dozen to 313 in 2010, which suggests that the newly defined competitive space and regulation has provided a new profit opportunity to potential entrepreneurs. ITCs' market entry reached a peak in 2008, when 46 new organizations registered as ITCs. Also, the average turnover per ITC doubled in the years 2008–2012, pointing to the fact that the opportunities for generating profits are significant, despite the rise in the competition. Strong points of ITCs' business formula are specialization, flexibility, and prices. ITCs typically specialize on non-acute, low-complexity, high-volume treatments that can be delivered without patient admission. Because of their small size and high specialization, ITCs do not require the same capital investment and costly infrastructure, and they can offer services similar as hospitals but against significantly lower costs—about 10–15%, which becomes particularly attractive for insurance companies. Their stand-alone nature furthermore allows ITCs to innovate their services and achieve more efficient and effective service delivery than hospitals. Between 2007 and 2010, the market share of ITCs in the specialized care market increased from 1% to 2.3%, in particular for plastic surgery, anesthesiology, allergology, orthopedics, dermatology, and ophthalmology. The relatively highest market shares are allergology, dermatology, ophthalmology, for which ITCs' market share amounts to more than 10%.

Interestingly, the relationship with hospitals is ambivalent. One aspect of it suggests fierce competition. ITCs have substantially increased competitive pressures for hospitals, which have systematically lost market share on a number of specialties. Hospitals in turn question the quality of services delivered by ITCs, and referrals by GPs to ITCs are still substantially lower than to incumbent hospitals. However, it appears also that ITCs and hospitals are strongly connected. In 2010, in more than 12% of the cases at least one ITC's manager or director was also affiliated to a hospital in a similar function. Moreover, more than 40% of ITCs directors simultaneously worked as specialists in a hospital at the time when the research took place. This suggests that more complex dynamics might be at play. Because of increasing financial pressures, hospitals might have concentrated on their core competences and strategically driven out some specialties to trusted outsourcing partners—the ITCs. At the same time, hospital medical specialists could have spotted a profit opportunity—generated by the combination of the new regulation, the hospitals' heavier infrastructure and hence high prices, and the presence of low-complexity, high-profit, non-acute treatments that could easily be delivered in an ambulatory setting. It seems therefore that medical specialist have been able to sense and seize an entrepreneurial opportunity and concretized it through the establishment of an increasing number of ITCs in the Dutch market.

Conclusions

In this chapter, we have explored the role of the institutional context on the efficiency and innovativeness of the healthcare industry. We have indicated that different countries utilize different healthcare systems. These systems can broadly be categorized as Beveridge-type or Bismarck-type systems. The former revolves around state ownership, while the latter is based on a (private) insurance system. The type of healthcare system is an important institutional factor driving the behavior of healthcare organizations, and over the years, several countries have blended elements of both types of systems and increasingly introduced competitive mechanisms into their healthcare sectors. The assumptions of competition in the healthcare domain are that it will improve the value created by organizations in the settings in two ways. First, competition is considered the optimal way to efficiently allocate resources. That is, providers in competitive markets are believed to produce their services as efficiently as possible. Second, competition should stimulate innovation in the sector, which will result in improved products and services for patients. In the healthcare industry, competition occurs in separate markets. Most prominently, it arises from the selective contracting process providers by purchasers. The evidence that competition improves the efficiency of healthcare markets is mixed. In terms of innovation and entrepreneurship, healthcare is a sector in which innovations are slow to disseminate and entry barriers are relatively high. Competitive reforms have, however, sought to lower these barriers and stimulate entrepreneurship within the sector.

References

Antonelli, C. 2009. The economics of innovation: from the classical legacies to the economics of complexity. *Economics of Innovation and New Technology*, 18(7), 611–646.

Arrow, K. J. 1963. Uncertainty and the welfare economics of medical care. *The American Economic Review*, 53(5), 141–149.

Baumol, W. J. 2002. *The Free-Market Innovation Machine: Analyzing the Growth Miracle of Capitalism*. Princeton, NJ: Princeton University Press.

Cutler, D. M. 2002. Equality, efficiency, and market fundamentals: The dynamics of international medical-care reform. *Journal of Economic Literature*, 40(3): 881–906.

Donelan, K., Blendon, R., Schoen, C., Davis, K., and Binns, K. 1999. The cost of health system change: Public discontent in five nations. *Health Affairs*, 18(3): 206–216.

Enthoven, A. C. 1993. The history and principles of managed competition. *Health Affairs*, 12(suppl. 1): 24–48.

Enthoven, A. C., and Tollen, L. A. 2005. Competition in health care: It takes systems to pursue quality and efficiency. *Health Affairs*, 24: W5.

Ferlie, E., Fitzgerald, L., Wood, M., and Hawkins, C. 2005. The nonspread of innovations: The mediating role of professionals. *Academy of Management Journal*, 48(1): 117–134.

Gaynor, M., Ho, K., and Town, R. J. 2015. The industrial organization of healthcare markets. *Journal of Economic Literature*, 53(2): 235–284.

Gaynor, M., and Town, R. J. 2012. *Competition in Health Care Markets*. Bristol, UK: The Centre for Market and Public Organisation.

Ingram, P., and Yue, L. Q. 2008. 6 structure, affect and identity as bases of organizational competition and cooperation. *The Academy of Management Annals*, 2(1): 275–303.

Kroneman, M., Boerma, W., van den Berg, M., Groenewegen, P. P., De Jong, J., and van Ginneken, E. 2016. Health systems in transition: The Netherlands. In R. Busse, J. Figueras, M. McKee, E. Mossialos, E. Nolte, and E. van Ginneken (Eds.), *Health Systems in Transition*. Copenhagen, Denmark: European Observatory on Health Systems and Policies.

Lipczynski, J., Wilson, J., and Goddard, J. 2005. *Industrial Organization: Competition, Strategy, Policy*, 2nd ed. Essex, UK: Pearson Education Limited.

Machlup, F. 1952. *The Economics of Sellers' Competition: Model Analysis of Sellers' Conduct*. Baltimore, MD: The John Hopkins Press.

Mossialos, E., Wenzl, M., Osborn, R., and Anderson, C. 2015. *2015 International Profiles of Health Care Systems*. Washington, DC: The Commonwealth Fund.

NZa. 2011. *Marktscan Medisch specialistische zorg: Weergave van de markt 2006–2011*. Utrecht, the Netherlands: Dutch Healthcare Authority.

NZa. 2012. *Monitor Zelfstandige Behandelcentra*. Utrecht, the Netherlands: Dutch Healthcare Authority.

OECD. 2017. *OECD Health Statistics 2017*. Retrieved from: http://www.oecd.org/els/health-systems/health-data.htm

Paulus, A., van Raak, A., van der Made, J., and Mur-Veeman, I. 2003. Market competition: Everybody is talking, but what do they say?: A sociological analysis of market competition in policy networks. *Health Policy*, 64(3): 279–289.

Porter, M. 1980. *Competitive Strategy: Techniques for Analyzing Industries and Competitors*. New York, NY: The Free Press.

Robinson, J. 1969. *The Economics of Imperfect Competition*. London, UK: Springer.

Schut, F. T., and Varkevisser, M. 2017. Competition policy for health care provision in the Netherlands. *Health Policy*, 121(2): 126–133.

Scott, R. W. 1995. *Institutions and Organizations*. Thousand Oaks, CA: Sage Publications Inc.

Smith, P. C., Anell, A., Busse, R., Crivelli, L., Healy, J., Lindahl, A. K., Westert, G., and Kene, T. 2012. Leadership and governance in seven developed health systems. *Health Policy*, 106(1): 37–49.

Sohn, M. W. 2002. A relational approach to measuring competition among hospitals. *Health Services Research*, 37(2): 457–482.

Toth, F. 2010. Healthcare policies over the last 20 years: Reforms and counter-reforms. *Health Policy*, 95(1): 82–89.

Van de Ven, W. P. M. M., and Schut, F. T. 2009. Managed competition in the Netherlands: Still work-in-progress. *Health Economics*, 18(3): 253–255.

Vektis, C.V. 2015. Zorgprisma Publiek: Hoe hoog zijn de totale zorgkosten in Nederland? In *Cognos*. Zeist, the Netherlands.

Westra, D., Angeli, F., Carree, M., and Ruwaard, D. 2017. Understanding competition between healthcare providers: Introducing an intermediary inter-organizational perspective. *Health Policy*, 121(2): 149–157.

Zweifel, P. 2017. Competition in the healthcare sector: A missing dimension. *European Journal of Health Economics*, 18: 135–138.

4 Beyond Competition

Exploring Collaboration for Entrepreneurship in Healthcare Organizations

Daniele Mascia, Francesca Pallotti, and Valentina Iacopino

Introduction

The macro-level perspective outlined in Chapter 1 clarified that the entrepreneurial ecosystem in healthcare is influenced by the socio-cultural, legal, and institutional environments, governmental policy, and patterns of technological advancements in which healthcare organizations are embedded. Altogether, these elements contribute to shape the general climate where several social actors—healthcare professionals, hospitals, biopharmaceutical companies, medical device manufacturers, and policymakers—operate and perform (e.g., Scott et al., 2000). According to this perspective, organizations are not closed, isolated entities, but rather they are open and highly embedded in a complex web of both competitive and collaborative interdependences (Uzzi, 1997; White, 2002).

There is increasing awareness that collaborative relationships are of quintessential importance in healthcare, especially in light of the current epidemiological scenario characterized by an increased prevalence and incidence of chronic diseases (cardiovascular problems, oncological diseases, metabolic disorders, etc.). Collaboration is important for coordination and integration of activities provided by different healthcare organizations, such as community hospitals, nursing homes, specialized hospitals, primary care physicians, etc. Prior literature has documented that both planned and unplanned collaborative partnerships are important to predict the quality and efficiency with which providers deliver service to consumers (e.g., Ferlie et al., 2003). However, the role that these collaborations play in the context of entrepreneurship initiatives has been overlooked so far.

Several cases in North American, European, and Asian countries have documented that, especially in large research hospitals and under certain conditions, groups of clinicians may give rise to initiatives aimed at exploiting and leveraging internal clinical knowledge, eventually contributing to the development of new products and innovation in the medical field. Hospitals are becoming more focalized on a narrow set of clinical capabilities (Clark and Huckman, 2012), and at the same time, more involved in an increased number of initiatives for the commercial exploitation of medical knowledge (Smith and Clark, 2010). These organizational trajectories are sustained through a complex network of collaborative initiatives, in which planned and unplanned arrangements can be established.

Against this backdrop, the chapter presents an organizational perspective that provides a rationale for the formation of collaborative relationships in the healthcare industry. We present the main forms of collaboration in healthcare, and then discuss how planned and unplanned collaborative initiatives can sustain knowledge exploitation initiatives undertaken in hospitals. Next, we introduce the concept of "centers of excellence" and discuss their role in the context of entrepreneurship in the healthcare domain. We conclude with a general discussion about the main contributions of the chapter.

Collaboration in Healthcare

Coordination among healthcare providers has become of fundamental importance, and it is likely to become unavoidable, given increasing levels of specialization and differentiation, which require an integrated approach to care delivery (Gittell and Weiss, 2004). For example, patients with serious acute or chronic conditions are likely to demand healthcare services offered by more than one provider. The fragmentation of patients' treatments resulting from the highly specialized nature of the system increases interdependence and implies extensive coordination and collaboration among healthcare providers across the system (Enthoven, 2009). Through the establishment of collaborative relations, individual and organizational actors obtain access to information, resources, and knowledge possessed by other individuals or organizations. In fact, lack of coordination—empirical evidence demonstrates—can result both in higher costs of service utilization at the system level, as well as in adverse patient outcomes, such as higher mortality and readmission rates (Lu and Lu, 2017, Tsai et al., 2015; Frandsen et al., 2015). As a consequence, interconnection is an essential concept to understand key drivers of success for organizations.

As in many other industries, organizations elicit a natural propensity to establish relationships with the reference environment, and to be interconnected to others through a wide set of both economic and social relations. Such linkages may consist of: (i) supply and/or financing relationships, such as shared human resources agreements; (ii) associative forms created for specific purposes (Westra et al., 2017b); (iii) strategic alliances; (iv) interlocking directorates; (v) informal relationships among individuals (Gulati et al., 2002); or (vi) joint ventures and consortia (e.g., Fottler et al., 1982; Barringer and Harrison, 2000). Those listed are not exhaustive nor mutually exclusive (Fottler et al., 1982), but are useful to justify the reasons for forming connections.

Furthermore, collaborative behaviors may imply change for organizations. Ownership and management style, human resources, and decision-making are some of the components which are of paramount importance for the choice of collaboration form. Some of them are riskier than others, because their impact on organizational variables is dramatic. This is why, sometimes, collaboration starts by the simplest and less risky approach—for example, by sharing services among partners—and then it progressively becomes stronger (Fottler et al., 1982).

Although different classifications describing the ways through which organizations connect with each other and activate collaborations exist, we recognize two guiding criteria. The first criterion is the distinction between planned and unplanned collaborative arrangements. Planned collaboration implies a high strategic involvement of partners and the definition of clear and specific strategic objectives. Unplanned collaborations are, instead, the result of contingent emerging needs of partners, and thus they appear less linked to well-defined strategic purposes. The second criterion concerns the extent to which relationships are formalized. Such degree may vary from partnerships based on formal documentation and contracts to less formalized, collaborative initiatives that are based on mutual trust and common values. Figure 4.1 presents four macro-categories of collaborative relationships defined according to the combination of the previously mentioned criteria. Such conceptualization likely oversimplifies the different collaboration forms; however, it represents a useful categorization for our further discussion. We next turn to planned forms of collaboration. The following section focuses on unplanned collaborative forms.

Planned Collaborations

Over the past few decades, hospital tendency toward integration increased, and developed both horizontally and vertically (Lawton and Parker, 2002; Bazzoli et al., 2004). Horizontal integration is linkages among organizations operating at the same stage of production, while vertical integration refers to collaboration types created among organizations located at different—but proximate—stage of production and distribution (Fottler et al., 1982). Several reasons are at the basis of this trend, whose goal was to improve the strategic flexibility (Ginn et al., 2006) and the achievement of higher level of efficiency, financial strength and a stronger market position (Burns and Pauly, 2002). First, being part of a system permits the exploitation of economies of scale and scope, for example by eliminating overlap in technological equipment. Second, hospital systems reduce administrative costs. Third, membership can confer advantages in terms of marketing and accessibility to healthcare services. Finally, relations enhance the level of stability and reliability of members and reduces patient uncertainty over the quality of care (Dranove et al.,

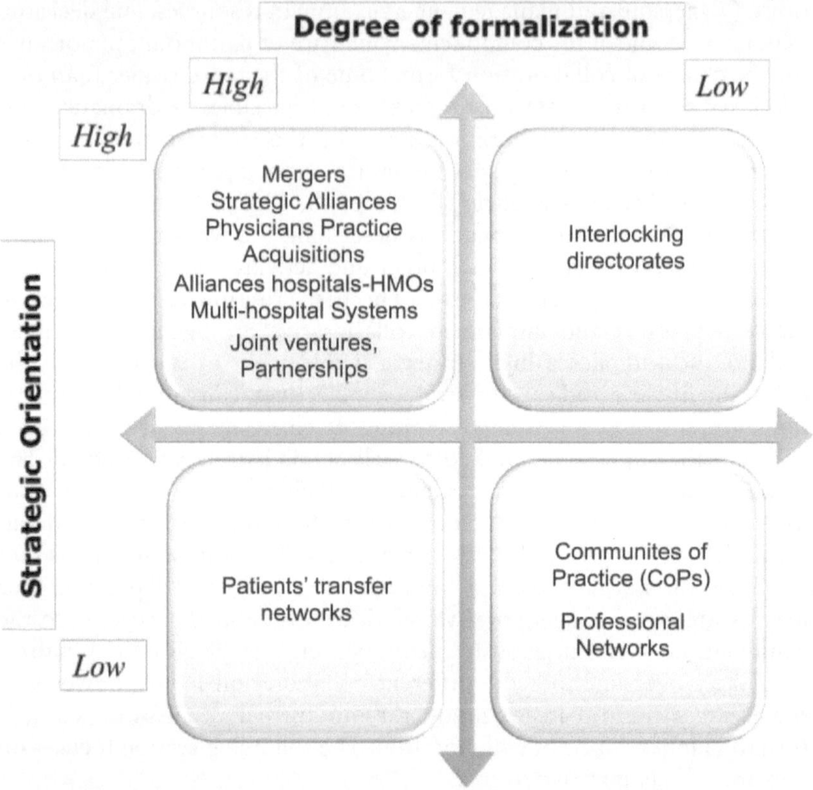

Figure 4.1 Classification of Collaboration in Healthcare

1996). For example, previous evidence has documented that, although the effects of a membership on patients' outcomes are generally limited, hospital's embeddedness in a geographically concentrated system can generate better clinical outcomes in terms of mortality (Madison, 2004).

Moreover, collaborative forms affect many important organizational assets. First, they play role in the propensity of people to cooperate and activate knowledge sharing channels and trust (Chen et al., 2013). In addition, inter-organizational linkages affect technological integration (Mahoney et al., 2007), which in turn positively influences clinical and organizational performance. To conclude, collaborative relations are natural vehicles for the diffusion of innovations and clinical practices, and ideal channels for sharing and implementation. They are valuable drivers for members' experiences and learning and play role in the enhancement of individual competences (Gulati et al., 2002).

Horizontal integration was the dominant design in the 1980s. Forms included the formation of Multi-Hospital Systems (MHSs), mergers, and strategic alliances among hospitals geographically concentrated to form local networks (Burns and Pauly, 2002). MHSs, made up of two or more affiliated hospitals partially or fully owned by a single company owner, is a suitable aggregation both for profit and non-profit hospitals (Cuellar and Gertler, 2003). It differs from a merger as far as hospitals in the system keep their separate identities and thus their ability to face community local needs (Bazzoli et al., 2004). From an empirical point of view, a lack of evidence is still observable on the advantages associated to horizontal integration. According to strategic management scholars, more research is needed to fully understand the characteristics of these systems (Luke, 2006). As a matter of fact, many of the financial benefits associated with integration, such as the opportunity to access capital in equity markets, are not suitable for non-profit hospitals (Burns and Pauly, 2002), and there is uncertainty around the assumption that MHSs positively contribute to the efficiency or hospital's market share.

More recent trends led some health systems, such as the NHS in UK, to advance also forms of vertical integration (Ferlie and McGivern, 2003), such as the Physician Practice Acquisitions (Bazzoli et al., 2004). Even in this case, several negative effects of integration were found, all associated with large financial loss due to adverse selection and scarce productivity. Further different forms of vertical integration have been implemented across countries, such as strategic alliances between hospitals and HMOs, but the outcomes were not those expected (Burns and Pauly, 2002). Residual forms of medical organizations diffused but then declined during the 1990s.

Further inter-organizational relations reside in partnerships and strategic alliances. While partnerships are a valuable tool to include non-public partners in the healthcare sector (Ferlie and McGivern, 2003), strategic alliances are "voluntary arrangements between firms, involving exchange, sharing or co-development of products, technologies and services" (Gulati, 1995: 619). Other relevant forms of collaborations in healthcare organizations are represented by interlocking directorates, a vehicle for inter-organization coordination and control (Zajac, 1988; Westra et al., 2017b), and joint ventures, which normally support organizations in accessing new markets, skills, and resources (Beamish and Lupton, 2009).

Relevant previous literature investigated the effects of collaboration and integration in healthcare; for instance, on hospital pricing (Melnick and Keeler, 2007), effectiveness (Yavas and Romanova, 2005) and performance (Judge and Dooley, 2006). Surprisingly, little evidence is available about the outcomes of this strategic choice. According to Dranove et al. (1996), horizontal integration generates greater efficiency in marketing activities, but not in the productivity. With particular reference to MHSs, scholars highlighted how the relationship between hospitals' membership and financial returns is still ambiguous (Tennyson and Fottler, 2000; Spetz et al., 2000), even in the case of creation of local and /or regional hospitals' clusters (Sikka et al., 2009).

Unplanned Collaboration in Healthcare

Less examined, but equally common, are those forms of collaboration involving emerging social relationships among healthcare providers (Provan et al., 2007; Barringer and Harrison, 2000; Antivachis and Angelis, 2015; Powell, 1990; Borgatti and Cross, 2003). Unlike contractual arrangements, unplanned coordination arises from the deliberate action of participants establishing repeated, enduring collaborations that facilitate achievement of collective goals. Such form of coordination is facilitated by trust, mutual awareness, personal relations, and shared knowledge among healthcare providers (de Figueiredo and Silverman, 2017; Gittell 2000).

The provision of healthcare services through patient referral systems provides an instructive example of an emergent social system (Lomi and Pallotti, 2012). By definition, patient referral systems are composed of individual or organizational actors that are linked by patient sharing relations. The distinctive feature of patient referral systems is the fact that participants are not necessarily connected by planned or hierarchical and employment relations (Provan et al., 2007; Barringer and Harrison, 2000; Antivachis and Angelis, 2015; Powell, 1990; Borgatti and Cross, 2003). Typically, patients are shared among system members as a result of deliberate decisions to involve partners in the process of care delivery.

Because of limited available data, most research on patient referral systems has focused on the analysis of interprofessional rather than inter-organizational networks, as two relatively recent reviews suggest (Chambers et al., 2012; Harris et al., 2012). In interprofessional networks, healthcare providers are individuals (e.g., primary care physicians, hospital specialists, nurses) collaborating by sharing patients within or outside organizational boundaries—see, for example, the works by Gittell (2002) and Hilligoss and Cohen (2013) on patient referrals between and within hospital units; and the work by Landon et al. (2012) on shared patient networks among physicians working across geographically defined administrative units, such as hospital referral regions. It is only over the past decade that research has devoted increasing attention to the analysis of patient referral networks among hospitals, in both emergency and acute empirical settings (among the most recent works, see Kitts et al., 2017; Lu and Lu, 2017; Stadtfeld et al., 2016; Lomi et al., 2014; Lomi and Pallotti, 2012; Veinot et al., 2012; Iwashyna and Courey, 2011).

In interhospital patient referral systems, patients are moved from one hospital (sender) to another (receiver) as a result of individual, yet interdependent, decisions to collaborate on joint problem-solving activities across organizational boundaries. Collaboration in these systems is unplanned when it is activated by a contingent clinical or medical problem. Such contingency becomes the antecedent for the formation of a collaborative relationship between partner hospitals.

The main reason behind interhospital patient referral, especially in emergency settings, concerns the lack of treatment capabilities at the sender hospital. Lu and Lu (2017), for example, describe the routing of patients with acute myocardial infarction (AMI), and explain that if the hospital admitting a patient with AMI symptoms is unable to offer adequate treatment procedures, then its staff immediately initiates a patient transfer process. The action of transferring patients is a fairly routinized process requiring not only a physical and technical infrastructure to make a transfer operationally possible, but also a relational infrastructure based on coordination and information sharing among healthcare providers (Veinot et al., 2012; Bosk et al., 2011; Iwashyna, 2012). The correct functioning of these infrastructures is essential for avoiding delays and maintaining continuity of medical care (Hains et al., 2011).

It has been suggested that patient referral networks produce signals of a relational collaboration between hospitals, which comprises "frequent, timely, accurate communication, as well as problem-solving, shared goals, shared knowledge, and mutual respect among healthcare providers" (Gittell, 2000: 807). The flow of patients among hospitals implies not only the transfer of financial resources, but also the transfer of clinical information and knowledge. As described in Kitts et al. (2017), the documentation that accompanies a transferred patient provides a learning opportunity for both the sending and the receiving hospital. For example, the medical staff of the receiving hospital might learn from receiving a patient who underwent an innovative procedure or treatment protocol in the sending hospital.

Because of these varied reasons, both the decision to transfer a patient, as well as the decision to receive a patient, imply a commitment of time, resources, and information sharing that is likely to transform a contingent event into an enduring relationship between hospitals. Prior studies have shown that physical distance, quality measures, personal relationships, and capabilities complementarities are fundamental factors determining the emergence and maintenance of interhospital patient referral relationships (Lu and Lu, 2017; de Figueiredo and Silverman, 2017; Iwashyna and Kahn, 2014). Far less examined, on the other hand, are the possible outcomes of these relationships at the patient, hospital and system levels. A few notable exceptions are available. For example, Mascia et al. (2015) have shown that patients who are transferred to hospitals occupying central positions in patient transfer networks are less likely to be readmitted for subsequent care and treatment. A recent study using 30-day readmission rates to evaluate the health outcome of interhospital transfer networks has shown that transfers to higher quality, physically proximate hospitals are likely to lead to better outcomes than transfers to hospitals belonging to the same MHS (Lu and Lu, 2017).

Another less formalized, unplanned form of coordination in healthcare is represented by the so-called Communities of Practice (CoPs). A

CoP is a community of individuals connected to one another in order to share specific knowledge, finally converging towards the adoption of a common language and identity (Brown and Duguid, 2001; Ferlie and McGivern, 2003). CoPs pertain to groups of individuals belonging to one or more organizations and/or professional communities, and are different from patient referrals in terms of contents of relationships and objectives. CoPs are emergent and voluntary, but their boundaries are more fluid, since the relationships among members can emerge (and dissolve) over time as far as knowledge exchange and resource commonalities are perceived as useful (Ferlie and McGivern, 2003).

Organizational Trajectories and Collaboration

Competitive and collaborative forces currently coexist in many healthcare systems around the world as a result of institutional reforms and interventions aimed at making the overall health system more affordable (Brandenburger and Nalebuff, 1996; Barretta, 2008; Westra et al., 2017a, 2017b). In the US, for example, the Patient Protection and Affordable Care Act was implemented during the presidency of Barack Obama to reduce the inequalities and inefficiencies of the system and to promote new forms of public insurance. Moreover, we observe interventions that aims to increase the level of regionalization in healthcare. Regionalized health systems are based on "hub and spoke" configurations, where resources are centralized, and information and patients tend to flow from peripheral facilities to larger clinical centers according to the patient's conditions and complexity (Glickman et al., 2010; Iwashyna and Kahn, 2014: 11). Regionalization is generally considered an effective model to improve efficiency, because it offers the opportunity to avoid duplication, share resources, coordinate efforts with authorities, and achieve consistency at local, regional, and national levels (Stoto, 2008). Moreover, it reduces competitive forces and increases the level of collaboration among providers at the same time.

The concurrent collaboration and competition (Westra et al., 2017a, 2017b; Mascia et al., 2012, 2015; Barretta, 2008; Peng and Bourne, 2009) is the result of pro-competitive reforms implemented in public health systems. In countries such as Canada, Italy, and the UK, several innovations have been adopted to introduce market forces to increase the level of competition among public (and private) providers. Simultaneously, providers were asked to keep ensuring the provision of basic health needs within the context of societal priorities dictated by the public character of the system.

Such trends had implications on the organizational models adopted in hospitals. Figure 4.2 illustrates two major trajectories of organizational evolution nowadays observed, all of which have important

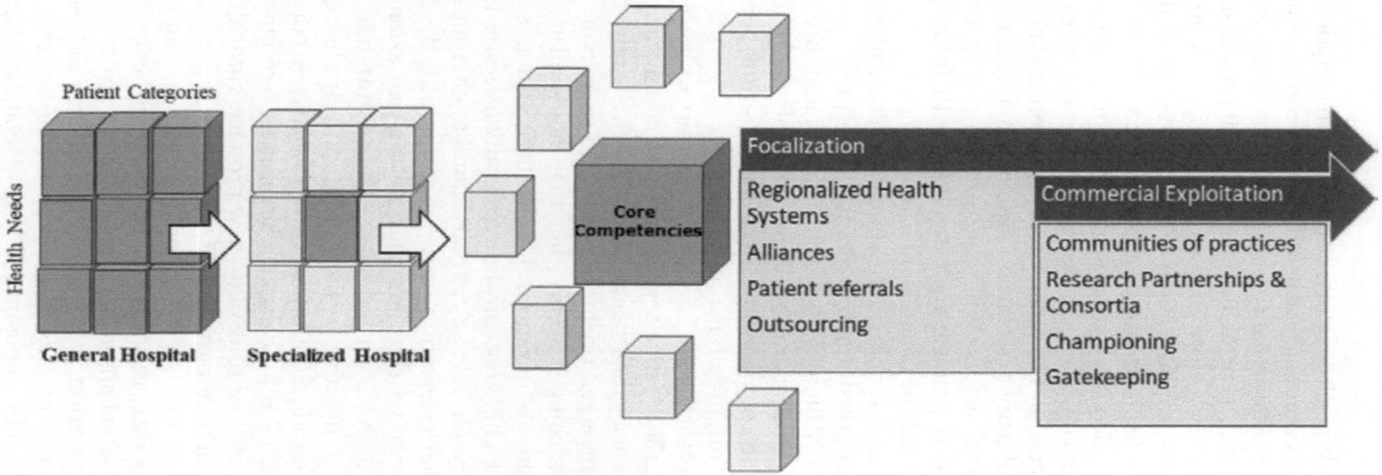

Figure 4.2 Organizational Evolution and Entrepreneurial Orientation of Healthcare Organizations

implications for collaboration initiatives in the healthcare domain (Cicchetti, 2002).

Focalization—a.k.a. selective reduction—is a first important trajectory adopted in hospitals that consists in a progressive (re)allocation of organizational resources on internal core competencies (Clark and Huckman, 2012). The traditional "general hospital" has been progressively replaced by specialized hospitals, more focused on particular health conditions (oncological diseases, cardiovascular problems, etc.) or well-defined categories of patients (e.g., pediatric, geriatric, etc.). The aim is twofold: on one hand, providers may concentrate the managerial attention and resources on those competencies that are functional to the delivery of high-quality services; on the other hand, they become more efficient in the development of activities that are not central and that can be better provided by external actors. While implementing such strategies, hospitals are asked to coordinate their activities with those run by other providers, and to combine the greater level of specialization with the continuity of care required for patient treatment. Several collaborative initiatives are thus established among specialized hospitals, nursing homes, medical centers, etc. Alliances and formal partnerships are the most preferred forms of such collaboration. However, unplanned patient referrals are likely adopted to complement formal collaborations according to the objectives that the organization aims to achieve.

The second trajectory is the increased propensity of hospitals to establish and leverage collaborative networks for the commercial exploitation of clinical competencies (Smith and Clark, 2010). We refer to this trajectory as the entrepreneurial orientation, which is more typically observed in research and teaching hospitals, but that can similarly characterize other kinds of health organizations. This strategy is often related to focalization because a higher concentration generally increases the allocation of organizational resources to a restricted number of groups/capabilities. The entrepreneurial orientation often coincides with the formation of small groups of hospital clinicians that, through an extensive network of collaborations both within and outside the organization, become particularly engaged and active in the exploitation of clinical knowledge (Lorenzoni and Grandi, 2000). Clinical knowledge is not only applied in the context of clinical processes; rather, it is used to innovate the current medical practice and to develop new products through an extensive network of collaborative partnerships. In this second trajectory, collaborative partnerships are largely adopted to generate and exploit new knowledge. In this case, relationships are pipes through which relevant knowledge is channeled among a diverse range of actors.

In the following section, we introduce the concept of "center of excellence" as an example of how hospital organizations rely on a combination of planned and unplanned forms of collaborations to sustain entrepreneurial activities.

Centers of Excellence in Healthcare

The term "center of excellence" has been used in different streams of literature. For example, in the context of international corporations, this term has been used to identify some peculiar categories of subsidiaries (Meyer-Kramer and Reger, 1999). In educational studies, the National Science Foundation has referred to this label to characterize particular universities and educational centers. In the more traditional healthcare literature, the term was used to designate providers focused on high volume, single specialty or conditions aimed at achieving volume efficiencies (Robinson, 2005). Here we refer to center of excellence as "a government-supported non-profit organization aimed at fostering university research potentials and building university-industry research relationship" as Ahn (1995: 248) first did. An increased interest by governmental institutions toward centers of excellence was observed in many countries, especially because of the role they play in the development of innovation through the creation of relationships between university and industry.

Lorenzoni and Grandi (2000) have used the term "center of excellence" to identify units and groups that, in the context of Italian universities, exhibit a distinctive capability to combine the development of scientific research with its concrete application and commercial exploitation. In the biomedical sector, they explicitly use the term "centers of excellence" to characterize those units and groups that are engaged in the development of new medical knowledge, at the same time stimulating the adoption of innovation in medical practice. These groups and units are often not formalized, and hence their boundaries do not correspond to typical hospital departments or clinical wards. Instead, they are groups of clinicians that spontaneously combine their knowledge resources to develop new medical knowledge and then exploit scientific results achieved. Small groups of hospital clinicians tend to expand over time into larger professional communities and networks of collaborative relationships, which involve relevant external partners such as other colleagues, private research laboratories, research foundations, and biopharmaceutical companies.

The centers of excellence have two distinctive features. First, their members are well-known in light of their scientific reputation, as demonstrated by their scientific track record in terms of publications, international research grants, research awards, etc. Furthermore, they rely on a *dual network structure*, in which both planned and unplanned collaborative relationships are used to both explore and exploit new medical knowledge. Figure 4.3 illustrates an example of such a dual network structure.

A group of well-known and widely recognized clinicians contribute to generate new knowledge through their extensive collaboration with peers in the professional community (exploration network). At the same

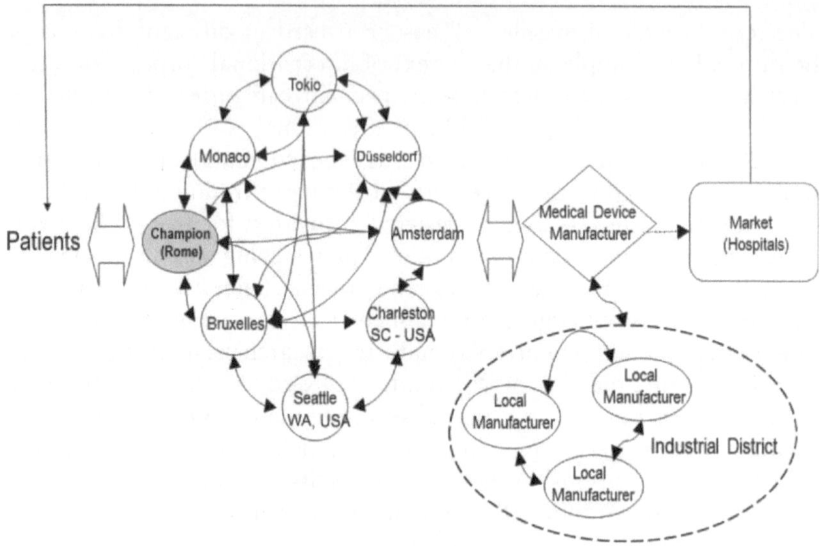

Figure 4.3 The Dual Structure of "Centers of Excellence" in Hospitals (adapted from Cicchetti and Profili, 2004)

time, collaborative ties are established with private corporations and venture capitalists to find new opportunities for the commercial exploitation of clinical knowledge (exploitation network). Partners may in turn refer to their own (local) networks to further develop and exploit their knowledge. This network structure helps the group to pursue its ambidextrous activities of exploration and exploitation (Wilden et al., 2018). The exploration and unplanned component characterizes the formation of a "communities of practices," i.e., emergent collaborative knowledge networks of individuals belonging to a professional community. This part of the network is formed on a voluntary basis, and its boundaries are continuously reshaped as far as new members enter or leave the community. Clinicians normally collaborate with other colleagues who have similar interests. They may be located in the same hospital but also in other research centers and universities, sometimes in other part of the world. In the exploitation phase, actors become over time engaged in the development of more formal collaborative relationships with external actors in order to have access to other resources that can useful for the commercial exploitation of medical knowledge.

The dual network structure is not stable, but instead is exposed to rapid fluctuations and oscillations (Burt and Merluzzi, 2016). Communities of practices, unplanned in nature, may evolve from unplanned, informal structures to more formalized collaborative initiatives such as, for example, formal projects or research consortia, etc. In a similar vein, planned and formal agreements (e.g., alliances) may crystallize into newly formed communities of practices or even change the boundaries of already existing communities. The dual network structure is also exposed to the oscillation of the focal organization in the choice of the most appropriate channel between the two components (explorative vs. exploitative) to achieve the contingent purpose.

Prior research suggests that the development of dual network structures is favored by different specific roles that emerge in centers of excellence (Lorenzoni and Grandi, 2000; Cicchetti, 2002). The first role, named "champion," is that of the scientific leader, namely that clinician who mainly contributes to the development of novel ideas and innovation in the group. The reputation and status of champions are usually documented by the quality of scientific publications (high impact factor, H-index, etc.) and by the role (s)he plays as principal investigator in international research programs and board member of institutions and governmental committees. This role is important for the development of both planned and unplanned components of the dual network.

The second role, called "gatekeeper," refers to those individuals who contribute to the creation of links with external partners in order to find new exploitation opportunities. The gatekeeper normally increases the visibility of all activities performed in the group and supports the selection of the "right" partner for the further development of existing ideas and solutions. (S)he spans the group and organizational boundaries, connecting the members of the group with external actors such as private corporations, research laboratories, and other institutions engaged in medical research. The role of gatekeepers also includes the recognition of external funding opportunities, including possible relationships with venture capitalists, business angels, and other actors interested to the commercial exploitation of clinical research. This role is especially important for the exploitation phase.

Finally, the "sponsor" helps the center of excellence to receive other important resources such as legitimacy and endorsement. Sustenance for the work of the group should be provided by administrators and executives before further exploitation activities with external actors are undertaken. Substantial support is also needed form external organizations and bodies such as the Ministry of Health, Ministry of Education and Research, and regional policymakers. This role is relevant for both exploration and exploitation.

The Center for Medical Innovation at Karolinska

Several activities and interventions sustain and accelerate the formation and further development of centers of excellence in healthcare. The complexity of collaborative relationships (different actors, fluidity of collaborations, etc.) that sustain knowledge exploitation initiatives requires substantial commitment by executives. The importance of medical innovation for both medical practice and clinical research has to be clearly acknowledged in the organizational vision and culture. Furthermore, a strategic approach in the management of collaborative partnerships has to be adopted for an effective development of centers of excellence within hospitals.

Around the world, there are several examples of health organizations in which centers of excellence are systematically identified and sustained. North America is rich with examples about the successful commercial exploitation of knowledge developed in medical schools and universities. Scant knowledge is instead available about successful initiatives undertaken in European countries, where the institutional framework regulating healthcare is different.

The Center for Medical Innovation (CMI) at the Karolinska Research Hospital in Stockholm, Sweden, represents a prototypical example of how managerial interventions can sustain the formation and development of the hospital's centers of excellence. CMI was created in 1996 with the aim of sustaining the commercial exploitation of clinical knowledge through the internal scouting of ideas and knowledge with the highest innovative potential and that can be of interest for external actors (private corporations, foundations, etc.). The main activities of the CMI are centered on: (i) supporting collaborative partnerships in the fields of strategic interest; (ii) creating initial contacts for collaboration; (iii) supporting scientists to establish fruitful collaboration with industrial partners; (iv) developing programs to facilitate interaction and knowledge sharing; and (v) stimulating entrepreneurship and innovation in the Karolinska Research Hospital.

CMI plays an important role in sustaining the development of the Karolinska's dual network structure through which exploration and exploitation activities are developed. Figure 4.4 provides a schematic representation of the model that CMI adopts to sustain the development of centers of excellence at Karolinska. *Mapping* is a first important activity that overall aims to identify the best clinical competencies available, as well as to localize centers of excellence within the hospital. Significant efforts are made to identify those groups of physicians who have reputation and are involved in formal research projects, ongoing scientific collaborations, etc., with other well-known peers. *Understanding* has to do with the internal selection of the best available knowledge and groups, along with their integration to achieve a critical mass. This may in turn become important for subsequent exploitation phases, for example in the case of applications for research grants or the formation of a collaborative partnership with private corporations. *Sponsoring* is devoted to bringing ideas and knowledge developed within the organization to the attention of external actors. Relevant sponsoring activities are aimed at protecting relevant knowledge through patents and other intellectual

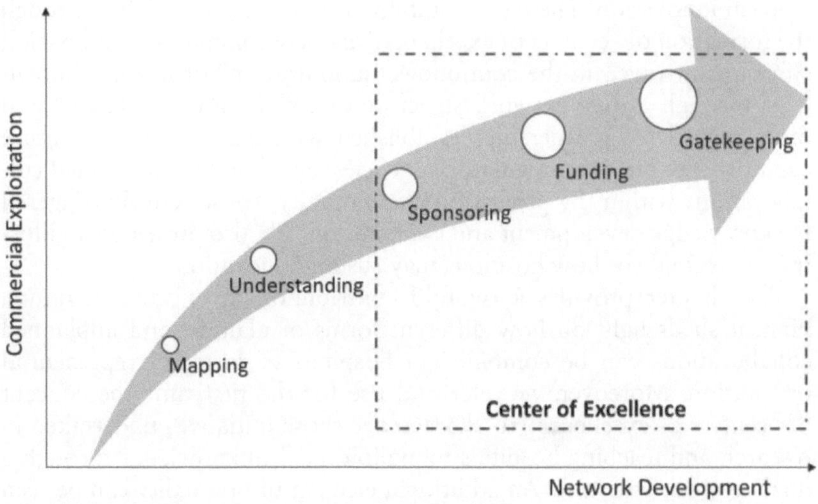

Figure 4.4 Steps for the Commercial Exploitation of Medical Knowledge

property rights. Moreover, presentations to external potential partners are organized for those ideas that are more likely to be transformed in innovation. Sponsoring includes also a constant dialogue with business angels, venture capitalists, etc. *Funding* concerns those activities that sustain the formalization of the centers of excellence, for example through the allocation of dedicated internal spaces (research labs, etc.) or the acquisition of avant-garde equipment and technologies. This may favor the co-location of partnering groups of clinicians. *Gatekeeping* comprises all those activities that directly address the commercial exploitation of clinical knowledge through the selection of industrial partners and the subsequent formalization of collaborative partnerships. Often, gatekeeping activities lead to the formation of biomedical new ventures in which the hospital is directly involved.

Conclusion

In this chapter, we have discussed how the organizational evolution of hospitals, and in particular their increasing entrepreneurial (re)orientation, can be sustained through a wide range of collaborative partnerships aimed at exploiting medical knowledge. Several forms of collaboration and integration can be adopted by healthcare organizations, including planned and unplanned forms. We identified two main trajectories characterizing the organizational change of hospitals, namely selective reduction and entrepreneurial orientation, and discussed how, under certain conditions, hospitals become more and more involved in the commercial exploitation of clinical knowledge, assuming a leading role for the development of medical innovation. These exploitation efforts often materialize through the formation of "centers of excellence," namely communities of hospital clinicians involved in the continuous "mobilization" of medical knowledge through a dual network structure of collaborations. Planned and more formalized partnerships established with manufacturers, venture capitalists, public labs, regulatory agencies, etc., but also unplanned collaborations within the professional community, are selectively triggered for knowledge development and exploitation. We also presented an illustrative example of how hospitals may sustain innovation.

The chapter provides a twofold contribution to existing literature. First, it sheds light on how different forms of planned and unplanned collaborations can be combined in hospitals to foster entrepreneurial orientation. Moreover, we refer and use for the first time the concept of "centers of excellence" to characterize those initiatives undertaken in research and teaching hospitals to exploit medical knowledge through a dual network structure. An additional element of originality can be seen in the dual perspective through which collaborations are linked to entrepreneurship initiatives in healthcare. We believe that this approach may pave the way for future healthcare entrepreneurship studies.

References

Ahn, S. 1995. A new paradigm in cooperative research between academia and industry in Korea, involving Centers of Excellence. *Technovation*, 15(4): 241–257.

Antivachis, N. A., and Angelis, V. A. 2015. Network organizations: The question of governance. *Procedia-Social and Behavioral Sciences*, 175: 584–592.

Barretta, A. 2008. The functioning of co-opetition in the health-care sector: An explorative analysis. *Scandinavian Journal of Management*, 24(3): 209–220.

Barringer, B. R., and Harrison, J. S. 2000. Walking a tightrope: Creating value through interorganizational relationships. *Journal of Management*, 26(3): 367–403.

Bazzoli, G. J., Dynan, L., Burns, L. R., and Yap, C. 2004. Two decades of organizational change in health care: What have we learned? *Medical Care Research and Review*, 61(3): 247–331.

Beamish, P. W., and Lupton, N. C. 2009. Managing joint ventures. *The Academy of Management Perspectives*, 23(2): 75–94.

Borgatti, S. P., and Cross, R. 2003. A relational view of information seeking and learning in social networks. *Management Science*, 49(4): 432–445.

Bosk, E. A., Veinot, T., and Iwashyna, T. J. 2011. Which patients, and where: A qualitative study of patient transfers from community hospitals. *Medical Care*, 49(6): 592–598.

Brandenburger, A., and Nalebuff, B. 1996. *Co-opetition*. New York, NY: Currency/Doubleday.

Brown, J. S., and Duguid, P. 2001. Knowledge and organization: A social-practice perspective. *Organization Science*, 12(2): 198–213.

Burns, L. R., and Pauly, M. V. 2002. Integrated delivery networks: A detour on the road to integrated health care? *Health Affairs*, 21(4): 128–143.

Burt, R. S., and Merluzzi, J. 2016. Network oscillation. *Academy of Management Discoveries*, 2(4): 368–391.

Chambers, D., Wilson, P., Thompson, C., and Harden, M. 2012. Social network analysis in healthcare settings: A systematic scoping review. *PLoS ONE*, 7(8): e41911.

Chen, D. Q., Preston, D. S., and Xia, W. 2013. Enhancing hospital supply chain performance: A relational view and empirical test. *Journal of Operations Management*, 31(6): 391–408.

Cicchetti, A. 2002. *L'organizzazione dell'ospedale*. Milano: Vita & Pensiero.

Cicchetti, A., and Profili, S. 2004. Il processo di creazione di conoscenza attraverso i centri di eccellenza: un caso di inerazione tra università e industria nel settore delle apparecchiature per la chirurgia endoscopica. In F. Fontana, and G. Lorenzoni (Eds.), *Il Knowledge Management*. Rome: Luiss University Press, 25–28.

Clark, J. R., and Huckman, R. S. 2012. Broadening focus: Spillovers, complementarities, and specialization in the hospital industry. *Management Science*, 58(4): 708–722.

Cuellar, A. E., and Gertler, P. J. 2003. Trends in hospital consolidation: The formation of local systems. *Health Affairs*, 22(6): 77–87.

de Figueiredo, J. M., and Silverman, B. S. 2017. On the genesis of interfirm relational contracts. *Strategy Science*, 2(4): 234–245.

Dranove, D., Durkac, A., and Shanley, M. 1996. Are multihospital systems more efficient? *Health Affairs*, 15(1): 100–104.

Enthoven, A. C. 2009. Integrated delivery systems: The cure for fragmentation. *American Journal of Managed Care*, 15: S284–S290.

Ferlie, E., and McGivern, G. 2003. *Relationships Between Health Care Organisations: A Critical Overview of the Literature and a Research Agenda*. London: Centre for Public Services Organisation.

Fottler, M. D., Schermerhorn, J. R., Wong, J., and Money, W. H. 1982. Multi-institutional arrangements in health care: Review, analysis, and a proposal for future research. *Academy of Management Review*, 7(1): 67–79.

Frandsen, B. R., Joynt, K. E., Rebitzer, J. B., et al. 2015. Care fragmentation, quality, and costs among chronically ill patients. *The American Journal of Managed Care*, 21: 355–362.

G. O., Lee, R. P., and Ellis, T. 2006. Community orientation, strategic flexibility, and financial performance in hospitals. *Journal of Healthcare Management*, 51(2): 111–121.

Gittell, J. H. 2000. Organizing work to support relational co-ordination. *International Journal of Human Resource Management*, 11(3): 517–539.

J. H. 2002. Coordinating mechanisms in care provider groups: Relational coordination as a mediator and input uncertainty as a moderator of performance effects. *Management Science*, 48(11): 1408–1426.

Gittell, J. H., and Weiss, L. 2004. Coordination networks within and across organizations: A multi-level framework. *Journal of Management Studies*, 41(1): 127–153.

Glickman, S. W., Delgado, M. K., Hirshon, J. M., et al. 2010. Defining and measuring successful emergency care networks: A research agenda. *Academy Emergency Medicine*, 17: 1297–1305.

Gulati, R. 1995. Social structure and alliance formation patterns: A longitudinal analysis. *Administrative Science Quarterly*, 40(4): 619–652.

Gulati, R., Dialdin, D. A., and Wang, L. 2002. Organizational networks. In Baum, J.A.C. (Ed.), *Companion to Organizations*, Malden, MA: Blackwell, 281–303.

Hains, I. M., Marks, A., Georgiou, A., and Westbrook, J. I. 2011. Non-emergency patient transport: What are the quality and safety issues? A systematic review. *International Journal for Quality in Health Care*, 23(1): 68–75.

Harris, J. K., Beatty, K. E., Barbero, C., Howard, A. F., Cheskin, R. A., Shapiro, R. M., and Mays, G. P. 2012. Methods in public health services and systems research: A systematic review. *American Journal of Preventive Medicine*, 42(5): S42–S57.

Hilligoss, B., and Cohen, M. D. 2013. The unappreciated challenges of between-unit handoffs: Negotiating and coordinating across boundaries. *Annals of Emergency Medicine*, 61(2): 155–160.

Iwashyna, T. J. 2012. The incomplete infrastructure for interhospital patient transfer. *Critical Care Medicine*, 40(8): 2470–2478.

Iwashyna, T. J., and Courey, A. J. 2011. Guided transfer of critically ill patients: Where patients are transferred can be an informed choice. *Current Opinion in Critical Care*, 17(6): 641–647.

Iwashyna, T. J., and Kahn, J. M. 2014. Regionalization of critical care. In D. C. Scales, and G. D. Rubenfeld (Eds.), *The Organization of Critical Care*. New York, NY: Springer, 217–233.

Judge, W. Q., and Dooley, R. 2006. Strategic alliance outcomes: A transaction-cost economics perspective. *British Journal of Management*, 17(1): 23–37.

Kitts, J. A., Lomi, A., Mascia, D., Pallotti, F., and Quintane, E. 2017. Investigating the temporal dynamics of interorganizational reciprocity: Patient exchange among Italian hospitals. *American Journal of Sociology*, 123: 850–910.

Landon, B. E., Keating, N. L., Barnett, M. L., Onnela, J. P., Paul, S., O'Malley, A. J., et al. 2012. Variation in patient-sharing networks of physicians across the United States. *JAMA*, 308(3): 265–273.

Lawton, R., and Parker, D. 2002. Barriers to incident reporting in a healthcare system. *Quality and Safety in Health Care*, 11(1): 15–18.

Lomi, A., Mascia, D., Vu, D. Q., Pallotti, F., Conaldi, G., and Iwashyna, T. J. 2014. Quality of care and interhospital collaboration: A study of patient transfers in Italy. *Medical Care*, 52(5): 407–411.

Lomi, A., and Pallotti, F. 2012. Relational collaboration among spatial multipoint competitors. *Social Networks*, 34(1): 101–111.

Lorenzoni, G., and Grandi, A. 2000. *I centri di eccellenza*. Working Paper, Department of Management, University of Bologna.

Lu, L. X., and Lu, S. F. 2017. Distance, quality, or relationship? Interhospital transfer of heart attack patients. *Production and Operations Management*. doi:10.1111/poms.12711 (Manuscript Published Ahead-of-Print).

Luke, R. D. 2006. Taxonomy of health networks and systems: A reassessment. *Health Services Research*, 41(3p1): 618–628.

Madison, K. 2004. Multihospital system membership and patient treatments, expenditures, and outcomes. *Health Services Research*, 39: 749–770.

Mahoney, C. D., Berard-Collins, C. M., Coleman, R., Amaral, J. F., and Cotter, C. M. 2007. Effects of an integrated clinical information system on medication safety in a multi-hospital setting. *American Journal of Health-System Pharmacy*, 64(18): 1969–1977.

Mascia, D., Angeli, F., and Di Vincenzo, F. 2015. Effect of hospital referral networks on patient readmissions. *Social Science & Medicine*, 132: 113–121.

Mascia, D., Di Vincenzo, F., and Cicchetti, A. 2012. Dynamic analysis of interhospital collaboration and competition: Empirical evidence from an Italian regional health system. *Health Policy*, 105(2): 273–281.

Melnick, G., and Keeler, E. 2007. The effects of multi-hospital systems on hospital prices. *Journal of Health Economics*, 26(2): 400–413.

Meyer-Kramer, F., and Reger, G. 1999. New perspectives on the innovation strategies of multinational enterprises: Lessons for technology policy in Europe. *Research Policy*, 28: 751–776.

Peng, T. J. A., and Bourne, M. 2009. The coexistence of competition and cooperation between networks: Implications from two Taiwanese healthcare networks. *British Journal of Management*, 20(3): 377–400.

Powell, W. 1990. Neither market nor hierarchy: Network forms of organization. *Research in Organizational Behavior*, 12(1): 295–336.

Research in Organizational Behavior 12: 295–336.

Provan, K. G., Fish, A., and Sydow, J. 2007. Interorganizational networks at the network level: A review of the empirical literature on whole networks. *Journal of Management*, 33(3): 479–516.

Robinson, J. C. 2005. Managed consumerism in health care. *Health Affairs*, 24(6): 1478–1489.

Scott, W. R., Ruef, M., Mendel, P., and Caronna, C. 2000. *Institutional Change and Healthcare Organizations: From Professional Dominance to Managed Care*. Chicago, IL: University of Chicago Press.

Sikka, V., Luke, R. D., and Ozcan, Y. A. 2009. The efficiency of hospital-based clusters: Evaluating system performance using data envelopment analysis. *Health Care Management Review*, 34(3): 251–261.

Smith, M., and Clark, R. 2010. Commercialization of innovations from the UK National Health Service. *International Journal of Technology Transfer and Commercialization*, 9(3): 238–254.

Spetz, J., Mitchell, S., and Seago, J. A. 2000. The growth of multihospital firms in California. *Health Affairs*, 19(6): 224–230.

Stadtfeld, C., Mascia, D., Pallotti, F., and Lomi, A. 2016. Assimilation and differentiation: A multilevel perspective on organizational and network change. *Social Networks*, 44: 363–374.

Stoto, M. A. 2008. Regionalization in local public health systems: Variation in rationale, implementation, and impact on public health preparedness. *Public Health Report*, 123: 441–449.

Tennyson, D. H., and Fottler, M. D. 2000. Does system membership enhance financial performance in hospitals? *Medical Care Research and Review*, 57(1): 29–50.

Tsai, T. C., Orav, E. J., and Jha, A. K. 2015. Care fragmentation in the post-discharge period: Surgical readmissions, distance of travel, and postoperative mortality. *JAMA Surgery*, 150: 59–64.

Uzzi, B. 1997. Social structure and competition in interfirm networks: The paradox of embeddedness. *Administrative Science Quarterly*, 42(1): 35–67.

Veinot, T. C., Bosk, E. A., Unnikrishnan, K. P., and Iwashyna, T. J. 2012. Revenue, relationships and routines: The social organization of acute myocardial infarction patient transfers in the United States. *Social Science & Medicine*, 75(10): 1800–1810.

Westra, D., Angeli, F., Carree, M., and Ruwaard, D. 2017a. Coopetition in health care: A multi-level analysis of its individual and organizational determinants. *Social Science & Medicine*, 186: 43–51.

Westra, D., Angeli, F., Carree, M., and Ruwaard, D. 2017b. Understanding competition between healthcare providers: Introducing an intermediary interorganizational perspective. *Health Policy*, 121(2): 149–157.

White, H. C. 2002. *Markets From Networks: Socioeconomic Models of Production*. Princeton, NJ: Princeton University Press.

Wilden, R., Hohberger, J., Devinney, T., and Lavie, D. 2018. Revisiting James March (1991): Whither exploration and exploitation? *Strategic Organization*. Forthcoming https://doi.org/10.1177/1476127018765031.

Yavas, U., and Romanova, N. 2005. Assessing performance of multi-hospital organizations: A measurement approach. *International Journal of Health Care Quality Assurance*, 18(3): 193–203.

Zajac, E. J. 1988. Interlocking directorates as an interorganizational strategy: A test of critical assumptions. *Academy of Management Journal*, 31(2): 428–438.

Part 2

Meso-Level Topics in Healthcare Entrepreneurship

5 The Role of Incubators and Accelerators in Healthcare Innovation

William Page, Massimo Garbuio, and Ralf Wilden

Introduction

Technological innovation has had a significant impact in providing substantial cost savings and efficiencies for healthcare providers and in advancing and innovating new healthcare practices and services. Within the healthcare system, they are typically related to product, process, or structure (Varkey et al., 2008). Many of these technological innovations do not usually come from traditional sources of innovation, such as the healthcare providers themselves, but rather come from increasingly small and agile entrepreneurial individuals or teams able to tackle healthcare problems and to innovate in a leaner and cost-efficient manner. In doing so, these entrepreneurs provide new innovative approaches to problems, utilize new skills and abilities, and are quicker at adapting to the issues being tackled. It is not surprising, therefore, that increasingly funding and resources are pouring into these startups, with digital health startups collectively raising over US$11.5 billion in 2017, surpassing the 2016 record of US$8.2 billion by almost UW$3.5 billion (StartUp Health, 2018).

Yet, despite the increasing public attention and funding available for startup entrepreneurs in general, many entrepreneurs and their startups in the healthcare sector do not have sufficient financing, resources, or expertise to transform their innovative ideas and solutions into successful businesses. New approaches to fostering and nurturing startup innovation have developed as one of the ways to address this issue. Recently, the establishment of new healthcare-related accelerators has provided healthcare entrepreneurs with access to a wide pool of complementary technological and business resources to enable them to fund and grow their startups. Although no commonly agreed-upon definition of accelerators exist, they are typically referred to as groups of experienced business people who provide services, office space, guidance, mentorship, networking, management services, knowledge, and expertise to nascent firms on an as-needed basis to help them succeed in the early stages of venture life (Fishback et al., 2007). There were 579 such accelerator programs in 2016 and they vary significantly in their structure and approach, with some focusing on a particular industry or sector while others may be industry agnostic (GUST, 2016)

Specifically, within the healthcare sector there are now over 90 accelerator programs focusing either solely on healthcare-related startups or which have the healthcare sector as one of their focus areas. These accelerators are utilizing new models and approaches by acting as an "enabler" in finding new ways to seek innovative solutions to problems being faced in the healthcare sector. Some of these accelerators are standalone entities such as StartUp Health, while others such as the Johnson & Johnson-sponsored Health and Wellness Technology Accelerator were established and owned by universities or were established by sponsoring healthcare corporates. These accelerators first emerged as a way that startups could assist in applying technology-driven solutions to some of the biggest problems being faced in healthcare. Depending on their structure, they can act in many ways like an outsourced innovation solution provider by bringing people together and give fledgling companies access to resources otherwise difficult to obtain.

By providing strategic guidance, mentoring, and access to healthcare experts, these accelerators aid in guiding entrepreneurs through the innovation and subsequent commercialization process. This is particularly useful in a healthcare sector that can be a complicated and a difficult landscape to navigate for new startup founders. Although the process of innovation is typically not a linear one, the majority of innovations go through the process of problem identification and idea generation, idea evaluation, development, first use, commercialization, and diffusion (Varkey et al., 2008). Accelerators provide an environment for these stages to be carried out within a stable and supportive ecosystem.

We believe that these new centers of innovation and ways to work with a range of startup partners offer a new way and approach for healthcare organizations to quickly and cost effectively innovate. The movement from traditional internal "closed" innovation sources to instead partnering with external sources offers significant opportunities to more effectively overcome specific innovation challenges being faced (Randhawa et al., 2016). There may be a correlation and link between the development of accelerators and the growth of open innovation adoption, although further research is needed on this. The role that these accelerators play as "enablers" is likely to increase as a greater number of healthcare organizations move from a focus on internal "closed innovation" to "open innovation" in partnership with these accelerators.

In this chapter, we start by providing an overview of the different types of entrepreneurial communities working within the healthcare innovation space before focusing on accelerators, which are the most recent and high-profile type of entrepreneurial community that has developed. We comprehensively discuss the different types of accelerators that have worked with healthcare organizations and startups. We then highlight the variety of ways in which they seek to revolutionize the healthcare industry. We use a number of practical and relevant examples to illustrate the different approaches that can be used.

Community Focused Innovation in Healthcare

Accelerators represent the latest development in a long line of startup communities and collaborations, aimed at assisting startups and other entrepreneurs to develop their ideas and businesses. The development of accelerators can be linked back to the development of other forms of startup communities such as physical co-working spaces or incubators (Hughes et al., 2007; Spinuzzi, 2012), science parks (Bakouros et al., 2002), regional hubs such as the Silicon Valley (Saxenian, 1996), and online communities. Within the healthcare space, these communities are often linked to universities and hospitals, from where many healthcare startups originate. Whether it is in a physical space or online, they have increasingly played a key role in creating, shaping, and disseminating technological and social innovations (Fichter, 2009), as evidenced by the growth in the number of incubators, science parks, and accelerators (see Figure 5.1).

Entrepreneurial communities within the healthcare sector come in many shapes and sizes. They can also represent different levels of aggregation, depending on the circumstances. Communities can develop, sometimes as part of a wider cluster ecosystem, where they cohabit or work together, sharing services and resources. This community is often a collection of varied members, in which organizations approach the

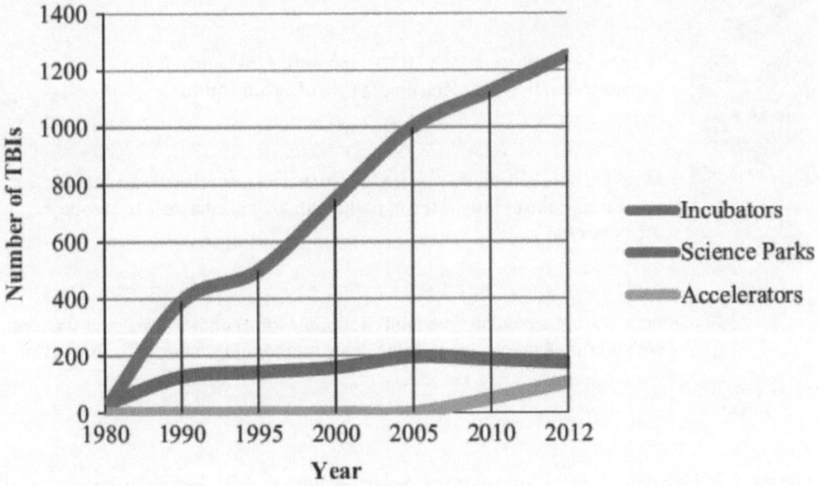

Figure 5.1 Growth of Incubators, Science Parks and Accelerators in the USA Since 1980 (Mian et al. 2016)

community as a strategic motivation and seek to leverage the community for organizational benefits (West and Lakhani, 2008). The inhabitants of these communities can range from new startups through to older, more established healthcare organizations. These communities can take the form of incubators, university sponsored technology transfer offices, or more recently, accelerators. Specifically, within the healthcare sector, the communities are often interlinked with universities, research institutes, and hospitals, who look to these communities as a way to commercialize the research or medical advancements undertaken. Figure 5.2 highlights how these communities have developed and changed over time as the structure, format, and values of the communities have changed from early stage research parks and incubators into university technology transfer offices and, more recently, accelerators.

Besides physical communities, another type of entrepreneurial community identified in the literature are the virtual "user communities" that have developed mostly online and act as a distributed group of individuals seeking to solve a general problem and/or develop a new solution supported by computer-mediated communication (Dahlander and Wallin, 2006; Chesbrough, 2006; Chesbrough and Appleyard, 2007; Nambissan and Sawhney, 2007; von Hippel, 2005; West and Gallagher, 2006). Technology has been a key enabler in the development of these user

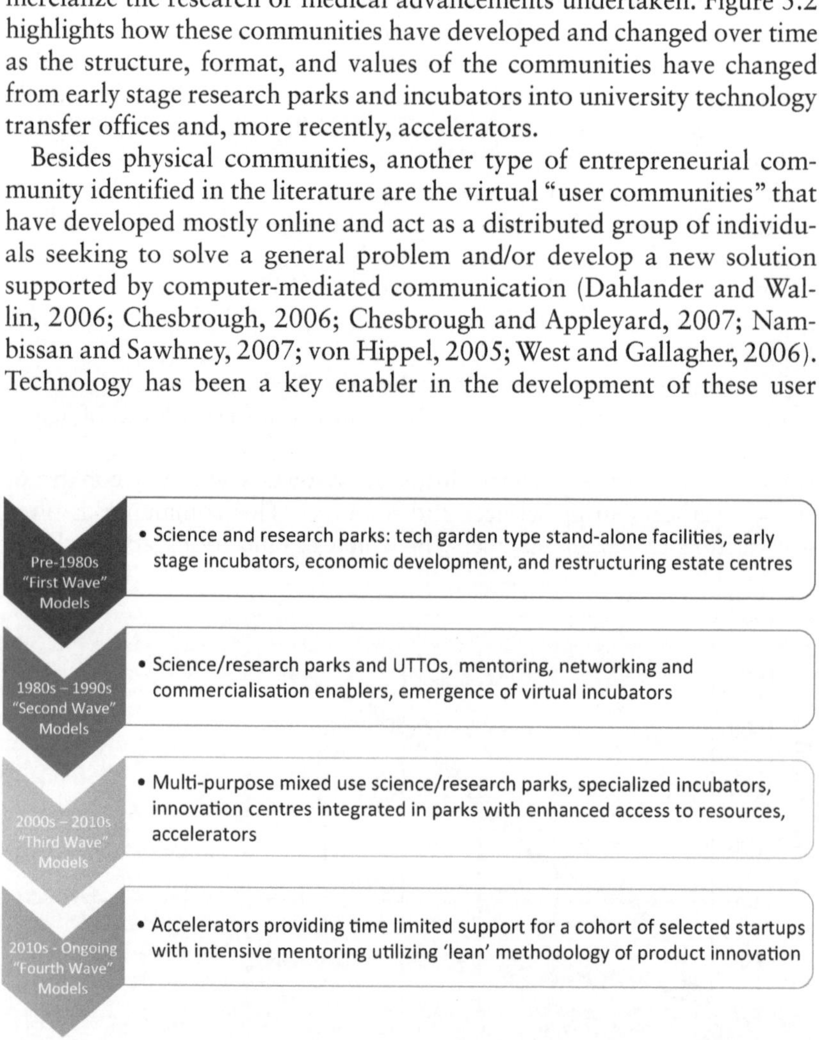

Figure 5.2 Historical Development of Science Parks, UTTOs, Incubators and Accelerators

Adapted and modified from Mian et al. (2016)

communities by giving them global accessibility and facilitating communication and interaction between contributors at a comparatively low cost. User communities have been perceived to be popular mechanism to integrate customers as part of the innovation process (Randhawa et al., 2016). Sometimes users voluntarily reveal their innovations and build on the work of others in a community in a democratic and cooperative manner (von Hippel, 2005). However, to date these user communities have been less active in the healthcare sector than in other sectors.

Incubators

Incubators are one of the oldest forms of such entrepreneurial communities and pre-date the emergence of accelerators by more than 30 years. They are often found in or near universities and provide inexpensive office space and mentorship (Christiansen, 2009). Incubators have been seen as centers helping young companies to grow in their early stages by providing them with a rental space, shared office, and assistance through business consulting services (Allen and Bazan, 1990). Allen and Bazan (1990) further refined this definition by viewing incubators as networks or organizations that provide skills, motivation, knowledge, experience in real estate, business services, and shared services.

Grimaldi and Grandi (2005) broke down incubators into two forms. The first provides basic tangible services and necessary support. The second form provides intangible resources to a startup on a short-term basis in order to assist the development of the startup. The time companies spend inside an incubator varies from a few days to a few months, and can also depend on the needs of the company (Lewis et al., 2011).

An uncertainty with the incubation process is how the success of the incubator can best be measured using factors that determine the outcome of business incubation (Dee et al., 2011). Despite the large number of studies, most research on business incubation remains anecdotal and excludes the incubated company's perspective, suffering from an informal research design and/or a limited theoretical approach (Theodorakopoulos et al., 2014). Another criticism has been that most studies take the perspective of the incubator, instead of the startup's perspective, with there still being a need to understand how and why incubated companies grow inside business incubators (Smilor and Gill, 1986). Given the assistance provided, several researchers have found that startups participating in an incubator or accelerator program have historically had a greater chance of success (Barrehag, 2012). Yet to date, no large-scale long-term longitudinal study has been undertaken to validate this.

There has been a large amount of academic research undertaken on incubators, due in part to incubators being one of the oldest forms of startup communities. Table 5.1 provides an overview of some of the

Table 5.1 Theoretical Lenses Employed to Study the Business Incubation Process (adapted from Mian et al., 2016)

Theoretical Lens Employed	*Authors*
New Venture Creation or Addressing Market Failure: The incubator compensates for perceived failures or imperfections in the marketplace to counter the problems caused by an inefficient allocation of resources	Plosila and Allen (1985) and Bollingtoft and Ulhoi (2005)
Resource-Based View: The incubator as an organization awarding a stoke of tangible and intangible resources to client firms that result in development of the client firms	McAdam and McAdam (2008) and Patton et al. (2009)
Stakeholder View: Incubators act as bridging mechanisms to implement the interest of key regional stakeholders	Mian (1997), Corona et al. (2006), Etzkowitz (2002), and McAdam et al. (2016)
Structural Contingency Theory: Incubation mechanisms are configured to fit the external environment and are tailored to local needs and norms	Ketchen et al. (1993) and Phan et al. (2005)
Social Network Theory: Incubation functions as a system for increasing client firms' internal and external network density, hence social learning	Totterman and Sten (2005) and Hansen et al. (2000)
Real Options View: Client firms are supported by a pool of available options through selection criteria based on fit with incubator strategy	Hackett and Dilts (2004)
Dyadic Theory: An interdependent co-production dyad where incubation assistance is co-produced by the incubator and the tenant entrepreneur	Rice (2002) and Warren et al. (2009)
Institutional Theory: The incubator's support mechanism, rules, and contracts offer a more structured approach to reduce uncertainty and risk and accelerate the process	Guerrero and Urbano (2012) and Phan et al. (2005)
Mechanisms-Driven Theory: The incubator implements its own internal policies through an understanding of the relations that are value laden and context specific within the incubator organization	Ali Junaid (2014) and Bergek and Norrman (2008)
Virtual Incubation View: The incubator offers knowledge brokering and information dissemination in the market space of ideas to develop innovation ventures	Nowak and Grantham (2000) and Gans and Stern (2003)
Absorptive Capabilities View: Incubators enhance and strengthen the absorptive capacity of new technology-based firms	Hutabarat and Pandin (2014) and Patton (2014)
Open Innovation View: Incubators act as an intermediary for the transfer of knowledge from large firms to society	Clausen and Rasmussen (2011) and Battistella et al. (2017)

theoretical lenses that have been employed to study the business incubation process within incubators.

Table 5.1 provides an overview of a number of different theoretical lenses that have been applied to understand incubators. However, the majority of the research to date has either focused on how incubators run or the functions of the incubator entity itself. Research has not yet looked comprehensively at the theoretical development from the point of view of the startups within the incubator itself and the rationale for them in entering into the incubator. More specifically, understanding how they perceive the benefits of working within the incubator, what resources or capabilities are provided to them by being a part of the incubator, and the importance of the relationships developed between the different startup members of the incubator remains underexplored. It is possible that the startups learn from one another and benefit from the collaborative environment of the incubator just as much as they benefit from the incubator itself. Further data from incubators, especially within the healthcare sector, may help to shed light on this.

Finally, Table 5.1 shows that due to the variety of research fields explored, the literature has become very dispersed and fragmented over time with no one author being a predominant researcher in the field of incubator and wider community-focused research. This is very different than other fields, such as open innovation, where Henry Chesbrough and Joel West have emerged as preeminent leading researchers within that field.

Development of Accelerators

Accelerators are different than incubators and technology parks, as they provide education, mentoring, and financial support for startup founders in a fixed short-term cohort-based approach (Hochberg, 2015). They are typically perceived to comprise experienced business people who provide services, office space, guidance, mentorship, networking, management services, knowledge, and expertise to nascent firms on an as-needed basis to help them succeed in the early stages of venture life (Fishback et al., 2007). The first recognized accelerator was Y-Combinator, which started in 2005 as an industry-agnostic accelerator. Like many other accelerators, it partnered with investors and venture capital funds in order to invest money into its companies at the beginning of their program. One of the reasons why early stage accelerators, such as Y-Combinator, were able to disrupt the existing startup funding models were partly due to the fact that new technologies had dramatically reduced the cost of starting new companies (Apodaca, 2013). Coupled together with an open, yet highly selective screening and application process with small batches or 'cohorts' of startups, this enabled the accelerator model to take off quickly as a new approach to encouraging innovation.

Yet, the emergence of healthcare-focused accelerators took longer to develop than those for other sectors. The development of healthcare-focused accelerators was also driven by a number of wider socio-economic, political, and technological changes, many of which were specific to the healthcare sector. In the US, which has the largest number of healthcare accelerators, the passing of the American Recovery and Reinvestment Act (ARRA) created billions of dollars in funding for technology focused healthcare solutions, while the passing of the Affordable Care Act (ACA), more commonly known as "Obamacare," expanded healthcare coverage and provided an impetus for an increase in demand for new health services and technologies (Apodaca, 2013). These specific healthcare-related legislative changes created an impetus for innovation within the healthcare sector and, when added together with the development of the accelerator model and other technological developments, led to the development of the first healthcare-related accelerators in 2011, as shown on Figure 5.3.

Another key factor that may have led to the rapid growth of accelerators in recent years is the growing recognition that in order to become more innovative firms of all sizes need to move away from a focus on internal "closed" innovation and instead embrace collaboration and exchange information with external stakeholders in order to leverage complementary assets and capabilities in what Chesbrough defines as "Open Innovation" (Chesbrough, 2003).

How Accelerators Operate

Accelerators differ in their objectives and their workings. Some programs require equity in the startups they assist, while others do not. Other

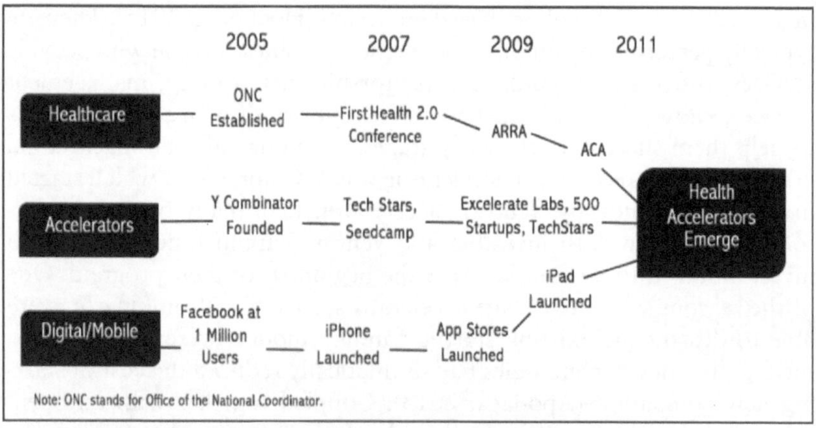

Figure 5.3 Notable Events Leading Towards the Emergence of Healthcare Focused Accelerators (2005 to 2011) (Apodaca, 2013)

accelerators, such as AVIA or the Johnson & Johnson-sponsored Health and Wellness Technology Accelerator, find startup solutions for the healthcare organization supporting or working with the accelerator. In many accelerators, healthcare-orientated organizations and companies partner with an accelerator to have access to healthcare focused startups that they may be interested in either working with or investing in. In this way, these early-stage strategic partnerships can operate as a deal-flow mechanism for the healthcare organizations to develop relationships with startups and figure out which firm may be a right fit for their organization.

Accelerators provide intensive, boot-camp-style training comparable to entrepreneurship classes at the collegiate level (Fishback et al., 2007). Boot-camp and accelerator contestants are selected from a pool of qualified candidates led by startup teams with interesting or innovative ideas. Their training is typically provided by successful entrepreneurs or corporates with specific experience in the healthcare sector or other areas where they need support. Like venture capitalists, accelerators fund along themes and in specific industries with which they are familiar or knowledgeable.

Accelerators assist with building the venture team, fine-tuning the idea, and mentoring the business from idea to prototyping through to product development. Within healthcare accelerators, they also provide additional services, such as access to specific health resources or potential patients for their product or service to be tested on. Small startups do not usually have access to these resources, so these services provided by accelerators play a crucial role in enabling the development and commercialization of the healthcare product faster than if it had been developed outside of the incubator or accelerator. The shape and form of many of these accelerators vary greatly from non-profit to corporate-sponsored accelerators taking startups ranging in size from half a dozen to over 100, typically over the period of around three months.

Six different types of accelerator models have been identified, which each have their own set of motivations for being established and rational for time and capital invested, with some accelerators operating more than one type of model or a blend of models within their accelerator (Suennen, 2014). The six models identified are:

- **Independent commercial model**—Typically independently run, either a for-profit (e.g., Healthbox) or non-profit (e.g., Rock Health) in structure; takes equity in startups; works closely with sponsoring corporates and focuses on creating companies with specific regard to who might be their customer, investor, or acquirer.
- **Enterprise-based innovation model**—Typically initiatives run by a company or a small group of companies, which generally provide grants and assistance.
- **Product or sector-specific model**—Typically formed around a specific problem or product area.

- **Economic Development model**—Typically focused on economic development with funds usually provided by local governments, corporates, and other stakeholders interested in building jobs in their community (e.g., BaseLaunch); they usually offer non-dilutive capital, longer-term rents than most accelerators and other perks to encourage startups to move to the area.
- **University-affiliated program**—These are widely varied programs ranging from tech transfer programs or offices to accelerators sitting within the sponsoring university, and they tend to have broader focus areas.
- **Collaboration platform**—These are a relatively new form of accelerator and are focused on creating partnerships between a sponsoring corporates and small startups (e.g., Health XL, Avia).

Accelerators Focusing on Healthcare

The majority of healthcare accelerators are focused on the fields of digital health, medical technology, healthcare services, healthcare IT, and genomics (Suennen, 2014). Early stage healthcare focused accelerators emerged in 2011 and copied the model used in other leading non-healthcare accelerators, such as Techstars and Y-Combinator, for their initial programs. However, healthcare-focused accelerators are now adapting these models and have increasingly focused on becoming enablers in the healthcare innovation sector by as acting as facilitators or conduits between the various stakeholders operating within the accelerator. In this way, accelerators acting within the healthcare industry sit and operate within a triangular network of the startups they are supporting (the "Supply"), the healthcare systems (the "Demand"), and venture capital funds (the "Finance"), as shown in Figure 5.4.

There are a number of key stakeholders within a typical healthcare-focused accelerator, as shown in Table 5.2. Each of the stakeholders have different needs, wants, and expectations in working with the accelerator. However, a shift appears to be taking place in the business models of many accelerators as they have increasingly refocused their services and activities away from concentrating on startups to instead assisting healthcare organizations with specific problems or innovation needs (Zehel, 2017). Depending on the accelerator, the role of the partner or sponsoring healthcare organizations and/or venture capital investors can be crucial as they increasingly play a role in determining whether the startups selected by the accelerator are developing products and services that are needed.

There are many examples of successful startups coming out of these programs. StartUp Health (2018) was one of the earliest accelerators, launched in 2011, and has supported over 200 companies to date spanning five continents, 18 countries, and more than 60 cities. To date, 12

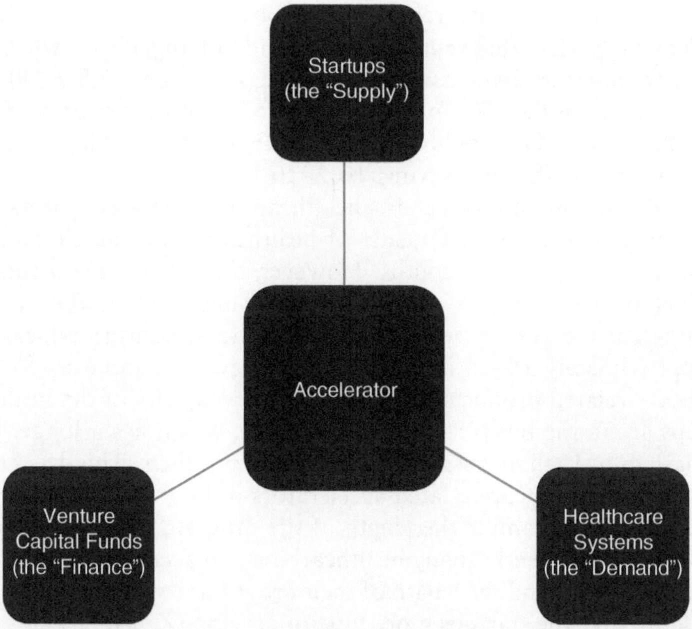

Figure 5.4 Healthcare Accelerator Triangular Network

Table 5.2 Key Stakeholders of the Healthcare Innovation Process

Stakeholders	*Needs, Wants and/or Expectations*
Physicians and Other Caregivers	Improved clinical outcomes, improved diagnosis and treatment
Patients	Improved patients' experience, improved physiological wellbeing, reduced waiting time, reduced delays
Organizations	Enhanced efficiency of internal operations, cost containment, increased productivity, and quality and outcomes improvement
Innovator Companies	Profitability, improved outcomes
Regulatory Agencies	Reduced risks and improved patient safety
Universities	Improved developing and trialing of research developed
Investment Funds and Other Investors	Access to new startups' ideas, innovations, and investment

Source: Adapted from (Omachonu and Einspruch, 2010)

of its companies have been acquired by companies—including Intel, WebMD, Under Armour, and Zimmer Biomet—and its companies have raised over US$800 million of funding since 2012.[1] StartUp Health's diverse portfolio is currently comprised of 40% "doctorpreneurs," 30%

female founders and one-third serial entrepreneurs.[2] Innovations include the Care4Today® cardiac rehabilitation program[3] and devices such as PneuX, which is a cuffed ventilation tube and inflating device which electronically monitors patients breathing and saves the NHS £700 every time it is used. In the UK alone, it is estimated that the use of innovative technologies and data could lead to the NHS in the making up to £22 billion worth of efficiency savings by 2020.[4]

One of the biggest changes for healthcare-focused accelerators is the length of their programs. Outside of healthcare, most accelerator programs typically last 3–4 months. However, this length is too short for most healthcare startups to develop their business and get their product to market, as the sales cycles within the healthcare industry typically last for approximately 18–24 months for health systems and even for basic healthcare-related products. Furthermore, the majority of the healthcare startups are in the business-to-business space, which has a longer buyer purchasing cycle than business-to-consumer products. This has created problems for healthcare-related accelerators in how they structure their accelerators, for example the length of the program and the investment structure. Consequently, many healthcare-related accelerators have made the decision to extend the length of their programs to six or more months in order to give the startups more time to develop (Zehel, 2017).

Table 5.3 provides an overview of the different types of accelerators and incubators currently focusing on the healthcare sector, highlighting whether or not they take an equity interest, the form of assistance provided, the length of the program cohort, focus areas, and partners, among other things. Early evidence suggests that accelerators have a positive impact on startup founders, helping them to learn rapidly, create powerful networks, and become better entrepreneurs (Miller and Bound, 2011). These benefits may be difficult to attain as easily through other methods or approaches adopted by startups. Some accelerators are notable for the high quality of both the mentors and startup teams they work with and the value they add to the corporates. Accelerators are also not as stigmatized as incubators (Miller and Bound, 2011), which have been perceived as providing a form of "life support" for startups by sustaining them longer than is necessary and in doing so failing to encourage startups to innovate successfully.

Yet, the quality of the mentors varies greatly between accelerators, and there remains no set of criteria or framework for how mentors should be accessed and selected before they are accepted into an accelerator program.

Aims and Objectives of Accelerators

The aims and objectives of accelerators are similar to incubators, with typical aims including creation of new jobs and businesses, fostering a climate of entrepreneurship; commercializing technology; diversifying, revitalizing, and accelerating growth of industry and local economies;

Table 5.3 Leading Healthcare-Focused Accelerators

Incubator/ Accelerator	*Location*	*Details*
StartUp Health	New York City (USA)	**Form of Assistance**—Takes an equity stake (average of 6%) in the companies they incubate rather than seeking fixed compensation or a percentage of sales revenue. Aims to fund 1,000 healthcare companies within the next decade to help transform the face of the healthcare industry. **Length of Program**—Three-year coaching program for digital health and wellness companies. **Cohort Size**—Approximately 10 per cohort. **Healthcare Focus**—During the incubation period, StartUp Health matches companies with a network of more than 10,000 health professionals and business people focused on improving digital health and wellness. Identification of gaps in care, new insurance models, new billing/payment models (including cost transparency), and risk adjustment optimization are all areas of interest. **Partners**—GE, AT&T, Pfizer, GE Ventures. **Successful Start-ups**—Medivo, CarePlanners, TalkSession, and Care at Hand.
Blueprint Health	New York City (USA)	**Form of Assistance**—Seed funding of US$20,000, several thousand dollars' worth of perks, office space, and networking in exchange for approximately 6% equity. **Length of Program**—Three-month program. **Cohort Size**—Twenty healthcare IT companies each year. **Healthcare Focus**—Blueprint Health focuses on companies developing tech projects directly for hospitals, physicians, and health plans rather than consumer-facing applications, which means deeper access to established customers. While many incubators assist early-stage companies, Blueprint Health is focused more on later-stage companies with more than half of its startups already having paying customers. **Partners**—Goodwin Procter, AstraZeneca, aetna, Samsung Advanced Institute of Technology, HP, CarePoint Health. **Successful Start-ups**—Decisive Health, BoardRounds, and MediQuire.
Health Wildcatters	Dallas (USA)	**Form of Assistance**—Companies receive an initial seed investment of between US$30,000 to US$380,000 for 8% equity. **Length of Program**—Twelve-week program. **Cohort size**—Approximately 10 per cohort. **Healthcare Focus**—Health Wildcatters focuses mainly on early-stage healthcare technology startups, including IT, SaaS, digital health, and mobile health companies. Aims to work with startups to quickly achieve a short-term objective—getting their prototype finished, securing a new investment, or launching the new product. **Partners**—Cigna, Validic, SHD (Scientific Health Development), Live Oak Partners, Ballast Point Ventures, and S3 Ventures,

(*Continued*)

Table 5.3 (Continued)

Incubator/ Accelerator	*Location*	*Details*
BaseLaunch	Switzerland	**Form of Assistance**—Financial support through BaseLaunch can be as high as CHF 10,000 per project. Up to three startups accepted for the second phase will receive the opportunity to secure a one-year grant of up to CHF 250,000 to generate data and reach business plan milestones in the labs at the Switzerland Innovation Park Basel Area. During the first phase, lasting three months, entrepreneurs work closely with the BaseLaunch team as well as a network of entrepreneurs-in-residence, advisors, and consultants to further develop their business cases. **Length of Program**—The program consists of two phases, which extend over a total period of 15 months. **Cohort Size**—Approximately 10–15 startups selected per year. **Healthcare Focus**—BaseLaunch aims to attract a broad range of healthcare-related startups from abroad to the Basel region of Switzerland. **Partners**—Novartis Venture Fund, Johnson & Johnson Innovation, and Pfizer; and partners with Digital Switzerland's Kickstart Accelerator.
CORPORATE-SPONSORED ACCELERATORS		
JLABS	Toronto (Canada); New York, San Francisco, San Diego, and the Texas Medical Center (USA); and Singapore	**Form of Assistance**—This accelerator is run by Johnson & Johnson and provides opportunities for founders to stay focused on advancing science and developing their product. No equity is taken in the startups selected. Companies residing at JLABS gain immediate access to core research facilities hosting specialized capital equipment, as well as shared administrative areas. Additionally, JLABS produces a year-round curriculum designed to assist innovators along the product development continuum. Provides access to core research facilities hosting specialized capital equipment, educational programs, operational capabilities, and a community of like-minded entrepreneurs. The Johnson & Johnson Innovation teams expand opportunities for venture capital funding, as well as the deal-making, therapeutic and technology area, product development, and commercialization expertise of Johnson & Johnson. **Length of Program**—Varies according to location, **Cohort Size**—Varies according to location, **Healthcare Focus**—Seeks out companies whose ideas align with its identified business priorities—pharmaceutical innovations in neuroscience, infectious diseases and vaccines, oncology, immunology and cardiovascular/metabolism, and medical/diagnostic devices for orthopedics, neurovascular surgery, vision care, diabetes, sports medicine, and aesthetics. The company also reviews ideas for healthcare IT innovations. **Partners**—Johnson & Johnson.

StartUp Health/SAP	New York City (USA)	**Form of Assistance**—Entrepreneurs are heavily supported by StartUp Health and SAP, with benefits including technical and business training, access to SAP's industry-leading cloud technologies, opportunities to pitch and present to potential customers. Provides up to US$50,000 in investment. **Length of Program**—No fixed time period, depends on company. **Cohort size**—Up to 15 startups per cohort. **Healthcare Focus**—Seeks to fund medical and healthcare IT startups that focus on one or more chronic diseases while helping healthcare providers address all aspects of population health management. **Partners**—SAP.
UNIVERSITY-SPONSORED INCUBATORS AND ACCELERATORS		
Biosci Labs	Rhode Island (USA)	**Form of Assistance**—Provides unique laboratory, office, and manufacturing space for medical product startups. **Length of Program**—Information not available. **Number of Start-ups**—Information not available. **Healthcare Focus**—unique networking, prototype development, and business strategy incubator created to support the technology startup community in Rhode Island and New England. **Partners**—Brown University Alpert Medical School, Rhode Island Hospital, and University of Rhode Island. **Successful Startups**—Information not available.
Austin Technology Incubator (ATI)	Austin, Texas (USA)	**Equity or non-equity**—Takes a small percentage stake in each company that is accepted. **Form of Assistance**—Does not provide funding but states that it provides access to talent that startups could not otherwise afford. **Length of Program**—This varies with each company. **Number of Start-ups**—Does not have a fixed number but states that it typically accepts only 8% of the companies that apply each year. **Healthcare Focus**—Focuses on medical devices, diagnostics, medical research tools, and new therapeutic options. **Partners**—University of Texas, Heart Hospital of Austin, the RICE Alliance for Technology and Entrepreneurship, and the Central Texas Angel Network. **Successful Start-ups**—Information not available

reducing company mortality rate; reducing unemployment; increasing university-incubation interaction; or simply fostering technology development (Bizzotto, 2003); (Mutambi et al., 2010); (Al-Mubaraki and Busler, 2011). Previous research suggests an increasing focus on healthcare sponsors of accelerators to use the accelerator as a way to solve or to work on a predefined problem (Suennen, 2014).

Some healthcare accelerators, such as the Johnson & Johnson-supported Health and Wellness Technology Accelerator and JLABS, are owned by healthcare organizations, so are closely aligned to their internal R&D needs, while others work in partnership with a variety of partners. Some leading non-healthcare-focused accelerators, such as TechStars, have set up accelerators specifically focusing on the healthcare sector. The Cedars-Sinai Accelerator, established in 2016 by Techstars, is a great example of this as over a period of two years it has assisted 28 startups on three continents to accelerate their ideas to product, and product to market (Cedars-Sinai Accelerator, 2018). It is no surprise then that the aims of accelerators vary according to the setup of the particular accelerator.

The earliest healthcare focused accelerators typically provided US$10,000–25,000 to their selected companies, either as grants or as an early-stage equity investment in the startup company in exchange for a percentage of equity in the startup. However, some accelerators now provide investments or grants of over US$100,000—with many leading accelerators, such as Healthbox and Rock Health, raising their own funds in order to compliment the capital committed. This has led to the belief that the more successful healthcare-focused accelerators are becoming more focused on seed funding and investment than on the accelerator being a training program (Suennen, 2014).

Impact of Accelerators on Startups

Early evidence suggests that accelerators have a positive impact on the startup founders, helping them to learn rapidly, create powerful networks and become better entrepreneurs (Miller and Bound, 2011). These benefits may be difficult to attain as easily through other methods or approaches adopted by startups. Some accelerators are notable for the high quality of both the mentors and startup teams they work with and the value they add to the corporates. Yet, the quality of the mentors varies greatly between accelerators, and there remains no set criteria or framework for how mentors should be assessed and selected before they are accepted into an accelerator program. Accelerators have also been perceived to have a positive impact on founders of the startups and are not as stigmatized as incubators (Miller and Bound, 2011), which have been perceived to provide a form of "life support" for startups by sustaining them longer than is necessary and in doing so failing to encourage startups to innovate successfully. Furthermore, they hypothesized that startups working with web or mobile related products are particularly suitable for accelerators due primarily to their low development costs.

Accelerators may also have a role to play in the wider ecosystem by acting as an intermediary between the mentors, investors and startups involved in the program. This creates a positive effect on the local ecosystem in which they operate, providing a focal point for introductions and building trust between founders, investors, and other stakeholders. According to Mian et al. (2016), accelerators are highly promising as a new post-startup incubator model for providing targeted assistance over a limited period (e.g., 3–6 months) to help young TBFs achieve sustained growth.

Conclusion

In this chapter, we have highlighted how new additions to the entrepreneurial ecosystem, in the form of incubator and especially accelerators, have become increasingly important enablers for entrepreneurship and innovation in the healthcare sector. We stress that healthcare companies need to work closely with accelerators to ensure that the right startups are accepted for the program and to diminish the likelihood of failure occurring. Accelerators are likely to become more important as a mechanism by which healthcare corporates are able to carry out due diligence on potential startup investments through working over a prolonged period of time with the startups within a stable collaboration space provided by the incubators and accelerators.

This chapter makes two contributions. First, it contributes to healthcare innovation literature by highlighting the important role that incubators and accelerators are now playing to healthcare companies and within the wider healthcare industry. It is argued that involving healthcare firms in the accelerator programs from an early stage may result in a greater startup success rate. Second, we contribute to the open innovation literature by highlighting the potential for this field of research to grow as a research area. The potential links between open innovation and accelerator literature have also been touched upon, but still require additional research. This is likely to increase as we see the number of startups successfully going through these accelerators and reaching commercialization expanding.

Notes

1. Crunchbase, 2018. StartUp Health. Available at: https://www.crunchbase.com/organization/startup-health.
2. Crunchbase, 2018. StartUp Health. Available at: https://www.crunchbase.com/organization/startup-health.
3. Johnson & Johnson, 2018. Janssen Healthcare Innovation Launches Care4Today™ Mobile Adherence. *Medication Reminder Platform*. Available at: https://

www.jnj.com/media-center/press-releases/janssen-healthcare-innovation-launches-care4today-mobile-adherence-medication-reminder-platform.

4. Youth Health Parliament, 2018. Innovation & the NHS: Time to start thinking like a startup?. London: 2020health, pp. 1–19. Available at: http://www.abhi.org.uk/media/1228/innovation-and-the-nhs-2020health-1.pdf.

References

Ali Junaid, A. 2014. A mechanisms-driven theory of business incubation. *International Journal of Entrepreneurial Behavior & Research*, 20(4): 375–405. doi:10.1108/IJEBR-11-2012-0133.

Allen, D. N., and Bazan, E. 1990. *Value Added Contribution of Pennsylvania's Business Incubators to Tenant Firms and Local Economies*. Pennsylvania, USA: Pennsylvania State University.

Al-Mubaraki, H. M., and Busler, M. 2011. Critical activity of successful business incubation. *International Journal of Emerging Sciences*, 1(3): 455–464.

Apodaca, A. 2013. *Greenhouse Effect: How Accelerators Are Seeding Digital Health Innovation*. Retrieved from https://www.chcf.org/wp-content/uploads/2017/12/PDF-GreenhouseSeedingDigitalHealth.pdf

Bakouros, Y. L., Mardas, D. C., and Varsakelis, N. C. 2002. Science park, a high tech fantasy?: An analysis of the science parks of Greece. *Technovation*, 22(2): 123–128. doi:10.1016/s0166-4972(00)00087-0.

Barrehag, L., Fornell, A., Larsson, G., Mårdström, V., Westergård, V., and Wrackefeldt, S. 2012. *Accelerating Success: A Study of Seed Accelerators and Their Defining Characteristics*. Gothenburg, Sweden: Chalmers University of Technology.

Battistella, C., De Toni, A. F., and Pessot, E. 2017. Open accelerators for start-ups success: A case study. *European Journal of Innovation Management*, 20(1): 80–111. doi:10.1108/ejim-10-2015-0113.

Bergek, A., and Norrman, C. 2008. Incubator best practice: A framework. *Technovation*, 28(1–2): 20–28. doi:10.1016/j.technovation.2007.07.008.

Bizzotto, C. E. N. 2003. *The Incubation Process*. Brazil: Gene Institute—infoDev Incubator Support Center (iDISC).

Bollingtoft, A., and Ulhoi, J. P. 2005. The networked business incubator: Leveraging entrepreneurial agency? *Journal of Business Venturing*, 20(2): 265–290. doi:10.1016/j.jbusvent.2003.12.005.

Cedars-Sinai Accelerator. 2018. Cedars-Sinai Accelerator. [online] Available at: http://www.techstarscedarssinaiaccelerator.com/ [Accessed 16 May 2018].

Chesbrough, H. W. 2003. *Open Innovation: The New Imperative for Creating and Profiting From Technology*. Boston, MA: Harvard Business School Press.

Chesbrough, H. W. 2006. *Open Business Models: How to Thrive in a New Innovation Landscape*. Boston, MA: Harvard Business School Press.

Chesbrough, H. W., and Appleyard, M. M. 2007. Open innovation and strategy. *California Management Review*, 50(1): 57–76.

Christiansen, J. D. 2009. *Copying Y Combinator: A Framework for Developing Seed Accelerator Programmes*. Cambridge: University of Cambridge.

Clausen, T., and Rasmussen, E. 2011. Open innovation policy through intermediaries: The industry incubator programme in Norway. *Technology Analysis & Strategic Management*, 23(1): 75–85. doi:10.1080/09537325.2011.537109.

Corona, L., Doutriaux, J., and Mian, S. 2006. *Building Knowledge Regions in North America: Emerging Technology Innovation Poles*. Cheltenham, UK: Edward Elgar Publishing.

Dahlander, L., and Wallin, M. W. 2006. A man on the inside: Unlocking communities as complementary assets. *Research Policy*, 35(8): 1243–1259. doi:10.1016/j.respol.2006.09.011.

Dee, N. J., Livesey, F., Gill, D., and Minshall, T. 2011. *Incubation for Growth: A Review of the Impact of Business Incubation on New Ventures With High Growth Potential*. NESTA Retrieved from http://nesta.org.uk/library/documents/IncubationforGrowthv11.pdf.

Etzkowitz, H. 2002. Incubation of incubators: Innovation as a triple helix of university-industry-government networks. *Science and Public Policy*, 29(2): 115–128.

Fichter, K. 2009. Innovation communities: The role of networks of promotors in Open Innovation. *R&D Management*, 39(4): 357–371. doi:10.1111/j.1467-9310.2009.00562.x.

Fishback, B., Gulbranson, C. A., Litan, R. E., Mitchell, L., and Porzig, M. 2007. Finding business idols: A new model to accelerate start-ups. *Ewing Marion Kauffman Foundation*, 2–8.

Gans, J. S., and Stern, S. 2003. The product market and the market for 'ideas': Commercialization strategies for technology entrepreneurs. *Research Policy*, 32(2): 333–350. doi:10.1016/s0048-7333(02)00103-8.

Grimaldi, R., and Grandi, A. 2005. Business incubators and new venture creation: An assessment of incubating models. *Technovation*, 25(2): 111–121. doi:10.1016/s0166-4972(03)00076-2.

Guerrero, M., and Urbano, D. 2012. The development of an entrepreneurial university. *Journal of Technology Transfer*, 37(1): 43–74. doi:10.1007/s10961-010-9171-x.

GUST. 2016. *Global Accelerator Report*. Retrieved from http://gust.com/global-accelerator-report-2015/.

Hackett, S. M., and Dilts, D. M. 2004. A systematic review of business incubation research. *The Journal of Technology Transfer*, 29(1): 55–82. doi:10.1023/B:JOTT.0000011181.11952.0f.

Hansen, M. T., Chesbrough, H. W., Nohria, N., and Sull, D. N. 2000. Networked incubators: Hothouses of the new economy. *Harvard Business Review*, 78(5): 74–+.

Hochberg, Y. V. 2015. *Accelerating Entrepreneurs and Ecosystems: The Seed Accelerator Model*. Paper presented at the Innovation Policy and Economy.

Hughes, M., Ireland, R. D., and Morgan, R. E. 2007. Stimulating dynamic value: Social capital and business incubation as a pathway to competitive success. *Long Range Planning*, 40(2): 154–177. doi:10.1016/j.lrp.2007.03.008.

Hutabarat Z., and Pandin, M. 2014. Absorptive capacity of business incubator for SME's rural community located in Indonesia's village. *Procedia: Social and Behavioural Sciences*, 115: 373–377.

Ketchen, D. J., Thomas, J. B., and Snow, C. C. 1993. Organizational configurations and performance: A comparison of theoretical approaches. *Academy of Management Journal*, 36(6): 1278–1313. doi:10.2307/256812.

Lewis, D. A., Harper-Anderson, A., and Molnar, L. A. 2011. *Incubating Success: Incubation Best Practices That Lead to Successful New Ventures*. Michigan, MI: U.S. Department of Commerce Economic Development Administration.

McAdam, M., and McAdam, R. 2008. High tech start-ups in University Science Park incubators: The relationship between the start-up's lifecycle progression and use of the incubator's resources. *Technovation*, 28(5): 277–290. doi:10.1016/j.technovation.2007.07.012.

McAdam, M., Miller, K., and McAdam, R. 2016. Situated regional university incubation: A multi-level stakeholder perspective. *Technovation*, 50–51: 69–78. doi:10.1016/j.technovation.2015.09.002.

Mian, S. A. 1997. Assessing and managing the university technology business incubator: An integrative framework. *Journal of Business Venturing*, 12(4): 251–285. doi:10.1016/s0883-9026(96)00063-8.

Mian, S. A., Lamine, W., and Fayolle, A. 2016. Technology business incubation: An overview of the state of knowledge. *Technovation*, 50–51: 1–12. doi:10.1016/j.technovation.2016.02.005.

Miller, P., and Bound, K. 2011. *The Startup Factories: The Rise of Accelerator Programmes to Support New Technology Ventures*. Retrieved from https://www.nesta.org.uk/publications/startup-factories.

Mutambi, J., Byaruhanga, J. K., Trojet, L., and Buhwezi, K. B. 2010. Research on the state of business incubation systems in different countries: Lessons for Uganda. *African Journal of Science, Technology, Innovation and Development*, 2(2): 190–214.

Nambissan, S., and Sawhney, M. 2007. *The Global Brain: Your Roadmap for Innovating Faster and Smarter in a Networked World*. Philadelphia: Wharton School Publishing.

Nowak, M. J., and Grantham, C. E. 2000. The virtual incubator: Managing human capital in the software industry. *Research Policy*, 29(2): 125–134. doi:10.1016/s0048-7333(99)00054-2.

Omachonu, V. K., and Einspruch, N. G. 2010. Innovation in healthcare delivery systems: A conceptual framework. *The Innovation Journal: The Public Sector Innovation Journal*, 15(1): Article 2.

Patton, D., 2014. Realising potential: The impact of business incubation on the absorptive capacity of new technology-based firms. *International Small Business Journal: Researching Entrepreneurship*, 32(8): 897–917.

Patton, D., Warren, L., and Bream, D. 2009. Elements that underpin high-tech business incubation processes. *Journal of Technology Transfer*, 34(6): 621–636. doi:10.1007/s10961-009-9105-7.

Phan, P. H., Siegel, D. S., and Wright, M. 2005. Science parks and incubators: Observations, synthesis and future research. *Journal of Business Venturing*, 20(2): 165–182. doi:10.1016/j.jbusvent.2003.12.001.

Plosila, W. H., and Allen, D. N. 1985. Small business incubators and public-policy: Implications for state and local development strategies. *Policy Studies Journal*, 13(4): 729–734. doi:10.1111/j.1541-0072.1985.tb01612.x.

Randhawa, K., Wilden, R., and Hohberger, J. 2016. A bibliometric review of open innovation: Setting a research agenda. *Journal of Product Innovation Management*, 33(6): 750–772. doi:10.1111/jpim.12312.

Rice, M. P. 2002. Co-production of business assistance in business incubators: An exploratory study. *Journal of Business Venturing*, 17(2): 163–187. Retrieved from https://doi.org/10.1016/S0883-9026(00)00055-0

Saxenian, A. 1996. Inside-out: regional networks and industrial adaptation in Silicon Valley and Route 128 cityscape. *A Journal of Policy Development and Research*, 2(2): 41–60.

Smilor, R. W., and Gill, M. D. 1986. *The New Business Incubator Linking Talent, Technology, Capital, and Know-how*. Ann Arbor, MA: Lexington Books.

Spinuzzi, C. 2012. Working alone together: Coworking as emergent collaborative activity. *Journal of Business and Technical Communication*, 26(4): 399–441. doi:10.1177/1050651912444070.

StartUp Health. 2018. *StartUp Health Insights Year End Report*. [online] New York, USA: StartUp Health, pp. 1–28. Available at: https://www.startuphealth.com/insights

Suennen, L. 2014. *Survival of the Fittest: Health Care Accelerators Evolve Toward Specialization*. Retrieved from https://www.chcf.org/wp-content/uploads/2017/12/PDF-SurvivalFittestAccelerators.pdf

Theodorakopoulos, N., Kakabadse, N. K., and McGowan, C. 2014. What matters in business incubation? A literature review and a suggestion for situated theorising. *Journal of Small Business and Enterprise Development*, 21(4): 602–622.

Totterman, H., and Sten, J. 2005. Start-ups: Business incubation and social capital. *International Small Business Journal*, 23(5): 487–511. doi:10.1177/0266242605055909.

Varkey, P., Horne, A., and Bennet, K. E. 2008. Innovation in health care: A primer. *American Journal of Medical Quality*, 23(5): 382–388. doi:10.1177/1062860608317695.

von Hippel, E. 2005. *Democratizing Innovation*. Cambridge, MA: MIT Press.

Warren, L., Patton, D., and Bream, D. 2009. Knowledge acquisition processes during the incubation of new high technology firms. *International Entrepreneurship and Management Journal*, 5(4): 481. doi:10.1007/s11365-009-0121-8.

West, J., and Gallagher, S. 2006. Challenges of open innovation: The paradox of firm investment in open-source software. *R & D Management*, 36(3): 319–331. doi:10.1111/j.1467-9310.2006.00436.x.

West, J., and Lakhani, K. R. 2008. Getting clear about communities in open innovation. *Industry and Innovation*, 15(2): 223–231. doi:10.1080/13662710802033734.

Zehel, J. 2017. *Healthcare Accelerators for Startups*. Retrieved from www.redoxengine.com/blog/healthcare-accelerators-for-startups.

6 Understanding Healthcare Innovation Through a Dynamic Capabilities Lens

Emre Karali, Federica Angeli, Jatinder S. Sidhu, and Henk Volberda

Introduction

Unsurprisingly, in the last decades the healthcare sector has drawn increasing attention of strategic management scholars, for at least two main reasons. First, the sector is highly dynamic. Change in demographics, such as population aging,[1] and related changes in epidemiologic profiles of patients, with the rise of chronic conditions,[2] determines continuous variations of population needs and demands, and a steady rise of healthcare expenditures.[3] In response, policy reforms have been enacted to curb costs, often via pro-competitive regulations (Van de Ven and Schut, 2008, 2009). This in turn produces changes in the type and number of stakeholders, such as governments, patient associations, insurance companies, pharmaceutical companies, suppliers of medical equipment, and value chain partners. The direction, type, and magnitude of changes and phenomena also strongly varies across countries, hence hampering generalizability of findings related to country-specific organizational and policy interventions (Retzlaff-Roberts et al., 2004; Ridic et al., 2012).

Against this already complex backdrop, in recent years we have witnessed a fast-paced rise of new technologies employed in the healthcare sector (Smith, 2004; Thielst, 2007; Kvedar et al., 2014). From electronic health records (Angst and Agarwal, 2009) to wearables (Piwek et al., 2016), mobile apps (Mosa et al., 2012), and telemedicine applications (Nicolini, 2011), patients have significantly amplified opportunities to monitor their own health status, access physicians, and monitor historical information. The emergence of eHealth applications (Black et al., 2011) changed the way in which health can be tracked and services can be provided, by promoting a more empowered and centered role of the patient (Barello et al., 2016). Social, technological, and demographic factors are changing our very understanding of how and where healthcare should be provided. Partly, this is spurred by the way in which technologies allow for different modalities of healthcare delivery (Blaya et al., 2010), partly by the rising costs of healthcare, which favors a policy and cultural change from inpatient to outpatient healthcare delivery settings

(Litvak and Bisognano, 2011), and partly because of increased attention to health literacy (Nutbeam, 2008).

Paradoxically, innovation—such as organizational, product, service, and technological innovations—within the healthcare sector is hard to introduce, because of especially the pluralistic and professional nature of healthcare organizations and their subjection to increased pressures on reducing costs rather than enhancing quality (Denis et al., 2001; Herzlinger, 2006; Porter and Teisberg, 2006). The eHealth technologies mentioned before provide a powerful illustration. Even when technologies are present, they often remain underutilized. Because of limited time, concerns surrounding confidentiality (Eng, 2002), mistrust (Rynning, 2007), or differences in organizational practices, professionals may choose not to consult or request information from other providers, even when eHealth makes it possible. The use of eHealth in hospital settings in particular often clashes with established work routines and decision-making patterns, which are mostly informal and *ad hoc* (Cresswell and Sheikh, 2013; Tjora and Scambler, 2009).

A substantial body of literature highlights, for example, how the introduction of electronic health records in hospitals is a complex undertaking, because of the context of implementation, content of the technology, and the implementation process (Boonstra et al., 2014). At the same time, the latest exploratory insights highlight that the use of eHealth applications poses a number of challenges for providers as well as patients, ranging from increased time spent on administrative activities, adverse effects on patient safety and workflows, usability problems, limited server access, and malfunctioning devices as a consequence of improper use or financial issues (Ossebaard et al., 2013). In order to make appropriate use of eHealth channels, patients need a critical mass of specialized knowledge to be able to use the information and communications technologies that eHealth consist of (Neter and Brainin, 2012). The underutilization of such technologies is also explained by scholars as related to the overlooking of patient-centered design (Berwick, 2009). Designing software that allows for the inclusion of different actors' needs and values is a competence that is essential to implement a utilized eHealth infrastructure. This competence turns into a crucial factor in determining the success or failure in the utilization of the implemented information challenge (Gregory et al., 2014).

A paradox emerges because the sector's level of dynamism and its important societal mandate to deliver the highest level of care implies a continuous and compelling need for innovation, which is however very difficult to introduce because of the complexity, plurality, and inherent professionalism of healthcare organizations. Drawing from the corporate and strategic entrepreneurship literature (Hitt et al., 2011; Yiu and Lau, 2008), by innovation we mean the consequence of corporate entrepreneurial activity that leads to the orchestration and alteration of resources and the initiation of new initiatives, rather than policy reforms. We utilize a dynamic capabilities lens in this chapter because of its potential to see how entrepreneurially initiated innovations can be brought about. A dynamic capability is the capacity of an organization to alter the way in which it makes its living, by altering its resource base in a purposeful manner (Helfat and Peteraf, 2009). The dynamic capabilities concept gives both insight into how organizations can reconfigure their resources, and hence their structure, and gives insight into the initiation process of new initiatives amidst environmental dynamism and contextual constraints (Ferlie et al., 2012; Helfat et al., 2007; Leung, 2012; Newbert, 2005; Teece, 2010, 2017; Wilden et al., 2016).

In the following section, we will first delineate the various concepts in the dynamic capabilities literature. We will subsequently explain how this literature is related to entrepreneurship, how it is applicable to the public sector in general, and consequently, healthcare in particular. By focusing on four distinct contextual characteristics of the healthcare sector, we will explain how innovation can be brought about in the healthcare sector.[4]

A Brief Introduction to the Dynamic Capability Framework

Background

The dynamic capabilities research stream focuses on the change of organizational resources in environments of varying dynamism for strategic purposes, such as innovation (Helfat and Winter, 2011; Teece, 2012; Schilke et al., 2017). This literature originates from the resource-based view (RBV) in that the use and reconfiguration of resources is central (Teece, 2007; Eisenhardt and Martin, 2000; Helfat et al., 2007; Schilke et al., 2017; Wilden et al., 2016). However, it extends the RBV in an important manner. The RBV was criticized for the absence of mechanisms through which resources could be adapted, especially in dynamic environments (Eisenhardt and Martin, 2000; Priem and Butler, 2001; Teece et al., 1997). In recent years, the literature has sought to address this concern and has provided insights into how organizations could strategically alter their resource base, for example, to acquire and (temporarily) sustain competitive advantage (Protogerou et al., 2011; Wilden and Gudergan, 2015; Schilke et al., 2017).

What Are Dynamic Capabilities?

Dynamic capabilities are, first of all, capabilities. Capabilities can be defined as consisting of one or multiple routines that are purposefully combined and directed towards a particular goal (Helfat and Peteraf, 2009; Di Stefano et al., 2014). Capabilities are thus purposeful (e.g., Dosi et al., 2000) and utilized, but are not equal to, routines (Helfat and

Peteraf, 2009). Furthermore, they are reliable and are repeated over time as otherwise no real capacity to perform an activity would exist (Helfat and Martin, 2015; Helfat and Winter, 2011). Finally, capabilities are minimally satisfactory, meaning that the outcome of the use of a capability "is recognizable as such" and "functions at least minimally as intended" (Helfat and Winter, 2011: 124). Dynamic capabilities then are capabilities that have as a goal to maintain or enhance the competitive edge of organizations in dynamic environments by altering the way in which these organizations make a living (Teece et al., 1997; Helfat and Winter, 2011). An important way in which dynamic capabilities do so, is by altering the resource base (Winter, 2003; Helfat et al., 2007; Helfat and Winter, 2011). These resources can be both tangible, such as equipment, machinery, and organizational structure, and intangible such as routines or other capabilities (Volberda and Karali, 2015). A dynamic capability could also be utilized to change aspects of an external environment (Teece, 2007; Helfat and Winter, 2011). For example, an organization could alter its institutional environment by exerting political influence (Barley, 2010).

Contrasting Dynamic Organizational Capabilities and Dynamic Managerial Capabilities

Dynamic capabilities have been argued to have an organizational and a managerial component (Teece et al., 1997; Eisenhardt and Martin, 2000; Adner and Helfat, 2003; Teece, 2007; Helfat and Martin, 2015; Helfat and Peteraf, 2009), of which the former can be defined as dynamic organizational capabilities and the latter as dynamic managerial capabilities. Scholars suggest that dynamic organizational capabilities represent the capacity of an organization as a whole to adapt to current challenges by altering its resource base, whereas dynamic managerial capabilities represent the capacity of a manager to orchestrate resources for this very purpose (e.g., Teece et al., 1997; Adner and Helfat, 2003; Helfat and Winter, 2011; Helfat and Martin, 2015). Thus, the locus of activity in the latter resides in the manager, which has important implications for the nature of the capability. Management-centered approaches are more suitable for challenges that are ill-structured than are approaches such as routines than draw from past knowledge (Simon, 1959). Also, managerial improvisation is argued to be a substitute for organizational routines in highly dynamic occasions, due to its higher capacity of bringing about novelty (Bingham and Eisenhardt, 2014), and thus leads to more incremental outcomes than management-based approaches, due to the fact that they are more routine, because of the need for coordination. compromise and averaging out of initiatives. Scholars have indicated that dynamic managerial capabilities (DMCs) are underpinned by managerial human capital (MHC), managerial social capital (MSC) and managerial cognition (MC), which are developed over time through the accumulation of experience (Adner and Helfat, 2003; Helfat and Martin, 2015). These underpinnings provide the capacity to strategic change and innovation, meaning that their composition translates into how DMCs are deployed and thus how strategic change and innovation takes place. MHC enables managers to act knowledgably, due to the accumulation of related knowledge via education and training (Hatch and Dyer, 2004; Colombo and Grilli, 2005; Marvel and Lumpkin, 2007). MSC allows managers to widen their pool of knowledge, by activating their network for the resolution of dilemmas (Portes, 1998; Tsai and Ghoshal, 1998; Andrews, 2010). Finally, MC is important for managers in that it is determinative of how problems are framed, understood and eventually addressed (Stubbart, 1989; Nadkarni and Barr, 2008; Eggers and Kaplan, 2013).

Whereas many moves of organizations are to some extent rooted in routines (Winter, 2003), this does not mean that each organizational or managerial act stems from routines or capabilities (Eggers and Kaplan, 2013). Some actions are executed only once or several times and, in these cases, the benefits from maintaining capabilities may not cover the expenses (Winter, 2003; Teece, 2012). In other cases, an organization might not have been able to develop desired capabilities, nor might managers possess them (Winter, 2003; Eggers and Kaplan, 2013). The possibility of organizational change and innovation without employing capabilities has led Winter (2003) to describe a direct alternative to dynamic capabilities, *ad hoc* problem solving. *Ad hoc* problem solving might be especially relevant in, for example, periods of economic crises or outbreaks of diseases that were not encountered before and therefore could not be dealt with by whatever resources organizations possess at the moment of the encounter. Think of the Ebola outbreak, where nurse Nina Pham had to act upon the outbreak of the disease without prior knowledge.[5] Eggers and Kaplan (2013) have described that in such cases in which suitable capabilities are absent, managerial cognition can be a substitute for, rather than an underpinning of, capabilities. In these situations, actions would have to stem from the capacity of management to read a situation and act upon it, without past relevant experience. Even though *ad hoc* problem solving and the substitutive potential of managerial cognition are very important and useful in certain cases, it is beyond the scope of this book chapter.

Functioning of Dynamic Capabilities

Dynamic capabilities scholars have made an important distinction between possessing dynamic capabilities and being able to achieve and sustain competitive advantage (Eisenhardt and Martin, 2000). They describe the way in which the relationship between dynamic capabilities and competitive advantage manifests itself as contingent on two things:

the deployment of dynamic capabilities and contextual factors (Teece, 2007; Helfat and Peteraf, 2009; Wilden and Gudergan, 2015).

Dynamic Capability Deployment

Dynamic capabilities need to be "deployed" in order to have any effect. Deployment in this regard means the actual "use" of a capability by an organization, in the case of dynamic organizational capabilities, or by management, in the case of dynamic managerial capabilities (Helfat and Peteraf, 2009). In the case of dynamic organizational capabilities, scholars have often pointed at the sensing-seizing-reconfiguring framework introduced by Teece (2007) as being exemplary of how dynamic capabilities could be deployed by organizations. This framework shows that dynamic capability deployment consists of three aspects, which altogether, if successfully deployed, can lead to effective strategic change and innovation.

Sensing, as described by Teece (2007), entails the identification and shaping of opportunities. Organizations can identify and shape such opportunities through, for instance, processes that direct internal R&D projects, or processes that tap developments in exogenous science and technology. Subsequently, what is identified and shaped needs to be seized. Teece (2007) has drawn attention to addressing new opportunities via investments and commercialization activities. For this purpose, an organization needs to ensure proper structures, procedures, designs and incentives that facilitate the seizing of opportunities. Examples are delineating the business model to optimize the value proposition and delivery, as well as selecting decision-making protocols to enhance decision-making effectiveness. Finally, Teece (2007) has drawn attention to the reconfiguration of organizations, based on opportunities sensed and seized. Sensing and seizing is likely to result in a path-dependent continuation of activities as successes are reaped (Sirén et al., 2012). In these cases, organizations have to be aware of the possible emergence of inertia and should be reconfiguring themselves whenever needed.

Dynamic Capabilities, Entrepreneurship, and Entrepreneurial Innovation

An important aspect of the dynamic capabilities literature is its inherent link with entrepreneurship (e.g., Al-Aali and Teece, 2014; Arend, 2014; Arthurs and Busenitz, 2006; Augier and Teece, 2008; Teece, 2012; Zahra et al., 2006). Among others, these scholars have pointed at the benefits of dynamic capabilities for new ventures and young MNEs. They also have described how entrepreneurial acts are an important aspect of any competitive advantage that might flow out of dynamic capability deployment within any organization. Dynamic capabilities, like any capabilities, come into existence through the accumulation and dissemination of knowledge

(Helfat and Peteraf, 2003; Zollo and Winter, 2002). In this regard, entrepreneurship appears to be key in the development of dynamic capabilities, as Zahra et al. (2006) have indicated that new ventures and established companies differ in terms of their nature of dynamic capability use and that in general, entrepreneurial activities lie at the center of organizational learning and the leveraging of (learned) resources and skills. Weerawardena et al. (2007) have shown that dynamic capabilities are also of vital importance to born globals, because they can enhance the speed and quality of the internationalization process. Augier and Teece (2009) have indicated that the entrepreneur plays a vital role for organizations in helping them introduce novelty and seek new resource combinations, while also helping them to promote and shape learning processes. Teece (2012) has argued that dynamic capabilities and entrepreneurial activities have a symbiotic relationship, meaning that the competitive advantage that might follow from effectively deploying dynamic capabilities might be rooted in the acts of corporate entrepreneurs and their entrepreneurial and creative acts. As a final example of the importance of the interrelation of dynamic capabilities and entrepreneurship, Arend (2014) has found that even young and small SMEs can have dynamic capabilities, as these capabilities can be imported by their founders. He states that younger SMEs seem to reap more of the benefits of dynamic capabilities due to the motivation of their employees. Arend (2014) also points out that smaller SMEs tend to reap less of dynamic capability benefits than bigger SMEs do, as the former seems to benefit more from economies of scale, product-differentiating dynamic capabilities, and a better choice regarding dynamic capability quality.

To sum up, past research has shown that dynamic capabilities are important for young SMEs, born globals and other entrepreneurial ventures, in the sense that dynamic capabilities enable these organizations to learn better, leverage their resource and skills, and consequently to outperform their competitors and rapidly grow (e.g., Arend, 2014; Weerawardena et al., 2007; Zahra et al., 2006). In a similar way, research has treated corporate entrepreneurship as a function that is in general important for basically any type of organization. Entrepreneurship has been treated as the source of novel resource combinations and outputs, while also being vital for the coordination and shaping organizational learning processes (Zahra et al., 2006; Teece, 2012). Consequently, dynamic capabilities are important to young and entrepreneurial ventures, whereas entrepreneurship is a vital aspect of the competitive advantage that might stem from dynamic capability deployment (Arend, 2014; Teece, 2012; Weerawardena et al., 2007; Zahra et al., 2006). Hence, throughout this chapter, whenever we refer the effect of dynamic capabilities on healthcare innovation, our descriptions are extremely relevant also for coordination, organization, and innovation within entrepreneurial ventures. Similarly, whenever we refer to managerial actions for bringing about change and innovation in the organizational structure or actions relating to new initiatives, we imply the entrepreneurial acts of managers through which they orchestrate, modify, and direct organizational resources and thus, organizations in general (Hitt et al., 2011; Teece, 2012).

Challenges of Dynamic Capabilities Deployment

Even though sensing, seizing, and reconfiguring have been identified as components of dynamic capabilities deployment, performing these activities is by no means a guarantee for success (Helfat and Peteraf, 2009). For example, as Eisenhardt and Martin (2000: 1108) put it, "there are better and worse ways to hit a golf ball." However, when professional golfers hit a ball in a bad way, one cannot say that these sportsmen are amateurs. Professional sportsmen will not always (be able to) play at their best, nor will all plays be successful. Similarly, organizations with dynamic capabilities can deploy these capabilities in sub-optimal ways, even though they might have the capacity for achieving something greater. The difference between the capacity and the realization is contingent on the deployment of dynamic capabilities. Sub-optimal deployment can have internal reasons as well as external reasons.

Internal factors are factors within the deploying organization that might hinder any effects dynamic capabilities deployment might have. An exemplary internal factor is bureaucracy. Bureaucratic features been known to problematize the production of novelty, because they can problematize decision-making or the actual enforcement of made decision (Teece, 2007). Another example is organizational culture. Certain cultures are known to be more resistant to change and innovation. Even though an organization or a management team might come up with a particular decision, these less embracing cultures can hinder the positive effect these decisions might have had on the organization (Kor and Mesko, 2013).

The success of dynamic capabilities deployment is also dependent on the context in which an organization resides. Organizations might have strategies and accompanied resources, but the actual benefit that can be reaped from these strategies and resources is dependent on whether such an organization is also able to utilize its capacity to the fullest (Helfat et al., 2007). Many organizations cannot, due to rules and legislations to which they must adhere. An example might be laws on competition within industries, hindering the level of innovation that might have been a consequence of such competition (Blind, 2012). Uber is another example of an organization that cannot utilize its capacity, in this case due to stringent laws regarding licenses of taxi drivers. In addition, environmental dynamism and competitiveness importantly affect the outcome of dynamic capabilities deployment and thus should be anticipated (Wilden et al., 2013; Schilke, 2014). Environmental dynamism has been known to erode the time over which benefits can be sustained. Therefore, these contexts may require more repeated dynamic capability deployment (Eisenhardt and Martin, 2000). Similarly, competitiveness intensity stresses the quality and repetition of dynamic capability deployment in the presence of competitors that perform similar tasks (Wilden and Gudergan, 2015). Figure 6.1 visualizes the conceptual framework underpinning this chapter.

Dynamic Capabilities in the Healthcare Sector

Dynamic Capabilities in the Public Sector

Research on dynamic capabilities has predominantly been theorized on and researched in private sector organizations, even though these capabilities can also be of vital importance to public sector organizations (Pablo et al., 2007). Scholars have emphasized that the distinction between the management of public and private organizations might not be that different (Boyne, 2002). Bozeman and Kingsley (1998) have emphasized that public sector organizations also take risks. Others have described that public organizations also need to and do utilize their internal resources to enhance their performance (Fernandez and Rainey, 2006). Public organizations face environmental competition and dynamism also, as they have to adapt constantly to changing rules and legislations, while some are also made to compete with other organizations to enhance efficiency (Boyne, 2002). Surely, organizational routines are embedded in contexts (Feldman et al., 2016) and consequently, change is context specific (Balogun and Hailey, 2008). Business models need to be innovated by maintaining a close fit with the environment in which the business is going to maneuver and the design of new initiatives should similarly entail a match of its resources with the positioned environment, in order to preserve fit (Sørensen and Stuart, 2000). Scholars have, for instance, pointed at the contextual differences across mainstream and social entrepreneurship (Dacin et al., 2011), even though in essence both require entrepreneurial activity in general. Similarly, the fact that public organizations also need to adapt themselves to an ever-changing dynamic environment means that Pablo et al. (2007) have advocated the applicability and suitability of the dynamic capabilities concept to the public sector as way in which public organizations could identify, enable, and manage the use of a dynamic capability.

Contextual Characteristics of the Healthcare Sector That Complicate and Necessitate Change and Innovation

Being part of the public sector, healthcare as a sector carries similar characteristics. At the same time, the healthcare sector is subject to its own contextual characteristics. Even though we will not delve into the root

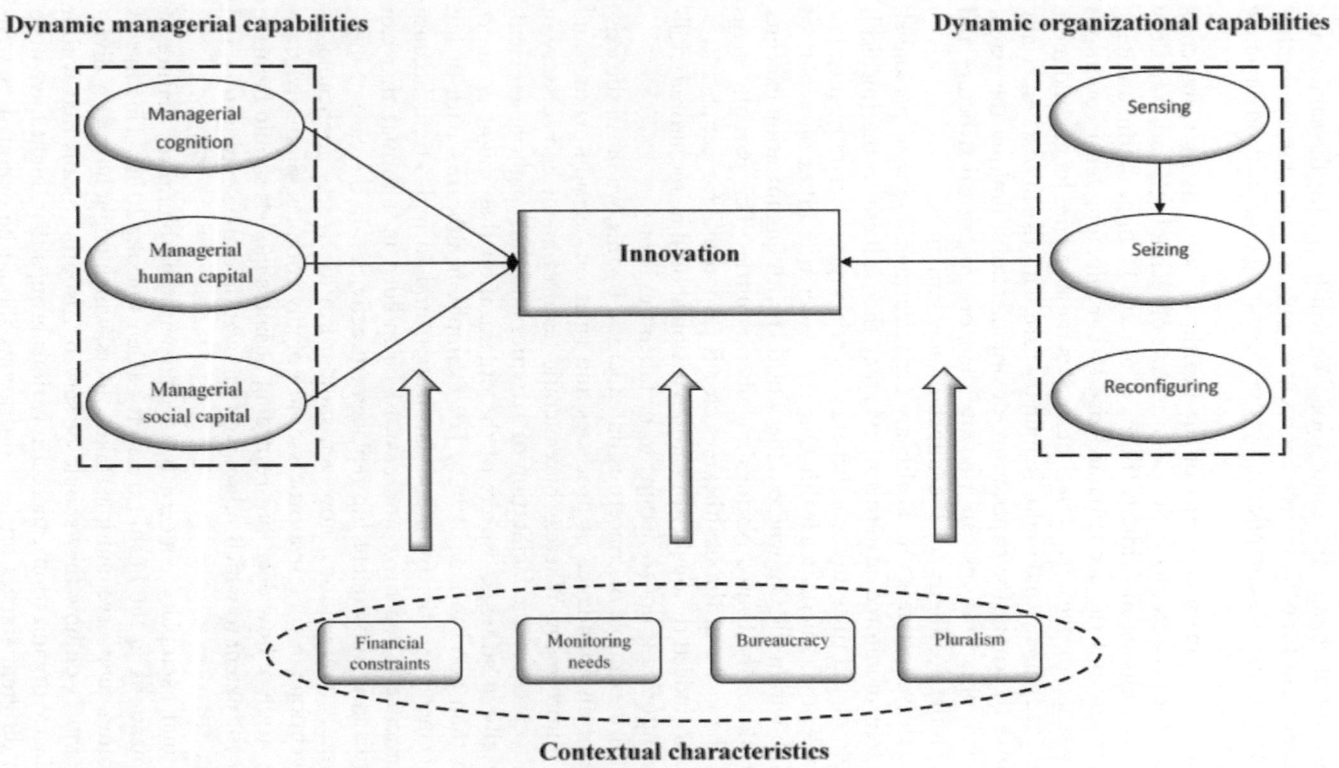

Figure 6.1 Conceptual Framework

causes of these constraints, we will utilize these constraints to enlighten how the contextual constraints of the healthcare sector may affect the propensity of change and innovation. We will focus, for the sake of the argument, on four distinctive contextual constraints within the healthcare sector that are complicating yet necessitating organizational change and innovation.

One of the main concerns of the healthcare sector is its rising costs due to, for instance, inefficiencies, the cost of technology, and unhealthy behaviors among individuals (Burns et al., 2011). In addition, an aging population and the accompanied rise of chronic, long-term conditions puts a strain on the cost of healthcare,[6] as these require longer and more specialized, timely, and multidisciplinary care. This rise in costs especially narrows the room for expenditure of organizations, limiting the extent to which organizations can innovate their organizational structure and limiting the possibility for the launch of new initiatives.

Another concern is that healthcare organizations, and their personnel, are often monitored in terms of whether they adhere to the (medical) guidelines and rules and whether they match targets on care quality. For example, the American Health Quality Association takes on a part of this job within the US, whereas the World Health Organization executes this task for the United Nations' member countries. This partially stems from the fact that the healthcare sector is responsible for people's lives. Whereas indeed the quality of care provision should be monitored, skillful monitoring is not something to be taken too lightly.

A third example of concern is bureaucracy. By this, we mean the existence of an abundance of processes and rules on decision-making and their enforcement. Whereas bureaucratic features might be necessary in certain cases for the facilitation of activities and thus might be efficient, especially in strategic aspects of the organization they might do more harm than good (Shane, 1992). For example, healthcare's path of hip replacement benefits from standardization and formalization, because the practice is repetitive and easy to be molded in a format that can be utilized in subsequent hip replacement activities. In the case of mental health interventions, however, standardization is less applicable, as interventions in cognitive processes are highly complex. Similarly, standardization of how decisions regarding business models should be made limits the extent to which subsequent innovation can be exploratory and radical.

A final exemplary concern has to do with the pluralistic nature of organizations in the healthcare sector (Denis et al., 2011). This means that often, they serve multiple stakeholders, which might have very divergent stances on how they should be served. Also, this means that within healthcare organizations, there are various groups that might have once again different stances on how operations should be operated. A well-known dilemma within hospitals is the existence of different professional groups and their subcultures, such as nurses, medical doctors, and professionals, and how to deal with their divergent interests, stances, and values regarding various issues (Denis et al., 2001; Jarzabkowski and Fenton, 2006). Such pluralism is known to lead to clashes between professional groups (Hall, 2005). Actors within different professions simply perceive conflicts and the approach towards resolution of such conflicts differently (Skjørshammer, 2002). As a result, in the relationship between various professional groups, power, politics, and the search for legitimacy are often very prevalent (Hoff and Rockmann, 2011).

Dynamic Capabilities in Healthcare Innovation

In this section, we aim to explain how dynamic capabilities could lead to innovation in the healthcare context, by magnifying how the aforementioned contextual characteristics of the healthcare sector may affect the deployment of dynamic organizational capabilities and dynamic managerial capabilities. Having shown the centrality of entrepreneurial actions to both concepts, this chapter brings insight into the interrelation of contextual characteristics and entrepreneurship.

Dynamic Organizational Capabilities and Healthcare Innovation

The dynamic capabilities concept describes that some innovation processes can be deployed at the organizational level (Teece, 2007). As these capabilities are rooted in routines (Schilke et al., 2017), they have a substantial aligning and coordinative routine aspect to them, because routines often span different people, various professions, and many departments (Becker, 2004; Collinson and Wilson, 2006; Feldman and Pentland, 2003; Zbaracki and Bergen, 2010). Whereas the innovation processes that dynamic capabilities comprise are patterned, the design of such processes and the coordination is highly dependent on entrepreneurial acts of orchestrating resources, funneling learning processes and consequently accommodating novelty production (Augier and Teece, 2008; Pentland and Feldman, 2008; Teece, 2012; Zahra et al., 2006).

An innovation process, as set in motion by dynamic capabilities, is argued to start with the identification of threats and opportunities through sensing capabilities (Teece, 2007). Angeli and Jaiswal (2016) discuss the case of the Aravind Eye Hospital in India, which coped with great inefficiencies in relation to acquiring intraocular lenses. The identification of this inefficiency, stemming from the purchasing of these lenses, could be seen as the manifestation of the organization's sensing capabilities. After identifying that the purchasing of technologies drives the cost of the delivery of healthcare services, the dynamic organizational capabilities literature first prescribes organizations to search for solutions. In this case, solutions should alleviate the financial burden of purchasing lenses on the organization. Think of alternative technologies or sharing of technologies with other hospitals in order to share costs and benefits. To be able to continuously do this, an organization needs procedures to tap into either internal R&D processes, or into external sources of opportunity discovery, such as patent repositories or conferences. The Aravind Eye Hospital sensed an opportunity for substituting the import of intraocular lenses for internal production. Sensing capabilities are thus the first step in the realization of healthcare innovation at the organizational level, as they ensure the identification of opportunities and threats that can be addressed through healthcare innovation.

After having sensed an opportunity or threat, the dynamic capabilities concept prescribes the investment in the development and commercialization of products and services that may leverage what is sensed (Teece, 2007). This may be done by investment in product and service innovation (Agarwal and Selen, 2009; Kindström et al., 2013), but may also require new ways of managing and operating through, for instance, business model innovation and management innovation (Birkinshaw et al., 2008; Hwang and Christensen, 2008; Teece, 2017). Regardless of the innovation mode, the identified opportunities should be committed to and pursued. For instance, hospital management might decide to transition from a model of departments to a model of care cycles, because they might have sensed that this is a best practice that should be adopted in order to deliver better care with fewer inefficiencies (Porter and Lee, 2013; Porter and Teisberg, 2006). As a matter of fact, many Dutch hospitals, such as the Franciscus Gasthuis and IJsselland hospitals, adopt such an approach. In these cases of seizing upon a sensed opportunity for transitioning to a care cycle model via innovation in the organizational structure, organizations would need to invest in the adoption of the innovation by delineating departments that are synergetic and combining them, their processes, and their people. Managers are key in the adoption of innovations (Damanpour and Schneider, 2009), as especially large transitions can be difficult in terms of preserving the fit of the innovation with the organization that tries to seize an opportunity (Sosa et al., 2004; Zott and Amit, 2008), as well as managing people's opposition towards newness (Haveman, 1993). In the latter case, managers often need to frame innovations (Edmondson, 2003) or streamline the adoption of an innovation at the organizational level (Sosa et al., 2004; Zott and Amit, 2008).

Finally, the focal organization should ready itself for transforming whenever a new opportunity might need to be pursued and seized (Teece, 2007). Successes might lead to inertia (Miller and Chen, 1994; Kim et al., 2006) and healthcare organizations need to be aware of this possibility and anticipate upon it by designing their organizations in a flexible (Volberda, 1996; Schreyögg and Sydow, 2010) and adaptive (Sørensen and Stuart, 2000) manner. Organizations might be decentralized (Mintzberg,

1979; Faguet, 2004) for this purpose, whereas learning processes might be installed to continuously trace whether the organization is in need of reconfiguration, based on predefined care quality indicators (De Vos et al., 2009; McIver et al., 2013). Extrapolating the example of the Aravind Eye Hospital in India, after having invested in the internal production of intraocular lenses, the hospital should reconfigure itself in such a manner that in the future it is able search for and invest in other needed resources and services. Similarly, the Franciscus Gasthuis hospital in the Netherlands should, after its shift to the care cycle system, reconfigure itself in such a way that it is able to accommodate new organizational forms in the future to reduce inefficiencies and enhance care effectiveness. In essence, the transformation phase is one of managerial and structural, rather than product or service innovation, in the sense that besides output, transformation requires an organization to "alter how it currently makes its living" (Helfat and Winter, 2011: 32).

Financial Constraints

The dynamic organizational capabilities literature brings us important insights on the contextual characteristics of the healthcare sector and its possible effects on innovation. The absence of financial room of many healthcare organizations is something that might harm their sensing. Alleviation of financial constraints might facilitate a larger input for the sensing phase of organizations, as IT systems might be consulted to automatize the way in which inefficiencies are tracked (McIver et al., 2013), or people might be able to access or visit locations where useful knowledge might be present or shared (Teece, 2007). Also, constraints are known to result in a broad, yet shallow, search (Garriga et al., 2013), possibly going at the cost of opportunity quality.

At the same time, research describes that sensing will be affected only partially, because there are many ways in which organizations could sense and not all of them require huge sums of money. Operational staff, such as nursing staff, is, for example, a great source of finding opportunities for improvement as they are at the frontline (Tucker and Edmondson, 2003). Even though operational staff is also bound by the financial limitations, research has shown that contextual constraints can spark novel approaches to circumvent the drawbacks of such constraints (Baker and Nelson, 2005; Desa and Basu, 2013). Similarly, the continuous reflective screening of current operations for imperfections is not something that needs to be expensive.

Effective sensing is often a matter of leadership (Garvin et al., 2008) and the organization making you feel supported and appreciated as part of a family (Bass and Avolio, 1993; Gong et al., 2009), in this way installing a culture that supports staff to voice their concerns and ideas (Edmondson, 2003). While the absence of financial means may harm an organization in the long run, as it may not be able to invest and hence preserve its competitiveness, over-abundance of financial means has it apparent risks, too. Management's task is thus to ensure that necessary investments can take place, while ensuring that especially also the opportunities and threats that require minimal resources are also identified, by appropriately incentivizing employees to sense in such a way, drawing their attention not only to those solutions that are complex and expensive, but also to simpler and more feasible solutions.

In terms of the seizing phase, financial constraints place a burden on the number of opportunities that can be pursued. Surely, not all opportunities require large investments. Inventive outcomes can flourish in more constrained environments (Hoegl et al., 2008). Investments could take the shape of low-cost activities, such as the installment of meetings that can shape strategies (Jarzabkowski and Seidl, 2008) and setting up a facilitative organizational environment (Jung et al., 2003). Financial constraints can also force healthcare organizations to make more efficient decisions due to the lower room for errors, making them more cautious and effective (Rosso, 2014). Again, these are more activities of orchestrating assets or utilizing contacts and networks, in that they require financial investment. In many cases, however, organizations might benefit from the presence of financial resources. For example, in order to seize the opportunities that are sensed, organizations often need to invest (Teece, 2007). Hospitals might need to purchase technologies and are bound by their financial freedom in their choice for equipment type and amount.

Still, even though the presence of financial assets opens up possibilities, at the same time it can result in inefficient expenditure or even not choosing the best possible alternative due to the lack of a stimulus (George, 2005). In the presence of financial constraints, procurers need to be more selective in their purchases. Similar technologies do not have to be priced similarly, thus an optimal level of financial constraints could favor healthcare organizations by forcing them to select better. Healthcare organizations that do not suffer from financial problems may want to consider self-imposed constraints to reap the benefits of forcing management to seize more innovatively. In addition, some technologies might be more "interesting" than "necessary." Thus, the postponement or withholding of procurement by placing constraints might in some cases be favorable as it might prevent unnecessary experimentation.

Finally, organizational transformation is also likely to only partially suffer from financial constraints. Academic literature prescribes that transformation has to do with the alteration of cultures (Cameron and Quinn, 2011), routines (Teece, 2012) and structures (Volberda et al., 2001). Besides the actual physical alteration of departmental structures, firing staff and the installment of new IT systems, much of organizational transformation has to do with the flexible design of departments (Volberda, 1996) to be able to adapt to new paths, incentivizing staff for proactively breaking away from the status quo and seeking new areas and supporting people in their quest for transformation (Crant, 2000; Hornung and Rousseau, 2007). People need to be made receptive to changes, in the present as well as in the future, and they should be managed accordingly. The financial strain on transforming the organization is thus limited in comparison to investing. Rather, it is about insight.

Monitoring

We have described that healthcare organizations are strongly subject to monitoring obligations, for instance in terms of reporting on their own activities to various stakeholders who evaluate them, which in turns translates into a continuous need for organizations to monitor of their own employees. Monitoring can have different forms, which can differently affect healthcare organizations.

Monitoring is likely to affect how organizations sense, seize, and reconfigure. First of all, internal monitoring draws away resources that could have been utilized for sensing opportunities (He and Wang, 2009; Liebeskind, 1997; McEvily et al., 2003). Even though it might be wise to spend this money on monitoring vital aspects of the provision of healthcare, the extent to which organizations are monitored should not be overstepped in order to prevent harm to their capacity to search (Greve, 2003) as less money can be invested into perfecting search activities. Second, in terms of external monitoring, people might not thoroughly sense in which areas experimentation is discouraged (Lee et al., 2004) or seizing is penalized (Kempner et al., 2005), because such initiatives reduce the incentive to sense. Thus, an organization's propensity to sense in areas where monitoring is tight might be less (He and Wang, 2009). Whereas monitoring is an important solution to the agency problem in which managers might not behave in the interest of the organization (Jensen and Meckling, 1976), excessive monitoring may harm the innovation process (Cardinal, 2001). Monitoring is known to restrict risk-taking behavior (Liebeskind, 1997; Cardinal, 2001) and improvisation (Barrett, 1998), thus reducing the extent to which organizations can deviate from their past. The right monitoring, thus, is the monitoring that restricts only the movement of organizations in the directions they should not be going in the first place while allowing employees the room to experiment and improvise, essentially not harming an organization's innovation capacity.

Monitoring is also important for the seizing and transforming aspects of dynamic organizational capabilities. Tight external monitoring might prevent the investment in certain products and services due to the risk of conflict with monitoring institutions. It is an issue that plays in the Netherlands, as insurance companies constrain the innovative capacity of health providers, by pushing the risks of innovating to these organizations.[7] In a similar way, tight internal monitoring could be interpreted as a sign of lack of confidence and lack of support for inventiveness (Parker et al., 2006), which might reflect itself in the choice of opportunities to pursue, as well as the way in which employees might decide to transform the organization.

In essence, monitoring can severely disturb the contribution of dynamic organizational capabilities to innovation, in the case that monitoring is too tight and thus harms innovation activities. Similarly, in the absence of monitoring, care quality might be gambled with in favor of the drive to innovate. Thus, regardless of its negative effect on dynamic organizational capability deployment, some degree of monitoring seems necessary. It is important to limit monitoring, however, to the preservation of care quality and not to those innovations that might not harm care quality per se or might even enhance care quality.

Bureaucracy

In discussing bureaucratic features of organizations, we refer to the definition of Adler and Borys (1996).

Davis et al. (2009) have found that the optimal structure lies in between too much and too little structure. As simple as this might seem, it appears to be very difficult to realize this in the healthcare sector amidst the desire to routinize and govern processes to provide reliability and minimize calamities, via for example the evidence-based medicine trend (Burns et al., 2011). Whereas formalization might in particular be beneficial in for medical operations, such as surgery, that are crucial to be followed exactly as is recorded in best-practice protocols, it might be better to abandon these structures in favor of, or at least complement them with, semistructures (Brown and Eisenhardt, 1997), such as simple rules (Bingham and Eisenhardt, 2011, 2014) in cases of processes that are more related to management and organization. For example, organizations that seek to identify new opportunities to address might want to complement formal instructions, procedures, and rules with more flexible simple rules to be able to allow more managerial involvement in the actual selection of the solution (Bingham and Eisenhardt, 2014; Wilden et al., 2013). In this sense, it is important to possess a repertoire of more detailed and simpler structures that together can provide efficiency but also can facilitate management.

Pluralism

Pluralistic organizations face dilemmas that many other organizations might not face. We focus in this section mainly on pluralistic organizations as those characterized by diffuse power and multiple objectives, while acknowledging also the importance of knowledge-based work in these types of organizations (Denis et al., 2011; Denis et al., 2007).

Pluralism might to some extent be present in all organizations, but research has often hinted at the stronger applicability of the pluralism concept to healthcare in general and hospitals in particular (Denis et al., 2007; Dunn and Jones, 2010). Here we exemplify the impact that pluralism can have on innovation within hospitals, underscoring the possible similarity of issues in other pluralistic healthcare organizations. Hospitals often do not innovate terms of developing products. Rather, they more often tend to innovate in terms of their organizational structure, management composition, or the embracing of new services (Aiken et al., 2000; Noordegraaf and Van der Meulen, 2008). As such, these categories will be the ones that we will focus on.

Hospitals are organizations embedded with a variety of people and professional groups. Within the same organization, various types of nurses (specialized versus general nurses), physicians (specialized versus physicians in training) and managers (medical and professional) are employed (Goodall, 2011). Each type of each group of employees differs from any other type within the same or within a different group. Differences can arise due to differences in, for instance, education, preferences, professional and departmental interests, and hierarchy (Fagermoen, 1997; Willem et al., 2007; Skjørshammer, 2002; Wardhani et al., 2009). To benefit the organization, decisions will need to take into account all of these differences (Pitts et al., 2010). These embracing decisions should flow out of an agreement between, if applicable, medical and professional managers, who often differ in how they approach management.

The diversity within hospitals necessitates the coordination of the different professional groups within the sensing process (Bruns, 2013). As different professions hold different beliefs and areas of expertise (Pratt et al., 2006), they might sense differently, resulting in a lack of synergy between the sensed opportunities themselves and also with the organization's goals. If governed effectively, however, diversity is known to potentially lead to novel opportunities (Wiersema and Bantel, 1992). Scholars suggest that management should pay attention to synergies in functional competence and preferences of workers (Bassett-Jones, 2005).

Subsequently, in terms of seizing and transforming, management faces the question of which opportunities to pursue, how to pursue these opportunities within their pluralistic environment, and consequently, how to adapt the organization in the face of environmental changes and needs. The development of services and the investment in opportunities might become a hard task within hospitals as power and politics is a prevalent theme (Hoff and Rockmann, 2011). Besides the aforementioned difficulty of agreement between medical and professional managers, within pluralistic organizations, one or multiple of the abundant stakeholders might pressure these managers so that the decision favors themselves, too. A similar issue is at hand in the case of transforming the organization. In pluralistic organizations, it is first of all important that varying groups are aligned (Brousseau et al., 1996). This alignment might be facilitated by initiatives that facilitate inter-group communication, as discourse is a means to find common ground (Salvato and Vassolo, 2017). These initiatives can include meetings (Jarzabkowski and Seidl, 2008), talk (Dittrich et al., 2016) or simply the establishment of a culture of questioning and dialogue (Hall et al., 2001). In addition, also here, the employment of procedures to aid in the agreement between managers on which opportunities to pursue and how to transform the organization is something that might help deal with the peculiarities of pluralistic settings (Denis et al., 2001). Too much trying to mold the pluralism, however, might limit the advantages of discourse between and improvisation of managers, and too much structure might decrease the quality of the decision-making process as managers might lack discretion as well as the opportunity to deviate from the past (Bingham and Eisenhardt, 2014).

There are some notable differences between innovation at the departmental and organizational levels. Often, within healthcare organizations, medical staff is more prevalent at the levels at which care is delivered, meaning that at the higher levels of the organization, relatively speaking, pluralism becomes much less of an issue due to the fact that there are fewer stakeholders, easing the balancing of interests (Reynolds et al., 2006). That being said, even at the higher levels, healthcare management does not cease to be a pluralistic setting (Moussa, 2011). In addition, top management teams can be highly diverse themselves (Nielsen, 2010), preserving the importance of managing pluralism in healthcare organizations. Also, whereas within department the decisions are related to a department only, decision at the organizational level are likely to influence multiple departments at once, increasing problem complexity (Simon, 1959). A merger between hospitals, as an extreme example, is likely to affect patient streams and departmental decision-making structures, such as in the case of the Blekinge hospital in Sweden, where organizational structure was altered and hospital accessibility decreased (Ahgren, 2008). Even though professional management does not compete with medical management at the organizational level to come to a decision, physicians do have an important say in the eventual decision as basically, without physicians there cannot be a hospital. Often, for this purpose, physicians can be found to be grouped as a separate unit within the hospital, as a per-specialty partnership called "maatschap" (Westra et al., 2016). Thus, even for decision-making at the organizational level, finding common ground across departments with various stakeholders indirectly remains to be a massive challenge, once again boiling down to extensive possibilities for meetings and bargaining.

Dynamic Managerial Capabilities and Healthcare Innovation

The dynamic managerial capabilities concept, on which we focus in this section, subtly differs from the dynamic organizational capabilities concept in the sense that it magnifies the role of the *manager* rather than the *organization*. As such, in this section, we will try to convey how, from a managerial perspective, innovation can be affected by the constraints of the healthcare sector.

Financial Constraints

We have described that financial constraints can both negatively and positively affect organizational innovation (Hoegl et al., 2008). Similarly, financial constraints can both negatively and positively affect the ability of managers to evoke innovation via dynamic managerial capabilities. As innovation is partly the product of the utilization of financial resources, the less the amount of financial resources, the less potential there is for a manager to experiment and innovate (George, 2005). That being said, as aforementioned, innovation can be achieved without spending much money and resource constraints can spark 'creativity' (Hewitt-Dundas, 2006). In both cases, the dynamic managerial capabilities literature prescribes that the interaction between MC, MHC, and MSC will prove to be crucial for the level of innovativeness, and thus also in financially constrained settings.

MC is fundamental for the comprehension of the problem at hand and the understanding of how such a problem might be addressed with the least amount of resources (Eggers and Kaplan, 2013). MC is important because it provides a partial solution through reasoning, beliefs, and emotion (Helfat and Martin, 2015), regardless of the financial room for innovation. However, under tighter constraints, the correct comprehension, dissection, and addressing of a problem will become more cognitively burdening (Liu et al., 2008). Subsequently, MHC and MSC provide two types of input, which together might determine the nature of financially constrained innovation (Adner and Helfat, 2003; Helfat and Martin, 2015). MHC is important for knowledgably being able to act upon an issue that is encountered. Within healthcare, this might be knowledge regarding how particular patients would like to be treated, or how certain innovations might impact the dynamics within a department. MHC is important to find solutions to the problem at hand through existing applications or past experience (Castanias and Helfat, 2001). However, financial constraints may limit the extent to which new knowledge can be acquired. Then, MSC is important for the influx of solutions to certain problems that might need to be solved, which could not be obtained by the manager herself or himself (Acquaah, 2007). The benefit of social capital can range from the seeds of an idea to the total solution to a problem. For example, in setting up a new hospital department, a manager might not know what type of patients might be expected, nor might this manager be aware how such a department might click with nascent departments. In both cases, MSC is crucial to acquire a solution, external to the manager, by asking colleagues or reaching out to comparable hospitals. Whenever solutions are scarce because resources are scarce, social capital might prove to be very useful in finding unconventional solutions in a relatively cheap manner. Still, financial constraints will harm the extension of social capital, as many ways of doing so, such as attending conferences and symposia, are dependent on financial resources.

Monitoring

Monitoring might hinder the capacity of healthcare managers to bring about innovations.[8] The main managerial issue with monitoring is that it might strain management cognitively (Liu et al., 2008), preventing management from innovating as its members would like to. Tight rules regarding operations might severely restrict the extent to which dynamic managerial capabilities can be effective. We have explained that contextual constraints could also spark innovative solutions (Rosso, 2014). Yet, an environment that does not facilitate managers' utilization of their capacity renders dynamic managerial capabilities useless (Teece, 2007). There is merit, obviously, in tight monitoring of medical practices and their quality criteria. However, a large part of healthcare organizations' performance stems from their organization, or could stem from their organization in the presence of a facilitative environment, meaning that monitoring should not interfere too much with management itself.

Excessive monitoring might affect the underpinnings of dynamic managerial capabilities in a variety of ways. MHC might be affected by measures that prohibit the possibilities for managers to be schooled or trained, because such activities might not be seen as directly useful or as needed. This has also implications for one's network, as many contacts can be acquired at educative institutions and conferences, translating into MSC. MSC might also be affected in terms of managers not wanting to utilize their social capital out of the fear that they would have to reach out to their contacts for nothing in case monitoring institutions would block the utilization of such contacts. Excessive monitoring strains MC, in the sense that the gap that arises from not being able to increase MHC and not being able to increase and utilize MSC needs to filled by means of the capacity of management to read the situation and act upon it, based on its current cognitive capacity.

Bureaucracy

Bureaucratic features of organizations have been a major hindrance for managers over the years, and in a similar fashion, they can also hinder the full potential of dynamic managerial capabilities deployment (Teece, 2007). There are risks in too much and too little structure, and research has indicated that semistructures favor decision-making and thus facilitate innovation more than tight procedures and rules might (Davis et al.,

2009; Bingham and Eisenhardt, 2011, 2014). Even through semistructures are not free of structure, the absence of structure poses the risk of undirected, experimental innovations that might do more harm than good (Strong and Volkoff, 2010).

Bureaucratic features can be useful, though, for healthcare managers in terms of enabling them to streamline more operational processes, such as patient admission, allowing these managers to preserve their cognitive capacity for more strategic activities, such as innovation (Becker, 2004), that might benefit more from semistructures, such as simple rules (Bingham and Eisenhardt, 2011). In terms of MC, semistructures leave plenty of room for managers to improvise and deviate from past paths accordingly, while at the same time providing these managers with best practices that direct their improvisational actions in possibly fruitful directions (Bingham and Eisenhardt, 2014; Sonenshein, 2016). Semistructures benefit also from the utilization of MSC, in the sense that they might provide suggestions by means of which managers could utilize or broaden their network. Think of guidelines that might indicate which people in the environment possess which types of medical knowledge and who within the organizations knows those people and thus can act as a connector. Similarly, guidelines on how such external knowledge can be internalized, or has been internalized in the past, eases the utilization of MSC by means of MC and increases MHC. Finally, semistructures might increase the extent to which managers can utilize their MHC. Without room to act, managers would not be able to utilize the knowledge they acquire from their education. The effect of this is that, possibly, the innovation process is harmed, because MHC in essence serves as an important source of input for the action that is eventually going to be undertaken through the interpretation of a problem at hand via MC. The absence of room for managerial discretion may also have as a consequence that managers might not be incentivized to acquire new knowledge through conferences, symposia or trainings. This might place a cap on the MHC, but may also limit MSC, as aforementioned, because these places are hotspots for broadening one's network.

Pluralism

Pluralism poses yet another challenge to the utilization of the capacity of managers to innovate, through dynamic managerial capability deployment. Pluralistic environments do so first by drawing managerial resources into the management of stakeholders (Reynolds et al., 2006). Managers need to interlink the various groups of employees with each other and safeguard their cooperation and preventing or fixing any intergroup conflicts (Denis et al., 2001). In addition, in the case of the desire to pursue a particular innovation, managers need to align interests of the various stakeholders its organization embeds (Brousseau et al., 1996). In seeking common ground across parties, the manager might need to economize on the innovation as cognitive resources are limited (Becker, 2004). Finally, managers in pluralistic organizations are likely to get caught in the task of cutting through hierarchies (Burns et al., 2011). Groups often do not have the same esteem and in the case certain groups climb the hierarchical ladder at the cost of others, managers might need to prevent these differences from harming intra-departmental communication and thus the innovation process (Bassett-Jones, 2005).

While pluralistic settings might burden managers, they might also grant managers broader sets of beliefs and mental representations due to a broader scope of interaction, aiding them in the development of more radical innovations (Eggers and Kaplan, 2013). In terms of MHC, pluralistic settings might prove to be a huge burden for those managers that might not have the education and experience to innovate within these settings. These managers will also likely not have the social capital through which they might address the pluralistic nature of these organizations by means of management innovation or structural innovation, because social capital is often built though past experiences and educations. However, the variety of people who pluralistic organizations embed may enlarge the social capital of management, due to the richness of their backgrounds and consequently the diversity of their networks. Table 6.1 summarizes the main lines of reasoning supporting the elaboration around the influence of dynamic organizational capabilities and dynamic managerial capabilities on innovation and entrepreneurial behavior.

Conclusion

In this chapter, the authors have tried to uncover how innovation could be realized in healthcare organizations. We have described that healthcare organizations are operating in a highly dynamic environment amidst demographic[9,10], institutional (Van de Ven and Schut, 2008, 2009), and technological changes (Acquaah, 2007; Kvedar et al., 2014; Smith, 2004; Thielst, 2007), while also being subject to different internal and external constraining contextual characteristics. In particular, we have shown that healthcare organizations are often subject to financial constraints, monitoring, bureaucracy, and pluralism. By utilizing a dynamic capabilities approach (Schilke et al., 2017), we have described how the contextual characteristics of the healthcare sector can influence the propensity to innovate of the organizations that have to operate amidst such characteristics.

In principle, all contextual constraints can limit the innovation potential of healthcare organizations, but can counterintuitively also enable efficiency and effectiveness in those organizations, provided that the execution is well performed. In general, it is important to grant freedom via the use of semistructures (Bingham and Eisenhardt, 2011, 2014) and

Table 6.1 Summary of Rationales Supporting the Influence of Dynamic Organizational Capabilities and Dynamic Managerial Capabilities on Innovation

	Dynamic organizational capabilities	*Dynamic managerial capabilities*
Exemplary seminal research	Teece et al. (1997), Eisenhardt and Martin (2000), Helfat et al. (2007), Teece (2007), Peteraf et al. (2013), Di Stefano et al. (2014)	Adner and Helfat (2003), Sirmon and Hitt (2009), Martin (2011), Kor and Mesko (2013), Helfat and Martin (2015)
Locus of innovation	The organization.	The manager/management.
Effect of financial constraints	May spark novel approaches, but restricts investment possibilities. Artificially constraining finances may result in pursuing novel approaches while leaving room for investment possibilities.	Many innovations are cheap. However, such innovations burden managerial cognition. Whereas managerial human capital and social capital are not harmed instantly, the future development of both is, as often this is dependent on financial resources.
Effect of monitoring	May preserve level of care quality if used appropriately. However, searching for and seizing opportunities may be discouraged if monitoring is too stringent and spills over to more strategic activities, reducing innovation potential.	May preserve level of care quality if used appropriately. Stringent monitoring may restrict knowledge acquisition and corresponding network size, leading to over-burdening managerial cognition and reduced innovation potential.
Effect of bureaucracy	May streamline operational processes, but may also limit search, experimentation, and investment if discretion is too restricted and thus not incentivized. Semistructures may prove to provide more flexibility, and thus be more beneficial for innovation.	May reserve cognitive capacity for innovation and streamlines operational processes if used appropriately. Innovation might benefit more from semistructures than from stringent rules.
Effect of pluralism	May benefit innovation through the benefits of diversity, but may consume large amounts of financial resources and time as the various interests of stakeholders need to be balanced and coordinated.	May benefit innovation through the benefits of diversity, but may consume large amounts of cognitive resources and time as the various interests of stakeholders need to be balanced and coordinated.

to not monitor obtrusively (Barrett, 1998; Cardinal, 2001) by focusing efforts on those aspects that are absolutely necessary for quality preservation, in order to not limit the capacity of an organization to innovate in a radical and exploratory manner. In addition, financial resources should be present to the extent that organizations do not have to economize on those innovations that can enhance their competitive position or quality of provided care (Hoegl et al., 2008). However, freedom, unobtrusive monitoring, and the provision of financial resources should not be to the extent that organizations forfeit the advantage or reliability, undergo unnecessary risks and waste resources. Procedures, routines, and rules can streamline processes by utilizing past knowledge and thus setting steps more convincingly (Becker, 2004), while financial restrictions can spark novelty (Rosso, 2014). Similar to the other contextual characteristics treated in this chapter, pluralism has two sides to it. On the one hand, pluralism complicates the innovation process because of the balancing and coordination of the various interests of the many stakeholders. On the other hand, pluralistic settings may benefit from the diversity of employees, potentially leading to a bigger network and more diverse insights.

The effects of the contextual characteristics can subtly differ across the managerial and organizational level and even within the managerial level itself. Most differences between management and organizational strategies will be between the top management on the one side and the frontline or middle management on the other side, as often the organization is a reflection of the top management team (Hambrick and Mason, 1984). Still, it is useful to acknowledge that this is not always the case, as there are many stakeholders—especially within healthcare organizations—that might affect the choices that are made by top management, or to which top management is subject (Banaszak-Holl et al., 2011; Hoff and Rockmann, 2011). Whereas we have mainly focused on the top management throughout this chapter, insights are also applicable for frontline and middle managers to the extent that they have been granted the room to contribute to innovation. Another difference between focusing on the top management team and the organization is such that managerial activities can be more radical of nature than organizational activities, as the latter are more collective activities, necessitating high levels of organizational support, which is difficult in pluralistic organizations such as those in the healthcare sector.

When the contextual characteristics of bureaucracy, financial constraints, and tight monitoring are enforced by top management, those affected by them are managers at the lower levels. However, when one of the many stakeholders, including those within the organization, set these constraints or influence them, the characteristics will also affect top management. Thus, especially in those cases when the top management does not reflect the organization, and is even affected by it, it is wise to pay close attention to the differences between the two, because of which we have looked in this chapter at both dynamic organizational (Teece, 2007) and managerial (Helfat and Martin, 2015) capabilities. Finally, in terms of pluralism, both management and the organization are concerned with aligning various professions and interests. Management can do so at the departmental, inter-departmental, or organizational level. Organizational level strategies, however, will be more focused on the latter two levels only because of the distance between the organization and the department and thus the inapplicability of those strategies for operational activities.

This chapter contributes to our comprehension of healthcare entrepreneurship and innovation in a variety of ways. First, we contribute by providing an analytical lens for looking at healthcare innovation, in terms of showing how the dynamic capabilities literature is a concept that is suitable at both the managerial and organizational level for examining the process of innovating, via the dynamic capabilities framework of Teece (2007) that dissects this process into sensing, seizing, and reconfiguring facets. Second, we show how innovations in healthcare organizations can be brought about amidst the contextual characteristics that healthcare organizations are subject to by applying this framework to those characteristics that we deem to be especially important for healthcare management and innovation. In this regard, we focus on bureaucracy, financial constraints, monitoring, and pluralism.

Notes

1. United Nations. 2015. *World population ageing*. Economics & Social Affairs. New York: United Nations, pp.1–164. Available at: http://www.un.org/en/development/desa/population/publications/pdf/ageing/WPA2015_Report.pdf
2. PwC. 2018. Chronic diseases and conditions are on the rise. Retrieved from https://www.pwc.com/gx/en/industries/healthcare/emerging-trends-pwc-healthcare/chronic-diseases.html
3. Healthdata.org. 2018. Global spending on health is expected to increase to $18.28 trillion worldwide by 2040, but many countries will miss important health benchmarks | Institute for Health Metrics and Evaluation. Retrieved from http://www.healthdata.org/news-release/global-spending-health-expected-increase-1828-trillion-worldwide-2040-many-countries
4. Chapter 7 also indicates how change and innovation within healthcare can be brought about and what activities are needed for this to be possible.
5. Engel, P. 2014. *Nurse at Ebola hospital: 'I can no longer defend my hospital at all'*. Business Insider. Retrieved from http://www.businessinsider.com/nurse-at-texas-health-presbyterian-speaks-about-ebola-crisis-2014-10?international=true&r=US&IR=T
6. United Nations. 2015. *World Population Ageing*. Economics & Social Affairs. New York: United Nations, pp. 1–164. Available at: http://www.un.org/en/development/desa/population/publications/pdf/ageing/WPA2015_Report.pdf

7. Kiers, B. 2017. *Banks and insurers turn financial risks into care*. Zorgvisie. Retrieved from https://www.zorgvisie.nl/banken-en-verzekeraars-wentelen-financiele-risicos-af-op-zorg/
8. Top managers might face less monitoring than managers at lower levels. Nevertheless, top management faces monitoring from the many stakeholders that the healthcare sector embeds. Consequently, we have decided to not make a distinction across management levels, also because research has shown that managers at all levels may contribute substantially to innovation—see Burgers and Jansen (2008) and Simsek et al. (2015).
9. United Nations. 2015. *World Population Ageing*. Economics & Social Affairs. New York: United Nations, pp. 1–164. Retrieved from http://www.un.org/en/development/desa/population/publications/pdf/ageing/WPA2015_Report.pdf
10. PwC. 2018. *Chronic diseases and conditions are on the rise*. Retrieved from https://www.pwc.com/gx/en/industries/healthcare/emerging-trends-pwc-healthcare/chronic-diseases.html

References

Acquaah, M. 2007. Managerial social capital, strategic orientation, and organizational performance in an emerging economy. *Strategic Management Journal*, 28(12): 1235–1255.

Adler, P. S., and Borys, B. 1996. Two types of bureaucracy: Enabling and coercive. *Administrative Science Quarterly*, 61–89.

Adner, R., and Helfat, C. E. 2003. Corporate effects and dynamic managerial capabilities. *Strategic Management Journal*, 24(10): 1011–1025.

Agarwal, R., and Selen, W. 2009. Dynamic capability building in service value networks for achieving service innovation. *Decision Sciences*, 40(3): 431–475.

Ahgren, B. 2008. Is it better to be big?: The reconfiguration of 21st century hospitals: Responses to a hospital merger in Sweden. *Health Policy*, 87(1): 92–99.

Aiken, L. H., Clarke, S. P., and Sloane, D. M. 2000. Hospital restructuring: Does it adversely affect care and outcomes? *Journal of Nursing Administration*, 30(10): 457–465.

Al-Aali, A., and Teece, D. J. 2014. International entrepreneurship and the theory of the (long-lived) international firm: A capabilities perspective. *Entrepreneurship Theory and Practice*, 38(1): 95–116.

Andrews, R. 2010. Organizational social capital, structure and performance. *Human Relations*, 63(5): 583–608.

Angeli, F., and Jaiswal, A. K. 2016. Business model innovation for inclusive health care delivery at the bottom of the pyramid. *Organization & Environment*, 29(4): 486–507.

Angst, C. M., and Agarwal, R. 2009. Adoption of electronic health records in the presence of privacy concerns: The elaboration likelihood model and individual persuasion. *MIS Quarterly*, 33(2): 339–370.

Arend, R. J. 2014. Entrepreneurship and dynamic capabilities: How firm age and size affect the 'capability enhancement—SME performance' relationship. *Small Business Economics*, 42(1): 33–57.

Arthurs, J. D., and Busenitz, L. W. 2006. Dynamic capabilities and venture performance: The effects of venture capitalists. *Journal of Business Venturing*, 21(2): 195–215.

Augier, M., and Teece, D. J. 2008. Strategy as evolution with design: The foundations of dynamic capabilities and the role of managers in the economic system. *Organization Studies*, 29(8–9): 1187–1208.

Augier, M., and Teece, D. J. 2009. Dynamic capabilities and the role of managers in business strategy and economic performance. *Organization Science*, 20(2): 410–421.

Baker, T., and Nelson, R. E. 2005. Creating something from nothing: Resource construction through entrepreneurial bricolage. *Administrative Science Quarterly*, 50(3): 329–366.

Balogun, J., and Hailey, V. H. 2008. *Exploring Strategic Change*. Essex, England: Pearson Education.

Banaszak-Holl, J., Nembhard, I., Taylor, L., and Bradley, E. H. 2011. Leadership and management: A framework for action. In L. R. Burns, E. H. Bradley, and B. J. Weiner (Eds.), *Shortell and Kaluzny's Healthcare Management: Organization Design and Behavior*. Clifton Park, NY: Delmar Cengage Learning.

Barello, S., Triberti, S., Graffigna, G., Libreri, C., Serino, S., Hibbard, J., and Riva, G. 2016. eHealth for patient engagement: A systematic review. *Frontiers in Psychology*, 6: 2013.

Barley, S. R. 2010. Building an institutional field to corral a government: A case to set an agenda for organization studies. *Organization Studies*, 31(6): 777–805.

Barrett, F. J. 1998. Coda—creativity and improvisation in jazz and organizations: Implications for organizational learning. *Organization Science*, 9(5): 605–622.

Bass, B. M., and Avolio, B. J. 1993. Transformational leadership and organizational culture. *Public Administration Quarterly*, 112–121.

Bassett-Jones, N. 2005. The paradox of diversity management, creativity and innovation. *Creativity and Innovation Management*, 14(2): 169–175.

Becker, M. C. 2004. Organizational routines: A review of the literature. *Industrial and Corporate Change*, 13(4): 643–678.

Berwick, D. M. 2009. What 'patient-centered' should mean: Confessions of an extremist. *Health Affairs*, 28(4): w555–w565.

Bingham, C. B., and Eisenhardt, K. M. 2011. Rational heuristics: The 'simple rules' that strategists learn from process experience. *Strategic Management Journal*, 32(13): 1437–1464.

Bingham, C. B., and Eisenhardt, K. M. 2014. Response to Vuori and Vuori's commentary on 'Heuristics in the strategy context'. *Strategic Management Journal*, 35(11): 1698–1702.

Birkinshaw, J., Hamel, G., and Mol, M. J. 2008. Management innovation. *Academy of Management Review*, 33(4): 825–845.

Black, A. D., Car, J., Pagliari, C., Anandan, C., Cresswell, K., Bokun, T., McKinstry, B., Procter, R., Majeed, A., and Sheikh, A. 2011. The impact of eHealth on the quality and safety of health care: A systematic overview. *PLoS Medicine*, 8(1): e1000387.

Blaya, J. A., Fraser, H. S., and Holt, B. 2010. E-health technologies show promise in developing countries. *Health Affairs*, 29(2): 244–251.

Blind, K. 2012. The influence of regulations on innovation: A quantitative assessment for OECD countries. *Research Policy*, 41(2): 391–400.

Boonstra, A., Versluis, A., and Vos, J. F. 2014. Implementing electronic health records in hospitals: A systematic literature review. *BMC Health Services Research*, 14(1): 370.

Boyne, G. A. 2002. Public and private management: What's the difference? *Journal of Management Studies*, 39(1): 97–122.

Bozeman, B., and Kingsley, G. 1998. Risk culture in public and private organizations. *Public Administration Review*, 109–118.

Brousseau, K. R., Driver, M. J., Eneroth, K., and Larson, R. 1996. Career pandemonium: Realigning organizations and individuals. *The Academy of Management Executive*, 10(4): 52–66.

Brown, S. L., and Eisenhardt, K. M. 1997. The art of continuous change: Linking complexity theory and time-paced evolution in relentlessly shifting organizations. *Administrative Science Quarterly*, 1–34.

Bruns, H. C. 2013. Working alone together: Coordination in collaboration across domains of expertise. *Academy of Management Journal*, 56(1): 62–83.

Burgers, H., and Jansen, J. J. 2008. Organizational ambidexterity and corporate entrepreneurship: The differential effects on venturing, innovation and renewal processes. *Frontiers of Entrepreneurship Research*, 28(19): 2.

Burns, L. R., Bradley, E. H., and Weiner, B. J. 2011. *Shortell and Kaluzny's Healthcare Management: Organization, Design and Behavior*. Clifton Park, NY: Delmar Cengage Learning.

Cameron, K. S., and Quinn, R. E. 2011. *Diagnosing and Changing Organizational Culture: Based on the Competing Values Framework*. San Francisco, CA: John Wiley & Sons.

Cardinal, L. B. 2001. Technological innovation in the pharmaceutical industry: The use of organizational control in managing research and development. *Organization Science*, 12(1): 19–36.

Castanias, R. P., and Helfat, C. E. 2001. The managerial rents model: Theory and empirical analysis. *Journal of Management*, 27(6): 661–678.

Collinson, S., and Wilson, D. C. 2006. Inertia in Japanese organizations: Knowledge management routines and failure to innovate. *Organization Studies*, 27(9): 1359–1387.

Colombo, M. G., and Grilli, L. 2005. Founders' human capital and the growth of new technology-based firms: A competence-based view. *Research Policy*, 34(6): 795–816.

Crant, J. M. 2000. Proactive behavior in organizations. *Journal of Management*, 26(3): 435–462.

Cresswell, K., and Sheikh, A. 2013. Organizational issues in the implementation and adoption of health information technology innovations: An interpretative review. *International Journal of Medical Informatics*, 82.

Dacin, M. T., Dacin, P. A., and Tracey, P. 2011. Social entrepreneurship: A critique and future directions. *Organization Science*, 22(5): 1203–1213.

Damanpour, F., and Schneider, M. 2009. Characteristics of innovation and innovation adoption in public organizations: Assessing the role of managers. *Journal of Public Administration Research and Theory*, 19(3): 495–522.

Davis, J. P., Eisenhardt, K. M., and Bingham, C. B. 2009. Optimal structure, market dynamism, and the strategy of simple rules. *Administrative Science Quarterly*, 54(3): 413–452.

Denis, J.-L., Dompierre, G., Langley, A., and Rouleau, L. 2011. Escalating indecision: Between reification and strategic ambiguity. *Organization Science*, 22(1): 225–244.

Denis, J.-L., Lamothe, L., and Langley, A. 2001. The dynamics of collective leadership and strategic change in pluralistic organizations. *Academy of Management Journal*, 44(4): 809–837.

Denis, J.-L., Langley, A., and Rouleau, L. 2007. Strategizing in pluralistic contexts: Rethinking theoretical frames. *Human Relations*, 60(1): 179–215.

Desa, G., and Basu, S. 2013. Optimization or bricolage? Overcoming resource constraints in global social entrepreneurship. *Strategic Entrepreneurship Journal*, 7(1): 26–49.

De Vos, M., Graafmans, W., Kooistra, M., Meijboom, B., Van Der Voort, P., and Westert, G. 2009. Using quality indicators to improve hospital care: A review of the literature. *International Journal for Quality in Health Care*, 21(2): 119–129.

Di Stefano, G., Peteraf, M., and Verona, G. 2014. The organizational drivetrain: A road to integration of dynamic capabilities research. *The Academy of Management Perspectives*, 28(4): 307–327.

Dittrich, K., Guérard, S., and Seidl, D. 2016. Talking about routines: The role of reflective talk in routine change. *Organization Science*, 27(3): 678–697.

Dosi, G., Nelson, R. R., and Winter, S. G. 2000. *The Nature and Dynamics of Organizational Capabilities*. Oxford: Oxford University Press.

Dunn, M. B., and Jones, C. 2010. Institutional logics and institutional pluralism: The contestation of care and science logics in medical education, 1967–2005. *Administrative Science Quarterly*, 55(1): 114–149.

Edmondson, A. C. 2003. Speaking up in the operating room: How team leaders promote learning in interdisciplinary action teams. *Journal of Management Studies*, 40(6): 1419–1452.

Eggers, J. P., and Kaplan, S. 2013. Cognition and capabilities: A multi-level perspective. *Academy of Management Annals*, 7(1): 295–340.

Eisenhardt, K. M., and Martin, J. A. 2000. Dynamic capabilities: What are they? *Strategic Management Journal*, 1105–1121.

Eng, T. R. 2002. eHealth research and evaluation: Challenges and opportunities. *Journal of Health Communication*, 7(4): 267–272.

Fagermoen, M. S. 1997. Professional identity: Values embedded in meaningful nursing practice. *Journal of Advanced Nursing*, 25(3): 434–441.

Faguet, J.-P. 2004. Does decentralization increase government responsiveness to local needs?: Evidence from Bolivia. *Journal of Public Economics*, 88(3–4): 867–893.

Feldman, M. S., and Pentland, B. T. 2003. Reconceptualizing organizational routines as a source of flexibility and change. *Administrative Science Quarterly*, 48(1): 94–118.

Feldman, M. S., Pentland, B. T., D'Adderio, L., and Lazaric, N. 2016. Beyond routines as things: Introduction to the special issue on routine dynamics. *Organization Science*, 27(3): 505–513.

Ferlie, E., Crilly, T., Jashapara, A., and Peckham, A. 2012. Knowledge mobilisation in healthcare: A critical review of health sector and generic management literature. *Social Science & Medicine*, 74(8): 1297–1304.

Fernandez, S., and Rainey, H. G. 2006. Managing successful organizational change in the public sector. *Public Administration Review*, 66(2): 168–176.

Garriga, H., Von Krogh, G., and Spaeth, S. 2013. How constraints and knowledge impact open innovation. *Strategic Management Journal*, 34(9): 1134–1144.

Garvin, D. A., Edmondson, A. C., and Gino, F. 2008. Is yours a learning organization? *Harvard Business Review*, 86(3): 109.

George, G. 2005. Slack resources and the performance of privately held firms. *Academy of Management Journal*, 48(4): 661–676.

Gong, Y., Huang, J.-C., and Farh, J.-L. 2009. Employee learning orientation, transformational leadership, and employee creativity: The mediating role of employee creative self-efficacy. *Academy of Management Journal*, 52(4): 765–778.

Goodall, A. H. 2011. Physician-leaders and hospital performance: Is there an association? *Social Science & Medicine*, 73(4): 535–539.

Gregory, P., Byrne, P., and Gabbay, M. 2014. Patient experiences of diabetes eHealth. *International Journal of Sociotechnology and Knowledge Development (IJSKD)*, 6(1): 1–17.

Greve, H. R. 2003. A behavioral theory of R&D expenditures and innovations: Evidence from shipbuilding. *Academy of Management Journal*, 46(6): 685–702.

Hall, A., Melin, L., and Nordqvist, M. 2001. Entrepreneurship as radical change in the family business: Exploring the role of cultural patterns. *Family Business Review*, 14(3): 193–208.

Hall, P. 2005. Interprofessional teamwork: Professional cultures as barriers. *Journal of Interprofessional Care*, 19(suppl. 1): 188–196.

Hambrick, D. C., and Mason, P. A. 1984. Upper echelons: The organization as a reflection of its top managers. *Academy of Management Review*, 9(2): 193–206.

Hatch, N. W., and Dyer, J. H. 2004. Human capital and learning as a source of sustainable competitive advantage. *Strategic Management Journal*, 25(12): 1155–1178.

Haveman, H. A. 1993. Follow the leader: Mimetic isomorphism and entry into new markets. *Administrative Science Quarterly*, 593–627.

He, J., and Wang, H. C. 2009. Innovative knowledge assets and economic performance: The asymmetric roles of incentives and monitoring. *Academy of Management Journal*, 52(5): 919–938.

Helfat, C. E., Finkelstein, S., Mitchell, W., Peteraf, M., Singh, H., Teece, D., and Winter, S. G. 2007. *Dynamic Capabilities: Understanding Strategic Change in Organizations*. Oxford, UK: John Wiley & Sons.

Helfat, C. E., and Martin, J. A. 2015. Dynamic managerial capabilities: Review and assessment of managerial impact on strategic change. *Journal of Management*, 41(5): 1281–1312.

Helfat, C. E., and Peteraf, M. A. 2003. The dynamic resource-based view: Capability lifecycles. *Strategic Management Journal*, 24(10): 997–1010.

Helfat, C. E., and Peteraf, M. A. 2009. Understanding dynamic capabilities: Progress along a developmental path. *Strategic Organization*, 7(1): 91–102.

Helfat, C. E., and Winter, S. G. 2011. Untangling dynamic and operational capabilities: Strategy for the (N) ever-changing world. *Strategic Management Journal*, 32(11): 1243–1250.

Herzlinger, R. E. 2006. Why innovation in health care is so hard. *Harvard Business Review*, 84(5): 58.

Hewitt-Dundas, N. 2006. Resource and capability constraints to innovation in small and large plants. *Small Business Economics*, 26(3): 257–277.

Hitt, M. A., Ireland, R. D., Sirmon, D. G., and Trahms, C. A. 2011. Strategic entrepreneurship: Creating value for individuals, organizations, and society. *The Academy of Management Perspectives*, 25(2): 57–75.

Hoegl, M., Gibbert, M., and Mazursky, D. 2008. Financial constraints in innovation projects: When is less more? *Research Policy*, 37(8): 1382–1391.

Hoff, T., and Rockmann, K. W. 2011. Power, politics, and conflict management. In L. R. Burns, E. H. Bradley, and B. J. Weiner (Eds.), *Shortell and Kaluzny's Healthcare Management: Organization Design and Behavior*. Clifton Park, NY: Delmar Cengage Learning.

Hornung, S., and Rousseau, D. M. 2007. Active on the job—proactive in change: How autonomy at work contributes to employee support for organizational change. *The Journal of Applied Behavioral Science*, 43(4): 401–426.

Hwang, J., and Christensen, C. M. 2008. Disruptive innovation in health care delivery: A framework for business-model innovation. *Health Affairs*, 27(5): 1329–1335.

Jarzabkowski, P., and Fenton, E. 2006. Strategizing and organizing in pluralistic contexts. *Long Range Planning*, 39(6): 631–648.

Jarzabkowski, P., and Seidl, D. 2008. The role of meetings in the social practice of strategy. *Organization Studies*, 29(11): 1391–1426.

Jensen, M. C., and Meckling, W. H. 1976. Theory of the firm: Managerial behavior, agency costs and ownership structure. *Journal of Financial Economics*, 3(4): 305–360.

Jung, D. I., Chow, C., and Wu, A. 2003. The role of transformational leadership in enhancing organizational innovation: Hypotheses and some preliminary findings. *The Leadership Quarterly*, 14(4–5): 525–544.

Kempner, J., Perlis, C. S., and Merz, J. F. 2005. Forbidden knowledge. *Science*, 307(5711): 854–854.

Kim, T.-Y., Oh, H., and Swaminathan, A. 2006. Framing interorganizational network change: A network inertia perspective. *Academy of Management Review*, 31(3): 704–720.

Kindström, D., Kowalkowski, C., and Sandberg, E. 2013. Enabling service innovation: A dynamic capabilities approach. *Journal of Business Research*, 66(8): 1063–1073.

Kor, Y. Y., and Mesko, A. 2013. Dynamic managerial capabilities: Configuration and orchestration of top executives' capabilities and the firm's dominant logic. *Strategic Management Journal*, 34(2): 233–244.

Kvedar, J., Coye, M. J., and Everett, W. 2014. Connected health: A review of technologies and strategies to improve patient care with telemedicine and telehealth. *Health Affairs*, 33(2): 194–199.

Lee, F., Edmondson, A. C., Thomke, S., and Worline, M. 2004. The mixed effects of inconsistency on experimentation in organizations. *Organization Science*, 15(3): 310–326.

Leung, R. C. 2012. Health information technology and dynamic capabilities. *Health Care Management Review*, 37(1): 43–53.

Liebeskind, J. P. 1997. Keeping organizational secrets: Protective institutional mechanisms and their costs. *Industrial and Corporate Change*, 6(3): 623–663.

Litvak, E., and Bisognano, M. 2011. More patients, less payment: Increasing hospital efficiency in the aftermath of health reform. *Health Affairs*, 30(1): 76–80.

Liu, X., Xiao, W., and Huang, X. 2008. Bounded entrepreneurship and internationalisation of indigenous Chinese private-owned firms. *International Business Review*, 17(4): 488–508.

Martin, J. 2011. Dynamic managerial capabilities and the multibusiness team: The role of episodic teams in executive leadership groups. Organization Science, 22(1), 118–140.

Marvel, M. R., and Lumpkin, G. T. 2007. Technology entrepreneurs' human capital and its effects on innovation radicalness. *Entrepreneurship Theory and Practice*, 31(6): 807–828.

McEvily, B., Perrone, V., and Zaheer, A. 2003. Trust as an organizing principle. *Organization Science*, 14(1): 91–103.

McIver, D., Lengnick-Hall, C. A., Lengnick-Hall, M. L., and Ramachandran, I. 2013. Understanding work and knowledge management from a knowledge-in-practice perspective. *Academy of Management Review*, 38(4): 597–620.

Miller, D., and Chen, M.-J. 1994. Sources and consequences of competitive inertia: A study of the US airline industry. *Administrative Science Quarterly*, 1–23.

Mintzberg, H. 1979. *The Structuring of Organisations: A Synthesis of the Research*. Eaglewoods Cliffs, NJ: Prentice-Hall.

Mosa, A. S. M., Yoo, I., and Sheets, L. 2012. A systematic review of healthcare applications for smartphones. *BMC Medical Informatics and Decision Making*, 12(1): 67.

Moussa, M. 2011. Communication. In L. R. Burns, E. H. Bradley, and B. J. Weiner (Eds.), *Shortell and Kaluzny's Healthcare Management: Organization, Design and Behavior*, 6th ed. Clifton Park, NY: Delmar Cengage Learning.

Nadkarni, S., and Barr, P. S. 2008. Environmental context, managerial cognition, and strategic action: An integrated view. *Strategic Management Journal*, 29(13): 1395–1427.

Neter, E., and Brainin, E. 2012. eHealth literacy: Extending the digital divide to the realm of health information. *Journal of Medical Internet Research*, 14(1).

Newbert, S. L. 2005. New firm formation: A dynamic capability perspective. *Journal of Small Business Management*, 43(1): 55–77.

Nicolini, D. 2011. Practice as the site of knowing: Insights from the field of telemedicine. *Organization Science*, 22(3): 602–620.

Nielsen, S. 2010. Top management team diversity: A review of theories and methodologies. *International Journal of Management Reviews*, 12(3): 301–316.

Noordegraaf, M., and Van der Meulen, M. 2008. Professional power play: Organizing management in health care. *Public Administration*, 86(4): 1055–1069.

Nutbeam, D. 2008. The evolving concept of health literacy. *Social Science & Medicine*, 67(12): 2072–2078.

Ossebaard, H. C., van Gemert-Pijnen, J. E., van Gemert-Pijnen, J., Peters, O., and Ossebaard, H. 2013. Introduction: The future of health care. *Improving eHealth*.

Pablo, A. L., Reay, T., Dewald, J. R., and Casebeer, A. L. 2007. Identifying, enabling and managing dynamic capabilities in the public sector. *Journal of Management Studies*, 44(5): 687–708.

Parker, S. K., Williams, H. M., and Turner, N. 2006. Modeling the antecedents of proactive behavior at work. *Journal of Applied Psychology*, 91(3): 636.

Pentland, B. T., and Feldman, M. S. 2008. Designing routines: On the folly of designing artifacts, while hoping for patterns of action. *Information and Organization*, 18(4): 235–250.

Peteraf, M., Di Stefano, G., and Verona, G. 2013. The elephant in the room of dynamic capabilities: Bringing two diverging conversations together. *Strategic Management Journal*, 34(12): 1389–1410.

Pitts, D. W., Hicklin, A. K., Hawes, D. P., and Melton, E. 2010. What drives the implementation of diversity management programs? Evidence from public organizations. *Journal of Public Administration Research and Theory*, 20(4): 867–886.

Piwek, L., Ellis, D. A., Andrews, S., and Joinson, A. 2016. The rise of consumer health wearables: Promises and barriers. *PLoS Medicine*, 13(2): e1001953.

Porter, M. E., and Lee, T. H. 2013. Why health care is stuck—and how to fix it. *Harvard Business Review*.

Porter, M. E., and Teisberg, E. O. 2006. *Redefining Health Care: Creating Value-based Competition on Results*. Cambridge, MA: Harvard Business Press.

Portes, A. 1998. Social capital: Its origins and applications in modern sociology. *Annual Review of Sociology*, 24(1): 1–24.

Pratt, M. G., Rockmann, K. W., and Kaufmann, J. B. 2006. Constructing professional identity: The role of work and identity learning cycles in the customization of identity among medical residents. *Academy of Management Journal*, 49(2): 235–262.

Priem, R. L., and Butler, J. E. 2001. Is the resource-based 'view' a useful perspective for strategic management research? *Academy of Management Review*, 26(1): 22–40.

Protogerou, A., Caloghirou, Y., and Lioukas, S. 2011. Dynamic capabilities and their indirect impact on firm performance. *Industrial and Corporate Change*, 21(3): 615–647.

Retzlaff-Roberts, D., Chang, C. F., and Rubin, R. M. 2004. Technical efficiency in the use of health care resources: A comparison of OECD countries. *Health Policy*, 69(1): 55–72.

Reynolds, S. J., Schultz, F. C., and Hekman, D. R. 2006. Stakeholder theory and managerial decision-making: Constraints and implications of balancing stakeholder interests. *Journal of Business Ethics*, 64(3): 285–301.

Ridic, G., Gleason, S., and Ridic, O. 2012. Comparisons of health care systems in the United States, Germany and Canada. *Materia Socio-medica*, 24(2): 112.

Rosso, B. D. 2014. Creativity and constraints: Exploring the role of constraints in the creative processes of research and development teams. *Organization Studies*, 35(4): 551–585.

Rynning, E. 2007. Public trust and privacy in shared electronic health records. *European Journal of Health Law*, 14(2): 105–112.

Salvato, C., and Vassolo, R. 2017. The sources of dynamism in dynamic capabilities. *Strategic Management Journal*, 1(1): 1–25.

Schilke, O. 2014. On the contingent value of dynamic capabilities for competitive advantage: The nonlinear moderating effect of environmental dynamism. *Strategic Management Journal*, 35(2): 179–203.

Schilke, O., Hu, S., and Helfat, C. 2017. Quo Vadis, dynamic capabilities? A content-analytic review of the current state of knowledge and recommendations for future research. *Academy of Management Annals*, (12)1: 390–439.

Schreyögg, G., and Sydow, J. 2010. Crossroads—organizing for fluidity? Dilemmas of new organizational forms. *Organization Science*, 21(6): 1251–1262.

Shane, S. A. 1992. Why do some societies invent more than others? *Journal of Business Venturing*, 7(1): 29–46.

Simon, H. A. 1959. Theories of decision-making in economics and behavioral science. *The American Economic Review*, 49(3): 253–283.

Simsek, Z., Jansen, J. J., Minichilli, A., and Escriba-Esteve, A. 2015. Strategic leadership and leaders in entrepreneurial contexts: A nexus for innovation and impact missed? *Journal of Management Studies*, 52(4): 463–478.

Sirén, C. A., Kohtamäki, M., and Kuckertz, A. 2012. Exploration and exploitation strategies, profit performance, and the mediating role of strategic learning: Escaping the exploitation trap. *Strategic Entrepreneurship Journal*, 6(1): 18–41.

Sirmon, D., and Hitt, M. 2009. Contingencies within dynamic managerial capabilities: Interdependent effects of resource investment and deployment on firm performance. Strategic Management Journal, 30(13): 1375–1394.

Skjørshammer, M. 2002. Understanding conflicts between health professionals: A narrative approach. *Qualitative Health Research*, 12(7): 915–931.

Smith, C. 2004. New technology continues to invade healthcare: What are the strategic implications/outcomes? *Nursing Administration Quarterly*, 28(2): 92–98.

Sonenshein, S. 2016. Routines and creativity: From dualism to duality. *Organization Science*, 27(3): 739–758.

Sørensen, J. B., and Stuart, T. E. 2000. Aging, obsolescence, and organizational innovation. *Administrative Science Quarterly*, 45(1): 81–112.

Sosa, M. E., Eppinger, S. D., and Rowles, C. M. 2004. The misalignment of product architecture and organizational structure in complex product development. *Management Science*, 50(12): 1674–1689.

Strong, D. M., and Volkoff, O. 2010. Understanding Organization—Enterprise system fit: A path to theorizing the information technology artifact. *MIS Quarterly*, 731–756.

Stubbart, C. I. 1989. Managerial cognition: A missing link in strategic management research. *Journal of Management Studies*, 26(4): 325–347.

Teece, D. J. 2007. Explicating dynamic capabilities: The nature and microfoundations of (sustainable) enterprise performance. *Strategic Management Journal*, 28(13): 1319–1350.

Teece, D. J. 2010. Technological innovation and the theory of the firm: The role of enterprise-level knowledge, complementarities, and (dynamic) capabilities. In *Handbook of the Economics of Innovation*, Vol. 1., Berkeley, CA: Elsevier, 679–730.

Teece, D. J. 2012. Dynamic capabilities: Routines versus entrepreneurial action. *Journal of Management Studies*, 49(8): 1395–1401.

Teece, D. J. 2017. Business models and dynamic capabilities. *Long Range Planning*.

Teece, D. J., Pisano, G., and Shuen, A. 1997. Dynamic capabilities and strategic management. *Strategic Management Journal*, 18(7): 509–533.

Thielst, C. B. 2007. The future of healthcare technology. *Journal of Healthcare Management*, 52(1): 7.

Tjora, A. H., and Scambler, G. 2009. Square pegs in round holes: Information systems, hospitals and the significance of contextual awareness. *Social Science and Medicine*, 68: 519–525.

Tsai, W., and Ghoshal, S. 1998. Social capital and value creation: The role of intrafirm networks. *Academy of Management Journal*, 41(4): 464–476.

Tucker, A. L., and Edmondson, A. C. 2003. Why hospitals don't learn from failures: Organizational and psychological dynamics that inhibit system change. *California Management Review*, 45(2): 55–72.

Van de Ven, W. P., and Schut, F. T. 2008. Universal mandatory health insurance in the Netherlands: A model for the United States? *Health Affairs*, 27(3): 771–781.

Van Van de Ven, W. P., and Schut, F. T. 2009. Managed competition in the Netherlands: Still work-in-progress. *Health Economics*, 18(3): 253–255.

Volberda, H. W. 1996. Toward the flexible form: How to remain vital in hypercompetitive environments. *Organization Science*, 7(4): 359–374.

Volberda, H. W., Baden-Fuller, C., and Van Den Bosch, F. A. 2001. Mastering strategic renewal: Mobilising renewal journeys in multi-unit firms. *Long Range Planning*, 34(2): 159–178.

Volberda, H. W., and Karali, E. 2015. Reframing the compositional capability: A resource-based view on 'a composition-based view of firm growth'. *Management and Organization Review*, 11(3): 419–426.

Wardhani, V., Utarini, A., van Dijk, J. P., Post, D., and Groothoff, J. W. 2009. Determinants of quality management systems implementation in hospitals. *Health Policy*, 89(3): 239–251.

Weerawardena, J., Mort, G. S., Liesch, P. W., and Knight, G. 2007. Conceptualizing accelerated internationalization in the born global firm: A dynamic capabilities perspective. *Journal of World Business*, 42(3): 294–306.

Westra, D., Angeli, F., Jatautaitė, E., Carree, M., and Ruwaard, D. 2016. Understanding specialist sharing: A mixed-method exploration in an increasingly price-competitive hospital market. *Social Science & Medicine*, 162: 133–142.

Wiersema, M. F., and Bantel, K. A. 1992. Top management team demography and corporate strategic change. *Academy of Management Journal*, 35(1): 91–121.

Wilden, R., Devinney, T. M., and Dowling, G. R. 2016. The architecture of dynamic capability research identifying the building blocks of a configurational approach. *The Academy of Management Annals*, 10(1): 997–1076.

Wilden, R., and Gudergan, S. P. 2015. The impact of dynamic capabilities on operational marketing and technological capabilities: Investigating the role of environmental turbulence. *Journal of the Academy of Marketing Science*, 43(2): 181–199.

Wilden, R., Gudergan, S. P., Nielsen, B. B., and Lings, I. 2013. Dynamic capabilities and performance: Strategy, structure and environment. *Long Range Planning*, 46(1–2): 72–96.

Willem, A., Buelens, M., and De Jonghe, I. 2007. Impact of organizational structure on nurses' job satisfaction: A questionnaire survey. *International Journal of Nursing Studies*, 44(6): 1011–1020.

Winter, S. G. 2003. Understanding dynamic capabilities. *Strategic Management Journal*, 24(10): 991–995.

Yiu, D. W., and Lau, C. M. 2008. Corporate entrepreneurship as resource capital configuration in emerging market firms. *Entrepreneurship Theory and Practice*, 32(1): 37–57.

Zahra, S. A., Sapienza, H. J., and Davidsson, P. 2006. Entrepreneurship and dynamic capabilities: A review, model and research agenda. *Journal of Management Studies*, 43(4): 917–955.

Zbaracki, M. J., and Bergen, M. 2010. When truces collapse: A longitudinal study of price-adjustment routines. *Organization Science*, 21(5): 955–972.

Zollo, M., and Winter, S. G. 2002. Deliberate learning and the evolution of dynamic capabilities. *Organization Science*, 13(3): 339–351.

Zott, C., and Amit, R. 2008. The fit between product market strategy and business model: Implications for firm performance. *Strategic Management Journal*, 29(1): 1–26.

7 Open Service Innovation for Healthcare Organizations

Ralf Wilden and Krithika Randhawa

Introduction

Healthcare service providers have experienced significant changes over the last decade (Thakur et al., 2012; Joiner and Lusch, 2016). Entrepreneurial activities and innovations have emerged from several industry players along the healthcare value chain. Besides significant innovations around new drugs and technologies (Faulkner and Kent, 2001; Folland et al., 2016) affecting healthcare services, other more service-related health innovations have significantly affected the industry. For example, online platforms have emerged that enable an increasing number of patients to use self-diagnosis tools and communicate with each other, often leading to patients challenging clinicians' advice, and the advent of wearable devices, such as smartwatches, which collect significant amounts of health-related data, has led to new health services and increasing patient "health literacy." Thus, healthcare service providers have to deal with both product and service innovations originating from outside their own firm boundaries. However, little do we know about how healthcare service providers could benefit from such external knowledge directly to improve their own service innovation processes (Bullinger et al., 2012). Thus, in this chapter we review innovation in healthcare in general and outline possible benefits for healthcare service providers of engaging in open service innovation activities.

Innovation, in general, comprises three aspects: (i) novelty, (ii) an application component, and (iii) an intended benefit (Länsisalmi et al., 2006). In its broadest definition, "innovation in healthcare is defined as those changes that help healthcare practitioners focus on the patient by helping healthcare professionals work smarter, faster, better and more cost effectively" (Thakur et al., 2012: 564). Driving and adopting innovation is a critical capability of healthcare service providers (Länsisalmi et al., 2006). Healthcare organizations, in general, often face significant hurdles when conducting innovation, for example, restrictive regulations and different expectations from varying stakeholders (such as patients, government, and suppliers) (Folland et al., 2016). Traditionally, innovation has been defined as introducing a new product, creating new markets, redefining an industry, redesigning production or processes, or acquiring a new source of supply (Schumpeter, 1934). Accordingly, much previous innovation research in general, and research on the healthcare industry more specifically, has focused on product manufacturers such as pharmaceutical companies and medical instrument manufacturers. Significantly less research has investigated service innovation, such the innovative activities of healthcare service providers (Nambisan, 2010). Furthermore, although healthcare service providers, such as hospitals, have been affected by technology and service innovations, many of these innovations have been developed by other members of the existing value chain, or even by newcomers (such as most health applications for mobile phones).

Given that much innovation occurs outside of healthcare providers, we urge healthcare organizations to reconsider their approach to innovation and work with outside partners. This is in line with previous research that has argued that healthcare organizations to include patients into their healthcare services to enhance the quality and value of their offerings (Nambisan and Nambisan, 2009). This has led to organizations establishing online health communities through which patients can interact with each other to offer support and share knowledge. However, only limited research has looked at how external stakeholders such as patients can be included the healthcare organizations innovation processes, which has been labeled open innovation (Bullinger et al., 2012). A departure from the traditional innovation paradigm, this novel approach to innovation stresses the importance of both internal and external paths to developing and commercializing inventions (Randhawa et al., 2016; Chesbrough, 2003b). For-profit organizations have increasingly adopted "open innovation" (OI) strategies by opening up their firm boundaries to foster collaboration and knowledge exchange with external partners to leverage complementary resources and capabilities, and to increase the commercialization speed of innovations (e.g., Chesbrough, 2003b; West and Gallagher, 2006).

Therefore, in this chapter, we will provide insights into open innovation in general, and open service innovation in particular, and discuss the possible benefits of using crowdsourcing, a popular open innovation mechanism in for-profit organizations, to drive innovative behavior in the healthcare industry, with a particular focus on healthcare service providers such as hospitals. To illustrate the possible workings and benefits of open innovation for healthcare, we will present an illustrative case vignette of The Royal Women's Hospital, a large Australian metropolitan healthcare provider, which we develop from vivid, concrete, and rich qualitative data (see, for example, Kleinbaum and Stuart, 2014).

Background

Innovation in Healthcare

Innovation is an important driver of firm growth and creates value for societies. Innovations in healthcare embody a distinctive and rather difficult case (Länsisalmi et al., 2006). Previous research has found that changing established medical practices and attitudes and behaviors of healthcare organizations and clinicians is challenging (Greco and Eisenberg, 1993; Shortell et al., 1998) due to substantial risks related to financial, social, and ethical issues (Collyer, 1994; Faulkner and Kent, 2001). The implementation of innovations is usually heavily regulated by laws (Faulkner and Kent, 2001). Furthermore, the typical value chain in healthcare (see Figure 7.1) comprises many different players at various stages of the value-generating process, making the process of healthcare innovation complex.

Innovation can be driven by any player along the value chain. Thus, innovation in healthcare can, for example, be a new product (e.g., a new drug or medical device), a new way of delivering a service (e.g., online health consultation), a service product innovation (e.g., a new insurance, medical equipment), or an innovative business model (e.g., online pharmacies). Thus, innovations in healthcare organizations are typically reflected in the introduction of new services, new ways of working, and/or new technologies (Länsisalmi et al., 2006). As outlined before, healthcare innovations are aimed at realizing an intended benefit (Länsisalmi et al., 2006). These benefits can be described in terms of benefits to the patient, and in terms of benefits to the healthcare provider. The former may comprise better health or less suffering from illness (Faulkner and Kent, 2001). The latter see benefits typically including improved internal operations efficiency and/or patient care quality (Länsisalmi et al., 2006).

Much innovation in the healthcare industry has traditionally been initiated by the manufacturers of healthcare products (e.g., drugs and medical devices), ultimately affecting providers, such as hospitals, and ultimately patients. Consequently, much research focus has been on innovation activities in medical devices for clinical diagnosis, intervention, and treatment of diseases, leading to significant advancement "in surgical equipments, non-invasive treatment methods, and radiological instruments as well as advancements in the pharmaceutical innovation (i.e., drug discovery) processes" (Nambisan, 2010: 163).

However, this has led to a paucity in research on patient-facing service providers and their innovative activities, which is especially concerning as it has been the healthcare providers who to a large extent control how innovations are used and affect patient treatment (Burns, 2012). Furthermore, research is needed in this area as "customer satisfaction and customer approval rates of many of our hospitals are at an all-time low" (Nambisan, 2010: 163). As outlined in Chapter 1 of this book, there has not been much cross-fertilization between healthcare and management research. Also, previous research has stressed that "Effective healthcare organizations facilitate the development of knowledge and emphasize market orientation" (Thakur et al., 2012: 564). Therefore, we suggest that opening up organizational boundaries, and thus being more

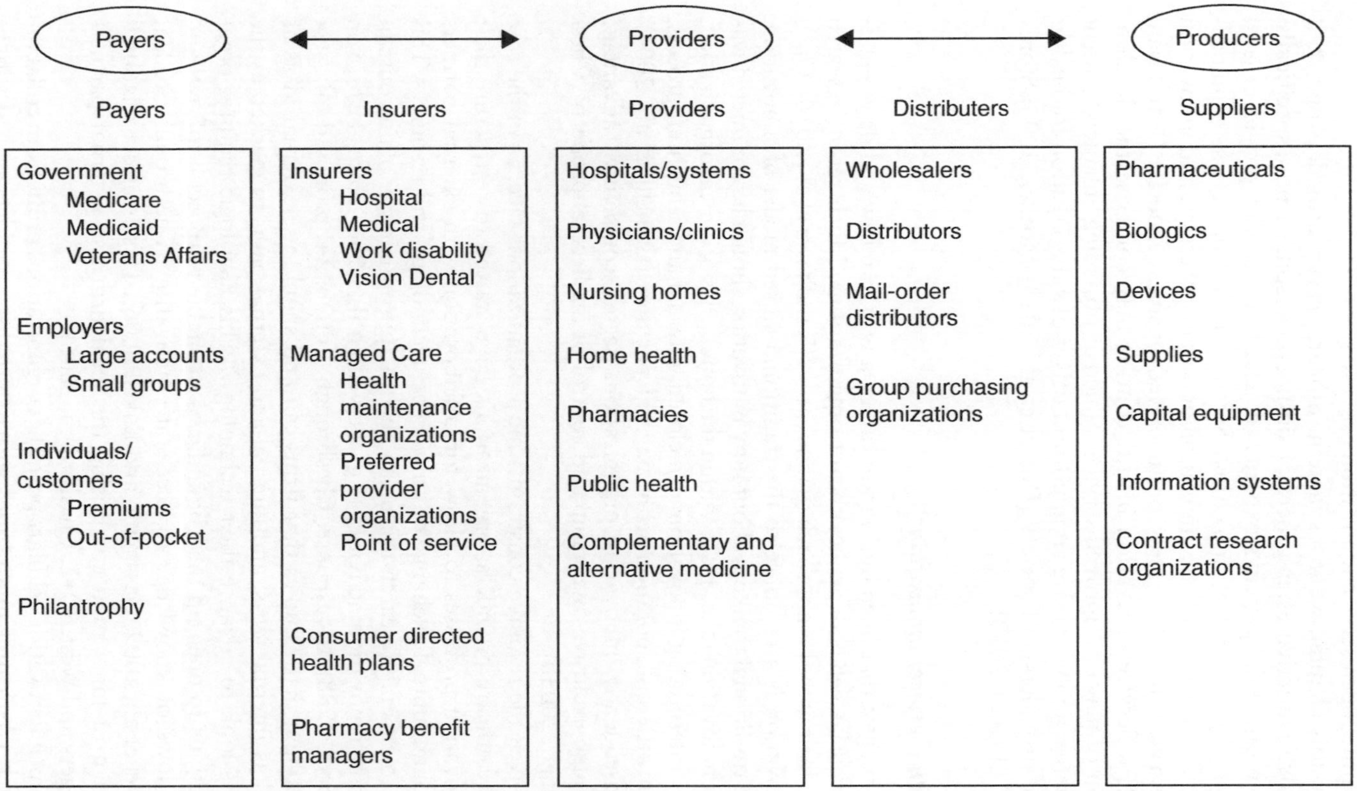

Figure 7.1 A Typical Value Chain in Healthcare (Burns, 2012)

market-oriented, can be achieved by healthcare service providers through adopting open service innovation processes.

In this chapter, we investigate healthcare service providers and their innovative activities, in general, focusing on hospitals, more specifically. To improve the patient's experience, healthcare service providers need to engage in service innovation. Service innovation refers to innovation in service products, innovation in service processes, and innovation in service firms (i.e., new or improved business models) (Nambisan, 2010). Service innovation in this context may comprise the development of new or improved services aimed at providing enhanced patient benefits, and which are an important driver of value creation for healthcare providers and society (Dotzel et al., 2013; Moeller, 2008; Storey and Hughes, 2013).

Open (Service) Innovation

We suggest that open innovation can be a way to renew and drive entrepreneurial behavior in healthcare organizations. Much recent research has dealt with this approach to innovation (Randhawa et al., 2016). Open innovation is a response to the traditional closed model of innovation. The traditional thinking about how innovation should be conducted was that innovation takes place within the boundaries of a focal organization, thus interpreting innovation as a closed, internal and sequential process, with little collaboration with external partners (Cainelli et al., 2004). Consequently, innovating organizations secure competitive advantage through exclusive ownership and control of intellectual property (Chesbrough, 2003b).

Given the resource constraints most organizations face, as in the case of healthcare providers, organizations have started to restructure their innovation processes to allow for collaboration with external partners through mutual exchange of knowledge, technology, and resources. This led to existing research not being able to appropriately explain contemporary innovation activities (e.g., Powell et al., 1996; Teece, 1986; von Hippel, 1988). In response, Chesbrough (2003b: 24) proposed OI as "a paradigm that assumes that firms can and should use external ideas as well as internal ideas, and internal and external paths to market, as the firms look to advance their technology." This new logic requires organizations to open up their boundaries to enable purposeful inflows and outflows of knowledge to accelerate innovation (Chesbrough, 2003a; Enkel et al., 2009; Gassmann and Enkel, 2006). This creates a relational system of innovation comprising the focal firm and external partners (Bogers and West, 2012; Chesbrough, 2006).

Open innovation scholars posit that organizations profit from collaboratively co-creating innovations with external stakeholders such as suppliers and customers (e.g., Chesbrough, 2003b; West and Gallagher, 2006).

Open innovation modes can be disaggregated into outbound, inbound, and coupled processes (West and Bogers, 2014; Enkel et al., 2009). Outbound or inside-out processes comprise the commercialization of internal knowledge, for example, through out-licensing technology (Lichtenthaler et al., 2010). Inbound or outside-in processes comprise the search and acquisition of knowledge from a various external sources, including suppliers and customers (e.g., Cassiman and Veugelers, 2006; Hughes and Wareham, 2010; Lau et al., 2010). Coupled processes combine outside-in and inside-out processes between complementary partners, as seen in interfirm alliances (de Araújo Burcharth et al., 2014; Greul et al., 2016). Previous research has provided us with valuable insights into the various means through which organizations can leverage external knowledge including interfirm R&D alliances and technology partnerships (e.g., Seldon, 2011; Vanhaverbeke et al., 2008), to novel approaches such as crowdsourcing for innovation (Poetz and Schreier, 2012; Afuah and Tucci, 2012). West and Bogers (2014) map research on inbound open innovation into a three-phase model of obtaining, integrating, and commercializing external innovations (Figure 7.2). Our focus in this chapter is on such outbound open innovation; that is, how healthcare providers can access and integrate external sources of innovation, in particular, by crowdsourcing from their consumer or patients.

Much previous research on open innovation, however, has investigated manufacturing and product-based businesses (Mina et al., 2014). Looking at the specific case of healthcare service providers, the majority of relevant innovations revolve around service innovation, albeit being supported by new technologies. Service innovations represent "a new service experience or service solution that consists of one or several of the following dimensions: new service concept, new customer interaction, new value system/business partners, new revenue model, new organizational or technological service delivery system" (den Hertog et al., 2010: 494). It is the very nature of services that they typically comprise a high degree of interactivity with various stakeholders, especially customers, across multiple "touchpoints" (Berry et al., 2006; Sampson and Spring, 2012),

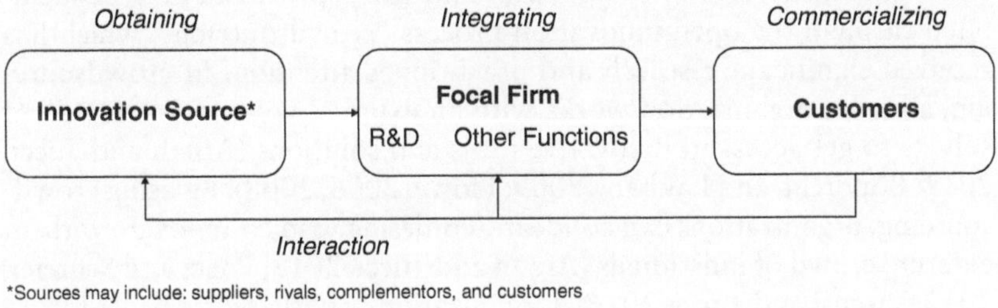

Figure 7.2 A Four-Phase Process Model for Leveraging External Sources of Innovation (West and Bogers, 2014)

and include multiple service ecosystem partners, such as suppliers (Kindström et al., 2013; Lusch et al., 2010). Furthermore, service innovation frequently heavily rests on input from customers to co-create output and value (Chesbrough, 2011a; Vargo and Lusch, 2004). Therefore, scholars have introduced the idea of open service innovation (Chesbrough, 2011a, 2011b), which rests on service co-creation logic which is aimed at developing novel solutions that focus on customer benefits rather than service features alone. This requires cooperating with value network stakeholders such as customers in the innovation process.

Chesbrough's (2011a, 2011b) work amalgamates the paradigms of open innovation and service innovation. The concept of open service innovation posits that, with services such as healthcare providing the growth vehicle in today's economy, applying a service-oriented logic to innovation can more effectively differentiate such business in the largely commoditized marketplace. The open innovation business model can be thus be applied to service businesses to leverage service innovation outcomes and one way to do this is to collaborate closely with customers across all stages of the innovation cycle. Chesbrough (2011a, 2011b) outlines four fundamental characteristics of open service innovation, which posits that organizations need to: (i) view themselves as open service businesses, (ii) invite customers to co-create innovations, (iii) collaborate with other value network entities to create economies of scale and scope in the open service innovation process, and (iv) create a platform business model to leverage their capabilities and competences in sustaining open service innovation.

Open Service Innovation Through Crowdsourcing

Co-creation with customers—and in the specific case of healthcare service providers, patients—is an important driver of successful service innovation (Lusch et al., 2010). In the context of healthcare, previous research has suggested that including the broader public and patients into healthcare R&D may both increase the quality and relevance of innovative outputs by providing additional knowledge that organizations may not have (Bullinger et al., 2012; Boote et al., 2010). Including large groups of external stakeholders into organizational R&D processes may be facilitated through the open innovation process "crowdsourcing," which has received significant research and practitioner attention. In crowdsourcing, a seeker organization works with an external voluntary "crowd" of solvers to get access to innovative ideas and solutions (Afuah and Tucci, 2012; Boudreau and Lakhani, 2009; Howe, 2006, 2008). By using crowdsourcing, organizations can co-ideate, co-design, and co-innovate with an external crowd of individuals (Afuah and Tucci, 2012; Poetz and Schreier, 2012; Viscusi and Tucci, 2016). Organizations can therefore benefit from the "wisdom of crowds" and their ability for social knowledge production (Surowiecki, 2005), by outsourcing previously internal innovation processes. This open innovation mechanism also allows to receive input from not only a few partners, but by a large group of individuals (Afuah and Tucci, 2012; Howe, 2006, 2008; Piller and West, 2014).

Previous research has found that crowdsourcing can help organizations to overcome the local search bias inherent in traditional innovation paradigms and to search for solutions outside their own boundaries to identify and make use of new sources of innovation (Lüthje et al., 2005). Crowdsourcing can be classified into: idea competitions (e.g., Piller and Walcher, 2006), innovation contests and tournaments (e.g., Boudreau et al., 2011; Terwiesch and Xu, 2008), and collaborative communities (e.g., Boudreau and Lakhani, 2009). Bullinger et al. (2012) represent a rare example of open service innovation research in healthcare. They studied an open health platform on rare diseases, which is used by stakeholders such as patients, family members, caregivers, and physicians. They find that external stakeholders have the innovative potential to provide significant input into healthcare research and can devise new products and services. Furthermore, Nambisan (2010) presents an exploratory case of an online health information system for patients, hosted by the Center for Health Enhancement Systems Studies at the University of Wisconsin–Madison. They identify critical aspects of knowledge creation (i.e., combination, internalization, externalization, and socialization) driving consumer-driven service innovation, which can be influenced by the healthcare organization.

Illustrative Case of How a Healthcare Services Provider Can Use Open Innovation

Approach

In line with Kleinbaum and Stuart (2014), we illustrate the value of open innovation in healthcare through a case vignette based on vivid and rich data. Rather than generating new theory, we synthesized and extended existing theory on open innovation and innovation in healthcare. Our illustrative case example may be characterized as "revelatory" (Yin, 1994). Recognizing the lack of case studies on the use of open innovation in the healthcare context, our aim was to present an illustrative case of a healthcare service provider that has successfully used open innovation to create value. Following recommendations in previous research (Patton, 1990), we sought to identify a healthcare service provider that could serve as an exemplary source of insights. We present the case of a large metropolitan hospital. The Royal Women's Hospital (the Women's), founded in Melbourne in 1856, is Australia's first and largest specialist public hospital dedicated to providing specialist care to women and newborns through a range of maternity, neonatal, gynecology, and cancer treatment services and support. For more than 160 years, the Women's has led the advocacy and advancement of women's health and wellbeing, and has created a proud legacy of excellence in care. Hospitals play a major role in evolving health economies, and healthcare service provision in hospitals are the most visible factor of total healthcare spending (Folland et al., 2016). We focus on the hospital's implementation of open service innovation through crowdsourcing initiatives, which is an ongoing process. We followed the case through its journey of open service innovation, and report on the hospital's transformation thus far, and its key upcoming initiatives to improve patient engagement in the co-design of services and decision-making.[1]

Illustrative Case Findings

The Royal Women's Hospital's motivation to engage in open service innovation was to improve patient experiences and patient, hospital, and statewide health outcomes, and to ultimately become a leader in these areas. Also, the hospital sought to achieve efficiencies that lead to a more sustainable organization. Finally, a main driver was that community expectations around healthcare have changed. Patients and other stakeholders increasingly take a consumer perspective on healthcare and thus have different expectations on the standards of their overall experience and their involvement in decision-making.

In continuing to build on its reputation as a high-performing hospital in the state of Victoria and being a recognized leader in women's and newborns' health, the Women's is known for constantly developing innovative ways of delivering responsive, patient-centric care and services. In doing so, the Women's is driven by its strategic goal "Our patients and consumers are at the heart of everything we do." Revolving around this strategic goal is its five-year strategic plan, which was developed in 2016 through extensive consultations with patients, consumers, and other community stakeholders, and has informed the development of new services and related resource decisions. The hospital has since spearheaded open service innovation initiatives in a structured way, to re-orient its approaches to care squarely on its patients and consumers. A key resource investment in this direction has been to put together a dedicated Patient and Consumer Experience team—comprising the chief experience officer, the director of patient and consumer experience and system improvement, and two others, coordinator and analyst—to develop a strategy and deliver on it. The director of patient and consumer experience, described how consumer engagement is at the core of their approach to open service innovation:

> Our goal is to involve people at the start of service design ... we have defined a patient and consumer experience strategy and that is based around robust experience design, how we measure and analyze

> experiences, how to implement change that is sustainable, how to make decisions that the consumer or user who is at the center of the decision is involved in those decisions.

To deliver on this goal, the team has developed an initiative called "Partnering with our People, Patients and Consumers," which is based on the International Association of Public Participation framework for collaboration, where the team's focus shifts from merely informing and engaging consumers, to actually empowering them to contribute across different levels of service and care that is provided. This approach has started a shift in the organization from:

> making service decisions in isolation to integrating the end-user upfront in designing services by mapping and implementing open service innovation projects ... so that we are making sure that from the start we know there is patient voice in the room and they are involved in the decision-making ... we want to ramp up this capability of the organization.

All open service innovation efforts have been aligned around their people strategies, as the director explains:

> As you would know in any organization the staff experience delivers patient experience—a really strong positive culture with a great staff experience, you are more likely going to have a better outcome for your customers or patients.

The emphasis has been on developing a culture of exceptional experience across the entire organization, and promoting the notion of having the patient outcome at the heart of everything that is done. To enable this, the team uses an online engagement platform that supplements the delivery of a face-to-face "Creating Exceptional Experience" course, to enhance the skills of frontline staff in personal reflection of attitude and attributes like listening skills, empathy, and bias/perception aimed at translating into better customer service and patient experience. So far, over the course of two years, the Women's have graduated over 750 staff and will continue to run the course over coming years to double this number. This has progressively helped in getting people on-board with the strategic plan and the shift towards open service innovation.

The same online intermediary platform is also used to engage on specific projects and develop a network of clinicians and staff through "the sharing of information and toolkits, forum discussion groups, feedback on services, education materials across multiple projects or programs." For example, the hospital launched a statewide leadership program on developing a framework for embedding the practice of strengthening hospital responses to family violence experienced by patients—an issue identified to disproportionately affect women and their children. A robust set of resources, tools, and training materials are shared publicly via the online platform site which, the intermediary executive confirmed has been successful in "capacity building for staff state-wide to identify instances of people at risk of family and domestic violence." Not only did it create a system-wide response to family violence among hospitals, but also opened up discussion within the broader community. The director also shared another effort in such online collaboration to promote open service innovation in healthcare:

> I have just started up a state-wide professional collaboration forum where we have an online discussion forum and the group of patient experience leaders across public health—we are all members, we get to jump in and discuss what we might be challenged with, ideas we might have, questions we might have.

Focus was also on instilling the decision-making and governance across the organization, which led to a refreshed approach to the well-established Consumer Advisory Committee, and increasing the patient representatives on other committees, and asking project teams to incorporate the consumer voice into their change programs. Overall, the effort was aimed at communicating across all levels that the hospital's move toward open service innovation is "not a project—this is a culture shift—it really is an ongoing program that needs structure and sustainability and capability and investment in the right people—and making sure it has a plan behind it that sustains it." This transformation is at the heart of the hospital's Strategic Plan, backed by the Board. The ensuing initiatives have been personally driven by the CEO, as the Director reveals:

> this is [our CEO's] legacy, this is her passion. Dr Sue Matthews is putting this up in the forefront as something that is extremely important in the leadership team, and the whole executive team is behind it.

In collaborating with patients and consumers, the focus has particularly been on increasingly moving towards crowdsourcing ideas from patients and consumers through the online engagement platform, to co-design services, and co-create value in ultimately providing an exceptional experience of healthcare. The nature of the open service innovation projects that the Women's involved patients and consumers ranged from simple service improvements to strategic issues on statewide initiatives on improving health outcomes for women and newborns.

For example, the hospital, in designing new name badges for staff and volunteers, used Nexus' online engagement platform to ask stakeholders including patients for their input on different design options, as "[we were keen] to know how patients might like staff introduced to them, and what information they would expect to see." The open service innovation intermediary that hosts the engagement platform shared this crowdsourcing initiative on its website, highlighting how the hospital team put together a well-designed and executed online project site to generate significant consumer interest, and achieve amazing results including 500 responses in less than day.

A more strategic co-design project was the Women's development of "Growing Together," an Australian-first parenting kit, that was backed by a $AU1.3 million funding from the State government, and was targeted at improving health literacy by providing new parents well-targeted, trusted, and evidence-based information about pregnancy and early parenting. The "Growing Together" parenting kit—initially comprising a comprehensive illustrated book, an app developed for smartphone and tablet, and a children's book—was designed by and for parents, and in doing so significant input was obtained from that consumer segment via an online engagement platform.

The hospital worked closely with the open service innovation intermediary to support their initiatives. One of the intermediary's executives shared how the Women's used the online platform to engage with parents on their specific needs after they left the hospital system, and in doing so:

> they went and asked what was the most exciting or strangest thing that happened with your new child at home ... they sought stories rather than just running surveys. This is where patient engagement is useful—understanding how people can give input at that meaningful point in time in their healthcare journey.

This co-design project has led to the development of a new service through a smartphone app for all new parents—not just patients of the Women's—which emerged out of their consultation with consumers, and is being trialed at the moment.

Besides online engagement, the hospital also used other face-to-face methodologies such as focus groups and videos for patient storytelling to integrate patient and consumer ideas in designing new services. A project has commenced using such an approach to patient involvement is around developing a new, real-time patient experience feedback loop from patients to frontline medical staff—nurses, midwives, doctors, physiotherapists—anyone who had contact with patients. The idea, once implemented, will provide more regular and consistent feedback from patients on their experience to allow a more agile response to the real pulse of the patients across all touchpoints. Another project that has been underway is focusing on improvements in waiting room experience, which also involved partnering with patients and staff to co-design a better waiting room experience.

Guidelines for Healthcare Services Provider When Using Open Innovation

Our ongoing research, together with other previous studies point to four important levers that entrepreneurial healthcare organizations should use to get the most out of their open innovation activities: (i) engage with and understand your patients, (ii) develop necessary organizational capabilities to guarantee success, (iii) develop an organizational culture and leadership that fosters open service innovation, (iv) develop a service-dominant orientation to stimulate open service innovation, and (iv) seek the support of open service innovation intermediaries.

1. Engage With and Understand Your Patients

Healthcare managers who want to implement open service innovation processes into their organization's portfolio can learn from valuable knowledge gained from existing open innovation and crowdsourcing research. One important advice is to get to know your patients and understand how to best engage them to co-create service innovation. Bullinger et al. (2012), investigating open innovation in healthcare specifically, find that efficient design of open health platforms need to account for the various types of participants (e.g., patients, family members, caregivers, physicians). As their communication content differs, we propose that the design of the platform should mirror these differences. Related research has provided us with insights into how, besides engaging with collaborative communities (Boudreau and Lakhani, 2009; West and Sims, 2017), organizations can also crowdsource innovation via idea competitions (e.g., Piller and Walcher, 2006), innovation contests, and tournaments (e.g., Boudreau et al., 2011; Terwiesch and Xu, 2008; Afuah and Tucci, 2012; Lüttgens et al., 2014). Focusing on the solver side (in our case, the patients) of the crowdsourcing process, studies have highlighted how we can enhance the motivation of solvers to participate in open innovation (e.g., Brabham, 2010) through incentives and award structures, managing the solver pool size (e.g., Boudreau et al., 2011; Terwiesch and Xu, 2008), solvers' professionalism (Füller et al., 2017), and solvers' technical marginality; that is, the distance between the solver's field of expertise and the problem domain (Jeppesen and Lakhani, 2010), and how these positively affect provided solutions (e.g., Boudreau et al., 2011; Terwiesch and Xu, 2008). Other work has shown how the extent of solvers' investment of cognitive, emotional, and physical energy into online interactions and experiences (i.e., solver engagement) shapes their creativity in crowdsourcing contests (Martinez (2015). These studies highlight that given that solvers (i.e., patients or consumers) who contribute to the innovation process are not formally tied to the seekers (i.e., the healthcare providers) as are their employees, there is a need for seekers to engage with the solvers closely to clearly define a solution space, attract their contributions, and direct and align their efforts with the seekers' motives (Hienerth et al., 2011; Lüttgens et al., 2014; Piezunka and Dahlander, 2015).

2. *Develop Necessary Organizational Capabilities to Guarantee Success*

The need for professionalization of practices relating to open service innovation is expressed, for example, in the National Safety and Quality Health Service (NSQHS) Standards by the Australian Commission on Safety and Quality in Health Care (ACSQHC). These state that leaders of a health service organisation implement systems to support partnering with patients, carers and other consumers to improve the safety and quality of care (2014). These guidelines stress governance and partnering with consumers as critical components of effective community engagement; that is, open innovation. Service innovation "is a multi-dimensional, organization-wide challenge to the managers charged with its design and implementation, and that a comprehensive conception of it is therefore essential" (Kindström et al., 2013: 1064). Therefore, it is important for organizations to develop necessary capabilities to conduct open service innovation. This professionalization of internal processes to manage open service innovation is important to conduct such processes more effectively and efficiently.

The dynamic capability framework may serve a starting point to better understand necessary capabilities to implement open service innovation within the organization. This framework has provided us with important insights into how organizations can identify opportunities, seize opportunities by making necessary investments and other resource commitments, and reconfigure the existing resource base in line with internal and external changes (Teece, 2007; Wilden and Gudergan, 2015; Wilden et al., 2013; Wilden et al., 2016). Kindström et al. (2013) suggest that these processes can be applied to the case of service innovation. They find that in terms of *sensing*, service organizations should deploy customer-linked service sensing, service system sensing, internal sensing, and technology exploration. In order to *seize* service innovation opportunities, they identify service interactions, managing the service delivery process, structuring the service development process, and adopting new revenue mechanisms as crucial processes. For example, in the healthcare context, clinicians are typically most familiar with experimental research methods to assess healthcare innovations. However, they have considerably more difficulty with evaluating innovations in organizational practices or how to structure innovations; these types of innovations often require different evaluation approaches derived from social science research, and which may not provide "hard" evidence, to service innovation opportunities, and thus may lack credibility in the eyes of clinicians (Pope and Mays, 2000). Finally, *reconfiguring* for service innovation comprises orchestration of the service system, balancing product- and service-innovation-related assets, and the development of a service-oriented mental model.

3. *Develop an Organizational Culture and Leadership That Fosters Open Service Innovation*

To further professionalize open service innovation within healthcare organizations, it is important to consider wider organizational aspects besides necessary firm capabilities. Previous research in innovation in healthcare is likely to be more successful if the organizational culture supports interactivity between employees (Fitzgerald et al., 2002). Furthermore, a culture of blame and secrecy (often driven by the health practitioners' inclinations to protect their individual independence and status) has been found to hinder organizational learning and innovations (Huntington et al., 2000). Furthermore, studies have shown that strong leadership driving motivation and participation of personnel and sufficient resources (financial, instrumental, and personal) all seem to be positively related to innovative culture and outcomes in healthcare organizations (e.g., Edmondson et al., 2001; Länsisalmi and Kivimäki, 1999).

The finding that firm culture and leadership is an important driver of or barrier to innovation is in line with findings in open innovation research (e.g., Randhawa and Wilden, 2016; Randhawa et al., 2018), which finds that a senior executive's buy-in as well as strategic intent, as well as a culture that is "open" to open innovation is critical to implement successful crowdsourcing projects. Several studies (e.g., Antons and Piller, 2015; Chesbrough and Crowther, 2006) have studied cultural and leadership barriers to open innovation through the lens of the "not-invented-here" syndrome (Katz and Allen, 1982). In general, scholars have acknowledged the role that organizational factors such as culture and leadership play in both the motivation and capability of organizations to openly collaborate with external partners, and hence the importance of aligning these with open innovation practices (e.g., West and Bogers, 2013; Gianiodis et al., 2010).

4. *Develop a Service-Dominant Orientation to Stimulate Open Service Innovation*

Besides culture and leadership, studies have shown that market orientation or customer-centricity is important for healthcare businesses (Thakur et al., 2012). First, a focus on the market and customers enables organizations to constantly collect information about target customers' (e.g., patients') needs and competitors' capabilities. Second, such a customer-focused approach also helps the business create customer value

(Slater and Narver, 1995). Furthermore, reinforcing our previous recommendation, Deshpande and Webster (1989) indicate that an appropriate organizational culture is the key for such customer-focused organizations to achieve their objectives. In a similar vein, researchers have stressed the importance of focusing on relationships, mutual trust, and win-win exchanges between the consumer (i.e., patient) and the producer (i.e., healthcare provider) by developing what has been referred to as service-dominant logic for healthcare (Joiner and Lusch, 2016). Such a managerial logic drives a service-dominant orientation, which has been defined as a way of conducting business that is based on guiding principles that emphasize value co-creation in service exchanges through collaboration with customers and other stakeholders (Lusch et al., 2007; Perks et al., 2012). Such a service-dominant orientation influences strategic decisions and actions within the organization (Noble et al., 2002; Wilden and Gudergan, 2017), and it will also help the organization embrace customer-centric thinking (Vargo and Lusch, 2004, 2011, 2016).

A traditional goods-dominant logic promotes separation between health providers and patients, viewing the provider as experienced, knowledgeable, and as the creator of value, while the patient is viewed as inexperienced and a passive consumer of value (Joiner and Lusch, 2016). As opposed to this, a service-dominant logic emphasizes commitment for dialogue and engagement between providers and consumers so as to co-create value through relational processes (Lusch and Nambisan, 2015; Payne et al., 2008). Going beyond mere market orientation, this logic highlights the significance of collaboration across all value network actors across the health ecosystem, and the role of service engagement platforms for the co-creation of innovation (Lusch and Nambisan, 2015; Miles, 2005; Vargo et al., 2015). From this perspective, service innovation in healthcare can be seen as a collaborative process involving the healthcare provider and the active participation of customers and other stakeholders in the health ecosystem (Vargo et al., 2015). Accordingly, healthcare providers such as hospitals need to develop and deploy resources and competences to co-create with consumers and other partners in the health service ecosystem (Lusch and Vargo, 2006) in enabling open service innovation for their clients. This process of resource integration for co-creation is supported by a service-dominant orientation.

5. Seek the Support of Open Service Innovation Intermediaries

Healthcare service providers may also consider the use of external agents to enable their open service innovation activities and connect them with their relevant stakeholder groups. Given resource constraints and the lack of capabilities in managing open service innovation (Ramaswamy and Gouillart, 2010), many organizations have used open innovation intermediaries to connect with customers and other stakeholders to drive (service) innovation (Mele and Russo-Spena, 2015; Sawhney et al., 2003). These intermediaries provide web-based platforms to facilitate collaboration and knowledge exchange between entities (Chesbrough, 2003b; Colombo et al., 2015), and assist in identifying, integrating and transferring ideas and solutions in various stages of their OI process (Diener and Piller, 2013; Lopez-Vega, 2009). Open innovation studies have highlighted key benefits of involving intermediaries, such as efficiency gains in knowledge search (Diener and Piller, 2013), better integration of technical expertise (Jeppesen and Lakhani, 2010) and customer knowledge (Verona et al., 2006), accessing external technology (Hargadon and Sutton, 1997), and reducing uncertainty in the innovation process (Zogaj et al., 2014).

Research has also examined intermediaries in the context of service innovation, to highlight how they develop and maintain long-lasting relationships with clients (Bessant and Rush, 1995; Howells, 2006), including in virtual settings (Verona et al., 2006) functioning as Knowledge Intensive Business Services, and enabling open service innovation (Randhawa and Wilden, 2016). These open innovation intermediaries form part of the service ecosystem and provide digital platforms to help clients crowdsource from online customer communities, and thus engage in open service innovation These open service innovation intermediaries are useful in extending the reach of their clients (healthcare service providers) to a large number of individuals (patients, consumers, and other stakeholders) and thus overcome the "local search bias" (Jeppesen and Lakhani, 2010; Verona et al., 2006) to provide access to a wide range of external ideas and solutions to feed into the service innovation process (Diener and Piller, 2013; Lopez-Vega, 2009). Healthcare providers can seek the support of such digital intermediaries to help leverage their open service innovation efforts in general (e.g., Howells, 2006; Sieg et al., 2010), and more specifically, to help them in crowdsourcing from online customer communities to co-design services (Lauritzen, 2017; Zogaj et al., 2014).

Conclusion

In this chapter, we discussed the value of implementing open service innovation into healthcare providers' innovation processes. We stress that healthcare managers need to consider five important levers when designing open service innovation initiatives: 1. engage with and understand your patients, 2. develop necessary organizational capabilities to guarantee success, 3. develop an organizational culture and leadership that fosters open service innovation, 4. develop a service-dominant orientation to stimulate open service innovation, and 5. seek the support of open service innovation intermediaries.

This chapter makes two contributions. First, it contributes to healthcare entrepreneurship and healthcare innovation literature by highlighting the value of open service innovation to healthcare organizations. It makes the case that implementing external stakeholders into the service innovation process provides benefits for healthcare service providers, which often face resource constraints and poor patient satisfaction ratings. Second, we contribute to the open innovation literature by highlighting the healthcare context as being a fruitful area of investigation. Although in this chapter we focused on the benefits of open innovation for healthcare service providers, the application of open innovation frameworks and findings of relevant studies on crowdsourcing, for example, may also be applied to other value network organizations such as pharmaceutical companies and health insurance providers.

Note

1. This case forms part of a larger research project, in which we collaborated with the largest open service innovation intermediary in the country and reviewed 18 of its clients. For this specific case, we interviewed the director of patient and consumer experience and system improvement from the Royal Women's hospital, and also two executives from Nexus—the open service innovation intermediary. We also collected data from secondary sources including online observation of the crowdsourcing project site of the Royal Women's, along with archival data from media articles and the hospital website.

References

Afuah, A., and Tucci, C. L. 2012. Crowdsourcing as a solution to distant search. *Academy of Management Review*, 37(3): 355–375.

Antons, D., and Piller, F. T. 2015. Opening the black box of 'not invented here': Attitudes, decision biases, and behavioral consequences. *The Academy of Management Perspectives*, 29(2): 193–217.

Australian Commission on Safety and Quality in Healthcare. 2014. National Safety and Quality Health Service Standard 2: Partnering with Consumers – Embedding partnerships in health care, November, Sydney: ACSQHC, viewed 18 April 2018 <https://www.safetyandquality.gov.au/wp-content/uploads/2014/11/Partnering-with-Consumers-Embedding-partnerships-in-health-care.pdf>

Berry, L. L., Shankar, V., Parish, J. T., Cadwallader, S., and Dotzel, T. 2006. Creating new markets through service innovation. *MIT Sloan Management Review*, 47(2): 56.

Bessant, J., and Rush, H. 1995. Building bridges for innovation: The role of consultants in technology transfer. *Research Policy*, 24(1): 97–114.

Bogers, M., and West, J. 2012. Managing distributed innovation: Strategic utilization of open and user innovation. *Creativity and Innovation Management*, 21(1): 61–75.

Boote, J., Baird, W., and Beecroft, C. 2010. Public involvement at the design stage of primary health research: A narrative review of case examples. *Health Policy*, 95(1): 10–23.

Boudreau, K. J., Lacetera, N., and Lakhani, K. R. 2011. Incentives and problem uncertainty in innovation contests: An empirical analysis. *Management Science*, 57(5): 843–863.

Boudreau, K. J., and Lakhani, K. 2009. How to manage outside innovation. *MIT Sloan Management Review*, 50(4): 69.
Brabham, D. C. 2010. Moving the crowd at threadless: Motivations for participation in a crowdsourcing application. *Information, Communication & Society*, 13(8): 1122–1145.
Bullinger, A. C., Rass, M., Adamczyk, S., Moeslein, K. M., and Sohn, S. 2012. Open innovation in health care: Analysis of an open health platform. *Health Policy*, 105(2): 165–175.
Burns, L. R. 2012. *The Business of Healthcare Innovation*. Cambridge: Cambridge University Press.
Cainelli, G., Evangelista, R., and Savona, M. 2004. The impact of innovation on economic performance in services. *The Service Industries Journal*, 24(1): 116–130.
Cassiman, B., and Veugelers, R. 2006. In search of complementarity in innovation strategy: Internal R&D and external knowledge acquisition. *Management Science*, 52(1): 68–82.
Chesbrough, H. W. 2003a. The era of open innovation. *MIT Sloan Management Review*, 44(3): 35–41.
Chesbrough, H. W. 2003b. *Open Innovation: The New Imperative for Creating and Profiting From Technology*. Boston, MA: Harvard Business School Press.
Chesbrough, H. W. 2006. *Open Business Models: How to Thrive in the New Innovation Landscape*. Boston: Harvard Business School Press.
Chesbrough, H. W. 2011a. Bringing open innovation to services. *MIT Sloan Management Review*, 52(2): 85–90.
Chesbrough, H. W. 2011b. *The Case for Open Service Innovation*. Open Services Innovation: Rethinking Your Business to Grow and Compete in a New Era, 5–20, San Francisco, CA.
Chesbrough, H. W., and Crowther, A. K. 2006. Beyond high tech: Early adopters of open innovation in other industries. *R&D Management*, 36(3): 229–236.
Collyer, F. 1994. Sex-change surgery: An unacceptable innovation? *The Australian and New Zealand Journal of Sociology*, 30(1): 3–19.
Colombo, G., Dell'Era, C., and Frattini, F. 2015. Exploring the contribution of innovation intermediaries to the new product development (NPD) process: A typology and an empirical study. *R&D Management*, 45(2): 126–146.
de Araújo Burcharth, A. L., Knudsen, M. P., and Søndergaard, H. A. 2014. Neither invented nor shared here: The impact and management of attitudes for the adoption of open innovation practices. *Technovation*, 34(3): 149–161.
den Hertog, P., van der Aa, W., and de Jong, M. W. 2010. Capabilities for managing service innovation: Towards a conceptual framework. *Journal of Service Management*, 21(4): 490–514.
Deshpande, R., and Webster Jr., F. E. 1989. Organizational culture and marketing: Defining the research agenda. *Journal of Marketing*, 53(1): 3–15.
Diener, K., and Piller, F. 2013. *The Market for Open Innovation: A Market Study of Intermediaries, Brokers, Platforms and Facilitators Helping Organizations to Profit From Open Innovation and Customer Co-creation*. Retrieved from http://frankpiller.com/oia-market-study-2013-market-for-open-innovation-support-to-top-6bn-in-2014/
Dotzel, T., Shankar, V., and Berry, L. L. 2013. Service innovativeness and firm value. *Journal of Marketing Research*, 50(2): 259–276.

Edmondson, A. C., Bohmer, R. M., and Pisano, G. P. 2001. Disrupted routines: Team learning and new technology implementation in hospitals. *Administrative Science Quarterly*, 46(4): 685–716.

Enkel, E., Gassmann, O., and Chesbrough, H. 2009. Open R&D and open innovation: Exploring the phenomenon. *R&D Management*, 39(4): 311–316.

Faulkner, A., and Kent, J. 2001. Innovation and regulation in human implant technologies: Developing comparative approaches. *Social Science & Medicine*, 53(7): 895–913.

Fitzgerald, L., Ferlie, E., Wood, M., and Hawkins, C. 2002. Interlocking interactions, the diffusion of innovations in health care. *Human Relations*, 55(12): 1429–1449.

Folland, S., Goodman, A. C., and Stano, M. 2016. *The Economics of Health and Health Care: Pearson International Edition*. Upper Saddle River, NJ: Routledge.

Füller, J., Hutter, K., Hautz, J., and Matzler, K. 2017. The role of professionalism in innovation contest communities. *Long Range Planning*, 50(2): 243–259.

Gassmann, O., and Enkel, E. 2006. Constituents of open innovation: Three core process archetypes. *R&D Management*.

Gianiodis, P. T., Ellis, S. C., and Secchi, E. 2010. Advancing a typology of open innovation. *International Journal of Innovation Management*, 14(4): 531–572.

Greco, P. J., and Eisenberg, J. M. 1993. Changing physicians' practices. *The New England Journal of Medicine*, 329: 1271–1274.

Greul, A., West, J., and Bock, S. 2016. Open at birth? Why new firms do (or don't) use open innovation. *Strategic Entrepreneurship Journal*, 1(1): 1–29.

Hargadon, A., and Sutton, R. I. 1997. Technology brokering and innovation in a product development firm. *Administrative Science Quarterly*, 716–749.

Hienerth, C., Keinz, P., and Lettl, C. 2011. Exploring the nature and implementation process of user-centric business models. *Long Range Planning*, 44(5): 344–374.

Howe, J. 2006. The rise of crowdsourcing. *Wired Magazine*, 14(6): 1–4.

Howe, J. 2008. *Crowdsourcing: How the Power of the Crowd Is Driving the Future of Business*. London: Random House.

Howells, J. 2006. Intermediation and the role of intermediaries in innovation. *Research Policy*, 35(5): 715–728.

Hughes, B., and Wareham, J. 2010. Knowledge arbitrage in global pharma: A synthetic view of absorptive capacity and open innovation. *R&D Management*, 40(3): 324–343.

Huntington, J., Gillam, S., and Rosen, R. 2000. Organisational development for clinical governance. *BMJ*, 321(7262): 679–682.

Jeppesen, L. B., and Lakhani, K. R. 2010. Marginality and problem-solving effectiveness in broadcast search. *Organization Science*, 21(5): 1016–1033.

Joiner, K., and Lusch, R. 2016. Evolving to a new service-dominant logic for health care. *Innovation and Entrepreneurship in Health*, 3(1): 25–33.

Katz, R., and Allen, T. J. 1982. Investigating the Not Invented Here (NIH) syndrome: A look at the performance, tenure, and communication patterns of 50 R&D Project Groups. *R&D Management*, 12(1): 7–20.

Kindström, D., Kowalkowski, C., and Sandberg, E. 2013. Enabling service innovation: A dynamic capabilities approach. *Journal of Business Research*, 66(8): 1063–1073.

Kleinbaum, A., and Stuart, T. 2014. Network responsiveness: The social structural microfoundations of dynamic capabilities. *The Academy of Management Perspectives*, 28(4): 353–367.

Länsisalmi, H., and Kivimäki, M. 1999. Factors associated with innovative climate: What is the role of stress? *Stress and Health*, 15(4): 203–213.

Länsisalmi, H., Kivimäki, M., Aalto, P., and Ruoranen, R. 2006. Innovation in healthcare: A systematic review of recent research. *Nursing Science Quarterly*, 19(1): 66–72.

Lau, A. K., Tang, E., and Yam, R. 2010. Effects of supplier and customer integration on product innovation and performance: Empirical evidence in Hong Kong manufacturers. *Journal of Product Innovation Management*, 27(5): 761–777.

Lauritzen, G. D. 2017. The role of innovation intermediaries in firm-innovation community collaboration: Navigating the membership paradox. *Journal of Product Innovation Management*, 34(3): 289–314.

Lichtenthaler, U., Ernst, H., and Hoegl, M. 2010. Not-sold-here: How attitudes influence external knowledge exploitation. *Organization Science*, 21(5): 1054–1071.

Lopez-Vega, H. 2009. *How Demand-driven Technological Systems of Innovation Work? The Role of Intermediary Organizations*. Proceedings of the DRUID-DIME Academy Winter 2009 Conference.

Lusch, R. F., and Nambisan, S. 2015. Service innovation: A service-dominant logic perspective. *MIS Quarterly*, 39(1): 155–175.

Lusch, R. F., and Vargo, S. L. 2006. Service-dominant logic: Reactions, reflections and refinements. *Marketing Theory*, 6(3): 281–288.

Lusch, R. F., Vargo, S. L., and O'Brien, M. 2007. Competing through service: Insights from service-dominant logic. *Journal of Retailing*, 83(1): 5–18.

Lusch, R. F., Vargo, S. L., and Tanniru, M. 2010. Service, value networks and learning. *Journal of the Academy of Marketing Science*, 38(1): 19–31.

Lüthje, C., Herstatt, C., and Von Hippel, E. 2005. User-innovators and 'local' information: The case of mountain biking. *Research Policy*, 34(6): 951–965.

Lüttgens, D., Pollok, P., Antons, D., and Piller, F. 2014. Wisdom of the crowd and capabilities of a few: Internal success factors of crowdsourcing for innovation. *Journal of Business Economics*, 84(3): 339–374.

Martinez, M. G. 2015. Solver engagement in knowledge sharing in crowdsourcing communities: Exploring the link to creativity. *Research Policy*, 44(8): 1419–1430.

Mele, C., and Russo-Spena, T. 2015. Innomediary agency and practices in shaping market innovation. *Industrial Marketing Management*, 44: 42–53.

Mina, A., Bascavusoglu-Moreau, E., and Hughes, A. 2014. Open service innovation and the firm's search for external knowledge. *Research Policy*, 43(5): 853–866.

Moeller, S. 2008. Customer integration: A key to an implementation perspective of service provision. *Journal of Service Research*, 11(2): 197–210.

Nambisan, P. 2010. Enabling consumer-driven service innovation in health care: The role of online Health Information Technologies (HIT). In *Information Technology and Product Development*. Boston, MA: Springer, 159–177.

Nambisan, P., and Nambisan, S. 2009. Models of consumer value cocreation in health care. *Health Care Management Review*, 34(4): 344–354.

Noble, C. H., Sinha, R. K., and Kumar, A. 2002. Market orientation and alternative strategic orientations: A longitudinal assessment of performance implications. *Journal of Marketing*, 66(4): 25–39.

Patton, M. 1990. *Qualitative Evaluation and Research Methods*. Thousand Oaks, CA: Sage Publications Newbury Park.

Payne, A. F., Storbacka, K., and Frow, P. 2008. Managing the co-creation of value. *Journal of the Academy of Marketing Science*, 36(1): 83–96.

Perks, H., Gruber, T., and Edvardsson, B. 2012. Co-creation in radical service innovation: A systematic analysis of microlevel processes. *Journal of Product Innovation Management*, 29(6): 935–951.

Piezunka, H., and Dahlander, L. 2015. Distant search, narrow attention: How crowding alters organizations' filtering of suggestions in crowdsourcing. *Academy of Management Journal*, 58(3): 856–880.

Piller, F. T., and Walcher, D. 2006. Toolkits for idea competitions: A novel method to integrate users in new product development. *R&D Management*, 36(3): 307–318.

Piller, F. T., and West, J. 2014. Firms, users, and innovation: An interactive model of coupled open innovation. In *New Frontiers in Open Innovation*. Oxford: Oxford University Press.

Poetz, M. K., and Schreier, M. 2012. The value of crowdsourcing: Can users really compete with professionals in generating new product ideas? *Journal of Product Innovation Management*, 29(2): 245–256.

Pope, C., and Mays, N. 2000. *Qualitative Research in Health Care*. Malden, MA: BMJ Books.

Powell, W. W., Koput, K., and Smith-Doerr, L. 1996. Interorganizational collaboration and the locus of innovation: Networks of learning in Biotechnology. *Administrative Science Quarterly*, 41: 116–145.

Ramaswamy, V., and Gouillart, F. 2010. Building the co-creative enterprise. *Harvard Business Review*, 88(10): 100–109.

Randhawa, K., and Wilden, R. 2016. *Online Intermediaries and Service Co-creation Capabilities: An Exploratory Case Study of Client Engagement for Open Innovation*. Paper presented to the 3rd World Open Innovation Conference, Barcelona.

Randhawa, K., Wilden, R., and Hohberger, J. 2016. A bibliometric review of open innovation: Setting a research agenda. *Journal of Product Innovation Management*, 33(6): 750–772.

Randhawa, K., Wilden, R., and West, J. 2018. Crowdsourcing Without Profit: The Role of the Seeker in Open Social Innovation. *R&D Management*, forthcoming.

Sampson, S. E., and Spring, M. 2012. Customer roles in service supply chains and opportunities for innovation. *Journal of Supply Chain Management*, 48(4): 30–50.

Sawhney, M., Prandelli, E., and Verona, G. 2003. The power of innomediation. *MIT Sloan Management Review*, 44(2): 77.

Schumpeter, J. A. 1934. *The Theory of Economic Development: An Enquiry Into Profits, Capital, Credit, Interest and the Business Cycle*. Cambridge, MA: Harvard University Press.

Seldon, T. 2011. Beyond patents: Effective intellectual property strategy in biotechnology. *Innovation: Management, Policy and Practice*, 13(1): 55–61.

Shortell, S. M., Bennett, C. L., and Byck, G. R. 1998. Assessing the impact of continuous quality improvement on clinical practice: What it will take to accelerate progress. *The Milbank Quarterly*, 76(4): 593–624.

Sieg, J. H., Wallin, M. W., and Von Krogh, G. 2010. Managerial challenges in open innovation: A study of innovation intermediation in the chemical industry. *R&D Management*, 40(3): 281–291.

Slater, S. F., and Narver, J. C. 1995. Market orientation and the learning organization. *Journal of Marketing*, 59(3): 63–74.

Storey, C., and Hughes, M. 2013. The relative impact of culture, strategic orientation and capability on new service development performance. *European Journal of Marketing*, 47(5/6): 833–856.

Surowiecki, J. 2005. *The Wisdom of Crowds*. New York: Anchor.

Teece, D. J. 1986. Profiting from technological innovation: Implications for integration, collaboration, licensing and public policy. *Research Policy*, 15: 285–305.

Teece, D. J. 2007. Explicating dynamic capabilities: The nature and microfoundations of (sustainable) enterprise performance. *Strategic Management Journal*, 28(13): 1319–1350.

Terwiesch, C., and Xu, Y. 2008. Innovation contests, open innovation, and multiagent problem solving. *Management Science*, 54(9): 1529–1543.

Thakur, R., Hsu, S. H., and Fontenot, G. 2012. Innovation in healthcare: Issues and future trends. *Journal of Business Research*, 65(4): 562–569.

Vanhaverbeke, W., Van de Vrande, V., and Chesbrough, H. 2008. Understanding the advantages of open innovation practices in corporate venturing in terms of real options. *Creativity and Innovation Management*, 17(4): 251–258.

Vargo, S. L., and Lusch, R. F. 2004. Evolving to a new dominant logic for marketing. *Journal of Marketing*, 68(1): 1–17.

Vargo, S. L., and Lusch, R. F. 2011. It's all B2B ... and beyond: Toward a systems perspective of the market. *Industrial Marketing Management*, 40(2): 181–187.

Vargo, S. L., and Lusch, R. F. 2016. Institutions and axioms: An extension and update of service-dominant logic. *Journal of the Academy of Marketing Science*, 44(1): 5–23.

Vargo, S. L., Wieland, H., and Akaka, M. A. 2015. Innovation through institutionalization: A service ecosystems perspective. *Industrial Marketing Management*, 44: 63–72.

Verona, G., Prandelli, E., and Sawhney, M. 2006. Innovation and virtual environments: Towards virtual knowledge brokers. *Organization Studies*, 27(6): 765–788.

Viscusi, G., and Tucci, C. L. 2016. Distinguishing 'crowded' organizations from groups and communities. In *Creating and Capturing Value Through Crowdsourcing*. Oxford, UK: Oxford University Press.

von Hippel, E. 1988. *The Sources of Innovation*. New York, NY: Oxford University Press.

West, J., and Bogers, B. 2014. Leveraging external sources of innovation: A review of research on open innovation. *Journal of Product Innovation Management*, 31(4): 814–831.

West, J., and Gallagher, S. 2006. Challenges of open innovation: The paradox of firm investment in open-source software. *R&D Management*, 36(3): 319–331.

West, J., and Sims, J. 2017. How firms leverage crowds and communities for open innovation. In A. Afuah, C. Tucci, and G. Viscusi (Eds.), *Creating and Capturing Value Through Crowdsourcing*. Oxford: Oxford University Press.

Wilden, R., Devinney, T. M., and Dowling, G. R. 2016. The architecture of dynamic capability research. *The Academy of Management Annals*, 10(1): 997–1076.

Wilden, R., and Gudergan, S. P. 2015. The impact of dynamic capabilities on operational marketing and technological capabilities: Investigating the role of environmental turbulence. *Journal of the Academy of Marketing Science*, 43(2): 181–199.

Wilden, R., and Gudergan, S. P. 2017. Service-dominant orientation, dynamic capabilities and firm performance. *Journal of Service Theory and Practice*, 27(4): 808–832.

Wilden, R., Gudergan, S. P., Nielsen, B. B., and Lings, I. N. 2013. Dynamic capabilities and performance: Strategy, structure and environment. *Long Range Planning*, 46(1–2): 72–96.

Yin, R. K. 1994. *Case Study Research: Design and Methods*. Thousand Oaks, CA: SAGE Publications, Inc.

Zogaj, S., Bretschneider, U., and Leimeister, J. M. 2014. Managing crowdsourced software testing: A case study based insight on the challenges of a crowdsourcing intermediary. *Journal of Business Economics*, 84(3): 375–405.

8 How Corporate Entrepreneurs Use Interfirm Collaboration in the Search for Emerging Knowledge in Biotech Innovation

Jan Hohberger and Ralf Wilden

Introduction

In this chapter, we focus on exploration activities in collaborative entrepreneurship by corporates (Zahra et al., 1999). Collaborative entrepreneurship is defined as "the creation of something of economic value based on new, jointly generated ideas that emerge from the sharing of information and knowledge" (Miles et al., 2006: 2). For entrepreneurs, knowledge is an important driver of innovation and has also been considered to be the most underutilized resource in organizations, one issue that may be resolved by using multi-firm collaborative networks (Miles et al., 2006; Ribeiro-Soriano and Urbano, 2009).

Explorative knowledge is especially central to drive innovation; however, it is difficult to access and use (Gupta et al., 2006; Rosenkopf and McGrath, 2011; Laursen, 2012; Wang and Hsu, 2014). Research rooted in evolutionary economics and organizational learning, in particular, suggests that emerging knowledge is critical for organizational adaptation and survival (March, 1991; Rosenkopf and McGrath, 2011). Various empirical studies have shown the positive influence of emerging knowledge on innovation outcomes and firm performance (Heeley and Jacobson, 2008; Ahuja and Lampert, 2001; Katila, 2002; Nerkar, 2003; Capaldo et al., 2014). For firms competing in innovation-intensive industries, to which healthcare-related industries such as biotechnology belong, continuous access to emerging knowledge (new ideas and technologies) is important to achieve success.

Despite the importance of research on exploration and emerging knowledge, these two phenomena are rarely investigated together and the relationship between emerging knowledge and explorative knowledge remains unclear. This is surprising, as firms use knowledge that is explorative and emerging at the same time. For example, with the emergence of the so-called "biotechnology revolution," firms in the pharmaceutical industry had to be capable of incorporating emerging technologies and scientific approaches into their development process (e.g., molecular genetics and rDNA technology) (Malerba and Orsenigo, 2002; Pisano, 2002). As such, firms had to be able to use emerging technologies in conjunction with the pharmaceutical realm of expertise but in addition to knowledge from rather different technological fields (such as informatics, physics, and biology) (Malerba and Orsenigo, 2002).

The biotechnology industry is an important industry within healthcare, which provides an ideal setting in which to study innovation- and learning-related phenomena for multiple reasons. First, it is characterized by high knowledge intensity and the continuous flow of emerging ideas and developments (Powell et al., 1996). The access to emerging knowledge is particularly important in the biotechnology industry because the field is still relatively young and evolving (e.g., in contrast to the more established structure of traditional pharmaceutical firms) (Pisano, 2002) and is characterized by rapid knowledge diffusion due to its basic science orientation (Gittelman and Kogut, 2003; Powell et al., 1996). Second, the need to access knowledge at a rapid pace is frequently stated as a primary reason for heavy reliance on inter-organizational collaboration in various forms (Powell et al., 1996; Arora and Gambardella, 1990; Rothaermel and Deeds, 2004), despite its potential disadvantages due to the increased managerial complexity and competitive behavior (Oliver, 2004).

Despite ample empirical investigation of explorative knowledge (Gupta et al., 2006; Rosenkopf and McGrath, 2011; Laursen, 2012) and a number of studies on emerging knowledge (Ahuja and Lampert, 2001; Katila, 2002; Hohberger, 2014; Capaldo et al., 2014; Petruzzelli and Savino, 2014), several questions are still left unanswered. For example, what is the relationship between emerging knowledge and explorative knowledge in the context of collaborative entrepreneurship? This study aims to address this issue. First, it argues that being explorative and emergent are two distinct but negatively related characteristics of knowledge. Following the initial work by March (1991) and recent investigations in evolutionary economics, "explorative knowledge" is defined as technologies with which the organization is "unfamiliar" (Phene et al., 2010; Rosenkopf and Almeida, 2003; Nerkar, 2003). This is distinct from the definition of "emerging knowledge," which refers to technological inputs that are recent in chronological terms and have only been developed in the recent past (Katila, 2002; Katila and Chen, 2008; Nerkar, 2003; Ahuja and Lampert, 2001). Second, based on the idea that collaborative entrepreneurship is particularly helpful to search and use knowledge (Powell et al., 1996; Liebeskind et al., 1996; Mowery et al., 1996), it argues that collaborative activities are positively linked to the use of emerging knowledge and positively moderate the negative relationship between explorative and emerging knowledge.[1]

By linking collaboration activities to the concepts of explorative knowledge and emerging knowledge, this study contributes in several ways to research on entrepreneurship, innovation, and collaboration.

First, and most broadly, it provides additional insight into the question of how emerging knowledge is searched and used, which remains a relatively underdeveloped area given its theoretical and empirical importance (Katila, 2002; Phene et al., 2005). Most of the existing research on emerging knowledge examines the effects of emerging knowledge on innovation outcomes (Heeley and Jacobson, 2008; Ahuja and Lampert, 2001; Nerkar, 2003; Capaldo et al., 2014; Petruzzelli and Savino, 2014), but far less is known about how firms are able to use emerging knowledge (Phene et al., 2005).

Second, this chapter helps to clarify the relationship between the explorative search and emerging knowledge. Researchers have often referred to the concepts of new, emerging, or explorative knowledge interchangeably even though they are distinct and convey different meanings (Gupta et al., 2006; Rosenkopf and McGrath, 2011; Ahuja and Lampert, 2001). Additionally, most of the empirical research investigates each concept individually and thereby discounts the complexity of the innovation process. By clearly differentiating between explorative and emerging knowledge, and examining the empirical relationship between them, this study helps to characterize and better describe the innovation process.

Third, the idea that interfirm collaborative entrepreneurial activities enhance the access and use of knowledge that is not readily available internally is frequently found in the alliance literature (Mowery et al., 1996; Inkpen, 2002; Rosenkopf and Almeida, 2003; Lavie et al., 2011; Wang, 2011). However, these studies focus mainly on cases of exploration on distant knowledge. This research investigates the learning advantages of collaboration and emerging knowledge. By demonstrating that collaboration can reduce the negative relationship between explorative and emerging knowledge due to risk sharing and knowledge access, this study extends the research on the benefits of collaboration in organizational learning situations.

The remainder of this chapter is structured as follows. After a brief theoretical contextualization of explorative and emerging knowledge, the hypotheses are developed. Then the methodology is explained, including a detailed description of the use of patent references to measure explorative and emerging knowledge. Following the presentation of the empirical results, the study ends with a discussion of the results, limitations, and future research.

Theory and Hypotheses

Knowledge-creation processes within organizations and ensuing use of new knowledge are closely related to the organization's learning and knowledge creation processes (Stopford and Baden-Fuller, 1994). In this context, previous research has stressed the importance of the firm's external environment including external organizations (Zahra et al., 1999).

The understanding that innovation and entrepreneurial activity are the results of a combination or recombination of knowledge parts can be traced back to the early work of Schumpeter (1934) and is still present in our current understanding of innovation (Fleming, 2001; Henderson and Clark, 1990). As a result, the search and use for knowledge, as well as the exploration and exploitation framework, hold a central position in innovation and strategy research (Gupta et al., 2006; Rosenkopf and McGrath, 2011). Often research refers to the seminal work of March (1991: 71), which lists a set of concepts to define exploration ("search, variation, risk taking, experimentation, play, flexibility, discovery, innovation") and exploitation ("refinement, choice, production, efficiency, selection, implementation, execution") or the late work of Levinthal and March (1993: 105), which highlights the focus on knowledge used by defining exploration as "the pursuit of new knowledge" and describing exploitation as "the use and development of things already known" (Wilden et al., 2018). The distinction between both understandings lies in the degree of familiarity with the object and the point of perspective. The first focuses on the chronological aspect of the new and does not make claims about the reference point, meaning that what is "new" is new to everybody. The second focuses on an experience- or familiarity-based understanding of "new" and therefore needs a reference point because people have different experiences—what is "new" to one person might not be "new" to somebody else. Several studies refer to the second understanding of "new" when they conceptualize explorative knowledge (Rosenkopf and Almeida, 2003; Rosenkopf and Nerkar, 2001; Phene et al., 2010; Benner and Tushman, 2003; Danneels, 2002); they refer to "exploration" or "distant search" as search that exposes the firm to not-yet-experienced or unfamiliar knowledge. Fewer studies focus on the chronological aspect and link it to the first definition (Katila, 2002; Nerkar, 2003; Katila and Chen, 2008). Based on their similarity, both exploration and emerging knowledge have been labeled as "new," but they are conceptually and empirically different concepts. To avoid any misunderstanding throughout the rest of the study, "exploration" refers to use of "unfamiliar knowledge," while "emerging knowledge" refers to knowledge inputs which have been developed in the recent past (Katila, 2002; Nerkar, 2003; Katila and Chen, 2008; Ahuja and Lampert, 2001; Petruzzelli and Savino, 2014).

Explorative and Emerging Knowledge

In order for entrepreneurial organizations to identify and sense opportunities, they need to engage in search activities (Shane and Venkataraman, 2000), whether they are driven by processes or the attention placed to the environment by top managers and entrepreneurs (Dong et al., 2016). Studies in organizational learning and evolutionary economics show that organizational knowledge search often focuses on familiar areas, and exploration removed from this familiar knowledge trajectory is inherently difficult (Rosenkopf and Almeida, 2003; Nelson and Winter, 1982; Stuart and Podolny, 1996). The underlying assumption is that managers cannot rationally evaluate a potential set of choices in uncertain and complex situations; instead, they base their decisions heavily on areas of practice and routines that are similar to their experience (Nelson and Winter, 1982). Choices thus tend to be path dependent and in the neighborhood of familiar activities, rather than those that may be the most attractive in terms of future success.

Like explorative activities, the use of emerging knowledge is more difficult than the use of older knowledge because emerging knowledge tends to be more tacit, uncertain, and ambiguous, as studies on firm innovation have shown (Kline and Rosenberg, 1986; Fleming, 2001; Nelson and Winter, 1982; Zander and Kogut, 1995). For example, Attewell (1992) claims that the implementation of emerging and complex knowledge often requires considerable individual and organizational adaptation. In contrast to technologies in use, which are normally understood and codified, emerging knowledge is more tacit because firms have not had time to codify the emerging knowledge and build competencies around it (Zander and Kogut, 1995; Katila, 2002). Furthermore, firms often need to modify emerging technologies before they are useful (Pavitt, 1984). For this reason, firms may even delay the adoption of emerging technologies until they gain sufficient understanding of those technologies (Attewell, 1992).

The inherent nature of emerging knowledge and explorative knowledge make it onerous for firms to use knowledge that is both explorative and emerging. The difficulties in exploration are enhanced by the more tacit, uncertain and ambiguous nature of emerging knowledge (Katila, 2002; Zander and Kogut, 1995). To stay at the forefront of emerging technologies in knowledge and learning is often a daunting task, even for firms operating in this knowledge domain. Not being familiar with this knowledge domain makes it an even more challenging task. Teece (1997), for example, argues that knowledge age and the degree of familiarity with it determines the cost of its transfer. Similarly, Hisey and Caves (1985) state that being unfamiliar with new activities increases the cost of information acquisition and absorption. These firm-level observations are somewhat mirrored by research on individual learning that shows that new skills are more quickly learned when the knowledge is similar to pre-existing skills (Zander and Kogut, 1995). In summary, even though it may be necessary to use for knowledge that is both explorative and emerging, it is difficult for firms to use for knowledge with these characteristics.

Hypothesis 1: The search of explorative knowledge relates negatively to the simultaneous search of emerging knowledge.[2]

Collaboration and Emerging Knowledge

Previous research considers firms to be entrepreneurial if they proactively collaborate with external partners (Antoncic, 2007), which has been termed 'collaborative entrepreneurship' (Miles et al., 2006). Engaging in collaborative activities is beneficial for the acquisition and use of external knowledge and helps to explore and overcome path dependency is widespread (Inkpen, 2002; Hamel, 1991; Rosenkopf and Almeida, 2003; Wang, 2011). Particularly research in the biotechnology sector and other high-technology industry has argued that the benefits of collaboration have a positive influence on entrepreneurial activities and ultimately innovation (Liebeskind et al., 1996; Powell et al., 1996; Rothaermel and Deeds, 2004; Baum et al., 2000; Almeida et al., 2011).[3] The advantages of accessing knowledge and leveraging existing knowledge are often cited as the main benefits of collaboration (Hoang and Rothaermel, 2010), but it is important to note that collaboration also contributes to the efficient application of that knowledge by: (i) increasing the efficiency of knowledge application, and (ii) improving the efficiency of knowledge utilization (Grant and Baden-Fuller, 2004; Dyer and Singh, 1998).

There are two main reasons why the use of collaboration is particularly suitable for the search and use of emerging knowledge. First, the pace and scope of innovation activities within high-technology industries make it impossible for firms to keep up with all recent developments. Firms consequently have to rely on external partners, which extend the limited knowledge reach of the firm beyond its boundaries (Powell et al., 1996), which in recent innovation research has often been labeled "open innovation" (Randhawa et al., 2016). This effect is multiplied in the case of emerging knowledge, since firms have to build the capacity to absorb or even recognize the emerging knowledge (Cohen and Levinthal, 1990). Partner firms not only potentially provide access to the knowledge, but they also help to scan and recognize available knowledge that may be particularly difficult to locate, assess, and understand; they then assist with the integration of this emerging knowledge (Kline and Rosenberg, 1986; Fleming, 2001).

Modern drug development in healthcare illustrates this situation nicely. The process of developing modern drugs is very expensive and is characterized by multiple scientific and technological challenges, along with competing solutions to these challenges (Pisano, 2002). The so-called molecular biotech revolution has increased this complexity (Malerba and Orsenigo, 2002). Given the dispersion of research activities in a new field, firms need to monitor, absorb, and evaluate knowledge quickly from different sources, and staying close to the cutting edge of science and technology is thus a daunting challenge for individual firms. In addition, it is difficult to combine all the necessary capabilities to develop a drug from the early research stages to the final regulatory trials within one firm; thus, firms in this sector frequently engage in collaborations of various kinds to stay at the forefront of innovation (Arora & Gambardella, 1990; Powell et al., 1996; F. T. Rothaermel & Deeds, 2004). Firms working under these conditions face high levels of uncertainty because it is difficult to determine ex ante that scientific and technological approaches are most likely to be successful (Liebeskind et al., 1996). Therefore, as Powell et al. (1996) argue, the locus of innovation has shifted from the firm to the sector and its various participants (for-profit firms, universities, research labs, hospitals, governmental institutions), and firms need collaborative mechanisms to participate in knowledge generation.

Second, the uncertain nature of emerging knowledge makes collaboration strategies particularly suitable for the use and acquisition of emerging knowledge, because the risk is shared between partners and options are provided for stepwise engagement in emerging areas (Grant and Baden-Fuller, 2004; Beckman et al., 2004; Eisenhardt and Schoonhoven, 1996). Collaborations facilitate a better understanding of the knowledge and reduce risks in its application; thus, firms that are uncertain about how to develop knowledge and innovation are more likely to engage in collaborations with other firms (Powell et al., 1996). Collaboration provides options to engage via small initial investments in unknown and emerging knowledge areas, which can be extended if desired. Grant and Baden-Fuller (2004) argue that early investment projects often provide the option to invest in subsequent phases, whereas late investments may result in a penalty or even the lockout of late investors. Following the option logic, high uncertainty, as in the case of emerging knowledge, increases the value of the option to engage in new areas, since the option value is partly determined by the uncertainty of the investment (Kogut, 1991; Grant and Baden-Fuller, 2004; McGrath, 1997). The risk-sharing and learning argument leads to the conclusion that emerging knowledge in the innovation process is more likely to be used via collaboration than it is without partners.

> Hence, hypothesis 2: Collaborative innovation activities relate positively to the search of emerging knowledge.

Collaboration and Explorative Knowledge

The problem regarding access to explorative knowledge that is not internally available (or only at a much higher cost) is the underlying rationale in several studies on collaboration (Mowery et al., 1996; Rothaermel and Deeds, 2004; Inkpen, 2002; Rosenkopf and Almeida, 2003; Phene et al., 2010; Baum et al., 2000). Thus, collaborations are a strategic tool that entrepreneurial firms can employ not only to fill gaps in their existing technologies, but also to move away from existing technological trajectories. For example, Rosenkopf and Almedia (2003) show that firms that could change their technological trajectory made extensive use of collaborations. Rothaermel and Deeds (2014) show how biotechnology firms use explorative collaborations at the beginning of the drug-development process to generate patents.

The fact that collaboration helps with the acquisition not only of emerging knowledge, as proposed in Hypothesis 2, but also of explorative knowledge, raises the question of how collaboration relates to knowledge that is explorative and emerging at the same time. This is perhaps one of the most difficult knowledge combinations because it blends the difficulties of both exploration and emerging knowledge. In this case, collaboration can be advantageous because it reduces the difficulty involved in the use of emerging and explorative knowledge simultaneously. The learning advantages of collaboration help to use emerging knowledge, as argued in Hypothesis 2, by: (i) extending the limited knowledge reach of the firm beyond its boundaries, (ii) risk sharing between partners and stepwise engagement, and (iii) by simultaneously providing advantages in the use of explorative knowledge (Rosenkopf and Almeida, 2003; Phene et al., 2010; Rosenkopf and Nerkar, 2001; Rothaermel and Deeds, 2004; Lavie and Rosenkopf, 2006; Stuart and Podolny, 1996). Rosenkopf and Almeida (2003) showed that the more complex, less codifiable, and less teachable the knowledge embodied within an innovation is, the greater the likelihood is that it will be transferred through collaboration. Therefore, the advantages of collaboration are particularly important in gaining access to emerging knowledge that is far from the firm's current knowledge base ("explorative"). Furthermore, it is important to note that risk sharing and stepwise engagement linked to collaborative activities provide benefits for firms even if the collaboration partner does not have a particular knowledge advantage. In cases where knowledge is emerging and explorative for both firms, engaging in collaborative activities can still reduce risk by providing the option of further investment in the future and thus makes collaboration more favorable.

> Hence, hypothesis 3: The negative relationship between the search of explorative knowledge and emerging knowledge is reduced in collaborative innovation activities.

Method

As outlined previously, the biotechnology industry is an important player within the healthcare industry, and it provides a suitable research context for our study, given its high knowledge intensity and the importance of securing access to emerging knowledge, which is in contrast to the more established traditional pharmaceutical industry (Pisano, 2002). Also, access to new knowledge quickly is a primary reason for the significant reliance on collaborative entrepreneurship (Powell et al., 1996; Arora and Gambardella, 1990; Rothaermel and Deeds, 2004). Finally, from a methodological standpoint, the biotechnology industry's reliance on patents to protect and generate profits (DeCarolis and Deeds, 1999; Cohen et al., 2000; Mansfield, 1986) makes the interpretation of patents more reliable than in other industries. The hypotheses are tested using a sample of 3,264 patents of 101 US biotechnology firms from the years 2000–2002. The usefulness of patent data has been shown in various studies in regards to innovation, knowledge flows, technological development, and localization of knowledge (Jaffe et al., 1993; Gittelman, 2008; Jaffe et al., 2000). Patent data provide a detailed and chronological picture of the innovation activities of firms, and their institutionalized applications and grant mechanisms increase their reliability.

Firms were selected from the BioScan database, which is an independent industry directory that offers a comprehensive range of company information (e.g., ownership, location, main products, collaboration, mergers, and acquisitions). To increase the comparability between firms and to gain access to control variables, private firms, large pharmaceutical companies with different product divisions, and research institutes are excluded from the sample. The disadvantage of this sample selection procedure is that it reduces the generalizability of the findings. However, the potential bias of excluding private firms is somewhat mitigated by the fact that biotechnology firms often become public in early stages of their lifecycle and financial reports provide company information for up to three years before the initial public offering date. Thus, the sample includes numerous very young and entrepreneurial firms.

In the next step, patents of the sample firm were downloaded from the Derwent Innovation Index (DWI).[4] To increase the interpretability of the patent data and to avoid the double counting of innovation activity, patent families were used to examine the innovation activities of firms. In general, a patent family comprises a set of patent applications, which are inter-related by either priority claims or PCT [Patent Cooperation Treaty] national phase entries, which normally comprise the same subject matter[5]

Dependent Variables

Similar to previous studies, citation lags are used to approximate emerging or mature knowledge (Phene et al., 2005; Hohberger, 2016; Fabrizio, 2007; Ahuja and Lampert, 2001). The citation lag is measured as the time span between the application date of the priority patent of a patent family and the average publication date of all cited patents. The publication date of the cited patent refers to the point in time when the previous knowledge was presented in the public domain and became available to other firms. The application date of the citing priority patent represents the moment in time when the learning process, based on the assimilation and utilization of knowledge, has been successful and leads to a new invention. This measure assumes that firms that have shorter citation lags use emerging knowledge, and that firms that have longer citation lags use more established knowledge. The average time span between the two points is measured in months.

Independent Variables

Collaborations

Collaborations are defined broadly as two or more firms working jointly in the production of a patent and application for the patent (Almeida et al., 2011; Kim and Song, 2007). It is measured as a patent family with at least one firm-assignee different from the applying firm. To avoid misinterpretation, it is important to account for merger and acquisition activities, subsidiary relationships, and name changes, which could lead to multiple assignees that do not represent collaboration between independent firms.

Importantly, this measure of collaboration does not capture the full collaborative activity of firms because it does not include unsuccessful collaborations, which do not yield a patent, or collaborations which do not result in co-patenting because partners have developed other means of rewarding their activities (Katz and Martin, 1997).[6] However, co-assigned patents are not uncommon in the biotechnology industry, as co-patenting is more frequent in industries with strong intellectual property regimes (Hagedoorn, 2003), and recent studies have stressed the collaborative characteristics of it. For example, in qualitative interviews with biotechnology inventors Almeida et al. (2011) show that co-patenting normally entails various characteristics of collaboration including face-to-face meeting, extensive discussion, exchange of ideas, and joint problem solving. Thus, co-patenting often encompasses the exchange of tacit knowledge (Maggioni and Uberti, 2009). Additional co-patenting inventors often have to accommodate and change their behaviors to their partners in order to build a common understanding, which is necessary for successful collaboration and the exchange knowledge (Hussler and Rondé, 2007). Thus, it is not surprising that Porter et al. (2005) argue that the generation of collaborative patents is costly and time-consuming, and thus, co-patenting represents a relatively strong type of collaboration. The complexity of collaboration co-patenting is also highlighted by Belderbos et al. (2013), who are not only showing the complexity of the involved process but also the fact that it is sometimes related to more valuable patents. Besides the collaborative nature of co-patenting this measurement has the important advantage that it precisely captures innovation-based collaborations and connects them to the participating actors (firms and inventors). This also helps to calculate valid controls of the underlying innovation activity.

Exploration

Because of its relevance in several research areas, scholars have conceptualized exploration and exploitation in various ways, for example, new or old partner (Beckman et al., 2004); old or new knowledge (Nerkar, 2003); or type of collaboration (Koza & Lewin, 1998; F. T. Rothaermel & Deeds, 2004). Based on the knowledge search focus of this study and definition of exploration, the similarity of searched knowledge is the criterion that characterizes exploration and exploitation. The lower the degree of similarity between an innovation and the pre-existing firm knowledge on which it is based, the more exploration-oriented is the knowledge. IPC codes of patent applications are used to classify innovation along the proximity of current technological trajectories and areas (Phene et al., 2010; Rosenkopf & Almeida, 2003). The measure compares the distribution of IPC patent classes (three-IPC-digit level) between the patent portfolios of the firm generating a patent with the distribution of the IPC classes of all the cited patent references of an underlying patent granted by the firm. It is important to note that every patent can cite several patents, which may each list several IPC classes.[7] Therefore, it is necessary to first calculate the distance (FE_{ijl}) between a citing firm's patent portfolio and a given reference of an underlying patent: $FE_{ilj} = \sqrt{\sum (p_{ki} - p_{kjl})^2}$, where p_{ki} represents the proportion of a patenting activity for a firm (i) in a given IPC subclass (k), and p_{kjl} shows the proportion of the IPC subclass (k) of cited references (l) of given patent (j). With this measure, the higher the distance figure, the less similarity there is between the patent portfolio of the citing firm and the cited patent. In a second step, the mean of all references (l) of a given patent (j) are calculated to gain the knowledge similarity between a patent (j) and the firm (FE_{ij}).

Controls

The *number of citations* per patent family is used to control the value of a patent (Hall, Jaffe, & Trajtenberg, 2005; Harhoff et al., 2003; Lanjouw, Pakes, & Putnam, 1998). Different studies have shown that *patent family size* is a good proxy for the value of an invention (Lanjouw et al., 1998; Harhoff et al., 2003; Cassiman et al., 2008). In this way, *patent family size* is used as a second measure to control for the value of a patent. Different technological and scientific fields have different cycle times (Fabrizio, 2007); therefore it is important to control for the technological area of an innovation when measuring citation lags across technological areas. This is particularly relevant for the biotechnology industry because it comprises various different scientific and technological areas (Pisano, 2002). The eight most frequent IPC codes are therefore used to control for the technological area. It is more difficult to combine a wide and large set of knowledge. Thus, the number of IPC codes for one patent family measures the technological scope of the patent. *Number of references* provides a measurement for the scope and amount of knowledge used in an innovation and approximates the knowledge inputs into a patent. Nerkar (2003) shows that the mix of old and new knowledge is critical and can influence patent value and the impact of innovations. The standard deviation of citation time per patent is therefore also included as a control variable (Citations Time Spread). We control for the *numbers of authors* (inventor) as it is a control for the size of the research team and the scope of the research project (Gittelman & Kogut, 2003), and it is also can influence innovation outcomes (Hohberger, et al. 2017).

To capture the observable and unobservable heterogeneity between firms, all models include fixed at the firm level (Greene, 2003). Additionally, despite the fact that the sample period is only three years, which makes significant changes in time-variant firm characteristics less likely, it is important to control for firm characteristics and activities which may change in this period and could influence results. *R&D investments* is used to approximate a firm's R&D inputs to the innovation process and the overall extent of a firm's innovation activities. A firm's *research intensity* (relative to firm size) is additionally controlled for. Innovation research has a long history linking firm size to innovation outcomes (Sorensen and Stuart, 2000). Thus, data on *firm size* (number of employees, total assets and total revenues) were collected from Compustat; however, due to the extremely high correlation between size variables ($r > 0.85$) and relatively higher correlation between employees and total assets compared to other control variables, only total revenues are used for further analysis. To account for changes in a firm's innovation direction, the overall level of exploration and average knowledge age are included as firm-level controls. Changes in a firm's overall collaboration activity could hint at a changed approach to the use of collaboration in the innovation process and innovation direction (Hohberger et al. 2017). Additionally, varying levels of collaboration experience and capabilities can influence the use or outcome of collaborations (Hoang and Rothaermel, 2010; Wang, 2011). Thus, the *number of collaborations* and the ratio of collaborative and non-collaborative patents in a given year ("*collaboration intensity*") are included in all models. Finally, the *number of patents* produced by the firm in a given year is used to capture the overall innovation activity. This is important because the level of innovation activity can influence the level of exploration and exploitation (Levinthal and March, 1981).

Model Specifications

Following previous research on citation lag (Phene and Tallman, 2002), this study applies a negative binomial regression model to estimate knowledge age. This approach assumes that the average citation lag represents non-negative integer values (if the average citation lag in a month is rounded to the full month). The negative binomial regression is an extension of the

Poisson regression, which relaxes the assumption that the sample variance equals the sample mean. It has the additional advantage that it accounts for an omitted variable bias while simultaneously estimating individual heterogeneity (Cameron and Trivedi, 1998) and is frequently applied in patent-based studies (Rosenkopf and Nerkar, 2001; Phene et al., 2005; Hess and Rothaermel, 2014; Fleming, 2001).

Results

Table 8.1 depicts the descriptive statistics and Table 8.2 the correlation matrix. The data reveal strong heterogeneity across the sample firms. For example, the sample includes firms from conception (induced in the founding year). Similarly, smaller firms may only produce one patent family per year, while bigger firms generate up to 241 patent families per year (mean 80.71). Firms also differ in their use of and relative propensity for collaboration. For example, the collaborative intensity in a given year ranges from 0 to 1, with a mean of 0.18. This heterogeneity is also apparent in the patent family level variables of which 569 are collaborative patent families and 2677 are non-collaborative activities. For example, patents have between 1 and 44 authors and between 0 and 307 forward citations.

Most correlation coefficients are at low or moderate levels, with the exception of the correlation between firm size and R&D investments (r = 0.716) The high correlation between these variables is not unexpected, as these controls are frequently highly correlated (e.g., Katila and Ahuja, 2002). High correlation can indicate problems of multicollinearity, which can lead to inflated confidence intervals and too small t-statistics. However, since high correlations do not necessarily lead to multicollinearity

Table 8.1 Descriptive Statistics

Variable	*Mean*	*Std. Dev.*	*Min*	*Max*
Citation Lag	37.59	30.03	1.00	258.00
R&D Intensity	165.16	88.84	1.31	1,292.78
R&D Investments	136,393.00	172,337.50	710.00	1,116,600.00
Firm Size	285,704.10	713,469.80	0.00	5,523,000.00
Average Knowledge Age	33.60	15.85	2.00	154.75
Average Firm Exploration	0.39	0.08	0.23	0.93
Number of Collaboration	10.85	11.01	0.00	37.00
Number of Patents	80.71	79.10	1.00	241.00
Collaboration Intensity	0.18	0.17	0.00	1.00
N IPC Codes	8.28	7.04	1.00	40.00
Patent Family Size	5.42	4.08	1.00	49.00
N. of Authors	4.62	4.95	1.00	44.00
N. of References	11.90	19.93	1.00	178.00
N. of Citations	4.52	14.92	0.00	307.00
Citations Time Spread	0.15	0.10	0.00	0.60
Firm Exploration	0.39	0.16	0.09	1.08
Collaboration Dummy	0.18	0.38	0.00	1.00

Table 8.2 Correlation Matrix

	Variable	*1*	*2*	*3*	*4*	*5*	*6*	*7*	*8*	*9*	*10*	*11*	*12*	*13*	*14*	*15*	*16*	*17*
1	Citation Lag	1.00																
2	R&D Intensity	–0.04	1.00															
3	R&D Investments (Ln)	–0.13	0.03	1.00														
4	Firm Size (Ln)	–0.05	–0.33	0.72	1.00													
5	Average Knowledge Age	0.47	–0.08	–0.27	–0.09	1.00												
6	Average Firm Exploration	0.23	–0.10	–0.34	–0.08	0.51	1.00											
7	Number of Collaboration	–0.14	–0.22	0.48	0.30	–0.35	–0.40	1.00										
8	Number of Patents (Ln)	–0.20	–0.08	0.59	0.40	–0.48	–0.48	0.71	1.00									
9	Collaboration Intensity	0.08	–0.10	–0.09	–0.09	0.17	0.12	0.10	–0.31	1.00								
10	N. IPC Codes (Ln)	–0.21	0.02	0.22	0.12	–0.19	–0.27	0.22	0.14	0.03	1.00							
11	Patent Family Size (Ln)	–0.10	0.02	0.00	0.01	0.03	0.07	–0.11	–0.19	0.12	0.59	1.00						
12	N. of Authors (Ln)	–0.05	0.08	0.05	0.01	–0.07	–0.15	0.10	0.01	0.07	0.32	0.25	1.00					
13	N. of References (Ln)	0.24	–0.02	–0.21	–0.08	0.25	0.34	–0.16	–0.17	0.02	–0.10	0.14	0.04	1.00				
14	N. of Citations (Ln)	0.03	0.00	–0.19	–0.14	0.14	0.15	–0.14	–0.27	0.17	0.12	0.25	0.18	0.22	1.00			
15	Citations Time Spread	–0.04	–0.01	–0.02	–0.01	–0.03	–0.02	0.00	0.03	–0.02	0.03	0.02	0.02	0.35	–0.01	1.00		
16	Firm Exploration	0.33	–0.05	–0.16	–0.04	0.22	0.48	–0.18	–0.21	0.05	–0.29	0.00	–0.08	0.32	0.06	0.07	1.00	
17	Collaboration Dummy	0.05	–0.04	–0.04	–0.04	0.08	0.06	0.04	–0.13	0.44	0.02	0.10	0.13	0.04	0.12	–0.03	0.09	1.00

Table 8.3 Negative Binomial Regression with Firm Fixed Effects

Model	*1*	*2*	*3*	*4*	*5*	*6*	*7*	*8*	*9*	*10*
	B/S.E.	*B/S.E.*	*B/S.E.*	*B/S.E.*	*B/S.E.*	*B/S.E.*	*B/S.E.*	*B/S.E.*	*B/S.E.*	*B/S.E.*
Research Intensity	0.00	0.00	0.00	0.00	0.00	0.00	0.00	0.00	0.00	–0.01
	0.00	0.00	0.00	0.00	0.00	0.00	0.00	0.00	0.00	0.01
R&D Investments (Ln)	–0.02	–0.03	–0.03	–0.03	–0.03	–0.04	–0.04	–0.03	–0.03	0.49
	0.03	0.03	0.03	0.03	0.03	0.03	0.03	0.03	0.03	0.74
Firm Size (Ln)	0.02	0.03	0.02	0.03	0.03	0.02	0.03	0.02	0.02	–0.16
	0.02	0.02	0.02	0.02	0.02	0.02	0.02	0.02	0.02	0.35
Average Knowledge Age	0.01***	0.01***	0.01***	0.01***	0.01***	0.01***	0.01***	0.01***	0.01***	0.85***
	0.00	0.00	0.00	0.00	0.00	0.00	0.00	0.00	0.00	0.04
Average Firm Exploration	0.03	–0.71**	–0.73***	–0.77***	–0.74***	–0.67**	–0.71**	–0.72**	–0.74***	–63.16***
	0.28	0.28	0.28	0.28	0.28	0.28	0.28	0.28	0.28	8.09
Number of Collaboration	0.00	0.00	0.00	0.00	0.00	0.00	0.00	0.00	0.00	–0.01
	0.00	0.00	0.00	0.00	0.00	0.00	0.00	0.00	0.00	0.07
Number of Patents	–0.04**	–0.04**	–0.04**	–0.04*	–0.04**	–0.04*	–0.04*	–0.04**	–0.04**	–0.40
	0.02	0.02	0.02	0.02	0.02	0.02	0.02	0.02	0.02	0.66
Collaboration Intensity	–0.05	–0.03	0.03	0.03	0.04	0.00	–0.01	0.03	0.02	2.26
	0.11	0.11	0.11	0.11	0.11	0.11	0.11	0.11	0.11	3.51
N. IPC Codes (Ln)	0.04	0.03	0.03	0.03	0.03	0.03	0.03	0.03	0.03	1.00
	0.02	0.02	0.02	0.02	0.02	0.02	0.02	0.02	0.02	0.96
Patent Family Size (Ln)	–0.15***	–0.15***	–0.15***	–0.15***	–0.15***	–0.12***	–0.12***	–0.15***	–0.15***	–5.98***
	0.02	0.02	0.02	0.02	0.02	0.02	0.02	0.02	0.02	0.85
N. of Authors (Ln)	0.00	0.00	0.00	0.00	0.00	0.01	0.01	0.00	0.00	0.25
	0.02	0.02	0.02	0.02	0.02	0.02	0.02	0.02	0.02	0.62
N. of References (Ln)	0.16***	0.15***	0.15***	0.15***	0.15***	0.15***	0.15***	0.15***	0.15***	4.36***
	0.01	0.01	0.01	0.01	0.01	0.00	0.00	0.01	0.01	0.49
N. of Citations (Ln)	–0.02	–0.01	–0.01	–0.01	–0.01	–0.01	–0.01	–0.01	–0.01	–1.05**
	0.01	0.01	0.01	0.01	0.01	0.01	0.01	0.01	0.01	0.44

Citations Time Spread	–0.42***	–0.51***	–0.52***	–0.53***	–0.52***	–0.11	–0.12	–0.51***	–0.52***	–29.32***
	0.14	0.13	0.13	0.13	0.13	0.12	0.12	0.13	0.13	4.77
Firm Exploration		0.91***	0.93***	1.00***	0.93***	0.95***	0.95***	0.93***	0.93***	50.38***
		0.08	0.08	0.09	0.08	0.08	0.08	0.08	0.08	3.65
Collaboration Dummy			–0.06*	–0.04				–0.08*	–0.08*	–0.13
			0.03	0.03				0.04	0.04	1.28
Collaboration Dummy x Firm Exploration				–0.36**						–13.65**
				0.17						6.89
Firm Collaboration					–0.09**					
					0.04					
University Collaboration					–0.01					
					0.05					
Collaboration Partners						–0.05*	–0.03			
						0.03	0.03			
Firm Exploration * Collaboration Partners							–0.25*			
							0.14			
Specific Collaboration Experience								0.01	0.01	
								0.01	0.01	
Firm Exploration x Specific Collaboration Experience									–0.04	
									0.04	
Technology Dummies	*Included*	*Included*	*Included*	*Included*	*Included*	*Included*	*Included*	*Included*	*Included*	*Included*
Firm Effect	fix	fix	fix	fix	fix	fix	fix	fix	fix	random
AIC	27533	27416	27414	27411	27414	27465	27463	27415	27416	30171
BIC	27679	27568	27572	27575	27578	27623	27628	27580	27586	30348
N	3246	3246	3246	3246	3246	3246	3246	3246	3246	3246

p < 0.1*; p < 0.05**; p < 0.01***

problems, the variance inflation factor (VIF) is calculated to directly examine the effect of the dependencies among the exploration variables on the variance of specific repressors. The highest VIF obtained is 7.34 (VIF average 2.55), which is substantially below the rule-of-thumb cut-off point of 10 (Ryan, 2008).[8] Additionally, firm size was removed from the all estimation to test the robustness of the models, but this did not change the results considerable.

Regression Results

Table 8.3 illustrates the results of the firm fixed effects negative binomial regression models and Model 1 shows the result for the control variables only. Several firm controls (R&D investment, R&D intensity, and number of collaborations) have no significant effect on knowledge age. Thereby, it is important to keep in mind that all models are performed with firm fixed effects (within estimator) and only for three years; this means that the variance within firm year observation is often low. Additionally, emerging knowledge is measure with average time span between the application date of the priority patent of a patent family and the average publication date of all cited patents. Thus, a positive coefficient reflects an increase in the average citation lag, which equals a negative relationship to emerging knowledge. From the patent-level controls, patent family size, number of references, citations time spread, and various IPC dummies are significant. Overall, the results for the control variables are highly consistent across the different models.

In Model 2, the exploration variable is examined. As expected, this variable is significantly positively related to emerging knowledge ($p < 0.01$), which supports Hypothesis 1. In Model 3, the collaboration dummy is added to test Hypothesis 2. The collaboration dummy is only weakly significant ($p = 0.055$), and thus has to be interpreted with care. To test Hypothesis 3, the interaction between collaboration activity and exploration is examined in Model 4. The results show a negative significant interaction effect ($p < 0.05$), which supports Hypothesis 3. The weak support of Hypothesis 2 is also reflected in the overall model fit examined by Akaike information criterion (AIC) and Bayesian information criterion (BIC). Following the AIC, the alliance dummy improves the model fit as well as the interaction effect. However, this is not the case for BIC, which shows that Model 2 has the highest fit. Ideally, both criteria should be aligned, but in the context of this study, it is better to include parameters than omitting significant parameters and, thus, the AIC is preferable.

To facilitate the interpretation of the results, the interaction effect of collaboration activity and exploration is plotted in Figure 8.1. The graph is based on Model 4, with all other variables kept on mean levels.[9] The graph shows that higher levels of explorative knowledge are positively related to emerging knowledge. It also shows that, at low levels of

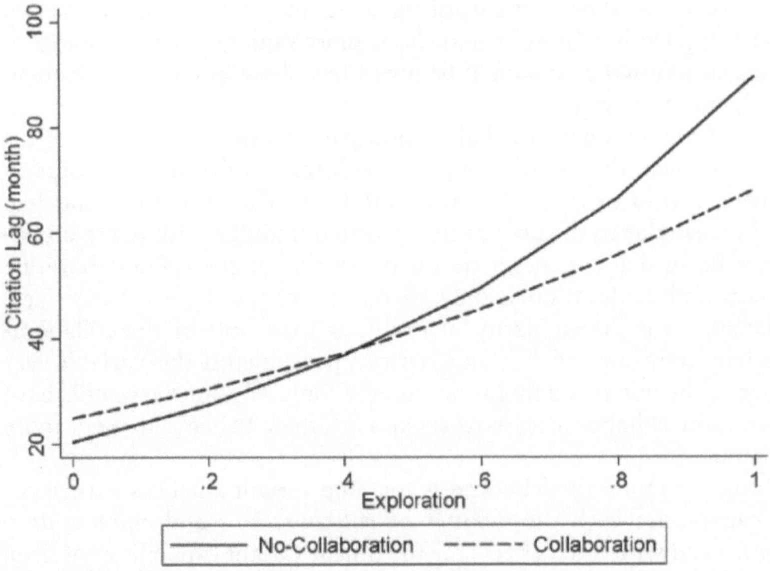

Figure 8.1 Interaction Graph

exploration, collaboration and firm-only innovation are very similar and collaborations are related to a slightly higher knowledge age. However, with increasing levels of exploration, collaborations are more related to emerging knowledge.

Exploration and Robustness Check

To examine the robustness of the findings and to facilitate the interpretation of the results, multiple additional tests were performed. First, previous research has shown that different partner types influence collaboration outcomes (Belderbos et al., 2004; Tether, 2002; Rothaermel and Deeds, 2006). Based on the fact that all collaborations in this sample are highly research-oriented, the most relevant distinction is between patent families with for-profit firms and universities/research institutes as collaboration partners, because earlier research has shown that firms need different capabilities to collaborate with universities and research firms, as they operate in very different organizational environments and also can influence innovation outcomes (Rothaermel and Deeds, 2006; Almeida et al., 2011; Murray, 2004; Bierly et al., 2009). To assess the different collaborations, three dummies were created: non-collaboration, collaboration with for-profit firms, and collaboration with the participation of university-research institutions. Results show that only firm collaboration is significantly different to non-collaboration and related to emergent knowledge (Model 5).[10] The non-significance of university collaboration is somewhat surprising, as Adams et al. (2006) show that university-scientific knowledge diffuses more rapidly than technological knowledge. However, it should be noted that these studies did not focus on collaborative activity.

Second, the number of collaboration partners may also influence the results; as such, the models were run with the number of collaboration partners instead of the collaboration dummy. The results of Models 6 and 7 are similar to the previously presented findings, with the main difference being that the interaction between the number of collaborating partners and exploration is only weakly significant ($p < 0.1$). A likely explanation for the similarity of results is that most of the collaborations have only one collaboration partner, which makes this variable very similar to the initial collaboration dummy (only 12% of the sample have two or more collaboration partners and less than 2% have three or more partners).

Third, the initial model controls for time variant alliances experience and capabilities with the *number of collaborations* and *collaboration intensity* and with fixed effects for the time invariant capabilities of firm. However, frequent interaction with a specific partner may also influence the results (Hoang and Rothaermel, 2010; Gulati et al., 2009). Thus, the partner-specific collaboration intensity, calculated as the ratio of repeated interaction with the same partner in a given year, and the interaction between partner-specific collaboration intensity and firm exploration are tested, in addition to the direct collaboration effect (Models 8 and 9). In both bases, the results show no significant effect for partner-specific collaboration intensity on major changes in the main findings.

Fourth, to test the robustness of the estimation method, the hypotheses are also tested with a Tobit random effects model. The Tobit regression is especially designed for continuous but truncated/censored data (e.g., citation lags cannot be negative) in which other (e.g., ordinary least squares [OLSs]) estimations may yield inconsistent estimators (Cameron and Trivedi, 1998). The main disadvantage of Tobit models is that, due to the incidental parameter problems, they only can be applied with random effects and not fixed effects to control for unobserved heterogeneity (Wooldridge, 2001). As shown in the fully specified estimation (Model 9), the results are generally in line with the negative binomial estimation, with the expectation of Hypothesis 2, which is not supported.

As a final robustness check, all regression models are run with the median citation lag instead of the mean. The median is less sensitive to outliers and better accounts for skewed distributions. The results based on the median values do not change substantially compared to the mean values. Hypotheses 1 and 3 are fully supported, whereas Hypothesis 2 only has weak support ($p < 0.1$). Additionally, the correlation between median and average emerging knowledge is high (0.9370), which indicates that outliers and the distribution of the citation lags do not bias the measurement.[11]

Discussion

For entrepreneurs in general, and in healthcare and biotechnology specifically, collaborative entrepreneurship can be an important tool to create and apply knowledge, and such entrepreneurship relies on "competence and experience, intrinsic motivation, trust among individuals and organizations, and the efficient, full sharing of ideas and information" (Miles et al., 2006: 2). This is even more relevant in the current landscape where the Internet of Things artificial intelligence are transforming the way that patient data is collected and analyzed, and the way decisions are made (Groves et al., 2013; Garbuio, 2018). This study contributes to research on collaborative entrepreneurship by investigating the relationships between emerging knowledge, explorative knowledge, and collaborative activities in the context of innovation in the context of the biotechnology industry. Based on the seminal work of March (1991) and previous research on knowledge search in high-technology industries (Katila, 2002; Phene et al., 2005; Rosenkopf and Almeida, 2003; Petruzzelli and Savino, 2014), this study advances our conceptual understanding of exploration by clarifying the difference between exploration and knowledge age. The distinction between these two concepts is important, because it represents two fundamentally different knowledge characteristics and it is difficult for firms to use knowledge which is explorative and emerging at the same time (Hypothesis 1). However, competitive pressure might force firms to use this type of knowledge.

Second, Hypothesis 2 states that collaborative activities are preferable when using emerging knowledge due to the benefits they offer in using emerging knowledge and their risk-sharing properties. However, this hypothesis is only weakly supported, and it cannot be claimed with certainty that collaboration influences the use of emerging knowledge. The weak results of the collaboration dummy are somewhat surprising, as most previous studies in the biotechnology sector highlight the benefits of collaboration for knowledge access and innovation (Arora and Gambardella, 1990; Liebeskind et al., 1996; Powell et al., 1996; Rothaermel and Deeds, 2004; Baum et al., 2000; Senker and Sharp, 1997; Almeida et al., 2011) and only a few studies provide a broader discussion of their disadvantages, which might explain the non-findings. One study with a stronger focus on the disadvantages of collaboration is the work of Oliver (2004), who argues that collaborations are essential for biotech firms, but complexity and competitive behavior can lead to negative results or even collaboration failure. This also supported by less biotechnology specific discussions on collaborations (Das and Teng, 1996; Gulati et al., 2000). However, probably more important for the question at hand, collaborations are based on an evolutionary process which requires collaborative learning and the development of collaborative capabilities over time (Inkpen, 2008; Doz, 1996; Zollo et al., 2002; Dyer and Singh, 1998). In an in-depth case study in the pharmaceutical industry, Doz (1996) argues that successful collaborations are highly evolutionary and undergo a sequence of interactive cycles of learning, re-evaluation, and readjustment. This process is necessary to develop common routines and language between two separate entities to enable the transfer of knowledge (Doz, 1996). However, not only is the development of these routines often difficult, but it also needs time, which can reduce the efficiency of knowledge transfer, particularly at the beginning of the collaboration.

Related, Dyer and Singh (1998) argue that through repeated interaction with partners, collaboration experience can help firms to achieve higher rents via collaboration-specific assets and through partner-specific absorptive capacity, which will help to generate collaborative rents via knowledge sharing and transfer. Thus, this study explored the influence of general and partner-specific collaboration experience and the use of emerging knowledge in an auxiliary analysis, but significant results. Therefore, it should be noted that previous empirical studies of collaboration experience have provided inconsistent results. For example, Gulati et al. (2009) find no support for increased value creation due to general collaboration experience and only limited support for the case of partner-specific experience in alliances, whereas Hoang and Rothaermel (2010) only find partial support for the positive effects of general alliance experience on joint alliance performance and even a marginally negative effect of partner-specific experience. Additionally, the sample time frame is relatively short to detect within firm differences.

Even though collaborations do not provide clear, direct advantages for emerging knowledge use, it is important to note that they reduce the negative relationship between explorative and emerging knowledge use and thereby still provide relevant advantages for firm (Hypothesis 3). In line with much of the literature on collaborations, the findings suggest that collaborations help to use knowledge that is distant, uncertain, and unfamiliar (Mowery et al., 1996; Rothaermel and Deeds, 2004; Inkpen, 2002; Rosenkopf and Almeida, 2003; Baum et al., 2000).

For managers, our results provide insights into how collaborations provide firms with a strategic alternative to local knowledge search; that is, collaborative entrepreneurship enables firms to break free of their local path-dependent search behavior and remain close to the knowledge frontier. This is particularly important in high-technology industries, where firms face constant competitive pressure to acquire emerging knowledge to stay close to the cutting edge of scientific and technological development. By uncovering the negative relationship between emerging knowledge and explorative knowledge, the study reveals the difficulties for firms to use emerging and explorative knowledge at the same time, as well as showing that collaboration is a tool that can address this problem.

The study focuses on innovation activities within publicly traded biotechnology firms, which are unique in their reliance on collaboration, innovation, patents, and the constant influence of scientific and technological developments (Powell et al., 1996; Arora and Gambardella, 1990; Rothaermel and Deeds, 2004), which limits the generalizability of the findings to other knowledge-intensive sectors and industries that rely on collaborative knowledge-sourcing strategies. Additionally, even though the sample includes very young and small firms, its potential bias against private firms may be particularly relevant in the context of emerging knowledge. In this context, universities and research centers were considered as partner firms, but not in the initial sample. These institutions in particular could have a stronger propensity to use emerging knowledge. However, the theoretical mechanism connecting exploration, emerging knowledge, and collaboration is not sector specific and is very likely to be transferable to other industries.

Patents are constructed in a complex institutional environment and built by strategizing actors (Gittelman, 2008; Jaffe et al., 2000; Duguet and MacGarvie, 2005). This study attempts to address the relevant caveats of patent data to increase validity and reliability, while still taking advantage of its unique possibilities. In general, this study attempts to address the relevant caveats of patent data to increase validity and reliability, while still taking advantage of its unique possibilities.

The regression analysis includes firm fixed effects, and various time-variant and invariant controls variables. Additionally, the use of patent data has the advantage of having a clear link between collaboration activity and collaboration outcome, and its order in time. Nevertheless, collaborations could be entered into with the very intent of gaining access to the latest knowledge and patents, in which case managerial intent clearly drives the use of emerging knowledge and collaboration. While firm fixed effects and control variables mitigate such concerns, they do not completely eliminate them. Care should thus be exercised when interpreting the observed relationship between collaboration activities and emerging knowledge as being causal.

While collaborations are one of the most important mechanisms for acquiring external knowledge, future studies may investigate the differences between mobility, acquisitions, or other forms of external knowledge acquisition. In particular, comparisons between acquisition and collaboration and the different underlying factors that influence emerging knowledge acquisition are worth studying, as these can provide direct guidance for managerial decision-making. By extending the research to non-industry specific collaborations, it would also be possible to investigate how firms achieve industry-level exploration. In general, the research on emerging knowledge is a rather under-researched area, considering its practical and theoretical importance, and it therefore offers substantial scope for future research.

This study extends research on emerging knowledge by analyzing how biotechnology firms can acquire the latest technological developments via interfirm collaboration. By clarifying the distinction between emerging knowledge and exploration, it adds a theoretically interesting and empirically relevant dimension to the search literature. The fact that collaborations can reduce the negative relationship between explorative and emerging knowledge extends the research into the benefits of collaboration in organizational learning situations and shows how firms can remain close to the frontier of innovation in technology- and science-driven industries.

Notes

1. Collaborations are defined as two or more firms working jointly in the production of an innovation.
2. The hypothesis does not imply directionality. Emerging knowledge and explorative knowledge are understood to be two dimensions of the knowledge used which have a negative relationship with each other.
3. Despite the overwhelming positive research findings on the relationship between collaboration and innovation in the biotechnology industry, it is important to mention that also in this sector, collaborations face complexity and competitive behavior, which can lead to negative results or even collaboration failure.
4. DWI provides access to a comprehensive database of international patent information comprising more than 37 million patent documents from 41 patent-issuing authorities worldwide, including all important industrial countries.
5. DWI is frequently used in innovation studies (e.g., Almeida et al., 2011; Gittelman, 2008; Gittelman and Kogut, 2003; Harhoff et al., 2003; Lanjouw and Schankerman, 2004). However, there exist alternative patent family databases with different definitions. "The OECD Directorate for Science, Technology and Industry" provides a detailed comparison of different patent family definitions and databases, which goes beyond the scope of this study (Martinez, 2010).
6. Katz and Martin (1997) discuss what constitutes a collaboration in the context of academic co-authorship; however, most of their arguments can also be applied to co-patenting.
7. The eight four-digit IPC classes are A61K, A61P, C07H, C07K, C12N, C12P, C12Q, and G01N.
8. The analysis of the eigenvalues supports the findings of the VIFs. The condition number is less than 30, which suggests that multicollinearity is not harmful to the results. The condition number is the condition index with the largest value; it equals the square root of the largest eigenvalue (λmax) divided by the smallest eigenvalue (λmin), where eigenvalues represent the variance of a linear combination of X variables.
9. The calculation is based on the margins command in Stata 11.
10. The difference between collaboration with for-profit firms and collaboration with university-research institutions was tested separately, but was also not significant.
11. The results can be requested from the authors.

References

Adams, J.D., Clemmons, R., and Stephan, P.E. 2006. *How Rapidly Does Science Leak Out*? NBER Working Paper No. 11997.

Ahuja, G., and Lampert, C. M. 2001. Entrepreneurship in the large corporation: A longitudinal study of how established firms create breakthrough inventions. *Strategic Management Journal*, 22: 521–543.

Almeida, P., Hohberger, J., and Parada, P. 2011. Individual Scientific Collaborations and Firm-level Innovation. *Industrial and Corporate Change*, 20: 1571–1599.

Antoncic, B. 2007. Intrapreneurship: A comparative structural equation modeling study. *Industrial Management & Data Systems*, 107: 309–325.

Arora, A., and Gambardella, A. 1990. Complementarity and external linkages: The strategies of the large firms in biotechnology. *Journal of Industrial Economics*, 38: 361–379.

Attewell, P. 1992. Technology diffusion and organizational learning: The case of business computing. *Organization Science*, 3: 1–19.

Baum, J. A. C., Calabrese, T., and Silverman, B. S. 2000. Don't go it alone: Alliance network composition and startups' performance in Canadian biotechnology. *Strategic Management Journal*, 21: 267–294.

Beckman, C. M., Haunschild, P. R., and Phillips, D. J. 2004. Friends or strangers? Firm-specific uncertainty, market uncertainty, and network partner selection. *Organization Science*, 15: 259–275.

Belderbos, R., Carree, M., and Lokshin, B. 2004. Cooperative R&D and firm performance. *Research Policy*, 33: 1477–1492.

Belderbos, R., Cassiman, B., Faems, D., et al. 2013. Co-ownership of intellectual property: Exploring the value-appropriation and value-creation implications of co-patenting with different partners. *Research Policy*, 43: 841–852.

Benner, M. J., and Tushman, M. L. 2003. Exploitation, exploration, and process management: The productivity dilemma revisited. *Academy of Management Review*, 28: 238–256.

Bierly, P. E., Damanpour, F., and Santoro, M. D. 2009. The application of external knowledge: Organizational conditions for exploration and exploitation. *Journal of Management Studies*, 46: 481–509.

Cameron, A. C., and Trivedi, P. K. 1998. *Regression Analysis of Count Data*. Cambridge: Cambridge University Press.

Capaldo, A., Lavie, D., and Petruzzelli, A. M. 2014. Knowledge maturity and the scientific value of innovations: The roles of knowledge distance and adoption. *Journal of Management*: 0149206314535442.

Cassiman, B., Veugelers, R., and Zuniga, P. 2008. In search of performance effects of (in)direct industry science links. *Industrial and Corporate Change*, 17: 611–646.

Cohen, W. M., and Levinthal, D. A. 1990. Absorptive capacity: A new perspective on learning and innovation. *Administrative Science Quarterly*, 35: 128–152.

Cohen, W. M., Nelson, R., and Walsh, J. 2000. *Protecting Their Intellectual Assets: Appropriability Conditions and Why U.S. Manufacturing Firms Patent (or Not)*. NBER Working Paper No. W7552.

Danneels, E. 2002. The dynamics of product innovation and firm competences. *Strategic Management Journal*, 23: 1095–1121.

Das, T. K., and Teng, B. S. 1996. Risk types and inter-firm alliances structures. *Journal of Management Studies*, 33: 827–843.

DeCarolis, M. D., and Deeds, D. L. 1999. The impact of stocks and flows of organizational knowledge on firm performance: An empirical investigation of the biotechnology industry. *Strategic Management Journal*, 20: 953–968.

Dong, A., Garbuio, M., and Lovallo, D. 2016. Generative sensing: A design perspective on the microfoundations of sensing capabilities. *California Management Review*, 58: 97–117.
Doz, Y. L. 1996. The evolution of cooperation in strategic alliances: Initial conditions or learning processes? *Strategic Management Journal*, 17: 55–83.
Duguet, E., and MacGarvie, M. 2005. How well do patent citations measure flows of technology? Evidence from French Innovation Surveys. *Economics of Innovation and New Technologies*, 14: 375–393.
Dyer, J. H., and Singh, H. 1998. The relational view: Cooperative strategy and sources of interorganizational competitive advantage. *Academy of Management Review*, 23: 660–679.
Eisenhardt, K. M., and Schoonhoven, C. B. 1996. Resource-based view of strategic alliance formation: Strategic and social effects in entrepreneurial firms. *Organization Science*, 7: 136–150.
Fabrizio, K. R. 2007. University patenting and the pace of industrial innovation. *Industrial and Corporate Change*, 16: 505–534.
Fleming, L. 2001. Recombinant uncertainty in technological search. *Management Science*, 47: 117–132.
Garbuio, M. 2018. *Artificial Intelligence in Healthcare Startups: Emerging Business Models*. Sydney, Australia: The University of Sydney Business School.
Gittelman, M. 2008. A note on the value of patents as indicators of innovation: Implications for management research. *Academy of Management Perspectives*, 22: 21–27.
Gittelman, M., and Kogut, B. 2003. Does good science lead to valuable knowledge? Biotechnology firms and the evolutionary logic of citation patterns. *Management Science*, 49: 366–382.
Grant, R. M., and Baden-Fuller, C. 2004. A knowledge assessing theory of strategic alliances. *Journal of Management Studies*, 41: 61–81.
Greene, W. 2003. *Econometric Analysis*. Englewood Cliffs, NJ: Prentice-Hall.
Groves, P., Kayyali, B., Knott, D., et al. 2013. *The 'Big Data' Revolution in Healthcare: Accelerating Value and Innovation*. Center for US Health System Reform—Business Technology Office.
Gulati, R., Lavie, D., and Singh, H. 2009. The nature of partnering experience and the gains from alliances. *Strategic Management Journal*, 30: 1213–1233.
Gulati, R., Nohria, N., and Zaheer, A. 2000. Strategic networks. *Strategic Management Journal*, 21: 2003.
Gupta, A. K., Smith, K. G., and Shalley, C. E. 2006. The interplay between exploration and exploitation. *Academy of Management Journal*, 49: 693–706.
Hagedoorn, J. 2003. Sharing intellectual property rights—An exploratory study of joint patenting amongst companies. *Industrial and Corporate Change*, 12: 1035–1050.
Hall, B. H., Jaffe, A., and Trajtenberg, M. 2005. Market value and patent citations. *RAND Journal of Economics*, 36: 16–38.
Hamel, G. 1991. Competition for competence and inter partner learning within international strategic alliances. *Strategic Management Journal*, 12: 83–104.
Harhoff, D., Scherer, F. M., and Vopel, K. 2003. Citations, family size, opposition and the value of patent rights. *Research Policy*, 32: 1343–1363.
Heeley, M. B., and Jacobson, R. 2008. The recency of technological inputs and financial performance. *Strategic Management Journal*, 29: 723–744.

Henderson, R. M., and Clark, K. B. 1990. Architectural innovation: The reconfiguration of existing product technologies and the failure of established firms. *Administrative Science Quarterly*, 35: 9–30.

Hess, A. M., and Rothaermel, F. T. 2014. When are assets complementary? Star scientists, strategic alliances, and innovation in the pharmaceutical industry. *Strategic Management Journal*, 32: 895–909.

Hisey, K. B., and Caves, R. E. 1985. Diversification strategy and choice of country: Diversifying acquisitions abroad by US multinationals, 1978–1980. *Journal of International Business Studies*, 16: 51–64.

Hoang, H., and Rothaermel, F. T. 2010. Leveraging internal and external experience: Exploration, exploitation, and R&D project performance. *Strategic Management Journal*, 31: 734–758.

Hohberger, J. 2014. Searching for emerging knowledge: The influence of collaborative and geographically proximate search. *European Management Review*, 11: 139–157.

Hohberger, J. 2016. Diffusion of science-based inventions. *Technological Forecasting and Social Change*, 104: 66–77.

Hohberger, J. 2017. Combining valuable inventions: Exploring the impact of prior invention value on the performance of subsequent inventions. *Industrial and Corporate Change*, 26: 907–930.

Hohberger, J., Almeida, P. and Parada, P. 2015. The direction of firm innovation: the contrasting roles of strategic alliances and individual scientific collaborations. *Research Policy*, 44(8): 1473–1487.

Hussler, C., and Rondé, P. 2007. The impact of cognitive communities on the diffusion of academic knowledge: Evidence from the networks of inventors of a French university. *Research Policy*, 36: 288–302.

Inkpen, A. C. 2002. Learning, knowledge management, and strategic alliances: So many studies, so many unanswered questions. In F. J. Contractor, and P. Lorange (Eds.), *Cooperative Strategies and Alliances*. Oxford: Pergamon.

Inkpen, A. C. 2008. Knowledge transfer and international joint ventures: The case of NUMMI and General Motors. *Strategic Management Journal*, 29: 447–453.

Jaffe, A. B., Trajtenberg, M., and Forgaty, M. S. 2000. *The Meaning of Patent Citations: Report on the NBER/Case-Western Reserve Survey of Patentees*. NBER Working Paper 7631.

Jaffe, A. B., Trajtenberg, M., and Henderson, R. 1993. Geographic localization of knowledge spillovers as evidenced by patent citations. *Quarterly Journal of Economics*, 108: 577–598.

Katila, R. 2002. New product search over time: Past ideas in their prime? *Academy of Management Journal*, 45: 995–1010.

Katila, R., & Ahuja, G. 2002. Something old, something new: A longitudinal study of search behavior and new product introduction. *Academy of Management Journal*, 45: 1183–1194.

Katila, R., and Chen, E. L. 2008. Effects of search timing on innovation: The value of not being in sync with rivals. *Administrative Science Quarterly*, 53: 593–625.

Katz, S. J., and Martin, B. R. 1997. What is a research collaboration? *Research Policy*, 26: 1–18.

Kim, C., and Song, J. 2007. Creating new technology through alliances: An empirical investigation of joint patents. *Technovation*, 27: 461–470.

Kline, S. J., and Rosenberg, N. 1986. An overview of innovation. In R. Landau, and N. Rosenberg (Eds.), *The Positive Sum Strategy: Harnessing Technology for Economic Growth*. Washington, DC: National Academy Press, 275–305.

Kogut, B. 1991. Joint ventures and the option to expand and acquire. *Management Science*, 37: 19–33.

Koza, M. P., and Lewin, A. Y. 1998. The co-evolution of strategic alliances. *Organization Science*, 9: 255–264.

Lanjouw, J. O., Pakes, A., and Putnam, J. 1998. How to count patents and value intellectual property: The uses of patent renewal and application data. *Journal of Industrial Economics*, 46: 405–432.

Lanjouw, J. O., and Schankerman, M. 2004. Patent quality and research productivity: Measuring innovation with multiple indicators. *Economic Journal*, 114(495): 441–465.

Laursen, K. 2012. Keep searching and you'll find: What do we know about variety creation through firms' search activities for innovation? *Industrial and Corporate Change*, 21: 1181–1220.

Lavie, D., Kang J., and Rosenkopf, L. 2011. Balance within and across domains: The performance implications of exploration and exploitation in alliances. *Organization Science*, 22: 1517–1538.

Lavie, D., and Rosenkopf, L. 2006. Balancing exploration and exploitation in alliance formation. *Academy of Management Journal*, 49: 797–818.

Levinthal, D., and March, J. G. 1981. A model of adaptive organizational search. *Journal of Economic Behavior & Organization*, 2: 307–333.

Levinthal, D. A., and March, J. G. 1993. The myopia of learning. *Strategic Management Journal*, 14: 95–112.

Liebeskind, J. P., Oliver, A. L., Zucker, L., et al. 1996. Social Networks, learning and flexibility: Sourcing scientific knowledge in new biotechnology firms. *Organization Science*, 7: 428–443.

Maggioni, M. A., and Uberti, T. E. 2009. Knowledge networks across Europe: Which distance matters? *The Annals of Regional Science*, 43: 691–720.

Malerba, F., and Orsenigo, L. 2002. Innovation and market structure in the dynamics of the pharmaceutical industry and biotechnology: Towards a history-friendly model. *Industrial and Corporate Change*, 11: 667–703.

Mansfield, E. 1986. Patents and innovation: An empirical-study. *Management Science*, 32: 173–181.

March, J. G. 1991. Exploration and exploitation in organizational learning. *Organization Science*, 2: 71–87.

Martinez, C. 2010. *Insight Into Different Types of Patent Families*. Paris: OECD Publishing.

McGrath, R. G. 1997. A real options logic for initiating technology positioning investments. *Academy of Management Review*, 22: 974–996.

Miles, R. E., Miles, G., and Snow, C. C. 2006. Collaborative entrepreneurship: A business model for continuous innovation. *Organizational Dynamics*, 35: 1–11.

Mowery, D., Oxley, J., and Silverman, B. 1996. Strategic alliances and interfirm knowledge transfer. *Strategic Management Journal*, 17: 77–91.

Murray, F. 2004. The role of academic inventors in entrepreneurial firms: Sharing the laboratory life. *Research Policy*, 33: 643–659.

Nelson, R. R., and Winter, S. 1982. *An Evolutionary Theory of Economic Change*. Cambridge, MA: Belknap Press/Harvard University Press.

Nerkar, A. 2003. Old is gold? The value of temporal exploration in the creation of new knowledge. *Management Science*, 49: 211–229.

Oliver, A. L. 2004. On the duality of competition and collaboration: Network-based knowledge relations in the biotechnology industry. *Scandinavian Journal of Management*, 20: 151–171.

Pavitt, K. 1984. Sectoral patterns of technical change: Towards a taxonomy and a theory. *Research Policy*, 13: 343–373.

Petruzzelli, A. M., and Savino, T. 2014. Search, recombination, and innovation: Lessons from haute cuisine. *Long Range Planning*, 47: 224–238.

Phene, A., Madhok, A., and Liu, K. 2005. Knowledge transfer within the multinational firm: What drives the speed of transfer? *Management International Review*, 45: 53–74.

Phene, A., and Tallman, S. 2002. Knowledge flows and geography in biotechnology. *International Journal of Medical Marketing*, 2: 241–254.

Phene, A., Tallman, S., and Almeida, P. 2010. When do acquisitions facilitate technological exploration and exploitation? *Journal of Management*, 38(3): 753–783.

Pisano, G. 2002. Pharmaceutical biotechnology. In B. Steil, D. G. Victor, and R. R. Nelson (Eds.), *Technological Innovation and Economic Performance*. Princeton, NJ: Princeton University Press.

Porter, Kelley, Kjersten Whittington, and W. W. Powell. 2005. The institutional embeddedness of high-tech regions. In *Clusters, Networks, and Innovation*, S. Breschi and F. Malerba (eds.). Oxford: Oxford University Press, pp. 261–296.

Powell, W., Koput, K. W., and Smith-Doerr, L. 1996. Interorganizational collaboration and the locus of innovation: Network learning in biotechnology. *Administrative Science Quarterly*, 41: 116–145.

Randhawa, K., Wilden, R., and Hohberger, J. 2016. A bibliometric review of open innovation: Setting a research agenda. *Journal of Product Innovation Management*, 33: 750–772.

Ribeiro-Soriano, D., and Urbano, D. 2009. Overview of collaborative entrepreneurship: An integrated approach between business decisions and negotiations. *Group Decision and Negotiation*, 18: 419–430.

Rosenkopf, L., and Almeida, P. 2003. Overcoming local search through alliances and mobility. *Management Science*, 49: 751–766.

Rosenkopf, L., and McGrath, P. 2011. Advancing the conceptualization and operationalization of novelty in organizational research. *Organization Science*, 22: 1297–1311.

Rosenkopf, L., and Nerkar, A. 2001. Beyond local search: Boundary-spanning, exploration and impact in the optical disc industry. *Strategic Management Journal*, 22: 287–306.

Rothaermel, F. T., and Deeds, D. L. 2004. Exploration and exploitation alliances in biotechnology: A system of product development. *Strategic Management Journal*, 25: 202–221.

Rothaermel, F. T., and Deeds, D. L. 2006. Alliance type, alliance experience and alliance management capability in high-technology ventures. *Journal of Business Venturing*, 21: 429–460.

Ryan, T. P. 2008. *Modern Regression Methods*. New York, NY: John Wiley & Sons.

Schumpeter, J. 1934. *Capitalism, socialism, and democracy*. New York: Harper & Row.

Senker, J., and Sharp, M. 1997. Organizational learning in cooperative alliances: Some case studies in biotechnology. *Technology Analysis & Strategic Management*, 9: 35–52.

Shane, S., and Venkataraman, S. 2000. The promise of entrepreneurship as a field of research. *Academy of Management Review*, 25: 217–226.

Sorensen, J. B., and Stuart, T. E. 2000. Aging, obsolescence, and organizational innovation. *Administrative Science Quarterly*, 45: 81–112.

Stopford, J. M., and Baden-Fuller, C. W. 1994. Creating corporate entrepreneurship. *Strategic Management Journal*, 15: 521–536.

Stuart, T. E., and Podolny, J. M. 1996. Local search and the evolution of technological capabilities. *Strategic Management Journal*, 17: 21–38.

Stuart, T.E. 2000. Interorganizational alliances and the performance of firms: A study of growth and innovation rates in a high technology industry. *Strategic Management Journal*, 21(8):791–811.

Teece, D. 1977. Technology transfer by multinational corporations: The resource cost of transferring technological know-how. *Economical Journal*, 87(1): 242–261.

Tether, B. S. 2002. Who co-operates for innovation, and why: An empirical analysis. *Research Policy*, 31: 947–967.

Wang, C.-H. 2011. The moderating role of power asymmetry on the relationships between alliance and innovative performance in the high-tech industry. *Technological Forecasting and Social Change*, 78: 1268–1279.

Wang, C.-H., and Hsu, L.-C. 2014. Building exploration and exploitation in the high-tech industry: The role of relationship learning. *Technological Forecasting and Social Change*, 81: 331–340.

Wilden, R., Hohberger, J., Devinney, T. M., et al. 2018. Revisiting James March (1991): Whither exploration and exploitation? *Strategic Organization* forthcoming.

Wooldridge, J. M. 2001. *Econometric Analysis of Cross Section and Panel Data*. Cambridge, MA: MIT Press.

Zahra, S., Nielsen, A., and Bogner, W. 1999. Corporate entrepreneurship, knowledge, and competence development. *Entrepreneurship: Theory & Practice*, 23: 169–189.

Zander, U., and Kogut, B. 1995. Knowledge and the speed of the transfer and imitation of organizational capabilities: An empirical-test. *Organization Science*, 6: 76–92.

Zollo, M., Reuer, J. J., and Singh, H. 2002. Interorganizational routines and performance in strategic alliances. *Organization Science*, 13: 701–712.

Part 3

Micro-Level Topics in Healthcare Entrepreneurship

9 Entrepreneurial Opportunities in Healthcare

A Cognitive Perspective

Massimo Garbuio and Nidthida Lin

Introduction

The discovery or creation of opportunities is one of the most discussed topics in entrepreneurial research (Schumpeter, 1934). A wealth of research has gone into identifying the preconditions of opportunity recognition, including the importance of prior knowledge and external conditions (Shane, 2000; Shepherd and DeTienne, 2005), as well as the thought processes that transform knowledge and observations of the environment into opportunities (Cornelissen and Clarke, 2010; Ucbasaran et al., 2009) and the impetus to act upon them (Dimov, 2007a).

However, entrepreneurship is still a relatively young scholarly discipline that has not yet settled on a research paradigm, and only recently many business schools have dedicated entrepreneurship majors and programs. Several attempts have been made to develop a coherent paradigm, focusing in particular on the cognitive mechanisms that frame an existing situation through the available knowledge and experience and identify opportunities. Proposals have ranged from the use of induction and deduction (Cornelissen and Clarke, 2010), the typical cognitive processes of the scientific method, to counterfactual thinking and mental simulation, which are the typical processes of creative people (Gaglio, 2004). More recently, a study has examined opportunity recognition through the concept of divergent thinking (Gielnik et al., 2014)—that is, the individual's general ability to generate multiple and original ideas.

Apart from cognitive processes, studies have shown that experience also plays a crucial role in the entrepreneur's recognition of opportunities. Through their unique experience, individuals develop their cognitive framework, which serves as a template in pattern recognition by classifying inputs in already known categories (Baron and Ensley, 2006). Hence, experienced entrepreneurs have been shown to be better at pattern recognition in identifying new business opportunities (Baron and Ensley, 2006; Ucbasaran et al., 2009).

The topic of opportunity creation and recognition is becoming of primary importance in the healthcare industry. With advances in computational systems, artificial intelligence, and mixed reality, there is a radical departure from how medical innovations are discovered. This ranges from nurses or doctors becoming entrepreneurs by opening a new clinic or home service, or a scientist at a university spinning off their research, to anyone being able to start a new business in the health tech sector. Telemedicine and remote consultations can deliver healthcare via mobile devices, challenging the conventional ideas of patient-carer relationships. Portable and wearable devices equipped with artificial intelligence can monitor and issue alerts to patients. The widespread use of smartphones in the past decade has given us only a small taste of how technology can rapidly transform a regular person into an informed patient. More options for patient-carer interactions are now possible and will only expand in the future. All this also requires a shift in the "mindset" of who can develop innovative opportunity (a physician, a technology person, or both), but also what problems are worth solving. In this chapter, we tackle these concepts by discussing the cognition behind the creation of entrepreneurial opportunities broadly and in healthcare more specifically.

The rest of this chapter proceeds as follows. First, we briefly introduce the main paradigm applied in entrepreneurship research with respect to opportunity: creation versus recognition. Then, we present a snapshot of exemplary works on the theoretical and empirical literature on the cognitive acts underpinning entrepreneurial opportunity creation and recognition. Next, we discuss the "contextual conditions," such as experience and expertise, which influence the processes of opportunity creation and recognition. Finally, we conclude the chapter with some thoughts and inspiration for future extensions of our model.

How Entrepreneurs Think Through New Opportunities

Entrepreneurial opportunities is one of the most discussed topics in entrepreneurship scholarship (Ardichvili et al., 2003; Short et al., 2010; Kirzner, 1973; Schumpeter, 1934). There has been an ongoing debate about the ontological nature of opportunities. More specifically, are opportunities objective artifacts waiting to be discovered by predisposed individuals, or do they arise from the subjective interpretation and the creative actions of individuals (Alvarez and Barney, 2010)? The nature of opportunities has important implications for our work. On the one side, *opportunity discovery/recognition* approach assumes that shocks in the environment (e.g., advances in technology, changes in consumer preferences or demographics) lead to competitive imperfections in the market and can be analyzed. Hence, opportunities present themselves and must be discovered by entrepreneurs. For opportunity recognition, strategy tools are useful and risk can be "computed" as we can assign probabilities to the various scenarios. On the other side, *opportunity creation* approach assumes that entrepreneurs create opportunities through a process of enactment, and hence opportunity creation is endogenous to entrepreneurs (Sarasvathy, 2001). In this case, strategy frameworks are not useful and even detrimental, and uncertainty is uncovered/solved over time. For opportunity creation, experimentation and ability to learn along the way are fundamental to create opportunities.

A wealth of conceptual and empirical research has also identified cognitive acts that entrepreneurs engage in their thought processes during the opportunity recognition. Here we present 11 conceptual and empirical studies[1] on the cognitive processes involved in opportunity recognition. Although not exhaustive, these studies present an overview of entrepreneurship articles that focus on the thinking aspects of entrepreneurial opportunity recognition. Tables 9.1 and 9.2 summarize these contributions.

We discuss in Table 9.2 five cognitive acts underpinning entrepreneurial opportunities.

Framing

Framing is the cognitive act of drawing associations and dissociations between the facts of a situation, assumptions, and precedents to produce a schema for their interpretation, which makes it possible to clarify the detailed requirements of the decision and determine the extent to which the proposed solution can satisfy them (Stumpf and McDonnell, 2002). Either through recognition of new ideas or a novel interpretation of the existing idea, framing is the act by which entrepreneurs identify a new problem or idea (Gao and Kvan, 2004). Schön (1983: 165) hypothesized that to "frame the problem of the situation, [practitioners] determine the features they will attend, the order they will attempt to impose on the situation, the directions they will try to change it." It is worth noting that this conceptualization of framing discussed here is taken from the

Table 9.1 Summary of Exemplar Conceptual Articles on Entrepreneurial Cognitive Acts

Conceptual Articles		*Cognitive Acts Examined in the Study*
Authors	*Year*	
Hill R.C. and Levenhagen M.	1995	– Analogical Reasoning
Gaglio C.M.	2004	– Mental Simulation – Counterfactual Thinking
Lumpkin G.T. and Lichtenstein B.B.	2005	– Reframing
Dimov D.	2007a	– Divergent Framing
Cornelissen J. and Clarke J.	2010	– Analogical Reasoning and Metaphors – Sensemaking
Dorst K.	2011	– Abductive Reasoning

Table 9.2 Summary of Exemplar Empirical Articles on Entrepreneurial Cognitive Acts

Empirical Articles		*Cognitive Acts in the Study*	*Empirical Method*	*Key Findings*
Authors	*Year*			
Baron R.A. and Ensley M.D.	2006	– Analogical Reasoning	Survey	Relative to novice entrepreneurs, experienced entrepreneurs have more clearly defined prototypes to recognize business opportunities. Experienced entrepreneurs also think of both danger and opportunity when looking for ideas.
Dyer J.H., Gregersen H.B. and Christensen, C.	2008	– Framing – Analogical Reasoning – Mental Simulation	Survey	Innovative entrepreneurs engage in associational thinking—one type of analogy—to come up with opportunities and display information seeking behaviors such as questioning, observing, experimenting, and networking, which helps them make novel associations and recognize opportunities.
Gregoire D.A., Barr P.S. and Shepherd D.A.	2010	– Framing – Analogical Reasoning – Mental Simulation	Verbal Protocol	The structural alignment process of opportunity recognition rests on entrepreneurs' mental comparison of new information with what they already know. In their efforts to recognize opportunities, entrepreneurs align first-order relationships (the functional operation of the technology and markets) and high-order relationships (the casual dynamics underpinning benefits and capabilities of the new technologies and the needs in a given market).
Jacobs C.D., Steyaert C. and Uberbacher F.	2013	– Sensemaking	Semi-Structured interview	Prospective sensemaking—the ability to predict demands of users in a future or hypothetical setting based on the existing situation—helps entrepreneurs conceptualize a future opportunity, state, or actor, which informs how a decision and action will be taken.
Gielnik M.M., Kramer A.-C., Kappel B. and Frese M.	2014	– Divergent Framing – Analogical Reasoning – Mental Simulation	Interview	The process of opportunity recognition corresponds to a larger extent to divergent thinking. Active information search enhances the positive effect of divergent thinking on opportunity identification, which in turn influences innovativeness of products and services contingent on active information search.
Dimov D.	2007b	– Divergent Framing	Online Experiment	Evaluating divergent, outside-the-box insights requires a divergent, multiple-perspective learning approach while evaluating convergent, logic-driven insights requires a convergent, disciplined learning approach.

design perspective and contrasts with framing in decision-making (Garbuio et al., 2015), in which framing emphasizes the analysis of the acts, outcomes, and contingencies associated with a particular choice (Tversky and Kahneman, 1981). Design frames are not analytical in the sense of decision-making; rather, the frame is generative in that it establishes a broad initial objective or small set of objectives in order to handle situations with conflicting constraints but also a potentially infinite number of solutions (Darke, 1979).

In entrepreneurship, a particular type of framing, so-called divergent framing, plays an important role in opportunity recognition. Divergent framing is a cognitive act in which entrepreneurs weaken and strengthen the problem and the solution frames by, for example, considering the goals that a product or service aims to achieve rather than focusing on the product and service itself. Divergent thinking involves the generation of possibilities that one might not ordinarily consider and, thus, involves a high level of abstraction (Finke, 1996, 1995). In divergent thinking, function follows form as the thinking flows outward. In an entrepreneurship study of undergraduate and MBA students, Dimov (2007b) matched the type of insights required for opportunity recognition with students' learning style. He found that evaluating outside-the-box insights requires a divergent, multiple-perspective learning approach.

Business people are generally preoccupied with "things": how to improve a product, how to change its package, how to change the composition of a cream to make it more effective. Thinking about a problem as an "object to improve" will not provide a springboard for innovation. A better frame for the situation of "improving a product" is improving "the way a goal is achieved"—that is, shifting the frame from "nouns/objects" to "verbs/functions." Divergent framing aims to enlarge the problem frames such that novel opportunities can be discovered. This technique emerged decades ago in experimental work by Taylor (1969) and in Langley's (2007) work on sensemaking.

Imagine that you are an entrepreneur in the healthcare industry who is passionate about delivering a better experience to patients. Should you think about how to design a better hospital, or should you redesign a specific treatment that is available for a condition? As compared to describing things, describing functions stimulates people to think in more creative terms about possible solutions. To note, the disruptive innovation framework starts from the concept of "job to be done" rather than with a product to be reinvented (Christensen and Raynor, 2003), similar to reframing a problem as a verb rather than a noun. Framing is relevant not only to the search for entrepreneurial opportunities, but also in identifying that the solution to a problem might be to tap into the markets of complementors or substitutors to create value for the final customer (Brandenburger and Nalebuff, 2011). Once the opportunities are identified in the "verb" mode, framing can take the entrepreneur back to a specific object or service to test in the marketplace, which, as in the case of complementors, might not be the initial object or service.

Interestingly, framing in healthcare might work in a counterintuitive way. Instead of starting with a broader frame, it might be necessary to start with a narrower frame (i.e., more focused question) and then enlarge it after a meaningful opportunity has been identified. For example, when thinking about artificial intelligence (AI) in healthcare, Christopher Khoury, vice president of the American Medical Association's environmental intelligence and strategic analytics unit, stated "It's really about selecting narrower tasks that computers can do better than humans."[2]

Another case in point is Smart Scheduling, which was known as Arsenal Health and bought by Athena Health in 2016 for US$1.7 million. Smart scheduling was started in 2012 by a team who met at the Massachusetts Institute of Technology hack-a-thon. The startup was driven by the question of "What if you could use data science to determine which patients are likely to show up and which ones will be no-shows and manage office appointments around those tendencies?" Using more than 700 variables and machine learning, the company was quickly able to achieve an accuracy of over 70%. This is an example of a new type of healthcare startups. Instead of attempting to solve big issues in healthcare, like curing cancers or diabetes, these startups are targeting more specific problems to improve medical experiences with technology. They work to streamline the processes and increase efficiencies as suggested by Bill Aulet, the director of The Martin Trust Center for MIT Entrepreneurship.[3]

The (re-)framing of entrepreneurial opportunity in healthcare can also appear through the use of a design thinking approach (Fraser, 2012; Garbuio et al., 2018) through a deep user understanding through primary research. For example, Fraser (2012) recount projects at the Princess Margaret Hospital in Canada were patients showed a need for "engagement" during the long period of wait for their treatment. The most common solution would have been thinking about how to shorten the wait time. Instead, the researcher reframed the opportunity as "turning lost time into found time by giving patients the means to make more productive use of their time (both while waiting for and during treatment) and engaging them emotionally, physically, intellectually, or spiritually" (p. 182). This new framing of the problem offered more solutions opportunities than simply looking at the problem as a matter of shortening time.

Another very typical reframing opportunity arises when we think about hospitals not only as a place of cure, but a place where people stay as if they were in a hotel. This reframing does indeed suggest an analogy hospital-hotel and sparks many sets of opportunities (Zygourakis et al., 2014).

Analogical Reasoning

Entrepreneurial scholarship has recognized analogical reasoning as one of the key cognitive acts through which entrepreneurs identify opportunities.

Analogical reasoning is the cognitive act that relies on drawing associations and dissociations between two "things."[4] In analogical reasoning, the properties of a source domain are transferred to a target domain based on an abstract conceptualization (mental representation) of similarity between the two domains (Holyoak and Thagard, 1995). Hill and Levenhagen (1995) suggest that analogies are important in sensemaking and sensegiving, as they help to articulate, communicate, and interpret entrepreneurs' mental models. Because analogies can be incomplete statements comparing one thing to another, they encourage inferences, cognitive flexibility, and adaptiveness to change. Similarly, Cornelissen and Clarke (2010) argue that prospective sensemaking is the result of an inductive use of analogies. Indeed, it has been well established that analogies are used for several purposes, including problem formulation (Visser, 1996), problem solving (i.e., ideation of solutions, inspiration) (Goel, 1997; Rowe, 1982), and uncertainty resolution over whether proposed solutions could work (Ball and Christensen, 2009).

Analogical reasoning has found clear resonance in empirical studies. Baron and Ensley (2006) surveyed 88 experienced and 106 novice entrepreneurs, and found that prototypes serve as templates or analogies that enable entrepreneurs to notice links between diverse events and trends. According to Baron and Ensley (2006), analogies and prototypes are part of a pattern-recognition process that allows entrepreneurs to see connections between apparently independent events. Analogies also play an important role in work on structural alignment—defined as the process of comparing new information with what is already known—in a study of executives' opportunity recognition (Grégoire et al., 2010).

In a study of entrepreneurs and innovative executives that explored the antecedents of associational thinking, Dyer et al. (2008) identified four types of behavioral patterns, some of which are related to cognitive acts. The first behavioral pattern is *questioning*, defined as the propensity of innovative people to challenge the status quo and ask "What if?" questions about the future. The second pattern is *observing*, or paying attention to even common experiences in the search for new ideas. Third, *experimenting* includes physical experimentation with objects, visiting new places and trying new things, and mentally experimenting with ideas. Fourth, the scholars identified *idea networking*, or actively engaging with others to find and test ideas, a process that triggers associations between disparate concepts (Berns, 2008).

Cognitive scientists differentiate between within-domain—that is, close field—and between-domain—that is, far field—analogies (Vosniadou and Ortony, 1989). Between-domain analogies are normally employed in problem formulation; analogies associated with uncertainty resolution are mainly within-domain; and solution-oriented analogies are a mixture of within- and between-domain (Christensen and Schunn, 2007). As a case in point, if you are identifying opportunities for a startup in the healthcare sector, you might be interested in exploring companies that have to operate with novel business models in very challenging environments. Consequently, you might want to look at how microorganisms in nature have survived hostile environments. While the opportunities for healthcare delivery and microorganisms surviving hostile environment may appear very different on the surface, these two problems might share some important characteristics. Once you identify an opportunity, you could explore the execution strategies of other startups and more mature businesses in the same sector to explain a revenue model. As we shall see in the next section, entrepreneurs make use of both within-domain and between-domain analogies.

One robust finding is that analogies that arise from sources drawn from domains far afield from the domain of the target situation generally result in more novel solutions (Chan et al., 2011; Fu et al., 2013; Dahl and Moreau, 2002; Kalogerakis et al., 2010). Introducing between-domain design cases to prime analogical reasoning results in novel solutions when the goals of the target situation are open (Tseng et al., 2008), while within-domain analogies provide a more time-efficient way to solve a problem (Casakin and Goldschmidt, 2000).

Mullins and Komisar (2009) extend the idea of within-domain and between-domain analogies by illustrating how businesses do not have to be revolutionary or start from scratch. They should use analogies with business ideas that worked (so-called analog) and business ideas that did not work well (so-called antilog) to think through business opportunities (Mullins and Komisar, 2009). Looking at both what worked and what did not work will allow entrepreneurs to learn from others' successes and avoid others' mistakes.

Analogical reasoning is recognized to be crucial for healthcare entrepreneurs. Marc Willard writes in the Entrepreneur magazine that using analogies is one of the four ways entrepreneurs can innovate in the health space. More specifically:[5]

> You'll have to look outside of healthcare, where IT generally lags 10 or 20 years behind other industries. Look to banking and investing, for instance. Modern banks have taken themselves almost entirely out of their customers' relationships with their money. While banks still have their traditional internal systems, consumers also have access to their finances on their phones and tablets, and banks compete to offer the best app. Or look at Betterment, which allows investors to skip a human financial advisor and have their investments handled by advanced algorithms.

Indeed, it seems that in comparison to other industries, healthcare research has thought about analogies for a long time. For example, healthcare has been systematically compared to retail, restaurants, media, banking, and education.[6] Others have described patients are analogous to packages, airplanes, and hotel guests.[7] Also, further analogies are explored with automakers (Kim et al., 2006) as well as other high-risk industries (Hudson, 2003; Carroll et al., 2002; Smith, 2007; Jahangirian et al., 2012).

Counterfactual Thinking

Counterfactual thinking refers to the ability to reason beyond known facts and question the status quo (Roese and Olson, 1993). Cognitive psychologists further specified counterfactual thoughts as logical statements that identify causes and effects (Markman and Weary, 1996; Roese, 1994). More specifically, constructing a counterfactual thought implicitly involves laying out a causal chain of events in a sequence of actions and mutating one step in the process to construct an alternate reality. To the extent that a mutation to an initial event undoes the occurrence of subsequent events, that initial event is seen as causally connected to what happened later (Wells et al., 1987). Running a counterfactual simulation in one's head is the mental equivalent of conducting an experiment. Like the experimental process, counterfactual thinking involves a logical consideration of relationships and causal associations between events (Einhorn and Hogarth, 1986; Mandel and Lehman, 1996).

Baron (2006) and Shane and Venkataraman (2000) claim that entrepreneurs do not or should not use too much counterfactual thinking because counterfactual thinking would stop entrepreneurs from acting upon opportunities because they will end up focusing on the possible negative scenarios that result from acting upon opportunities. However, Gaglio (2004) sustains that counterfactual thinking is a key cognitive acts in entrepreneurial opportunity recognition, and suggests that entrepreneurs use counterfactual thinking to help make educated guesses and identify casual connections.

The structure of a counterfactual can be categorized as either additive or subtractive. Additive counterfactual refers to the addition of antecedent elements to reconstruct reality, while subtractive counterfactual involves the subtraction of antecedent elements when reconstructing reality (Roese and Olson, 1993). For instance, an individual who does poorly on a math exam and considers "If only I had brought my calculator, I would have done better" has generated an additive counterfactual. Conversely, the statement "If only I had not had a beer last night, I would have done better" has generated a subtractive counterfactual (Wong et al., 2009). Subtractive counterfactual mindsets activate a relational processing style in which people consider the associations and relationships among stimuli and facilitate creative associations and information search and sharing at both the individual and group levels (but information sharing is only increased when the subtractive counterfactual mindset is created at the group, and not the individual, level). In contrast, additive counterfactual mindsets activate an expansive processing style that broadens conceptual attention and facilitates performance on idea generation tasks. According to Gaglio (2004), in the opportunity identification process, there are reasons to believe that people who develop creative innovative ideas about future products and services show a preference or counterfactuals constructed using addition.

Abductive Reasoning

Abductive reasoning is the form of logical reasoning that is the lifeblood of the creation of desired futures (Dorst, 2011; Roozenburg, 1993; Kolko, 2010). Abductive reasoning plays a key role in cognition because the observations and data that innovators rely on tend to be grounded in tacit socio-cultural dynamics rather than in market research-based data (Rosenman and Gero, 1998; Verganti, 2003). Similarly, entrepreneurs often rely on their experiences or socio-cultural trends rather than on market research on the specific needs and wants of customers (Ardichvili et al., 2003). An abductive reasoning takes a specific set of observations and generates a hypothesized answer to the question, "What product or service has a meaning that explains these observations?"

Unlike deductive and inductive reasoning, which seek to produce logically true conclusions, abduction is a form of logical reasoning that introduces a hypothesis to try to explain observations or data (Peirce, 1998, 1931). As the most commonly used reasoning in science, abductive reasoning allows us to predict results (the act of discovery given the "what" and "how"/working principle) and propose working principles (i.e., hypotheses) to explain the observed outcome (the act of justification given the "what" and outcome). Abductive reasoning is a basic reasoning pattern, which proposes the most plausible and parsimonious explanation for observations.

Dorst (2011) proposes two forms of abductive reasoning. In the first form of abduction, both the desired value (outcome) and the working principle (rule) that will help achieve the desired value are known. A "what" (an object, service, or system) is missing and the potential solution space. This form of abduction is also called *explanatory abduction*. We usually employ exploratory abduction when we have to explain some unexpected observation (outcome/value), such as the cause of an observed patient's dissatisfaction.

In the second form of abduction, neither the working principle (rule) nor the "what" are known; only the desired value (outcome) is known. In this situation, entrepreneurs should abductively propose both the "what" and the means of achieving it. Roozenburg (1993) refers to this form of abduction as *innovative abduction*. In the context of entrepreneurship, innovative abduction explains the unexpected information (outcome/value) by introducing a new opportunity ("what") that responds to the unexpected information and the conditions (working principle) that, if true, underpins the reason for the opportunity itself. During the process of opportunity recognition, the function or value of a proposed product or service may be known, as may be the technologies needed to achieve the desired outcomes, but the final product or service is not known.

In our research, we interviewed Matteo Berlucchi, serial entrepreneur and CEO of Your.MD, an app that uses artificial intelligence to guide individuals to find the best and most relevant health information for free. Interestingly, the development of the ideas as well as the monetization of the business followed a pattern of abduction in two steps (see also, Dong et al. (2016)). In the first step, the idea of addressing a critical problem through mobile phone apps came up.

> With mobile phones becoming ubiquitous and providing you with computing power on your hands and an easy connection to centralized computing power, there must be a way to get people the health information they need for free when they need it.... There must be a way to do something to improve healthcare using mobile phones, for the masses.[8]

Only after the original value creation idea was formed did the usual methodological approach of analyzing the market start. One insight was realizing that healthcare is very far behind other industries when it comes to digitization and transfer of control to the end user, which has clearly been the biggest shift in other industries. Here is when Berlucchi started to think about solving the problem in a very patient-centric way.

In a second step, abductive reasoning was used to identify the business model. Specifically, Berlucchi started to notice that health-related searches in Google are among the most common searches online, but also the most highly paid advertisement searches. However, search engines do not necessarily provide the most accurate information or diagnosis, and indeed it is not a curated marketplace of healthcare information. Indeed, hence the terms "Google syndrome" or "Google doctor." At the same time, specialized clinics started to inquire about providing paid advertisement to target specific customers who were looking for answers that they could provide with clinical consultations. For the clinic, it was a cheaper way to advertise and to a very targeted customer group. Hence was born OneStop Health, a curated network of trustworthy healthcare providers. With OneStop Health, Your.MD has created the first one-stop shop in digital health to empower patients to take control of each stage of their healthcare, from understanding their symptoms to finding the best treatment.

In summary, abductive reasoning allows innovative healthcare entrepreneurs to create a map from a set of desired meanings to the space of the product or service that embodies those meanings (Dong et al., 2016). This is not to say that coming up with innovative ideas does not entail deductive or inductive logic. Rather, abductive reasoning is the form of logical reasoning that permits innovative people to deal with situations when problems are neither completely stated nor definitively formulated, but must be determined from information-rich observations whose underlying principles may be poorly understood. A typical example is when you have a new technology, but the use and business cases are missing or unclear. You are required to make a set of hypothesis of what might be, and these can be formulated through a process of observations as well as trial and error.

Mental Simulation

Mental simulation is defined as the act of reassessing past events and imagining future environments prior to making decisions and taking action (Sanna, 2000). According to Gaglio (2004), mental simulation is another key cognitive act of entrepreneurs (together with counterfactual thinking). It allows emotions to be re-experienced and processed to aid in coping, and it also helps individuals to anticipate physical and social environments by envisioning strategies and tactics to make accurate estimates and enable goal achievement. While framing and anagogical reasoning are more commonly activated to generate novel problem or solution formulations, mental simulation facilitates the resolution of uncertainty over problem and solution formulation (Ball and Christensen, 2009).

Supported by mental imagery (Kavakli and Gero, 2001) and mental models, mental simulation supports the potential entrepreneur in the evaluation of different possible outcomes before these same questions are asked by, for example, an angel investor or a venture capitalist. The role of mental simulation in manifesting solutions and then pruning nonviable alternatives shares similarities with the practice of prototyping (Youn-Kyung et al., 2008), suggesting that mental simulations are a mental form of prototyping.

Mental simulation is instantiated when: (i) there is incomplete knowledge about an anticipated future into which the solutions, such as the business model, will be introduced, and (ii) the space of problem and solution formulations entails a large number of possibilities. Mental simulation is nonetheless an essential cognitive act for imagining how a solution might work in a world that is not the same one we know.

This is particularly true when we are looking at understanding scenarios that are wicked as well as complex because of all the constrains that are present in an industry, such as the role of blockchain in healthcare. Deployment of blockchain solutions entails substantial changes in the way healthcare practitioners store and assess information, as well as the amount of information that is available to them; mental simulation is brought in to consider the effects caused by change in elements. As the complexity of business model requirements increases, more mental simulations (Ball et al., 2010) and analogies may occur, suggesting that both of these cognitive acts appear to be important ways in which entrepreneurs can deal with uncertainties.

Consider an instance in which the value of mental simulation for entrepreneurs in the healthcare domain is crucial. Suppose that you have invented a smart pillow, which can detect sleeping disorders. This is a fairly common student projects in engineering and interaction design courses (Zhang et al., 2013), but has also been developed into several commercial applications, including Beddit (Paalasmaa et al., 2012), which was bought by Apple in 2017. Whereas Beddit is a consumer product, your team has developed a system that is comparable to the gold standard of sleep monitoring and sleep disorder diagnosis—that is, polysomnography (PSG), but is completely non-invasive. You would ask such questions as: Who is the buyer? Who are you creating value for? What can you do with the data that you can collect from the device given that sleeping disorders are also preconditions of several other diseases (McCall et al., 2009; Hansen et al., 2013)? You then start running a series of mental simulations, asking such questions as: Will hospitals pay for it? Will Medicare cover the costs? Will aged care facilities be willing to pay for it, since aged care individuals suffer from sleeping disorders more than other populations? What about shift workers? Should the device just diagnose, or also monitor? Does it need to provide "action"? Will insurance companies make use of the data and be willing to pay for it? Once you start running through these questions, you'll soon realize that whereas the market is rather large given the amount of population with sleeping disorders, the willingness to pay has serious constraints given the need to cover the costs through the public health system as well as the restrictions on change insurance premiums on the basis of the sleeping health of the patient. As such, you might realize that non-invasive medical-grade sleep diagnosis devices might remain a university student's project rather than a reality.[9] Instead, consumer level products such as Beddit have a space in the market.

Frameworks, such as the one proposed by Mullins and Komisar (2009), can provide a useful approach for creating testable hypotheses about specific elements of a business models for which answers are unknown but can be found by setting up tests in the marketplace, if not mentally.

Contextual Conditions of Entrepreneurial Opportunities

While we focus our discussion on cognitive acts underpinning opportunity recognition, entrepreneurial cognition goes beyond thought processes. Two key contextual conditions play an essential role in constraining or enabling the cognitive acts we discussed.

The first is the experience and knowledge the entrepreneur accumulates over time (Shepherd and DeTienne, 2005). It is thought that, over time, entrepreneurs develop a "knowledge corridor" (Ronstadt, 1989) that focuses their attention on certain opportunities but not others (Shane and Venkataraman, 2000; Venkataraman, 1997). For example, in analogical reasoning, expertise in a field has been shown to have an impact on the relational patterns between target and source domains, a finding that needs to be considered in further theory development and empirical testing. Novice entrepreneurs tend to make analogies based upon surface similarity between the source and target cases, whereas experienced entrepreneurs more routinely make analogies based on principles and underlying patterns (i.e., structural or deep similarity) (Ball et al., 2004; Ahmed and Christensen, 2009). Consequently, novices tend to use analogies to transfer structural information, such as "copying" the shape of a flower onto a building, rather than reasoning about the purpose of the flower's shape in repelling environmental hazards so as to transfer its shape as a strategy for a building that encounters similar environmental conditions.

The role of experience can also be explained through the process of sensemaking which occurs when we make sense of new inputs—typically the unusual, the confusing, and the unexpected rather than the everyday or the routine (Maitlis, 2005)—on the basis of past experiences (Weick, 1995). In opportunity recognition, a particular type of sensemaking, so-called prospective sensemaking, has emerged. Prospective sensemaking is an attempt to create meaningful opportunities and a structure for the future by imagining some desirable state (Shrivastava et al., 1996). Because it focuses on the future, prospective sensemaking is particularly useful in the context of new venture creations (Shrivastava et al., 1996).

The second is made up of external circumstances, such as technological invention and connection with communities. As a social skill, opportunity recognition requires more than knowing the right information and how to use the cognitive acts. Participation in communities for knowledge creation has been found to be a key characteristic of innovators (Powell et al., 1996). Indeed, the discovery of opportunity is not a single-person and single-insight attribution (Dimov, 2007a), but rather the result of a process in which a set of unitary, distinct events lead to the emergence of a pattern (Oliver and Roos, 2005). This is particularly relevant in technology entrepreneurship, which has been found to be more effective when it is built on the efforts of many (Garud and Karnøe, 2003). Van Burg and Romme (2014) can provide guidance on the broader settings on the social aspects of entrepreneurial cognition that surround our model.

Moving Research on Healthcare Opportunities Forward

The literature has yet to converge on a finite and exhaustive set of cognitive acts that explain how entrepreneurs process information while recognizing a business opportunity (Keh et al., 2002; Short et al., 2010; Moroz and Hindle, 2012). Most studies also fail to identify how overarching concepts, such as divergent and convergent thinking and sensemaking, clearly relate to more fine-grained concepts, such as analogical thinking and mental simulation. Our review of the literature also highlights a lack of discussion of two key cognitive acts, framing and abduction, in the process of entrepreneurship opportunity recognition.

Another area for future research is the critical role of external circumstances on opportunity recognition. Although changes in these circumstances are typically viewed as opportunities (Shane, 2000),[10] too much experience and knowledge are found to hinder entrepreneurs from identifying promising new opportunities (Ucbasaran et al., 2009)—a fruitful area for future research.[11] The social aspects of opportunity identification, such as connection with the community, are also ripe for study.

In this chapter, as previously stated, we did not discuss the impact of external circumstances (Shane, 2000), the amount and type of prior knowledge (Shepherd and DeTienne, 2005), or the emotional states (Baron, 2008) on opportunity recognition. We also did not discuss the potential use of heuristics and biases (Busenitz and Barney, 1997; Dosi and Lovallo, 1997). Further theoretical work is needed to explicate the number of opportunities identified (Arenius and De Clercq, 2005), their degree of innovativeness (Grégoire et al., 2010), and ultimately action on perceived opportunities (Levie and Autio, 2008). The recent evidence-based review of entrepreneurship provided by Van Burg and Romme (2014) will provide with some inspiration on these elements.

Discussion and Conclusion

Cognition as discussed in this chapter is not comprised of a finite set of cognitive acts employed in various situations. One appealing aspect of these cognitive acts is that they demystify notions of creative insight. Fluency in an ordinary set of cognitive acts can support the framing of a novel problem space, driven by distant analogical references, and the formation of corresponding solutions, by reducing psychological uncertainty using within-domain analogies and mental simulation.

Through the perspective discussed in this chapter, we also aim to provide further insights into the debate on the nature of entrepreneurial opportunities; that is, on whether they await to be discovered or they are created by a process of enactment (Alvarez and Barney, 2010). The cognitive acts discussed in this chapter suggest novel ways to use classical analysis tools for the examination of external shocks in the process of discovering opportunities. For example, they allow changing the frame of the industry and the frame of the problem to be solved from different points of view (e.g., customers, suppliers, competitors). They also invite to use analogies from other industries to solve user problems and create abductive hypotheses from scattered observations (Garbuio et al., 2017). These same cognitive acts provide key insights on the process of opportunity creation by, for instance, systematically using abductive reasoning in the generation of hypotheses from the data that has been generated, rather than the pure application of a systematic process (e.g., experimentation). No matter whether we believe that opportunities are discovered rather than created, or vice versa, the cognitive acts go at the core of novelty and help in the discovery or creation of novel solution.

The use of information technology and mobile applications have become essential in the healthcare industry, and greater attention is placed by both venture capitalists as well as corporate venture arms on the development of health tech startups (see CB Insight research on Health Tech, for example). As data from healthcare providers becomes ubiquitous, entrepreneurs are capitalizing on a tremendous opportunity to make sense of this data. Innovative startups are utilizing "big data" to offer solutions that improve quality, lower costs, and streamline access to healthcare services. They are using blockchain technologies as well as artificial intelligence, building on readily available services like Microsoft Cognitive Services. The key question is what is the value of data, and as a result, what is the business model of a data-driven healthcare startups. In this chapter, we conclude that to design business models that solve these problems, more attention is required on the cognitive side of understanding problem searching and solution design from both a technological and a business model perspective.

Notes

1. Published before 2017.
2. https://wire.ama-assn.org/practice-management/ai-teamed-physicians-intelligence-could-improve-care
3. www.bostonglobe.com/business/2014/07/13/high-tech-cure-for-doctors-scheduling-pains/ylLD4Fwar8EElFJ32frI9I/story.html
4. Some authors claim that these can be driven by metaphors, as well. The concepts of analogy and metaphor are often confused. The association of meanings through analogy is more functional and mostly carried out through rational thinking, while the association of meanings through metaphor is often driven by intuition and involves images. In our discussion, we focus on analogies as the most researched type in design, as well as entrepreneurial cognition.
5. www.entrepreneur.com/article/286008
6. www.beckershospitalreview.com/hospital-management-administration/what-can-healthcare-learn-from-other-industries-5-lessons.html
7. https://caremilestones.com/2013/11/11/are-your-patients-more-like-packages-planes-or-hotel-guests/
8. Interview date: October 2017.
9. This example is drawn from a real case.
10. Serendipity may play an important role on opportunity discovery. Serendipitous discovery can be defined as the search activity that leads to the discovery of something that the person was *not* looking for (Dew, 2009). It is built on three blocks: the domain of prior knowledge, the domain of systematic search, and the domain of contingency (i.e., events that are not logically necessary, that could not have occurred, that happened by chance, or without known causes).
11. The type of knowledge has also an impact on the radicalness of the ideas. Marvel and Lumpkin (2007) studied a sample of 145 technology entrepreneurs

and found that "innovation radicalness was positively associated with formal education and prior knowledge of technology, but negatively associated with prior knowledge of ways to serve markets" (p. 807). That is, "the less technology entrepreneurs know about ways to serve a market, the greater their chances of using technology knowledge to create breakthrough innovations within it" (p. 807).

References

Ahmed, S., and Christensen, B. T. 2009. An in situ study of analogical reasoning in novice and experienced design engineers. *Journal of Mechanical Design*, 131(11): 111004.

Alvarez, S. A., and Barney, J. B. 2010. Entrepreneurship and epistemology: The philosophical underpinnings of the study of entrepreneurial opportunities. *Academy of Management Annals*, 4(1): 557–583.

Ardichvili, A., Cardozo, R., and Ray, S. 2003. A theory of entrepreneurial opportunity identification and development. *Journal of Business Venturing*, 18: 105–123.

Arenius, P., and De Clercq, D. 2005. A network-based approach on opportunity recognition. *Small Business Economics*, 24(3): 249–265.

Ball, L. J., and Christensen, B. T. 2009. Analogical reasoning and mental simulation in design: Two strategies linked to uncertainty resolution. *Design Studies*, 30(2): 169–186.

Ball, L. J., Onarheim, B., and Christensen, B. T. 2010. Design requirements, epistemic uncertainty and solution development strategies in software design. *Design Studies*, 31(6): 567–589.

Ball, L. J., Ormerod, T. C., and Morley, N. J. 2004. Spontaneous analogising in engineering design: A comparative analysis of experts and novices. *Design Studies*, 25(5): 495–508.

Baron, R. A. 2006. Opportunity recognition as pattern recognition: How entrepreneurs 'connect the dots' to identify new business opportunities. *Academy of Management Perspectives*, 20(1): 104–119.

Baron, R. A. 2008. The role of affect in the entrepreneurial process. *Academy of Management Review*, 33(2): 328–340.

Baron, R. A., and Ensley, M. D. 2006. Opportunity recognition as the detection of meaningful patterns: Evidence from comparisons of novice and experienced entrepreneurs. *Management Science*, 52(9): 1331–1344.

Berns, G. 2008. *Iconoclast: A Neuroscientist Reveals How to Think Differently*. Cambridge, MA: Harvard Business School Press.

Brandenburger, A. M., and Nalebuff, B. J. 2011. *Co-opetition*. Crown Publishing Group, USA.

Busenitz, L. W., and Barney, J. B. 1997. Differences between entrepreneurs and managers in large organizations: Biases and heuristics in strategic decision-making. *Journal of Business Venturing*, 12(1): 9–30.

Carroll, J., Rudolph, J., and Hatakenaka, S. 2002. Lessons learned from non-medical industries: Root cause analysis as culture change at a chemical plant. *Quality and Safety in Health Care*, 11(3): 266–269.

Casakin, H. P., and Goldschmidt, G. 2000. Reasoning by visual analogy in design problem-solving: The role of guidance. *Environment and Planning B: Planning and Design*, 27(1): 105–119.

Chan, J., Fu, K., Schunn, C., Cagan, J., Wood, K., and Kotovsky, K. 2011. On the benefits and pitfalls of analogies for innovative design: Ideation performance based on analogical distance, commonness, and modality of examples. *Journal of Mechanical Design*, 133(8): 081004.

Christensen, B., and Schunn, C. 2007. The relationship of analogical distance to analogical function and preinventive structure: The case of engineering design. *Memory & Cognition*, 35(1): 29–38.

Christensen, C. M., and Raynor, M. E. 2003. *The Innovator's Solution: Creating and Sustaining Successful Growth*. Cambridge, MA: Harvard Business School Press.

Cornelissen, J. P., and Clarke, J. S. 2010. Imagining and rationalizing opportunities: Inductive reasoning and the creation and justification of new ventures. *Academy of Management Review*, 35(4): 539–557.

Dahl, D. W., and Moreau, P. 2002. The influence and value of analogical thinking during new product ideation. *Journal of Marketing Research*, 39(1): 47–60.

Darke, J. 1979. The primary generator and the design process. *Design Studies*, 1(1): 36–44.

Dew, N. 2009. Serendipity in entrepreneurship. *Organization Studies*, 30(7): 735–753.

Dimov, D. 2007a. Beyond the single-person, single-insight attribution in understanding entrepreneurial opportunities. *Entrepreneurship Theory and Practice*, 31(5): 713–731.

Dimov, D. 2007b. From opportunity insight to opportunity intention: The importance of person-situation learning match. *Entrepreneurship Theory and Practice*, 31(4): 561–583.

Dong, A., Garbuio, M., and Lovallo, D. 2016. Generative sensing. *California Management Review*, 58(4): 97–117.

Dorst, K. 2011. The core of 'design thinking' and its application. *Design Studies*, 32(6): 521–532.

Dosi, G., and Lovallo, D. 1997. Rational entrepreneurs or optimistic martyrs? Some considerations on technological regimes, corporate entries, and the evolutionary role of decision biases. In R. Garud, P. R. Nayyar, Z. B. Shapira, and J. G. March (Eds.), *Technological Innovation: Oversights and Foresights*. Cambridge: Cambridge University Press, 41–68.

Dyer, J. H., Gregersen, H. B., and Christensen, C. 2008. Entrepreneur behaviors, opportunity recognition, and the origins of innovative ventures. *Strategic Entrepreneurship Journal*, 2: 317–338.

Einhorn, H. J., and Hogarth, R. M. 1986. Judging probable cause. *Psychological Bulletin*, 99(1): 3.

Finke, R. A. 1995. Creative insight and preinventive forms. In R. J. Sternberg, and J. E. Davidson (Eds.), *The Nature of Insight*. Cambridge, MA: MIT Press, 255–280.

Finke, R. A. 1996. Imagery, creativity, and emergent structure. *Consciousness and Cognition*, 5(3): 381–393.

Fraser, H. M. 2012. *Design Works: How to Tackle Your Toughest Innovation Challenges Through Business Design*. Ontario, Canada: University of Toronto Press.

Fu, K., Chan, J., Cagan, J., Kotovsky, K., Schunn, C., and Wood, K. 2013. The meaning of 'near' and 'far': The impact of structuring design databases and the effect of distance of analogy on design output. *Journal of Mechanical Design*, 135(2): 021007–021007.

Gaglio, C. M. 2004. The role of mental simulations and counterfactual thinking in the opportunity identification process. *Entrepreneurship Theory and Practice*, 28(6): 533–552.

Gao, S., and Kvan, T. 2004. An analysis of problem framing in multiple settings. In J. S. Gero (Ed.), *Design Computing and Cognition '04*. Dordrecht: Springer Science+Business Media, 117–134.

Garbuio, M., Dong, A., Lin, N., Tschang, F., and Lovallo, D. 2018. Demystifying the genius of entrepreneurship: How design cognition can help create the next generation of entrepreneurs. *Academy of Management Learning & Education*, 17(1): 41–61. doi:10.5465/amle.2016.0040.

Garbuio, M., Lovallo, D., Porac, J. F., and Dong, A. 2015. A design cognition perspective on strategic option generation. In G. Gavetti, and W. Ocasio (Eds.), *Advances in Strategic Management*, Vol. 32. Bingley, UK: Emerald, 437–465.

Garbuio, M., Mazzoleni, I., and Eisenbart, B. 2017. Bio-inspired design: Explicating the value of bio-inspiration. In *Conference Proceedings of the Design Management Academy*, Vol. 1. Hong Kong: Design Research Society, 23–42.

Garud, R., and Karnøe, P. 2003. Bricolage versus breakthrough: Distributed and embedded agency in technology entrepreneurship. *Research Policy*, 32(2): 277–300.

Gielnik, M. M., Kraemer, A.-C., Kappel, B., and Frese, M. 2014. Antecedents of business opportunity identification and innovation: Investigating the interplay of information processing and information acquisition. *Applied Psychology: An International Review*, 63(2): 344–381.

Goel, A. K. 1997. Design, analogy, and creativity. *IEEE Expert*, 12(3): 62–70.

Grégoire, D. A., Barr, P. S., and Shepherd, D. A. 2010. Cognitive processes of opportunity recognition: The role of structural alignment. *Organization Science*, 21(2): 413–431.

Hansen, I. H., Marcussen, M., Christensen, J. A., Jennum, P., and Sorensen, H. B. 2013. *Detection of a Sleep Disorder Predicting Parkinson's Disease*. Paper presented at the 35th Annual International Conference of the IEEE, Engineering in Medicine and Biology Society (EMBC), 2013.

Hill, R. C., and Levenhagen, M. 1995. Metaphors and mental models: Sensemaking and sensegiving in innovative and entrepreneurial activities. *Journal of Management*, 21(6): 1057–1074.

Holyoak, K. J., and Thagard, P. 1995. *Mental Leaps: Analogy in Creative Thought*. Cambridge, MA: MIT Press.

Hudson, P. 2003. Applying the lessons of high risk industries to health care. *Quality and Safety in Healthcare*, 12(suppl. 1): i7–i12.

Jacobs, C. D., Steyaert, C., and Ueberbacher, F. 2013. Anticipating intended users: prospective sensemaking in technology development. *Technology Analysis & Strategic Management*, 25(9): 1027–1043.

Jahangirian, M., Naseer, A., Stergioulas, L., Young, T., Eldabi, T., Brailsford, S., Patel, B., and Harper, P. 2012. Simulation in health-care: Lessons from other sectors. *Operational Research*, 12(1): 45–55.

Kalogerakis, K., Lüthje, C., and Herstatt, C. 2010. Developing innovations based on analogies: Experience from design and engineering consultants. *Journal of Product Innovation Management*, 27(3): 418–436.

Kavakli, M., and Gero, J. S. 2001. Sketching as mental imagery processing. *Design Studies*, 22(4): 347–364.

Keh, H. T., Foo, M. D., and Lim, B. C. 2002. Opportunity evaluation under risky conditions: The cognitive processes of entrepreneurs. *Entrepreneurship Theory & Practice*, 27(2): 125–148.

Kim, C. S., Spahlinger, D. A., Kin, J. M., and Billi, J. E. 2006. Lean health care: What can hospitals learn from a world-class automaker? *Journal of Hospital Medicine*, 1(3): 191–199.

Kirzner, I. M. 1973. *Competition and Entrepreneurship*. Chicago, IL: University of Chicago Press.

Kolko, J. 2010. Abductive thinking and sensemaking: The drivers of design synthesis. *Design Issues*, 26(1): 15–28.

Langley, A. 2007. Process thinking in strategic organization. *Strategic Organization*, 5(3): 271.

Levie, J., and Autio, E. 2008. A theoretical grounding and test of the GEM model. *Small Business Economics*, 31(3): 235–263.

Lumpkin, G. T., and Lichtenstein, B. B. (2005). The role of organizational learning in the opportunity-recognition process. *Entrepreneurship theory and practice*, 29(4): 451–472.

Maitlis, S. 2005. The social processes of organizational sensemaking. *Academy of Management Journal*, 48(1): 21–49.

Mandel, D. R., and Lehman, D. R. 1996. Counterfactual thinking and ascriptions of cause and preventability. *Journal of Personality and Social Psychology*, 71(3): 450.

Markman, K. D., and Weary, G. 1996. The influence of chronic control concerns on counterfactual thinking. *Social Cognition*, 14(4): 292–316.

Marvel, M. R., and Lumpkin, G. T. 2007. Technology entrepreneurs' human capital and its effects on innovation radicalness. *Entrepreneurship Theory and Practice*, 31(6): 807–828.

McCall, W. V., Kimball, J., Boggs, N., Lasater, B., D'Agostino, R. B., and Rosenquist, P. B. 2009. Prevalence and prediction of primary sleep disorders in a clinical trial of depressed patients with insomnia. *Journal of Clinical Sleep Medicine: JCSM: Official Publication of the American Academy of Sleep Medicine*, 5(5): 454–458.

Moroz, P. W., and Hindle, K. 2012. Entrepreneurship as a process: Toward harmonizing multiple perspectives. *Entrepreneurship Theory and Practice*, 36(4): 781–818.

Mullins, J., and Komisar, R. 2009. *Getting to Plan B: Breaking Through to a Better Business Model*. Cambridge, MA: Harvard Business Review Press.

Oliver, D., and Roos, J. 2005. Decision-making in high-velocity environments: The importance of guiding principles. *Organization Studies*, 26(6): 889–913.

Paalasmaa, J., Waris, M., Toivonen, H., Leppäkorpi, L., and Partinen, M. 2012. *Unobtrusive Online Monitoring of Sleep at Home*. Paper presented at the 2012 Annual International Conference of the IEEE, Engineering in Medicine and Biology Society (EMBC).

Peirce, C. S. 1931. *Collected Papers of CS Peirce*, C. Hartshorne, P. Weiss, and A. Burks (Eds), 8 vols. Cambridge, MA: Harvard University Press.

Peirce, C. S. 1998. *The Essential Peirce, Volume 2: Selected Philosophical Writings, 1893–1913*. Bloomington, IN: Indiana University Press.

Powell, W. W., Koput, K. W., and Smith-Doerr, L. 1996. Interorganizational collaboration and the locus of innovation: Networks of learning in biotechnology. *Administrative Science Quarterly*, 41(1): 116–145.

Roese, N. J. 1994. The functional basis of counterfactual thinking. *Journal of Personality & Social Psychology*, 66(5): 805–818.

Roese, N. J., and Olson, J. M. 1993. The structure of counterfactual thought. *Personality & Social Psychology Bulletin*, 19(3): 312–319.

Ronstadt, R. 1989. The corridor principle. *Journal of Business Venturing*, 3(1): 31–40.

Roozenburg, N. F. 1993. On the pattern of reasoning in innovative design. *Design Studies*, 14(1): 4–18.

Rosenman, M. A., and Gero, J. 1998. Purpose and function in design: From the socio-cultural to the techno-physical. *Design Studies*, 19(2): 161–186.

Rowe, P. G. 1982. A priori knowledge and heuristic Reasoning in architectural design. *JAE*, 36(1): 18–23.

Sanna, L. J. 2000. Mental simulation, affect, and personality a conceptual framework. *Current Directions in Psychological Science*, 9(5): 168–173.

Sarasvathy, S. D. 2001. *Effectual Reasoning in Entrepreneurial Decision Making: Existence and Bounds*. Paper presented at the Academy of Management Proceedings.

Schön, D. A. 1983. *The Reflective Practitioner: How Professionals Think in Action*. New York, NY: Basic Books.

Schumpeter, J. A. 1942. *Socialism, capitalism and democracy*. New York: Harper and Brothers.

Shane, S. 2000. Prior knowledge and the discovery of entrepreneurial opportunities. *Organization Science*, 11(4): 448–469.

Shane, S., and Venkataraman, S. 2000. The promise of entrepreneurship as a field of research. *Academy of Management Review*, 25(1): 217–226.

Shepherd, D. A., and DeTienne, D. R. 2005. Prior knowledge, potential financial reward, and opportunity identification. *Entrepreneurship Theory and Practice*, 29(1): 91–112.

Short, J. C., Ketchen, D. J., Shook, C. L., and Ireland, R. D. 2010. The concept of 'opportunity' in entrepreneurship research: Past accomplishments and future challenges. *Journal of Management*, 36(1): 40–65.

Shrivastava, P., Gioia, D. A., and Mehra, A. 1996. Sensemaking in organizations. *Academy of Management Review*, 21(4): 1226–1230.

Smith, M. D. 2007. Disruptive innovation: Can health care learn from other industries? A conversation with Clayton M. Christensen. *Health Affairs*, 26(3): w288–w295.

Stumpf, S. C., and McDonnell, J. T. 2002. Talking about team framing: Using argumentation to analyse and support experiential learning in early design episodes. *Design Studies*, 23(1): 5–23.

Taylor, D. 1969. Creative design through functional visualization. *Journal of Creative Behavior*, 3(2): 212–214.

Tseng, I., Moss, J., Cagan, J., and Kotovsky, K. 2008. The role of timing and analogical similarity in the stimulation of idea generation in design. *Design Studies*, 29(3): 203–221.

Tversky, A., and Kahneman, D. 1981. The framing of decisions and the psychology of choice. *Science*, 211(4481): 453–458.

Ucbasaran, D., Westhead, P., and Wright, M. 2009. The extent and nature of opportunity identification by experienced entrepreneurs. *Journal of Business Venturing*, 24(2): 99–115.

Van Burg, E., and Romme, A. G. L. 2014. Creating the future together: Toward a framework for research synthesis in entrepreneurship. *Entrepreneurship: Theory and Practice*, 38(2): 369–397.
Venkataraman, S. 1997. The distinctive domain of entrepreneurship research: An editor's perspective. In J. Katz, and R. Brockhaus (Eds.), *Advances in Entrepreneurship, Firm Emergence, and Growth*, Vol. 3, Bingley, UK: Emerald, 119–138.
Verganti, R. 2003. Design as brokering of languages: Innovation strategies in Italian firms. *Design Management Journal (Former Series)*, 14(3): 34–42.
Visser, W. 1996. Two functions of analogical reasoning in design: A cognitive-psychology approach. *Design Studies*, 17(4): 417–434.
Vosniadou, S., and Ortony, A. 1989. Similarity and analogical reasoning: A synthesis. In S. Vosniadou, and A. Ortony (Eds.), *Similarity and Analogical Reasoning*. New York, NY: Cambridge University Press, 1–7.
Weick, K. E. 1995. *Sensemaking in Organizations*. Thousand Oaks, CA: Sage.
Wells, G. L., Taylor, B. R., and Turtle, J. W. 1987. The undoing of scenarios. *Journal of Personality and Social Psychology*, 53(3): 421.
Wong, E. M., Galinsky, A. D., and Kray, L. J. 2009. The counterfactual mind-set: A decade of research. In *Handbook of Imagination and Mental Simulation*, Taylor & Francis Group, USA, 161–174.
Youn-Kyung, L., Erik, S., and Josh, T. 2008. The anatomy of prototypes: Prototypes as filters, prototypes as manifestations of design ideas. *ACM Transactions Computer-Human Interaction*, 15(2): 1–27.
Zhang, J., Zhang, Q., Wang, Y., and Qiu, C. 2013. *A Real-Time Auto-Adjustable Smart Pillow System for Sleep Apnea Detection and Treatment*. Paper presented at the 2013 ACM/IEEE International Conference on Information Processing in Sensor Networks (IPSN).
Zygourakis, C. C., Rolston, J. D., Treadway, J., Chang, S., and Kliot, M. 2014. What do hotels and hospitals have in common? How we can learn from the hotel industry to take better care of patients. *Surgical Neurology International*, 5(Suppl. 2): S49.

10 The Antecedents of Healthcare Social Entrepreneurship

Jeroen Gruiskens, Jarrod Ormiston, Federica Angeli, and Onno C.P. van Schayck

Introduction

Over the past few decades, a new organizational model of healthcare social entrepreneurship has emerged, focusing on generating social value rather than focusing on generating financial revenue (Austin et al., 2006; Dees et al., 2001; Mair and Marti, 2006). Social entrepreneurs are viewed as key change agents capable of supporting failing and overburdened health systems by providing accessible and affordable healthcare, reducing socio-economic inequalities, and improving social determinants of health (Drayton et al., 2006; Harting et al., 2011). Social entrepreneurial action has proven effective in meeting healthcare needs where institutions or markets fail while being more innovative than its public counterparts, and as a result, is an increasingly common practice in healthcare systems (Roy et al., 2013; Lim and Chia, 2016). Empirical studies aimed specifically at social entrepreneurship in healthcare are, however, scarce (see for exception, Roy et al., 2013). There is a significant gap therefore in understanding the antecedents of social entrepreneurial action in healthcare. This chapter aims to address this gap.

Although research on the field of social entrepreneurship is gaining rapid attention from scholars from diverse fields (Short et al., 2009; Choi and Majumdar, 2014), research is limited to conceptual and theoretical papers, with few evidence-based papers devoted to antecedents or consequences of social entrepreneurial action (Zahra et al., 2009; Lepoutre et al., 2013). As a result, the antecedents of this promising new organizational model are poorly understood (Fowler, 2000; Zahra et al., 2009). Recent studies have suggested determinants of the micro-, meso-, and macro-level influence on the emergence of social entrepreneurs in various contexts (Dacin et al., 2010; Stephan et al., 2015; Chandra and Shang, 2017), though additional research on the antecedents of social entrepreneurship is required to understand "the qualitative aspects about who becomes a social entrepreneur, what their objectives are, and how they understand social entrepreneurial action" (Lepoutre et al., 2013: 696). This chapter is guided, therefore, by the following research question: What are the antecedents of social entrepreneurial action in healthcare? Gaining a deeper understanding of the antecedents of social entrepreneurial action enables us to foster social entrepreneurial action in healthcare systems while allowing us to educate aspiring social entrepreneurs better.

Our research aims to enrich present perspectives on the antecedents of social entrepreneurial action by drawing on the emerging literature on institutional biographies, which describes the accumulation of tangible and intangible resources that individuals gain through their personal lives and professional careers (Lawrence et al., 2011). Our study examines the biographical narratives of 57 healthcare social entrepreneurs from the Ashoka Network, a renowned worldwide social entrepreneurial consortium. Using Gioia's two-step methodology (Gioia et al., 2013), the chapter proposes four antecedents of social entrepreneurial action: multidisciplinarity, exposure, connectedness, and pro-social behavior.

Our paper proceeds as follows. First, we discuss prior research on antecedents of entrepreneurial action and show how exploring institutional biographies will deepen our understanding of the antecedents of social entrepreneurial action in healthcare. Second, we describe the methodology used for analyzing the antecedents of social entrepreneurship in health. We then outline our findings on the antecedents of social entrepreneurship and continue with a discussion of our findings in the context of prior and contemporary research on entrepreneurial antecedents. We conclude our discussion by presenting the implications of our study, along with recommendations for future research and acknowledgement of the limitations of our study.

Antecedents of Social Entrepreneurial Action

In contemporary studies on the antecedents of the entrepreneurial process, three prominent theoretical perspectives are used to help explain to emergence of entrepreneurship (Fisher, 2012). These most prevalent, generalizable, and impactful theories are based on either (i) causation logic (Shane and Venkataraman, 2000; Fisher, 2012), which views entrepreneurs as engaging in planned, strategic, and linear behavior based on the assumption of a predictable future; (ii) effectual logic (Duening et al., 2012; Perry et al., 2012; Sarasvathy, 2001, 2008), which asserts to be the inverse of causational logic, and views entrepreneurs as using means already at their disposal for new product development and new venture creation; and (iii) bricolage logic (Baker and Nelson, 2005; Senyard et al., 2009), an action-oriented approach, which views entrepreneurs as recombining resources already available to overcome resource constraints and "make do with what is at hand."

Despite these differing perspectives on entrepreneurial action, all three approaches are influenced to some extent by the micro-foundations (traits, prior knowledge, motivation, intention, and cognitive processes leading to opportunity recognition; see also Chapter 9 on the cognitive aspects of opportunity creation in healthcare) of the entrepreneur (Perry et al., 2012; Sarasvathy, 2001). Both individual and contextual conditions are thereby important in the recognizing, evaluating, judging, and pursuing new ideas (McMullen et al., 2007; Plummer et al., 2007; Shane, 2003). Combined with the subjective interpretations of the contextual circumstances, pervasive social norms, intuition, experiences, and cognitive resources of the entrepreneur, entrepreneurs create beliefs about the potential value and viability of opportunities (Corbett, 2005; Gregoire et al., 2010; Meek et al., 2010; Mitchell et al., 2007), which ultimately is a key driver of entrepreneurial behavior (Felin and Zenger, 2009; McMullen and Shepherd, 2006). As entrepreneurial processes are based on idiosyncratic knowledge, experience, cognitive processes, and motivation, opportunity beliefs are highly individual and thus individual level variables are key determinants of whether entrepreneurial action occurs (Dimov, 2010; Wood et al., 2014).

Despite the abundance of research conducted on the antecedents of entrepreneurial action, research on the antecedents of social entrepreneurship is scarce and largely restricted to intentions, motivations, and cognitions. Mair and Noboa (2006) suggest social entrepreneurial intentions are influenced by four antecedents: (i) componence, (ii) empathy, (iii) cognition, and (iv) moral judgment; and two enablers: (i) self-efficacy and (ii) social support. These four antecedents lead to behavioral intentions translating into social entrepreneurial behavior, which can be predicted by prior experiences (Hockerts, 2017). These findings have been supported by more recent research conducted by Miller et al. (2012), which found that compassion is a strong motivational and emotional driver of social entrepreneurship. Alternatively, Lee and Battilana (2013) argue that imprinting from previous work experience influences the evolution of hybrid venture creation. Taken together, early research on social entrepreneurial antecedents suggests that personality traits, contextual enablers, and prior experiences are key factors, echoing insights from the traditional entrepreneurship literature. To gain a more cohesive understanding of the interplay between individuals, their context, and their histories, we adopt the theoretical lens of institutional biographies.

Institutional Biographies

A major critique on entrepreneurial research over the last two decades surrounds the narrow focus of many theoretical and empirical papers, which lack contextual relevance (Watson, 2013). Welter (2011) acknowledges the progress made so far, but points out that "although entrepreneurship research has made progress in acknowledging context, this specifically applies to contextualising theory, less to theorising context."

These critiques lead to calls for the shift in the focus of entrepreneurial research to involve a more comprehensive understanding of context (Wiklund et al., 2011; Zahra and Wright, 2011). Watson (2013) suggests that such a process would involve research of four interlinked dimensions: (i) entrepreneurial action or Steyaert's (2007) concept of entrepreneuring, (ii) identity work and changing life orientations (defining who the individual is and how this changes over time), (iii) institutional logics (defined as "socially constructed, historical patterns of cultural symbols and material practices ... by which individuals and organizations provide meaning to their daily activity" (p. 413)), and (iv) effectuation and emergence. Combing these four dimensions highlights how entrepreneurial action emerges in the interplay between the individual, the organization, and the institutional context

Following Watson (2013), we argue that understanding how institutions shape entrepreneurial action is necessary to gain a contextual appreciation of the emergence of social entrepreneurship in health. Healthcare social entrepreneurs are faced with a situation of institutional complexity (Greenwood et al., 2011) that stems from the competing medical professionalism and business-like healthcare logics (Reay and Hinings, 2009). The tensions that arise from conflicting and competing institutions in both the internal and external environment of organizations shape the emergence of entrepreneurial action (Bertels and Lawrence, 2016; Besharov and Smith, 2014). As a result, the presence of both internal and external tensions between conflicting and competing logics highlights the importance of focusing on the actions of individuals in institutions, as organizations are inhabited by individuals that have "complex, heterogeneous relationships to institutional logics that go beyond their organizational roles" (Bertels and Lawrence, 2016: 340).

Bertels and Lawrence (2016) argue that "institutional biographies" (p. 1) are able to provide a clear and concrete conceptualization between the relationship of individuals and institutions. Institutional biographies contain information on how "individuals influence and have been influenced by institutions" (p. 9), through identifying "the key [institutional] factors that may constrain and enable individual opportunities to engage in organizational practices" (p. 16) (Finch et al., 2017). Entrepreneurial action can thereby be understood as institutional work comprised of the "practices of individual and collective actors at creating, maintaining, and disrupting institutions" (Lawrence et al., 2011: 1). Institutional biographies shed light on institutional work occurring within institutions, providing a template for "action, cognition and emotion" (p. 3), and institutional biographies grant individuals access and influence to institutions due to portfolios accumulated throughout their life history (Lawrence et al., 2011; Viale, 2009). The analysis of institutional biographies of social healthcare entrepreneurs will therefore expose a comprehensive overview of possible antecedents of their entrepreneurial action.

Methodology

In our exploratory study, we conducted a thematic analysis of publicly available biographies of social entrepreneurs in healthcare. The use of biographical narratives is particularly useful in the development of constructs, as they allow for recurrent themes to emerge over a large number of cases (Ritchie and Lewis, 2003). Analyzing biographical narratives allows for an understanding of the motives, beliefs, and behaviors of individuals, as well as offering unique insights into people's own perspective of these psychological phenomena (Rennie, 2012; Ritchie and Lewis, 2003). As biographical narratives do not necessarily describe historical truth, but rather refract the past, biographical narratives are subject to interpretation by both the storyteller and the researcher (Riessman, 2005).

Our study aims to understand how certain individuals become social entrepreneurs: we therefore aim to understand how their motives, beliefs, and behaviors and their institutional biographies shape entrepreneurial action. In doing so, we add to the research available on antecedents of social entrepreneurship and gain a deeper understanding of the micro-, meso-, and macro-determinants of social entrepreneurial behavior. The "entrepreneurial narrative" captured in publicly available biographies has been increasingly explored over the last decade, and is considered as a viable approach in entrepreneurial research (Chandra and Shang, 2017). Recently, such an approach has been extended to social entrepreneurial research in both quantitative and qualitative studies (Chandra and Shang, 2017; Meyskens et al., 2010).

Ashoka and Ashoka Fellows

The biographies of social entrepreneurs for this study were accessed through the Ashoka Network, a renowned social entrepreneurial consortium. The Ashoka Network was established in 1981 and provides mentoring, funding, support, and a large network to its members (Ashoka, 2017). With over 3,000 members, the Ashoka network is seen as an international authority on the subject of social entrepreneurship (Ashoka, 2017; Kidd et al., 2015). A social entrepreneur must be nominated to become a member of the Ashoka Network, and although thousands of nominations are made each year, only a select few are lauded as an Ashoka Fellow after a rigorous, multi-round process (Ashoka, 2017; Meyskens et al., 2010). Ashoka Fellows are selected according to five criteria: (i) possession of a new idea, (ii) creativity, (iii) entrepreneurial quality, (iv) social impact of the idea, and (v) ethical fiber (Ashoka, 2017). After nomination based upon these five criteria, a multi-stage iterative process of interviews and site visits by Ashoka volunteers and peer (social) entrepreneurs, and a board review, will assess if the nominated social entrepreneur fits the criteria and aligns with Ashoka's mission. Upon selection, a profile is composed derived from data contributed by the social entrepreneur and the Ashoka staff involved with the selection procedure. The profile contains written sections on the idea, problem, strategy, and personal history of the Fellow. When Fellows are admitted to the worldwide network of Ashoka, the profiles are made public on the Ashoka website (www.ashoka.org).

Our study accesses these publicly available profiles of Ashoka Fellows. Previous studies using these profiles have reported that the available profiles are relatively homogenous and a reliable, trustworthy source of information (Chandra and Shang, 2017; Meyskens et al., 2010). Meyskens et al. (2010) conducted a content analysis based upon the statistical analysis of 70 biographical profiles of Ashoka Fellows to demonstrate similarities between social entrepreneurs and traditional entrepreneurs when compared through a resourced-based view (RBV) lens. In a recent study, Chandra and Shang (2017) adopted a mixed-method approach to classify understand the emergence of social enterprises. Therefore, our methodology is based upon the notion that the Ashoka biographies contain valid information for conducting a qualitative analysis of the entrepreneurial narratives. We note, however, that the biographical profiles have an inherent bias towards celebrating the social entrepreneur, given that they are composed based on information provided to Ashoka by the social entrepreneurs themselves and are added to by observations made by Ashoka staff in the selection process.

To capture a selection of narratives relevant for the aim of our study, we searched specifically for healthcare social entrepreneurs on the Ashoka website, using the search term "healthcare." The search resulted in 57 profiles. Other search terms, such as more non-specific, general terms like "health," resulted in large numbers of profiles (N=357), which we deemed unsuitable for the purpose of this study. However, future studies might wish to expand their study to explore whether our study is generalizable. We began our study by building a database containing all the profiles of 57 entrepreneurs (N=57). One profile was excluded from the analysis due an incomplete profile text. Profiles were predominantly written about male social entrepreneurs (N=40, female: N=17), and in contrast to reports about social entrepreneurial activity occurring in developed contexts (Terjesen et al., 2012), the entrepreneurs were predominantly active in low- and middle-income regions (South America: N=12, South Asia: N=12, Africa: N=14). The concentration in low- and middle-income regions can be explained by the geographic focus of Ashoka's mission.

Analyzing Narratives

A unique opportunity arises from the use of these profiles, as the profiles contain biographical narratives which provide the social entrepreneurs' perspective on the antecedents related to becoming a social entrepreneur. The profiles enable us to generate narrative data, which can be used for thematic analysis and allow us to build new concepts (Ritchie and Lewis, 2003). Developing new theoretical concepts, which may both add upon existing concepts or add to new theory development, involves sophistication of constructs through a dialectical process between the informant of the narrative, in our study being the social entrepreneur, and the authors of this paper acting as interpreting researchers (Guba and Lincoln, 1994; Ritchie and Lewis, 2003). The dialectical process favors thematic analysis of the data, making use of developed constructs to inform abductive theory development (Dubois and Gadde, 2017; Gioia et al., 2013). As abductive theory development has been described as prone to a lack of rigor and quality, we adopted Gioia's two-step methodology for our thematic analysis, which has been extensively described as a valid qualitative method used for including rigor into qualitative research projects (Gioia et al., 2013). By adopting Gioia's (2012) approach we ensure a dynamic process, in which we move back and forth between the data and the analysis of the data. Our approach can thus be described as a continuous, investigative, heuristic dialogue between the narratives provided by the informers (the social entrepreneurs) and the authors of this paper. This dialogue is emphasized in our two-step methodology. We will describe our two-step approach in the next paragraph.

First, the first author compiled a database containing all relevant biographies from the Ashoka website, and completed the first round of coding. The first author then conducted a first order analysis and produced a set of first order categories and concepts. Next, during a second order analysis and coding, the first author adopted a more knowledgeable stance, exposing relations between first order concepts and second order themes, formulated on a more theoretical level (Gioia et al., 2013). During the development of a workable set of themes and concepts, a certain level of theoretical saturation was reached, the second order themes were gathered into second order aggregate dimensions. All coding was filed in a different database and the first order concepts, second order themes and second order aggregate dimensions were collected and organized in a data structure, which exposed interrelationships existing between the found themes. The databases and the data structure were then presented to the second and third author for review. After the second and third authors provided their own analyses of the coding, the first author then turned back to the biographical database and performed a second coding round, using the feedback of the second and third authors. During weekly meetings, the first author and the second author worked within an iterative, dialectical process, to structure the first order concepts, second order themes and second order aggregate dimensions more coherently. We allowed the data to evolve while analysis proceeded, having the third author audit our results, directing our analysis from an objective position. When the first and second authors agreed upon a consisting and coherent data structure, representative of the quotes found in the narratives, all authors were presented with the data structure. Then, all authors brainstormed on the thematic analysis conducted and sophisticated the construct into a data structure upon which all authors agreed. The first author then arranged the data used in the thematic analysis into a data table, linking the quotes found in the narratives to the first order concepts, second order themes and second order aggregate dimensions as presented in this chapter.

The iterative, dynamic process of building the data structure used to analyze the narratives from a theoretical perspective produced 635 overlapping first order categories. By moving back and forth through the data and the coding, we were able to build a data structure containing 27 first order concepts, 14 second-order themes related to the first order concepts, distilled into four aggregate separate dimensions associated with becoming a social entrepreneur: multi-disciplinarity, exposure, connectedness, and pro-social behavior. The first order concepts, second order themes, and second order dimensions are arranged in the data structure presented in Figure 10.1.

Subsequently, we arranged the first order concepts, second order themes and second order aggregate dimensions into a data table, linking the data structure to the narratives by presenting representative and compelling quotes found in the narratives as supportive evidence for our data structure. The data table is given in Table 10.1 below.

The data table was used by the authors to gain a comprehensive overview on the data generated and was processed into the following findings section.

Findings

To understand how institutional biographies influence the individual antecedents of social entrepreneurial action in healthcare, we conducted a first order analysis to produce a set of first order categories and concepts. This was followed by subsequent second order analysis and the development of second order themes, and finally the generation of second order aggregate dimensions. This section outlines each aggregate dimension, providing exemplar quotes from the entrepreneurial narratives.

Multi-Disciplinarity: Learning, Teaching, Analyzing, Developing, and Sharing Knowledge

Appreciating Education

Education seems to be a prominent and recurrent theme in the narratives of the social entrepreneurs included in our study. Social entrepreneurs seem to recognize education as a building block for constructing systems

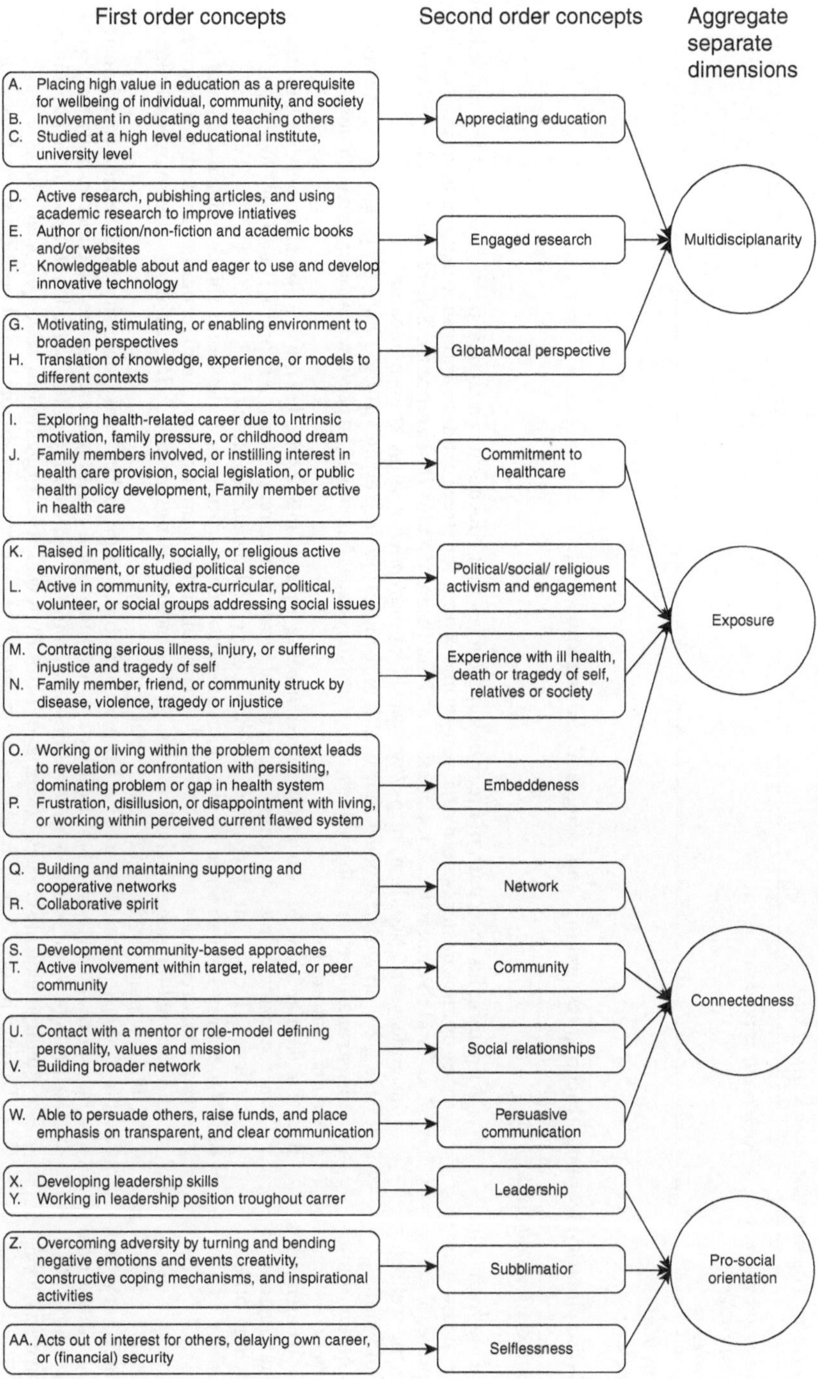

Figure 10.1 Data Structure

Table 10.1 Data Table of Generated Data

Dimensions, Themes, Categories, and Data	
Second order themes and first order categories	*Representative data*
Overarching dimension:	
Multi-disciplinarity: learning, teaching, researching, analyzing, and sharing knowledge	
1. Appreciating education	
A. Placing high value in education as a prerequisite for the wellbeing of individual, community, and society	A1. "Mirroring his own path in life, Rokhim believes that education can change people's lives. It has moved him to set up the Master School as a non-formal school for street children and other marginalized children in 2007 and to establish the foundation of Bina Insan Mandiri (Assistance for Self-reliant People) to organize his endeavors." (Rokhim) https://www.ashoka.org/en/fellow/nurokhim-nurokhim A2. "He grew up with the belief that health and education are key means for a nation's progress and it was this strong belief that shaped his career at later stages." (Daniel) https://www.ashoka.org/en/fellow/daniel-amoun-louis
B. Involvement in educating and teaching othe	B1. "Dr. Kumar knew he wasn't interested in being a practicing doctor. He quit his job after only six months to start teaching, while also engaging in social work as a secretary for the People's Union for Civil Rights in Calicut." (Dr. Kumar) https://www.ashoka.org/en/fellow/suresh-kumar B2. "Dr. Dakuyo is also ensuring the next generation of practitioners understands the benefits and uses of traditional remedies. He has designed a curriculum for a three-year training program on herbal medicine in the national languages—the first class of 40 students just graduated." (Dr. Dakuyo) https://www.ashoka.org/en/fellow/pando-z%C3%A9phirin-dakuyo
C. Studied at a high-level educational institute, university level	C1. "In 2009, he decided to study a Masters of Public Health at Harvard University. Both during this time at Harvard, as well as at a Stanford biomedical innovation program, Santiago became increasingly interested in technology based, scalable innovations within the health sector, and he found his interest in facilitating access to quality medical services." (Santiago) https://www.ashoka.org/el/fellow/santiago-ocejo-torres C2. "During the next few years Albert went on to obtain degrees in sociology and political science, as well as a series of Master's degrees and a Doctorate at Harvard University, all related to different aspects of public health, health policy and healthcare management." (Albert) https://www.ashoka.org/en/fellow/albert-jovell

2. Engaged research	
D. Active research, publishing articles, and using academic research to improve initiatives	D1. "Jorge found that little research had been performed on the topic of adolescent fatherhood and that there were no programs addressing it. Committed to the development of a program dealing with this major issue, Jorge won a MacArthur Foundation grant and put his master's thesis conclusions into practice as Papai." (Jorge) https://www.ashoka.org/en/fellow/jorge-lyra D2. "Before returning to India in 2002, Ashwin worked on the team that sequenced the Human and Mouse Genomes at Celera Genomics, based in Rockville, Maryland. At Celera, he was instrumental in coordinating multidisciplinary teams to compile and analyze the human and mouse genomes, which resulted in the production of two publications in the leading international scientific journal, SCIENCE." (Ashwin) https://www.ashoka.org/ko/fellow/ashwin-naik
E. Author of fiction/non-fiction & academic books and/or websites	E1. "Mohammad is a serial entrepreneur with a proven track record of innovation in the field of computing and medicine. He has written and published six books and is a trained physician and an IT programmer.... He then set up a website called MedicalApproaches.org which allowed him to distribute the book free of charge and received thousands of downloads from around the world." (Mohammed) https://www.ashoka.org/en-gb/fellow/mohammad-al-ubaydli E2. "Most recently, Francesca further solidified her position as global thought leader by publishing a book translated to *Fight and Smile: A Story of Love and Science*." (Francesca) https://www.ashoka.org/el/fellow/francesca-fedeli
F. Knowledge about and eager to use and develop innovative technology	F1. "Apart from contributing to several innovations in technology, Sameer.... Interested in biotechnology.... He decided to re-focus Neurosynaptic's work to create technology that would increase rural citizen's access to primary healthcare. Initially, Sameer believed the problem to be purely technological. After two years of trying to layer the technology over the N-Logue infrastructure, it became clear that healthcare delivery required a different approach. It was at this critical time that Sameer defined his role as co-creator of the telemedicine field." (Sameer) https://www.ashoka.org/en-gb/fellow/sameer-sawarkar F2. "This experience convinced Dr. Chauhan that appropriately utilized technology could serve as a powerful tool to increase access to health.... He used the technology provided by MIT to increase access to health in villages.... He began using mobile technology (which was just becoming popular in India) to consult with patients." (Dr. Chauhan) https://www.ashoka.org/el/fellow/partap-chauhan

(*Continued*)

Table 10.1 (Continued)

Dimensions, Themes, Categories, and Data	
Second order themes and first order categories	*Representative data*
3. Global-local perspective	
G. Motivating, stimulating, or enabling environment to broaden perspectives	G1. "From this perch, Mark was able to get to know 300 anti-poverty "theories of change." Then, as he puts it, "in the middle of this work, I was asked to join the board of the National Campaign to Prevent Teen and Unplanned Pregnancy, which I joined from a traditional women's reproductive rights perspective. I had one of those 'aha!' moments in a board meeting" (Mark) https://www.ashoka.org/el/fellow/mark-edwards G2. "After sharing with his father, who had relocated the family to the UAE for work, that he would go to Egypt to pursue his medical degree, his dad advised him to move at the age of fifteen so he could finish high school in Egypt, and meet young people studying all subjects before entering the medical faculty in university." (Mohamed) https://www.ashoka.org/el/fellow/mohamed-zaazoue
H. Translation from knowledge, experience, or morals to different contexts	H1. "Her work in Argentina was so successful that she reached national impact by formulating and ensuring the passage of a National Diabetes Law and by getting one of the public insurers to adopt her diabetes program. . . . She recently moved back to Cochabamba, Bolivia, where she is refining her model to include an express nutritional component and adapting it to the bleaker Bolivian context." (Patricia) https://www.ashoka.org/en/fellow/patricia-blanco H2. "After studying for a period in the United States, she returned to Cairo in 1984 and found that ultrasound—by this time widely used in some other countries—was not yet available in Egypt. She brought the technique home with her and set about the task of establishing training centers in Cairo hospitals." (Magda) https://www.ashoka.org/el/fellow/magda-iskander

Overarching dimension:

Exposure: encounters, confrontation and experience with the social problems

4. Commitment to healthcare	
I. Exploring health-related career due to intrinsic motivation, family pressure, or childhood dream	I1. "Throughout his life, Jorge has maintained a deep-rooted commitment to enable the lasting treatment and recovery of people with similar mental health conditions as he has." (Jorge) https://www.ashoka.org/en/fellow/jorge-cardoso I2. "Patricia says that she knew she wanted to be a doctor from the age of 5." (Patricia) https://www.ashoka.org/en/fellow/patricia-blanco
J. Family members involved or instilling an interest in healthcare provision, legislation, or public health policy development	J1. "As a child, Sanjeev followed his father—a leader in the Government of India and the World Health Organization's effort to eradicate small pox in India—and his mother who was an OB/GYN to underserved populations on their rounds, and from that young age he knew that he would grow up to use medicine to help those in need." (Sanjeev) https://www.ashoka.org/en/fellow/sanjeev-arora J2. "With a father and grandfather who are doctors, Mohamed always knew he would also put on the white coat." (Mohammed 2) https://www.ashoka.org/el/fellow/mohamed-zaazoue
5. Political/social/religious activism and engagement	
K. Raised in politically, socially, or religious active environment or studied political science	K1. "Since he was a child, he remembers sitting in on meetings of the teachers' union that his father conducted at home. Exposure to these environments drew him to a number of different political movements beginning at age of 17." (Dr. Kumar) https://www.ashoka.org/el/fellow/suresh-kumar K2. "Amitai's drive to help people stemmed from the socialist educational doctrine of his parents who came to Jerusalem from the kibbutz life and from witnessing the horrors and misfortunes of war throughout his Air Force career in the Israeli army." (Amitai) https://www.ashoka.org/en/fellow/amitai-ziv
L. Active in community, extra-curricular, volunteer, political, or social groups addressing social issues during career	L1. "Edith started the Telluride Sexual Awareness Program in schools, where she created sex-ed curriculum for teachers (to train students) based on safe sex rather than abstinence, which was the political sentiment of the time." (Edith) https://www.ashoka.org/el/fellow/edith-elliott L2. "During school, her participation in debate, drama, and science clubs, as well as her involvement with the Rotary Club and community-based projects gave her exposure to a variety of people, sharpened her sense of justice, and shaped her people-oriented personality." (Stella) https://www.ashoka.org/el/fellow/stella-iwuagwu

(*Continued*)

Table 10.1 (Continued)

Dimensions, Themes, Categories, and Data	
Second order themes and first order categories	*Representative data*
6. Experience with inequalities, injustice, ill health, death or tragedy of self, relatives or society	
M. Contracting serious illness, injury, or suffering injustice and tragedy of self	M1. "Rita feels deeply the social stigma that surrounds childlessness: for 16 years, she and her husband have tried to conceive a child. Early on, as she struggled with her own circumstance, she looked around and saw that many couples were childless." (Rita) https://www.ashoka.org/el/fellow/rita-sembuya M2. "Silke Mader gave birth to prematurely born twins. Her daughter died soon after birth and her surviving son weighed only 500 grams. Upon giving birth, Silke had to deal with both the grief of losing a child and the fear that her son might not survive"(Silke) https://www.ashoka.org/en/fellow/silke-mader
N. Family member, friend, or community struck by disease, violence, tragedy, or injustice	N1. "In 1992, while finishing his doctorate at Harvard far from home, Albert received a phone call informing him that his father had been diagnosed with cancer." (Albert) https://www.ashoka.org/en/fellow/albert-jovell N2. "Her life changed profoundly when her son Mario was born. Through her journey dealing and managing her son's stroke, Francesca grew stronger, more determined and began to think bigger." (Francesca) https://www.ashoka.org/en/fellow/francesca-fedeli
7. Embeddedness	
O. Working or living within the problem context leads to revelation or confrontation with persisting, dominating health problems, social problems, or gap in health system	O1. "While executive director of a healthcare center in an urban, underserved, and high-crime neighborhood of Pittsburgh, Jeff was not prepared for what he would see in the shadows of the region's premiere health institution: death, disease, abuse, and neglect. Infants starving to death from poverty and families torn apart by cancer, stroke, and heart disease seemed intractably ingrained in the community." (Jeff) https://www.ashoka.org/ja/fellow/jeff-palmer O2. "Julie went to Yale University, where she studied political science, and it was during this time that she was exposed to the inequities between developing and developed countries. During an election-monitoring mission she led in Nairobi during the 2007 elections, she witnessed firsthand the series of events that sparked the post-election violence that led to the death of over 3,000 people. Following her experience in Kenya, Julie went on an exchange to Mali and experienced yet another facet of the gross equities that characterize developing nation" (Julie) https://www.ashoka.org/en/fellow/julie-carney

P. Frustration, disillusion, or disappointment with living or working within perceived current flawed system	P1. "With a desire to understand how the impact could be created in healthcare at significant scale Prasanta joined a large international development agency in Delhi in 1998 as a program director. After a few years Prasanta was disillusioned with the top-down approach of the organization which unintentionally increased inequities by leaving out those most poor. He saw that the approach pioneered by the Arole's was not considered by the largest actors, in part, because there was not enough research and strategies created for them to embrace it." (Prasanta) https://www.ashoka.org/en-gb/fellow/prasanta-kishore-tripathy P2. "Upon graduation, Bénédicte naturally entered a neurological department in a Parisian hospital and was shocked to discover the inefficiencies of the system. She was particularly revolted that patients and families were so poorly considered." (Bénédicte) https://www.ashoka.org/el/fellow/b%C3%A9n%C3%A9dicte-d%C3%A9fontaines
Overarching dimension:	
Connectedness: being part of a bigger ecosystem	
8. Network	
Q. Building and maintaining supporting and cooperative networks	Q1. "He then organized more than 200 pharmacists to integrate the products into the formal pharmaceutical distribution network." (Dr. Dayuko) https://www.ashoka.org/en/fellow/pando-z%C3%A9phirin-dakuyo Q2. "Jeff began building a coalition targeting each of the nonprofit organizations in the region that aimed their programs and services toward at-risk populations. What emerged became Coordinated Care Network—a loose affiliation of 13 organizations that shared common values and principle, and, above all else, wanted to create better outcomes for the city's poorest citizens." (Jeff) https://www.ashoka.org/id/fellow/jeff-palmer
R. Collaborative spirit	R1. "He is also gifted with an extremely collaborative spirit, continually engaging others about his model, relating to people on all levels, from legislators down to drug-addicted patients." (Sanjeev) https://www.ashoka.org/el/fellow/sanjeev-arora R2. "After much lobbying and negotiation, she convinced her own Montefiore Hospital in New York to take on a partnership to help develop dialysis centers in Nigeria. With them on board, she began to pursue all the others necessary to realize her goals." (Tosan) https://www.ashoka.org/el/fellow/tosan-oruwariye
9. Community	
S. Developing community-based approaches	S1. "Dr. Sai later became cognizant that mortality was highest among younger children and poor children who did not go to school. Seeking to directly reach migrant workers and communities in slums, she started community-based work on preventive neo-natal and child care; to raise the agency of mothers in children's health." (Dr. Sai) https://www.ashoka.org/el/fellow/balijepalli-sailakshmi S2. "While still working full time, Mark began developing a methodology for community-based healthcare.... Today, Mark is a recognized thought leader in the field of social prescribing and community-based healthcare." (Mark) https://www.ashoka.org/el/fellow/mark-swift

(*Continued*)

Table 10.1 (Continued)

Dimensions, Themes, Categories, and Data	
Second order themes and first order categories	*Representative data*
T. Active involvement within target, related, or peer community	T1. "He got involved with the homosexual community and found himself helping and supporting friends with HIV/AIDS.... Organizing community meetings and fundraising to obtain medicines and equipment." (Rodrigo) https://www.ashoka.org/en/fellow/rodrigo-pascal T2. "Eldred is driven by his personal experiences as a drug user who managed to quit and stay clean.... After he came back to Mumbai, he decided to set up his own team of workers and volunteers and thus began his journey into the creation of a long term, targeted health and recovery program for the drug user community." (Eldred) https://www.ashoka.org/el/fellow/eldred-tellis
10. Social relationships	
U. Contact with a mentor or role-model defining personality, values, and mission	U1. "While Dr. Chauhan studied Ayurveda at the University of Delhi he had the opportunity to be mentored by his teacher for over five years who instilled the importance of making healthcare as easily accessible and affordable for India's population." (Partap) https://www.ashoka.org/el/fellow/partap-chauhan U2. "Carlos did go on to study medicine, and in that time, he was able to meet pioneers in the field of Family Medicine in Venezuela, and viewed them very much as mentors.... One of those mentors, whom he met through his neighborhood association, was Dr. Pedro Iturbe who was responsible for eradicating Tuberculosis in the state of Zulia and who had treated Carlos's grandfather.... Since then, other mentors, like Ashoka Fellow Elías Santana, have continued to show him the importance of passion for one's work and perseverance." (Carlos) https://www.ashoka.org/en/fellow/carlos-atencio
V. Building broader networks	V1. "During this time Prasanta visited Jamkhed to meet Raj and Mabelle Arole; an event that inspires his current work. Prasanta says, "They trusted people, they gave information, they respected everyone, they told the truth, and in turn the people of Jamkhed and the villagers nearby were adapting to the complexities of a changing world with exceptional grace and self-respect." (Prasanta) https://www.ashoka.org/en-gb/fellow/prasanta-kishore-tripathy V2. "He started to identify himself as an agent of social change and piece together his technical skills with his vision for an improved society." (Martín) https://www.ashoka.org/en/fellow/martin-guzman

11. Persuasive communication	
W. Able to persuade others, raise funds, and place emphasis on clear and transparent communication	W1. "His expertise as a specialist and an academic gives him a foundation from which to deliver results on the ground—and credibility to persuade his peers and spread his model." (Pedro) https://www.ashoka.org/en-gb/fellow/pedro-chan%C3%A1 W2. "Andrea has worked tirelessly to highlight the issue of transport in global health, working with bilateral donors, global institutions and philanthropists to secure the investment and funding to put systems in place." (Andrea) https://www.ashoka.org/el/fellow/andrea-coleman
Overarching dimension:	
Pro-social orientation: social values, behavior and thoughts encompassing social and humanistic belief-system	
12. Leadership	
X. Developing leadership skills	X1. "As a leader, Sanjeev is admired by his team, who see him as a mentor, a motivator and an inspiration, always encouraging innovation and initiative at all levels of the staff." (Sanjeev) https://www.ashoka.org/el/fellow/sanjeev-arora X2. One renowned healthcare expert described working with her: "And along comes this involved mother who gets experts, politicians and patients to work effectively. None of us have the time or distance to do so—she oversees the system and gave herself permission to guide us towards real large changes. We all follow." (Silke) https://www.ashoka.org/en/fellow/silke-mader
Y. Working in leadership positions throughout career	Y1. "He has also been a leader in his area of specialization at the national and international level: serving as Executive Secretary of the Latin American Society of Abnormal Movement; organizing an Americas-wide congress of neurology; as regional Vice-President of the World Neurology Foundation; and as founder and President of Group of Friends of Parkinson's." (Pedro) https://www.ashoka.org/en-gb/fellow/pedro-chan%C3%A1 Y2. "which he did for six years before taking a job as Managing Director of Clarkson Notcutt Insurance Brokers—an opportunity to apply his entrepreneurial skills at a much higher level and with more resources to work with." (Sam) https://www.ashoka.org/en/fellow/sam-agutu

(*Continued*)

Table 10.1 (Continued)

Dimensions, Themes, Categories, and Data	
Second order themes and first order categories	*Representative data*
13. Sublimation	
Z. Overcoming adversity by turning and bending negative emotions and events into creativity, constructive coping mechanisms, and inspirational activities	Z1. "She felt a lingering guilt, wondering if the preterm birth was somehow her fault. Silke felt isolated and her many questions were left unanswered. At that time parental support of any kind did not exist, neither were parents involved in the day-to-day care for their baby. Silke, a trained kindergarten teacher, could not believe there was no one to turn to and decided to change the situation. . . . soon became chairwoman of the national self-help association for the care of preterm infants, which she led from 2003 to 2009." (Silke) https://www.ashoka.org/en/fellow/silke-mader Z2. "Two years into these projects Albert himself was diagnosed with cancer. Instead of abandoning his idea, he decided to accelerate his efforts. During his treatment he coordinated the Patient's Rights Declaration and the successful launch of the Patients Forum. Albert has since recovered from his main cancer treatments through a very intense process in which he, as a patient, became an active part of his own medical team." (Albert) https://www.ashoka.org/en/fellow/albert-jovell
14. Selflessness	
AA. Acts out of interest for others, often delaying own career or risking own personal (financial) security	AA1. "For instance, when the state of Gujarat was affected by an earthquake that killed 20,000 people, Dr. Sai left for relief work missed her postgraduate entrance exams. Similarly, upon graduation in 2008, she missed a job interview to work for the flood relief in Bihar." (Dr. Sai) https://www.ashoka.org/el/fellow/balijepalli-sailakshmi AA2. "After working for the NHS for over seven years, Mark left his job to pursue his passion and turn his experience and vision into an organization. It was a big step and a financial risk, sacrificing a high salary and pension scheme and with a limited household income." (Mark) https://www.ashoka.org/pt-br/fellow/mark-swift

able to sustain the wellbeing of the individual, community and society at large. As the social entrepreneurs place high value in education, their acknowledgement of its value as a prerequisite for a healthy individual, community, or society seems to reflect their mission:

> Mirroring his own path in life, Rokhim believes that education can change lives. It has moved him to set up the Master School as a non-formal school for street children and other marginalized children in 2007.
>
> (Rokhim)

We found that social entrepreneurs were often involved in activities and positions where they would be educating or teaching others. Their mission, knowledge, or beliefs would be transferred to others, reflecting their own belief that transference of the knowledge about what works in a given situation is key to improving the lives of others living in similar situations:

> Dr. Dayuko is also ensuring the next generation of practitioners understands the benefits and uses of traditional remedies. He has designed curriculum for a three-year training program on herbal medicine in the national languages—the first class of 40 students just graduated.
>
> (Dr. Dayuko)

The social entrepreneurs themselves were mostly highly educated at a university level, which gave them access to knowledge, technology, and information that they were able to use later in their career. Not only does it speak for a high level of intelligence, but also of a certain degree of their willingness and eagerness to learn:

> In 2009, he decided to study a Masters of Public Health at Harvard University. Both during his time at Harvard, as well as at a Stanford biomedical innovation program, Santiago became increasingly interested in technology based, scalable innovations within the health sector, and he found his interest in facilitating access to quality medical services.
>
> (Santiago)

Engaged Research

We found several compelling stories of highly successful researchers becoming social entrepreneurs, while also publishing papers in influential academic journals. Some of them used their research as a starting point for their enterprises, backing their venture with evidence-based data:

> Jorge found that little research had been performed on the topic of adolescent fatherhood and that there were no programs addressing it. Committed to the development of a program dealing with this

> major issue, Jorge won a MacArthur Foundation grant and put his master's thesis conclusions into practice as Papai.
>
> (Jorge)

The craftsmanship of authoring knowledge in such a way it makes a compelling read for peers is a trait reflected by social entrepreneurs such as Mohammed:

> Mohammad is a serial entrepreneur with a proven track record of innovation in the field of computing and medicine. He has written and published six books and is a trained physician and an IT programmer.... He then set up a website called MedicalApproaches.org which allowed him to distribute the book free of charge and received thousands of downloads from around the world
>
> (Mohammed)

Aside from producing knowledge and making it available to others, awareness and recognition of knowledge and innovation by others is mentioned as both as a means to an end and as a goal in itself. Not only are the social entrepreneurs highly educated and aware of knowledge, they are able to use their education and knowledge to aid their mission:

> This experience convinced Dr. Chauhan that appropriately utilized technology could serve as a powerful tool to increase access to health.... He used the technology provided by MIT to increase access to health in villages.... He began using mobile technology (which was just becoming popular in India) to consult with patients.
>
> (Dr. Chauhan)

Global-Local Perspective

Social healthcare entrepreneurs were found to be individuals possessing the ability to expand their own constructs of the world, adding accumulated perspectives throughout life to their own construct. Their open-mindedness originating from the contexts in which they developed their constructs of the world, influences the ability of the person to actually become a social entrepreneur able to approach problem situations from multiple vantage points. Sometimes parents would stimulate the social entrepreneur to broaden their perspectives on the world before pursuing their career. In other cases, the contextual environment of the social entrepreneur enabled the expansion of world-views dramatically:

> From this perch, Mark was able to get to know 300 anti-poverty "theories of change." Then, as he puts it, "in the middle of this work, I was asked to join the board of the National Campaign to Prevent

> Teen and Unplanned Pregnancy, which I joined from a traditional women's reproductive rights perspective. I had one of those 'aha!' moments in a board meeting.
>
> (Mark)

Inherently connected to having a wide perspective is the ability to translate knowledge, experience, or morals and values from one context to another. The ability to see things from a multitude of angles enables the social entrepreneur to adapt and modify concepts to different contexts, which is often represented in narratives as the translation of solutions available in developed countries to developing countries:

> After studying for a period in the United States, she returned to Cairo in 1984 and found that ultrasound—by this time widely used in some other countries—was not yet available in Egypt. She brought the technique home with her and set about the task of establishing training centers in Cairo hospitals.
>
> (Magda)

We found social entrepreneurs to be individuals capable of multidisciplinarity: an intrinsic motivation, willingness, eagerness, and ability to learn, teach, research, analyze, and share knowledge with others with the aim of improving the lives and wellbeing of individuals, communities, or society at large.

Exposure: Encounters, Confrontation and Experience With Social Problems

Commitment to Healthcare

Almost every narrative of the social entrepreneurs we investigated mentioned a previous healthcare-related career, mostly being a medical doctor before becoming a social entrepreneur. Motivated by either their own confrontation with sickness and disease, family pressure, or pursuit of a childhood dream, social entrepreneurs often made their career choice early on in their lives:

> Throughout his life, Jorge has maintained a deep-rooted commitment to enable the lasting treatment and recovery of people with similar mental health conditions as he has.
>
> (Jorge)

> Her father, Patricia's grandfather was a doctor whom she never knew. Patricia says that she knew she wanted to be a doctor from the age of 5.... Patricia was diagnosed with Type 1 diabetes in 1984. The next

> year, she graduated from medical school and chose to specialize in endocrinology and diabetes.
>
> (Patricia)

It is notable that much of the determination or motivation to get involved in healthcare may also be related to family members being involved in healthcare themselves. Narratives often mentioned a parent or more distant family member being a medical doctor, or somehow being involved in healthcare policy making:

> As a child, Sanjeev followed his father—a leader in the Government of India and the World Health Organization's effort to eradicate small pox in India—and his mother who was an OB/GYN to underserved populations on their rounds, and from that young age he knew that he would grow up to use medicine to help those in need.
>
> (Sanjeev)

Political/Social/Religious Activism and Engagement

Characterizing the change-making nature of many social entrepreneurs is their activism, often linked to their upbringing. Frequently, narratives mention the social entrepreneur being brought up in a politically, socially, or religious active environment. Such upbringing seems to have infused the social entrepreneurial passion:

> Since he was a child, he remembers sitting in on meetings of the teachers' union that his father conducted at home. Exposure to these environments drew him to a number of different political movements beginning at age of 17.
>
> (Dr. Kumar)

Similar to political, social or religious activism is the involvement of social entrepreneurs in their environment, expressed by extra-curricular activities, or membership of volunteer, political or social groups addressing social issues:

> "During school, her participation in debate, drama, and science clubs, as well as her involvement with the Rotary Club and community-based projects gave her exposure to a variety of people, sharpened her sense of justice, and shaped her people-oriented personality.
>
> (Stella)

Experience With Inequalities, Injustice, Ill Health, Death, or Tragedy of Self, Relatives, or Society

Social entrepreneurs also tell compelling stories of their own suffering or suffering of others witnessed firsthand. War, human rights violations, devastating illnesses, or pervasive socio-economic inequalities seem to be triggers for the social entrepreneurs in developing a personal attachment to these issues:

> Silke Mader gave birth to prematurely born twins. Her daughter died soon after birth and her surviving son weighed only 500 grams. Upon giving birth, Silke had to deal with both the grief of losing a child and the fear that her son might not survive
>
> (Silke)

> and from witnessing the horrors and misfortunes of war throughout his Air Force career.... This experience opened up Amitai's eyes to a new world of human suffering, a sense of social rights and social values. His experience with war also brought about the realization that he wanted to transition from the killing industry to the healing industry.
>
> (Amitai)

Embeddedness

Attachment or involvement with a problematic social context, as expressed by embeddedness within the social issues is a common thread through the narratives of social entrepreneurs. Their lives become intertwined with the social context in which they live or work, thereby exposing them to the problem:

> While executive director of a healthcare center in an urban, underserved, and high-crime neighborhood of Pittsburgh, Jeff was not prepared for what he would see in the shadows of the region's premiere health institution: death, disease, abuse, and neglect. Infants starving to death from poverty and families torn apart by cancer, stroke, and heart disease seemed intractably ingrained in the community.
>
> (Jeff)

As their lives are embedded in the social context in which the social entrepreneur lives or works, frustration, disillusion, or disappointment seems to separate them from place, allowing the social entrepreneur to resist against the embeddedness, thereby not accepting the status quo:

> Upon graduation, Bénédicte naturally entered a neurological department in a Parisian hospital and was shocked to discover the inefficiencies of the system. She was particularly revolted that patients and families were so poorly considered.
>
> (Bénédicte)

Throughout the narratives, it appears that exposure to social problems by means of encounters, confrontation, and experience with the social problems plays a consistent role in paving the way for future social entrepreneurial behavior.

Connectedness: Being Part of a Bigger Ecosystem

Networks

Not unlike their commercial counterparts, social healthcare entrepreneurs show remarkable ability to build and maintain supporting and cooperative networks:

> He then organized more than 200 pharmacists to integrate the products into the formal pharmaceutical distribution network.
>
> (Dr. Dayuko)

As the main objective of social entrepreneurs is having a social impact, collaboration seems to be key to their success in setting up networks that support their ventures. Involving others, having them take part in their mission and getting them engaged in reaching their mutual objectives appears to be possible due to the collaborative spirit of the entrepreneur:

> He is also gifted with an extremely collaborative spirit, continually engaging others about his model, relating to people on all levels, from legislators down to drug-addicted patients.
>
> (Sanjeev)

Community

Placing a high value on involvement of the local community, the social entrepreneurs seem to be cognizant of the strength of community-based approaches in addressing community health issues. As a result, their employed business models favor community-based approaches:

> While still working full time, Mark began developing a methodology for community-based healthcare.... Today, Mark is a recognized thought leader in the field ... and community-based healthcare.
>
> (Mark)

Getting an understanding of the community is essential to any community-based approach. Many social entrepreneurs already are involved in their target community by either living circumstances or peer association:

> He got involved with the homosexual community and found himself helping and supporting friends with HIV/AIDS.... Organizing community meetings.
>
> (Rodrigo)

Social Relationships

Throughout the lives of the social entrepreneurs, mentors or role-models seem to have a great influence on defining their personality, values, and mission. Whether it be a parent or a professional contact, these individuals have a profound impact on the lives of the social entrepreneurs, reflected in their current work:

> Carlos did go on to study medicine, and in that time, he was able to meet pioneers in the field of Family Medicine in Venezuela, and viewed them very much as mentors.... One of those mentors, whom he met through his neighborhood association, was Dr. Pedro Iturbe who was responsible for eradicating Tuberculosis in the state of Zulia and who had treated Carlos's grandfather.... Since then, other mentors, like Ashoka Fellow Elías Santana, have continued to show him the importance of passion for one's work and perseverance.
>
> (Carlos)

The importance of social relationships reflects on their tendency to build broader networks by including the inspiration of others, having them influence the personal work of the social entrepreneur:

> During this time Prasanta visited Jamkhed to meet Raj and Mabelle Arole; an event that inspires his current work. Prasanta says, "They trusted people, they gave information, they respected everyone, they told the truth, and in turn the people of Jamkhed and the villagers nearby were adapting to the complexities of a changing world with exceptional grace and self-respect.
>
> (Prasanta)

Persuasive Communication

Social entrepreneurs seem to have strong skills in persuading others, and being able to raise funds without compromising clear and transparent communication:

> His expertise as a specialist and an academic gives him a foundation from which to deliver results on the ground—and credibility to persuade his peers and spread his model.
>
> (Pedro)

> Andrea has worked tirelessly to highlight the issue of transport in global health, working with bilateral donors, global institutions and philanthropists to secure the investment and funding to put systems in place.
>
> (Andrea)

Through network-building, community involvement, social relationships, and persuasive communication, social entrepreneurs invoke a sense of connectedness, being part of a greater ecosystem, which grants them both the support and ability to perform their work.

Pro-Social Orientation: Social Values, Behavior, and Thoughts Encompassing Social and Humanistic Belief Systems

Leadership

Social entrepreneurs often appear to be natural leaders, enacting their leadership by acquired skills or natural charisma, making professional experts follow their lead:

> One renowned healthcare expert described working with her: "And along comes this involved mother who gets experts, politicians and patients to work effectively. None of us have the time or distance to do so—she oversees the system and gave herself permission to guide us towards real large changes. We all follow.
>
> (Silke)

Matching their ability to lead and make others follow them is their involvement in leadership roles throughout their career, enabling them to make use of their ability to lead and thus having a large impact through the organizations they lead:

> He has also been a leader in his area of specialization at the national and international level: serving as Executive Secretary of the Latin American Society of Abnormal Movement; organizing an Americas-wide congress of neurology; as regional Vice-President of the World Neurology Foundation; and as founder and President of Group of Friends of Parkinson's.
>
> (Pedro)

Sublimation

Sublimation refers to the ability to overcome adversity by turning and bending negative emotions and events into creative, constructive coping mechanisms, and inspirational activities make up the most compelling stories found in the narratives. Rather than becoming a victim, suffering from an exploited weakness, social entrepreneurs tend to become stronger through adversity, becoming empowered:

> She felt a lingering guilt, wondering if the preterm birth was somehow her fault. Silke felt isolated and her many questions were left unanswered. At that time parental support of any kind did not exist,

> neither were parents involved in the day-to-day care for their baby. Silke, a trained kindergarten teacher, could not believe there was no one to turn to and decided to change the situation.... Silke soon became chairwoman of the national self-help association for the care of preterm infants, which she led from 2003 to 2009.
>
> (Silke)

Selflessness

Another key element of the nature of social entrepreneurs is reflected by a selfless nature. The social entrepreneur acts out of interest of others, delaying personal gain or career and risking personal (financial) security in order to help others less fortunate than them, resulting in inspiring stories:

> For instance, when the state of Gujarat was affected by an earthquake that killed 20,000 people, Dr. Sai left for relief work missed her postgraduate entrance exams. Similarly, upon graduation in 2008, she missed a job interview to work for the flood relief in Bihar.
>
> (Dr. Sai)

Perhaps the most emotionally compelling evidence found for a tendency to show an intrinsic pro-social orientation comes from the narratives which present social entrepreneurs as being natural leaders, or in some cases, "heroic"-like individuals, who, out of selflessness, enact in favor of those less fortunate than themselves, making use of extraordinary resilience and other merits and favorable personality traits. As a result, social entrepreneurs involved in this study have deeply rooted social values, expressed in their behavior and thoughts, encompassing social and humanistic belief systems.

Discussion

Our study of social entrepreneurial action in healthcare has revealed antecedents on both the individual level and the contextual level. These antecedents form complex relationships, which suggest social entrepreneurial action in this sector is a multifaceted phenomenon. The antecedents drawn out in this study indicate that social entrepreneurial action predominantly is preceded and evoked by effectual logic and bricolage, and to a lesser extent by causational logic. Thus, social entrepreneurial action emerging through, predominantly, effectual logic is driven by and synergetic interaction of antecedents on the micro-, meso-, and macro-levels. We are able to summarize our research by stating that when an embedded individual with a pro-social, multidisciplinary nature is exposed to social problems, the individual will shape their tangible and intangible resources through connectedness and a pro-social orientation into social entrepreneurial action.

Through the analysis of the narratives of Ashoka Fellows, treating the narratives as institutional biographies, our study revealed 14 antecedents of social entrepreneurial action which form four aggregate dimensions: (i) multi-disciplinarity, (ii) exposure, (iii) connectedness, and (iv) pro-social orientation. The aggregate dimensions can be seen as overarching gateways through which antecedents are subsequently combined, and ultimately lead to social entrepreneurial action (see Figure 10.2). It appears social entrepreneurs encounter these antecedents throughout their lives as the process of social entrepreneurial action unfolds.

The antecedents of social entrepreneurial action interact in a continuous and creative process leading to social entrepreneurial action. Social entrepreneurial action does not, however, require all antecedents explored in this study to be present, suggesting multiple combinations of antecedents are capable of evoking social entrepreneurial action among both lay- and expert-entrepreneurs. However, even though social entrepreneurs arise from all socio-economic layers of society, Ashoka Fellows in the healthcare sector predominantly seem to be highly educated and directly or indirectly involved in healthcare, suggesting an appreciation of education and commitment to healthcare to be the most important antecedents for social entrepreneurial action in healthcare.

Although there seems to be a degree of priority/hierarchy between the level of influence each antecedent can have on developing social entrepreneurial action, the aggregate dimensions and antecedents help explain the importance of the relationship between the individual social entrepreneur and his or her direct and indirect contextual environment. Expanding to broader theories of entrepreneurship, the model presented in Figure 10.2 matches the individual-opportunity nexus theory of entrepreneurship (Grimes et al., 2013; Arend, 2013), which stipulates the channeling of individual factors by institutional factors and drawn out by institutional opportunities, in which the entrepreneur is an embedded agent. Furthermore, our model is supportive of connecting the micro-level to the meso- and macro-levels in theorization of entrepreneurial action (Battilana, 2006; Dacin et al., 2010; Mair, 2010; Stephan et al., 2015). We argue that social entrepreneurial action is effectuated by dimensions that influence antecedents on the micro-, meso-, and macro-levels, and thus originates at the individual-opportunity nexus when an enabling matrix of antecedents is accumulated throughout the life and career of a potential social entrepreneur, as depicted in Figure 10.2.

In addition to confirming the findings of prior related work, our study advances existing theories on antecedents of social entrepreneurial action. In particular, our findings move beyond conventional push or pull theories such as seeing/experiencing social problems versus career development (Yitshaki and Kropp, 2016; Yiu et al., 2014), develops a

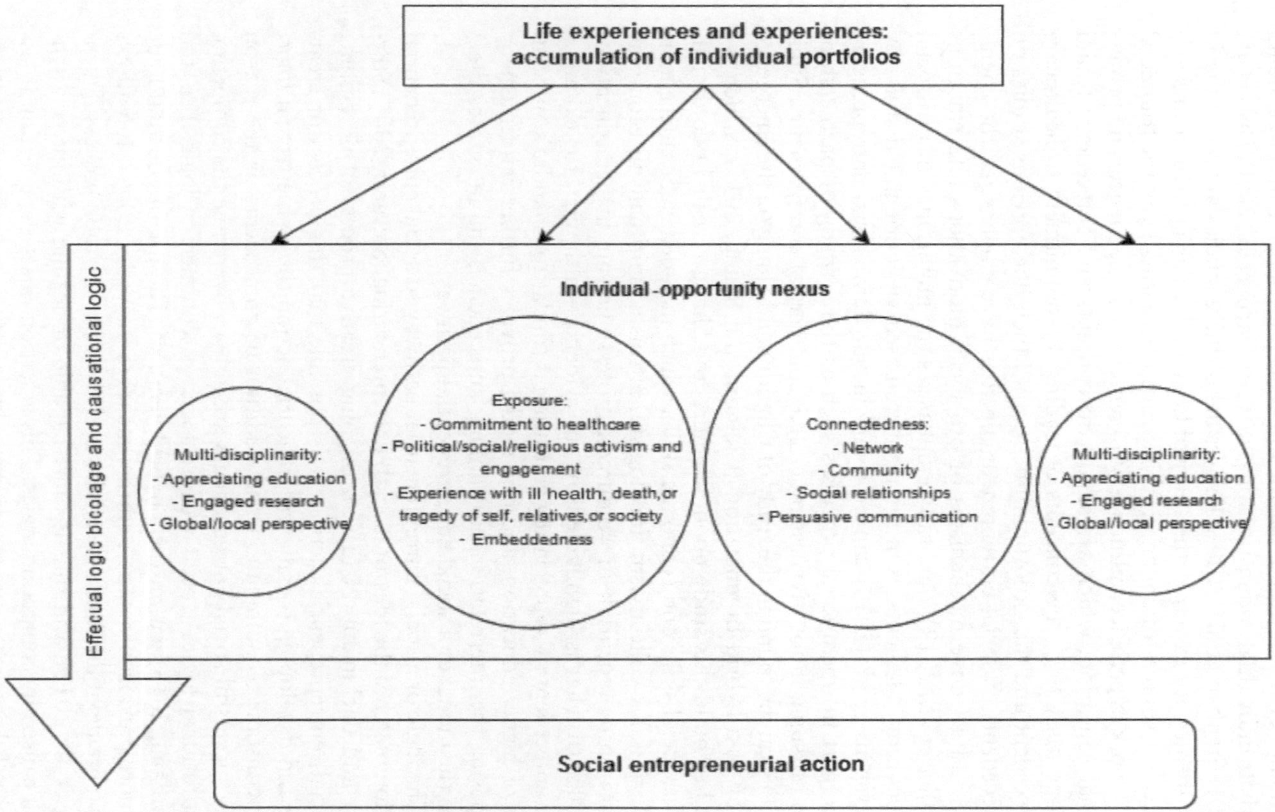

Figure 10.2 The Process of Social Entrepreneurial Action

comprehensive view on the motivation of social entrepreneurs (Germak and Robinson, 2014; Lee and Battilana, 2013; Miller et al., 2012), and combines evidence on the nature and concept of social entrepreneurship with its individual and institutional drivers (Dacin et al., 2010; Dees et al., 2001; Stephan et al., 2015). The results of these studies are recurring in our themes: for example, the study of Lee and Battilana (2013) found evidence for sources of commercial imprints originating from the founders' own work experience, influence of parental work experience, and professional education, which are similar to concepts and antecedents found in our study (e.g., the concepts of leading to commitment to healthcare antecedent and the exposure dimension). Much like previous studies on antecedents of social entrepreneurship that have emphasized the cognitive and affective mechanisms of pro-social motivations and emotions (Miller et al., 2012), our study emphasizes the importance of pro-social orientation. Elements from the resource-based view orientated study by Meyskens et al. (2010) can be found in our data: social entrepreneurs take part in operational processes such as the forming of partnerships and pursuing innovativeness much like commercial entrepreneurs. Similarities can be found in the study of Chandra and Shang on the emergence of SE-as-a-hybrid organization (Chandra and Shang, 2017), which we used to build this study upon. Chandra and Shang revealed two dimensions, social skills and economic skills, which included eight antecedents (social skills: collectivism, ideologism, altruism, spiritualism; economic skills: entrepreneurialism, resources, professionalism, higher education) similar to what is highlighted by our evidence—although, for example, our antecedent of appreciating education is similar to Chandra's antecedent of higher education, and our model provides further refinement by exposing the interrelationships among antecedents, and integrates them into the model of a social entrepreneurial pathway.

The logic of a social entrepreneurial pathway to social entrepreneurial action matches the idea of (social) entrepreneuring (Steyaert, 2007; Steyaert and Bachmann, 2012): an ongoing creative process of developing (social) entrepreneurial action. It is possible that this process of creating and developing social entrepreneurial action through effectual logic, the constant recombination and addition of antecedents, is the reason why successful social entrepreneurs are able to overcome the competing institutional logics (social welfare logic vs. commercial logic; Lee and Battilana, 2013) within their hybrid ventures. The use of effectual logic is more prevalent in expert entrepreneurs (Sarasvathy, 2008), and allows for more flexibility and reflectivity in the venture creation process (Duening et al., 2012), and thus is more capable of dealing with internal tension caused by competing logics. This assertion raises the question if less successful entrepreneurs use different logic in their new venture creation. Interestingly, while effectuation is a logic most often used by expert entrepreneurs (Sarasvathy, 2008), our data suggest that most Ashoka Fellows are lay entrepreneurs with healthcare careers, who then adopt effectual logic due to the antecedents of their social entrepreneurial action or have an innate talent for entrepreneurship. However, due to the qualitative methodology used in this study, more research is needed to draw out any inference regarding this observation.

Limitations of the Study

Our last assertion highlights a major limitation of our study. By focusing on Ashoka Fellows, our study only included narratives from highly successful entrepreneurs, and thus focuses on the so-called hero stories, which are inherently biased towards success and self-elevation. It is possible that less successful entrepreneurs have different life stories, and thus different institutional biographies. For example, many of the included narratives tell us stories about highly educated individuals, often raised in enabling environments, either due to financial or social stimulants. It is possible that these antecedents are exclusive to social entrepreneurs such as Ashoka Fellows, and thus the study is at risk of presenting a certain tendency to lean towards social entrepreneurs which have fewer obstacles to overcome when enacting social entrepreneurial action. Other social entrepreneurs might present themselves with different life stories, and thus different antecedents, which could lead to the adoption of different logics in their new venture creation process. However, we argue that the use of the Ashoka Fellow biographies did provide us with reliable data to base our research upon. The biographies do contain the perspectives of the Ashoka Fellows themselves, and thus contain the antecedents of their action as they perceived them. Therefore, treating these biographies as institutional biographies, we were able to isolate enabling factors that entrepreneurs themselves feel as important. However, using a qualitative research methodology for study does not allow for causational inference, and thus we argue further research is required to assess whether success of social entrepreneurship is related to certain antecedents and whether similar or different antecedents result in social entrepreneurial action among less known or less successful social entrepreneurs.

Furthermore, the biographies we used in the analysis do not grasp social entrepreneurship as "boundary work" (Lindgren and Packendorff, 2006), as they do not explain where, how, and why "radical social change" without compromising inclusivity and sustainability (Dees et al., 2001; Steyaert and Bachmann, 2012) is initiated by individuals. Nor do these biographies reflect the counter-narratives to the heroic meta-narrative of social entrepreneurship (Dey and Steyaert, 2010; Dempsey and Sanders, 2010) in which social entrepreneurship has been detrimental to lives of either the constituents as well as the social entrepreneur itself. This could be linked to the before mentioned use of profiles of highly successful Ashoka Fellows, which have a tendency to stem from enabling environments, and thus might be less related to counter-narratives. Although compassion is given as a possible reason for negating the counter-narratives of social entrepreneurship (Miller et al., 2012), involving narratives and counter-narratives would help explain in more detail the reasons why some social entrepreneurs are willing to incur tremendous cost of the self to achieve welfare for others or, as Licht states, how the "self-utility that may accrue to the actor is affected by the utility accruing to others" (Licht, 2010: 839). Including biographies rich with counter-narratives would thus help us answering critical questions on the why of social entrepreneurial action.

Finally, our sample was rather selective. More expansive research is needed to confirm our results within a larger population and inclusive of social entrepreneurs who are identified as collective/team-based (Chandra and Shang, 2017). However, due to our methodology, our study can be considered robust enough to provide evidence to warrant further investigation into the topic.

Implications and Future Research

Our study confirms previously reported data on the antecedents of social entrepreneurship and provides a first model on the emergence of social entrepreneurial action in healthcare on which future research might build. Our model may inform policymakers on creating favorable contextual environments for stimulating social entrepreneurship and help social entrepreneurs positively shape their organizational model and develop their own skills, personality, and behavior associated with successful social entrepreneurs. Furthermore, our model may help impact investors in screening social entrepreneurs, and help profile their biographies in the assessment of their potential. Future research should focus on whether our proposed model is generalizable to different sectors and is not purely limited to healthcare. Healthcare is a sector where altruism and social behavior is more common, and therefore, antecedents found in this study might be more apparent in that sector. To our knowledge the contemporary field of inquiry on social entrepreneurship in healthcare is small, and our study opens the way for more in-depth exploration of the phenomenon, moving beyond the theoretical field and elevating research towards more practical application. For example, additional inquiry into the handling and use of the competing logics prevalent in healthcare social entrepreneurship might reveal additional insights into organizational models capable of synergizing apparent competing logics rather than having them impede the entrepreneurial process.

The research conducted further suggests that existing theories on effectual reasoning are applicable to research on social entrepreneurship. Also, we suggest that the individual-opportunity theory is related to the emergence of social entrepreneurial action, and might provide answers to the when, how and why of social entrepreneurial action, which confirms previous statements made by Arend (2013) and Grimes et al. (2013). Future studies might be directed at exploring how the extrapolation of these and other theorizations in commercial entrepreneurship might be applicable to social entrepreneurship, as well.

Despite the previously mentioned limitations, our results hold significant value in guiding future research on the topic of social entrepreneurial action. The exposed antecedents ought to provoke the interest of researchers who occupy themselves with the questions of the where, why, and how of social entrepreneurship, and provides sufficient evidence to warrant in-depth investigation of the presented antecedents. Further studies could be directed on revealing more causational relationships between factors driving the emergence of social entrepreneurship.

References

Arend, R. J. 2013. A heart-mind-opportunity nexus: Distinguishing social entrepreneurship for entrepreneurs. *Academy of Management Review*, 38(2): 313–315. doi:10.5465/amr.2012.0251.

Ashoka. 2017. www.ashoka.com.

Austin, J., Stevenson, H., and Wei-Skillern, J. 2006. Social and commercial entrepreneurship: Same, different, or both? *Entrepreneurship Theory and Practice*, 30(1): 1–22. doi:10.1111/j.1540-6520.2006.00107.x.

Baker, T., and Nelson, R. E. 2005. Creating something from nothing: Resource construction through entrepreneurial bricolage. *Administrative Science Quarterly*, 50(3): 329–366. doi:10.2189/asqu.2005.50.3.329.

Battilana, J. 2006. Agency and institutions: The enabling role of individuals' social position. *Organization*, 13(5): 653–676. doi:10.1177/1350508406067008.

Bertels, S., and Lawrence, T. B. 2016. Organizational responses to institutional complexity stemming from emerging logics: The role of individuals. *Strategic Organization*, 14(4): 336–372. doi:10.1177/1476127016641726.

Besharov, M. L., and Smith, W. K. 2014. Multiple institutional logics in organizations: Explaining their varied nature and implications. *Academy of Management Review*, 39(3): 364–381. doi:10.5465/amr.2011.0431.

Chandra, Y., and Shang, L. 2017. Unpacking the biographical antecedents of the emergence of social enterprises: A narrative perspective. *Voluntas*, 28(6): 2498–2529. doi:10.1007/s11266-017-9860-2.

Choi, N., and Majumdar, S. 2014. Social entrepreneurship as an essentially contested concept: Opening a new avenue for systematic future research. *Journal of Business Venturing*, 29(3): 363–376. doi:10.1016/j.jbusvent.2013.05.001.

Corbett, A. C. 2005. Experiential learning within the process of opportunity identification and exploitation. *Entrepreneurship Theory and Practice*, 29(4): 473–491. doi:10.1111/j.1540-6520.2005.00094.x.

Dacin, P. A., Dacin, M. T., and Matear, M. 2010. Social entrepreneurship: Why we don't need a new theory and how we move forward from here. *Academy of Management Perspectives*, 24(3): 37–57. doi:10.5465/Amp.2010.52842950.

Dees, J. G., Emerson, J., and Economy, P. 2001. *Enterprising Nonprofits: A Toolkit for Social Entrepreneurs*. New York, NY: John, Wiley & Sons.

Dempsey, S. E., and Sanders, M. L. 2010. Meaningful work? Nonprofit marketization and work/life imbalance in popular autobiographies of social entrepreneurship. *Organization*, 17(4): 437–459. doi:10.1177/1350508410364198.

Dey, P., and Steyaert, C. 2010. The politics of narrating social entrepreneurship. *Journal of Enterprising Communities: People and Places in the Global Economy*, 4(1): 85–108.

Dimov, D. 2010. Nascent entrepreneurs and venture emergence: Opportunity confidence, human capital, and early planning. *Journal of Management Studies*, 47(6): 1123–1153. doi:10.1111/j.1467-6486.2009.00874.x.

Drayton, W., Brown, C., and Hillhouse, K. 2006. Integrating social entrepreneurs into the 'health for all' formula. *Bulletin of the World Health Organization*, 84(8): 591–591. doi:10.2471/Blt.06.033928.

Dubois, A., and Gadde, L. E. 2017. 'Systematic combining': An approach to case research. *Journal of Global Scholars of Marketing Science*, 27(4): 258–269. doi: 10.1080/21639159.2017.1360145.

Duening, T., Shepherd, M., and Czaplewski, A. 2012. How entrepreneurs think: Why effectuation and effectual logic may be the key to successful enterprise entrepreneurship. *International Journal of Innovation Science*, 4: 205–216.

Felin, T., and Zenger, T. R. 2009. Entrepreneurs as theorists: On the origins of collective beliefs and novel strategies. *Strategic Entrepreneurship Journal*, 3(2): 127–146. doi:10.1002/sej.67.

Finch, D., Deephouse, D. L., O'Reilly, N., Foster, W. M., Falkenberg, L., and Strong, M. 2017. Institutional biography and knowledge dissemination: An analysis of Canadian Business School faculty. *Academy of Management Learning & Education*, 16(2): 237–256. doi:10.5465/amle.2015.0130.

Fisher, G. 2012. Effectuation, causation, and bricolage: A behavioral comparison of emerging theories in entrepreneurship research. *Entrepreneurship Theory and Practice*, 36(5): 1019–1051. doi:10.1111/j.1540-6520.2012.00537.x.

Fowler, A. 2000. NGDOs as a moment in history: Beyond aid to social entrepreneurship or civic innovation? *Third World Quarterly*, 21(4): 637–654.

Germak, A. J., and Robinson, J. A. 2014. Exploring the motivation of nascent social entrepreneurs. *Journal of Social Entrepreneurship*, 5(1): 5–21.

Gioia, D. A., Corley, K. G., and Hamilton, A. L. 2013. Seeking qualitative rigor in inductive research: Notes on the Gioia Methodology. *Organizational Research Methods*, 16(1): 15–31.

Greenwood, R., Raynard, M., Kodeih, F., Micelotta, E. R., and Lounsbury, M. 2011. Institutional complexity and organizational responses. *Academy of Management Annals*, 5: 317–371.

Gregoire, D. A., Barr, P. S., and Shepherd, D. A. 2010. Cognitive processes of opportunity recognition: The role of structural alignment. *Organization Science*, 21(2): 413–431.

Grimes, M. G., McMullen, J. S., Vogus, T. J., and Miller, T. L. 2013. Studying the origins of social entrepreneurship: Compassion and the role of embedded agency. *Academy of Management Review*, 38(3): 460–463.

Guba, E. G., and Lincoln, Y. S. 1994. *Competing Paradigms in Qualitative Research*. Thousand Oaks, CA: SAGE.

Harting, J., Kunst, A. E., Kwan, A., and Stronks, K. 2011. A 'health broker' role as a catalyst of change to promote health: An experiment in deprived Dutch neighbourhoods. *Health Promotion International*, 26(1): 65–81.

Hockerts, K. 2017. Determinants of social entrepreneurial intentions. *Entrepreneurship Theory and Practice*, 41(1): 105–130.

Kidd, S. A., Kerman, N., Cole, D., Madan, A., Muskat, E., Raja, S., ... McKenzie, K. 2015. Social entrepreneurship and mental health intervention: A literature review and scan of expert perspectives. *International Journal of Mental Health and Addiction*, 13(6): 776–787.

Lawrence, T., Suddaby, R., and Leca, B. 2011. Institutional work: Refocusing institutional studies of organization. *Journal of Management Inquiry*, 20(1): 52–58.

Lee, M., and Battilana, J. 2013. *How the Zebra Got Its Stripes: Imprinting of Individuals and Hybrid Social Ventures*. Cambridge, MA: Harvard Business School.

Lepoutre, J., Justo, R., Terjesen, S., and Bosma, N. 2013. Designing a global standardized methodology for measuring social entrepreneurship activity: The Global Entrepreneurship Monitor social entrepreneurship study. *Small Business Economics*, 40(3): 693–714.

Licht, A. N. 2010. *Entrepreneurial Motivations, Culture, and the Law*. Dordrecht: Springer.

Lim, Y. W., and Chia, A. 2016. Social entrepreneurship improving global health. *Jama-Journal of the American Medical Association*, 315(22): 2393–2394. doi:10.1001/jama.2016.4400.

Lindgren, M., and Packendorff, J. 2006. *Entrepreneurship as Boundary Work: Deviating From and Belonging to Community*. Cheltenham, UK: Edward Elgar Publishing.

Mair, J. (2010). *Social Entrepreneurship: Taking Stock and Looking Ahead*. IESE Business School Working Paper No. WP-888.

Mair, J., and Marti, I. 2006. Social entrepreneurship research: A source of explanation, prediction, and delight. *Journal of World Business*, 41(1): 36–44. doi:10.1016/j.jwb.2005.09.002.

Mair, J., and Noboa, E. 2006. *Social Entrepreneurship: How Intentions to Create a Social Venture Get Formed*. New York: Palgrave MacMillan.

McMullen, J. S., Plummer, L. A., and Acs, Z. J. 2007. What is an entrepreneurial opportunity? *Small Business Economics*, 28(4): 273–283. doi:10.1007/s11187-006-9040-z.

McMullen, J. S., and Shepherd, D. A. 2006. Entrepreneurial action and the role of uncertainty in the theory of the entrepreneur. *Academy of Management Review*, 31(1): 132–152.

Meek, W. R., Pacheco, D. F., and York, J. G. 2010. The impact of social norms on entrepreneurial action: Evidence from the environmental entrepreneurship context. *Journal of Business Venturing*, 25(5): 493–509. doi:10.1016/j.jbusvent.2009.09.007.

Meyskens, M., Robb-Post, C., Stamp, J. A., Carsrud, A. L., and Reynolds, P. D. 2010. Social ventures from a resource-based perspective: An exploratory study assessing global Ashoka Fellows. *Entrepreneurship Theory and Practice*, 34(4): 661–680. doi:10.1111/j.1540-6520.2010.00389.x.

Miller, T. L., Grimes, M. G., McMullen, J. S., and Vogus, T. J. 2012. Venturing for others with heart and head: How compassion encourages social entrepreneurship. *Academy of Management Review*, 37(4): 616–640. doi:10.5465/amr.2010.0456.

Mitchell, R. K., Busenitz, L. W., Bird, B., Gaglio, C. M., McMullen, J. S., Morse, E. A., and Smith, J. B. 2007. The central question in entrepreneurial cognition research 2007. *Entrepreneurship Theory and Practice*, 31(1): 1–27. doi:10.1111/j.1540-6520.2007.00161.x.

Perry, J. T., Chandler, G. N., and Markova, G. 2012. Entrepreneurial effectuation: A review and suggestions for future research. *Entrepreneurship Theory and Practice*, 36(4): 837–861. doi:10.1111/j.1540-6520.2010.00435.x.

Plummer, L. A., Haynie, J. M., and Godesiabois, J. 2007. An essay on the origins of entrepreneurial opportunity. *Small Business Economics*, 28(4): 363–379. doi:10.1007/s11187-006-9036-8.

Reay, T., and Hinings, C. R. 2009. Managing the rivalry of competing institutional logics. *Organization Studies*, 30(6): 629–652. doi:10.1177/0170840609104803.

Rennie, D. L. 2012. Qualitative research as methodical hermeneutics. *Psychological Methods*, 17(3): 385–398. doi:10.1037/a0029250.

Riessman, C. K. 2005. *Narrative Analysis*. Huddersfield: University of Huddersfield.

Ritchie, J., and Lewis, J. 2003. *Qualitative Research Practice: A Guide for Social Science Students and Researchers*. London: SAGE Publications.

Roy, M. J., Donaldson, C., Baker, R., and Kay, A. 2013. Social enterprise: New pathways to health and well-being? *Journal of Public Health Policy*, 34(1): 55–68. doi:10.1057/jphp.2012.61.

Sarasvathy, S. D. 2001. Causation and effectuation: Toward a theoretical shift from economic inevitability to entrepreneurial contingency. *Academy of Management Review*, 26(2): 243–263. doi:10.2307/259121.

Sarasvathy, S. D. 2008. *Effectuation: Elements of Entrepreneurial Expertise: New Horizons in Entrepreneurship Research*. Cheltenham, UK: Edward Elgar Publishing.

Senyard, J., Baker, T., and Davidsson, P. 2009. Entrepreneurial bricolage: Towards systematic empirical testing. *Frontiers of Entrepreneurship Research*, 20(5), A5.

Shane, S. E. 2003. *The Individual-Opportunity Nexus*. Boston, MA: Springer.

Shane, S. E., and Venkataraman, S. 2000. The promise of entrepreneurship as a field of research. *Academy of Management Review*, 25(1): 217–226. doi:10.5465/amr.2000.2791611.

Short, J. C., Moss, T. W., and Lumpkin, G. T. 2009. Research in social entrepreneurship: Past contributions and future opportunities. *Strategic Entrepreneurship Journal*, 3(2): 161–194. doi:10.1002/sej.69.

Stephan, U., Uhlaner, L. M., and Stride, C. 2015. Institutions and social entrepreneurship: The role of institutional voids, institutional support, and institutional configurations. *Journal of International Business Studies*, 46(3): 308–331. doi:10.1057/jibs.2014.38.

Steyaert, C. 2007. 'Entrepreneuring' as a conceptual attractor? A review of process theories in 20 years of entrepreneurship studies. *Entrepreneurship and Regional Development*, 19(6): 453–477. doi:10.1080/08985620701671759.

Steyaert, C., and Bachmann, M. 2012. *Listening to Narratives*. Northampton: Edward Elgar Inc.

Terjesen, S., Lepoutre, J., Justo, R., and Bosma, N. 2012. *Global Entrepreneurship Monitor Report on Social Entrepreneurship*.

Viale, T. S. 2009. *The Institutional Portfolio (Alberta School of Business Working Paper)*. Edmonton: University of Alberta.

Watson, T. J. 2013. Entrepreneurship in action: Bringing together the individual, organizational and institutional dimensions of entrepreneurial action.

Entrepreneurship and Regional Development, 25(5–6): 404–422. doi:10.1080/08985626.2012.754645.

Welter, F. 2011. Contextualizing entrepreneurship-conceptual challenges and ways forward. *Entrepreneurship Theory and Practice*, 35(1): 165–184. doi:10.1111/j.1540-6520.2010.00427.x.

Wiklund, J., Davidsson, P., Audretsch, D. B., and Karlsson, C. 2011. The future of entrepreneurship research. *Entrepreneurship Theory and Practice*, 35: 1–9.

Wood, M. S., McKelvie, A., and Haynie, J. M. 2014. Making it general: Opportunity individuation and the shaping of opportunity beliefs. *Journal of Business Venturing*, 29: 252–272.

Yitshaki, R., and Kropp, F. 2016. Motivations and opportunity recognition of social entrepreneurs. *Journal of Small Business Management*, 54(2): 546–565. doi:10.1111/jsbm.12157.

Yiu, D. W., Wan, W. P., Ng, F. W., Chen, X., and Su, J. 2014. Sentimental drivers of social entrepreneurship: A study of China's Guangcai (Glorious) program. 社会创业与情操驱动力: 中国光彩事业研究. *Management and Organization Review*, 10(1): 55–80.

Zahra, S. A., Gedajlovic, E., Neubaum, D. O., and Shulman, J. M. 2009. A typology of social entrepreneurs: Motives, search processes and ethical challenges. *Journal of Business Venturing*, 24(5): 519–532. doi:10.1016/j.jbusvent.2008.04.007.

Zahra, S. A., and Wright, M. 2011. Entrepreneurship's next act. *Academy of Management Perspectives*, 25(4): 67–83. doi:10.5465/amp.2010.0149.

Index

Page numbers in italics indicate figures and in bold indicate tables on the corresponding pages.